THE GAME MASTER'S BOOK OF
LEGENDARY
DRAGONS

EPIC NEW DRAGONS, DRAGON-KIN AND MONSTERS, PLUS CULT, CLASS,
COMBAT AND MAGIC OPTIONS FOR 5TH EDITION RPG ADVENTURES

DILLON ✳ HAECK ✳ HÜBRICH
LEWIS ✳ PINTO

THE GAME MASTER'S BOOK OF
LEGENDARY DRAGONS

CONTENTS

"If you're a casual gamer, Game Master or full-time RPG enthusiast, this book is for you. It presents an exciting, mythical and fantastical world of dragons designed to enhance your gaming experience in ways you never imagined."

—*Chris Seaman*
DUNGEONS & DRAGONS AND MAGIC: THE GATHERING ARTIST
chrisseamanart.com

FOREWORD

DRAGONS PERMEATE OUR MYTHOLOGY ON A GLOBAL SCALE. All inhabited continents include some form of these beasts in their folklore, from Europe to the Far East. The idea of massive reptilian creatures inhabiting the edge of civilization crosses cultures and is one of the threads that binds us together as human beings. Our literary history is replete with dragons serving as the archetypal foe that opposes the hero from the *Argonautica* in antiquity to the tales of Beowulf and King Arthur. And dragons grew in popularity in the 20th century in the stories of authors such as C.S. Lewis, Ursula K. Le Guin, Robert A. Heinlein and famously the evil red dragon Smaug from my favorite childhood book, *The Hobbit*, by J.R.R. Tolkien.

Given all of these factors, it is no surprise that when my father, Gary Gygax, created the fantasy role-playing genre, he chose to name that revolutionary new game Dungeons & Dragons. Dragons are the stuff of legends, so this tome could not be more aptly named than it is: *The Game Master's Book of Legendary Dragons.*

Let's face it, if you love fantasy role-playing gaming like me (and since you're reading this foreword the chances are that you do share my passion for gaming), you are fascinated with dragons. And why shouldn't you be? When I think of my favorite fantasy artwork, it includes dragons. Larry Elmore's rendering of the red dragon on the iconic Basic D&D red box, Clyde Caldwell's Tiamat, Erol Otus's Basic D&D cover—or a personal favorite that I commissioned from Jeff Easley for Gary Con VI, "An Aerial Duel," depicting a flying wizard battling a dragon. Something about these mystical beings touches our souls, ignites our sense of adventure and sends our imagination soaring on massive bat-like wings.

Some of my earliest memories around the gaming table are of listening to the likes of Rob Kuntz and my dad talking about their adventures in the World of Greyhawk. Each one of them had gone searching through dangerous territory in the wilderness to find and subdue a dragon. Rob played the evil hero, Lord Robilar, who overcame a green dragon and forced it into his service. Mordenkainen, a powerful archmage played by my father, gained control of a pair of ancient red dragons. It was a mark of prestige to be able to conquer and control a being of such raw power.

Don't you want to have one of these magical beasts at your beck and call?

It's clear that the people who put together this resource are fascinated with dragons too. It's packed with information and ideas that will bring dragons to the forefront of your favorite fantasy role-playing game. Inside, you'll find a selection of ancient wyrms with colorful stories that bring their personalities to life and make it easier for the Game Master to understand and play them. From the fearsome Balaur and Balleg, both left twisted and filled with rage at the wizards that cruelly subjected them to tortures to gain power, to the intriguing and compelling Fury, Dragon Queen of Hell, and the wise Kiennavalris whom you can use to add layers of story to your campaign. In addition to the more than two dozen of these Legendary Dragons, the book includes a new character class, spell enhancements, the dräken race, information about hunting dragons, dragon cults, new magic items and even rules to manage aerial combat.

Dragons have a special place in our folklore, mythology and fantasy gaming. I encourage you to have fun using this book to reinvigorate the role that dragons play in your campaign and watch how much fun your players have interacting with them.

LUKE GYGAX
Founder of Gary Con

COME NOT BETWEEN THE DRAGON AND HIS WRATH.

–William Shakespeare

INTRODUCTION

WELCOME TO
THE GAME MASTER'S BOOK
OF LEGENDARY DRAGONS...

We've all been there. You pore over monster manuals, searching for a compelling creature with which to test, taunt and otherwise terrify your players. You gauge stat blocks and customize your creation, even practicing your sinister snarl in the mirror so you can bring it to life at your table. But as you look at your reflection, embodying an ancient draconic menace with a subtle lip curl and a Rasputin-like accent, it begins to dawn on you that you have no idea who this dragon is. What he wants from your party. Why he would even exist in your world. As a GM, you know what the dragon can do—but you're plagued by the question that hangs over any quality actor: "What's my motivation?"

Now, thanks to *The Game Master's Book of Legendary Dragons*, you'll have the answers to this and many other questions about dragons and the impact they have on the world around them.

What This Book Is

The Game Master's Book of Legendary Dragons is meant to provide information on more than two dozen unique dragons, with rich histories, motivations and strategies that anyone can add to any sandbox. Your players will also find ways to boost spells with harvested dragon scales or organs and even play a new dragon-related race. Perhaps a player wants to become a dragon rider or join a dragon-hunting faction that uses airships to track down and destroy evil dragons. The content contained within this book can provide mechanics for both, offering a staggering number of options for anyone who loves dragons as much as we do.

This book is a resource meant to inspire. There is so much more to a dragon than the overwhelming power of their breath weapon or the color of their scales. Dragons are not ordinary creatures. They are highly intelligent, equally charismatic and in most cases long-lived. They have unique goals, a plethora of personalities and are steeped in lore and allure built up over their centuries of roaming the realm. They are more than a stat block. This was one of the primary reasons for the development of this book. We wanted to elevate dragons to the level they deserve and provide a deep understanding of what makes each dragon unique, special, even awe-inspiring. With each dragon comes their backstory, details related to their lair as well as encounter conditions and tactics. This information is intended to serve as a tool for you to craft your own stories as opposed to the story in total. In short: These creatures are still your characters, and you should take them wherever you and your party decide they need to go. Like all legends, they change a bit based on who is presenting the tale.

Each Legendary Dragon featured is distinct, and you are encouraged to choose one that's appropriate for your current campaign. Even a new campaign can feature one or several dragons as a major antagonist in your game's storyline. Need a dragon of war? Go with Balaur. Want a dragon that is a step beyond the fabled and fierce tarrasque? Select Zuth. Need to save the princess, but with a twist? Choose Immryg-Umryss. There is a good chance a Legendary Dragon in this book will suit your desire to tell any number of stories, ensuring you're giving all your players a memorable experience.

What This Book Is Not

The Game Master's Book of Legendary Dragons is not just a big book of dragons with stats or variations of the same dragons found in other 5th Edition sourcebooks. Our approach with this book was to go much deeper with lore to give you inspiration. Entire campaigns can be built around a single Legendary Dragon's own rich, detailed history, but you can also lay the foundation for a one-shot encounter with one of these creatures if your party is simply spoiling for an unforgettable fight.

None of the dragons within are variations of the more common and familiar types of dragons in 5th Edition. These dragons have proper names, histories and motivations that transcend metallic or chromatic stereotypes. While many traditional and familiar 5e dragons are already quite formidable, Legendary Dragons are one-of-kind and well-deserving of their epic status. That said, most basic dragons are not suitable for encounters with lower level players, and in that way, the Legendary Dragons featured in this book do align with their more generic cousins. These creatures could kill a low-level party with a single breath (weapon), so use them at your discretion.

This is not railroad information. Each dragon entry provides the "Goldilocks zone" of intel so you can have enough information to run them well while still leaving room for your unique interpretation.

How to Use This Book

The Game Master's Book of Legendary Dragons was created using the System Resource Document for the 5th Edition of the world's most popular tabletop roleplaying game. The lore within could undoubtedly be used for other well-known games, but the stats are optimized for 5e. The license for the SRD is printed for your convenience on pg. 234. Passing references to material from this resource have been marked in **bold** (monsters or NPCs), are in *italics* (spells) or ***both*** (magic items). All other content is new and created specifically for this book.

It is encouraged that new GMs explore the SRD so they can best understand the basic rules of the game. With that foundation of knowledge, you can more readily translate the specifics of each dragon presented to your world. As you weave your own narrative, consider the impact any one of these creatures may have on a kingdom's economy (pg. 159), travel (pg. 170) or on the land itself (Gallomarg [pg. 33], Kut-Echinae [pg. 70] and Zuth [pg. 116] are great examples of this).

When you use this book, you'll be able to choose from several of the Legendary Dragons featured within. Do you need a unique dragon for a particular part of your world? A large city, forest, mining town or seaside village? Chances are good you will find a dragon that fits your needs. Do you require a powerful NPC to guide your group or thwart their best-laid plans?

A shapeshifting Legendary Dragon may just fit the bill. Most of these dragons would function well as a powerful "end of the campaign" finale.

Dragons are smart. Perhaps smarter than you. That's OK—you're only human. In order to more effectively challenge your players, plan a little strategy ahead of time. Dragons know the look of a healing spell, the tell-tale signs of a powerful warrior or trappings of a would-be wizard. They can discern who the strong, skilled or spellcasting are with a simple considered gaze, and they're not above ripping a cleric apart, fairness or honor be damned. Legendary Dragons have lived a long time, and they didn't do so by fighting to the bitter end. They will flee as necessary, forcing your party to give chase, perhaps over several months, if that's what's required to bring in a bounty.

A Legendary Dragon is rarely caught flat-footed. Several tactics are provided within these pages to help run them to their maximum potential, and each dragon features unique abilities, lairs and legendary actions. Some have minions or companions to tip them off of any PC activity that threatens a dragon's plans or if they encroach upon its lair, and others have regional effects that will make things even harder on your party. If your players have fought dragons before, they may be in for a big shock.

And look, we see what you're thinking. "But these dragons are so powerful. My players won't stand a chance!" Perhaps. In some cases, assuredly. But...

You can always start small. If a Legendary Dragon is introduced to an adventuring party early into their careers, it should be set up for a future encounter. It can become a memorable part of the grand story. A dragon (or several dragons) can weave in and out of the adventurers' lives over several months or years. Imagine the Legendary Dragon as a slow drumbeat—a steady pulse in the background that is always there, guiding your group to glory or attempting to subvert them at every turn. Not every Legendary Dragon needs to be tangled with. In fact, several dragons could be very helpful to an adventuring party just starting their journey. Glitz, Jörmungand, Kiennavalyriss, Kundal, Naghi, Umunairu, Vanadon-Necroth, Volthaarius, Vyraetra and Zuth are all neutral or even good-aligned. That's not to say there won't be a conflict with any of these Legendary Dragons. Still, the dragon's demeanor or outlook may give the party a chance to be creative in how they interact. Some Legendary Dragons might even request help from adventurers.

The writers of this book haven't forgotten about players, either. Imagine creating a character directly tied to a dragon's regional magic. As the character matures, this proximity of birth manifests unusual and exceptional powers. Your players can become a dräken with a combination of abilities unique to them and them alone. No two dräken are alike, as each region's draconic magic affects different characters in many divergent ways. The roll tables associated with draconic mutations are so diverse and numerous that the possible outcomes will ensure a one-of-a-kind character players can bring to life at your table.

A player can also become a dragon rider that utilizes a dragon companion as a loyal mount and sidekick by rolling up a PC using the Dragon Rider class exclusive to this book. As the player character progresses into higher and higher levels, so does their draconic companion, and the bond that forms between dragon and rider is strong enough to sunder an entire kingdom (though you may be inclined to balance it at your own table if you feel other PCs are getting a little jealous).

Your party can choose to go professional and become fearsome dragon hunters. Be sure to encourage them to keep it a secret, though. Dragons loathe the practice (for a good reason!) and have exacted revenge upon dragon hunters and their communities many, many times before. They can learn from veteran hunters who have the fortitude to take on these fabled beasts or play as those archetypes themselves. Dragon hunters are seasoned adventurers, and those who still remain are likely to share invaluable knowledge on how to take on an ancient leviathan like Anoth-Zuul.

Or take to the skies! This book includes mechanics that enable players to take to the air and navigate an airship in order to more doggedly pursue their quarry. Additionally, after the players master the ability to hunt dragons, they can be rewarded by selling valuable harvested dragon parts or enhancing spells with the dragon components. It's nice to know there's a payoff when a dragon is defeated. But be sure to keep it confidential, as this trade is highly illegal in many areas of the world. Buying and selling dragon parts is a black market venture (at least unless you decide it isn't), but if your party is crafty and intelligent, there is plenty of coin to be had.

We invite you to enjoy the contents of *The Game Master's Book of Legendary Dragons*. We hope you find the Legendary Dragons within to be an inspiration to you and your players for many years to come. Or at least until the first TPK.

Happy adventuring!

LEGENDARY DRAGONS

A STAGGERING COLLECTION OF CUNNING AND CHARISMATIC CHROMATIC (AND METALLIC AND IN SOME CASES COMPLETELY UNDEAD) DRAGONS.

ANOTH-ZUUL, MUMMIFIED DRAGON QUEEN

In the lands of Graal, the name Anoth-Zuul strikes terror into souls both young and old. It is not the great dragon queen they fear so much, however, as the zealous cultists who worship her mummified remains. With her dual heart in an unholy clay jar and her body wrapped in clinging magical rags, the great dragon queen is a source of power that fuels the foul rituals of Anoth-Zuul's deranged supplicants. This is, however, not a fate the mighty dragon would have chosen for herself, and should she ever rise again, she will be more powerful than any thought possible.

As the story goes, Anoth-Zuul was betrayed by a loyal retainer—Nemoz—who tended to her during her hibernation. As her two hearts still beat, Nemoz tenderly carved them from her breast over the course of several weeks and placed portions of each into a desecrated clay vessel. A ritual was performed to ensure she would remain in perpetual sleep for at least 101 years. Only then would she fully regain consciousness, an unholy specter of her powerful form.

Only that's not exactly what happened.

Nemoz's original plans were to use the mummified dragon as a sepulchre of magic and make himself immortal, placing his faith in the ritual he had paid so dearly for. But an unpredictable result of the ritual allowed Nemoz to use Anoth-Zuul's body to channel unholy magic from the negative material plane and fuel his own diabolic machinations. Decades passed. Nemoz grew in strength, and his body barely aged. From his power, a cult celebrating the power of the dragon as well as unlife was born. While Anoth-Zuul slept, Nemoz extended his own life—and the lives of his servants—through the use of this vile magic. The great dragon queen lay in agony, trapped in lasting torpor as a mummified tool of the cult, biding her time.

Nemoz was ultimately slain by his own daughter—Revora—who granted herself the rank of high priestess of the cult of Anoth-Zuul and spread her message far and wide through the darker corners of the land. Those who were powerless in their regular lives turned to the cult for the strength to slay their husbands, jailers, lords, masters and anyone else who would exploit them. Rumors of the cult spread throughout Graal, and terror consumed those who refused to submit to it. The cult's servants were called harridans (regardless of gender) and people feared the cultists could be living anywhere rebellious behavior was present. Anoth-Zuul slept.

Unbeknownst to the cult, Anoth-Zuul grew in power in her undeath. Nemoz had thought he was draining the great dragon while channeling magic through her. But her age and wisdom served her even in death. She stored some vile magic inside her form, granting her powers beyond the reach of dragons or mummies. And though she has not yet fully woken from her slumber, something stirs within. It is in this limbo-like state that Anoth-Zuul has become a weapon of the cult.

As high priestess, Revora possesses the vessel. She has the power to wake Anoth-Zuul from time to time to enact painful acts of violence against those who are too powerful for the cultists alone. And with this power, she keeps the dragon under her control.

While under the cult's power, Anoth-Zuul cannot rain death upon the cultists. At least not yet. She remains a tool of the cult, serving the high priestess and destroying her enemies wherever she demands. But this could change. Once the clay vessel storing portions of her dual heart is broken, she will be free of the prison Revora keeps her in. Perhaps then, the dragon queen will have her vengeance on Revora. And the cult. And every other living thing.

Hook

Revora and the cult use the myth of Anoth-Zuul to great effect. Often they attack in the dead of night and slay someone of importance—a guild leader for instance—to send word to abusers that they will not tolerate the misuse of power. But sometimes they get it wrong and kill someone who doesn't deserve to die. Fear of their power spreads nonetheless, and inside the land of Graal, the cult is a terrifying force.

Any number of horrifying tales can drag the party into a story about Anoth-Zuul and the cult. Such a story should be a lengthy adventure involving numerous victims, witnesses and trails of blood. If the party gets too close, loyal cultists would be dispatched. And when that doesn't work, Anoth-Zuul would be summoned to finish them off.

Encounter Conditions

A confrontation with Anoth-Zuul is nearly always at night and always against those the cult believes have it coming. Revora is power-hungry. While her aim is to balance the scales of power by harming abusers, she now has a taste for it and takes up arms against whomever she pleases. Graal has become a nightmare of a place where any person could be next. And while people do not know who is behind the cult, they know the name and some have seen the great dragon when it comes to dispense "justice."

The land has become bleak, and hope for a better tomorrow is gone.

An entire campaign can be built around the party residing in Graal, living in constant fear and growing up to vanquish the cult. Or they can stumble upon the story like any other traditional encounter. In many ways, the cult drives Anoth-Zuul's actions, unless she shakes the shackles of the dual-heart vessel.

The cult's activities should draw the party into the story and her appearance should shock and terrify them. If Revora (use **archmage** stats with a **lich** spell list) sends her to kill the party, she will present a formidable challenge. If the party attempts to engage Anoth-Zuul when she is within 120 feet of the dual-heart vessel, they will understand the full breadth of the power wielded by the cult.

Tactics

When Revora sends Anoth-Zuul to enact her will, she does so without much consideration of tactics. Anoth-Zuul is a giant, monstrous flamethrower of a weapon to be hurled indiscriminately at her enemies. Revora has never seen resistance to her methods and has therefore never had to learn a better way. But while Anoth-Zuul is nearly mindless, she is not foolish. Even though Revora controls her, Anoth-Zuul does not behave in a way that exposes her weaknesses (if this can be avoided).

Those who would do her the most harm are her first targets. Trapping enemies behind a *wall of force* is a favorite tactic of Anoth-Zuul, if the clay vessel is close enough. The wall ensures the party won't bother her for a while, as she flanks her enemies from another direction.

Depending on the encounter the game master creates for Anoth-Zuul, Revora and the cultists may be present. They would certainly be a thorn in the party's collective sides during a fight, picking off anyone who is undefended or distracting the most powerful warriors using ad hoc weapons and commando tactics (developed from years of their raids).

Treasure

Anoth-Zuul herself is unlikely to have any treasure, but the cult is wealthy enough for a thousand peasants. Over the years, they have collected countless small treasures from their victims. Gems, coffers, coins, relics, heirlooms and even the occasional magic item have all found their way into the cult's hoard. Journals of misdeeds are also kept, as well as maps of dozens of people's homes—targets for the cult's unyielding vengeance.

These treasures are secured across the city in makeshift vaults and storage centers, all controlled or manipulated by the cult. The party might get a glimpse of these storage centers, providing another opportunity for adventure and investigation.

Anoth-Zuul's Dual Heart

The dual-heart vessel used to control Anoth-Zuul functions as a lair for her. It weighs 100 lbs, has an AC of 20, 100 hit points and is enchanted to withstand area of effect damage from natural or arcane effects. If the vessel of hearts were destroyed, the magic associated with controlling Anoth-Zuul would dissipate and she would be free.

When fighting within 120 feet of the dual-heart vessel, provided it is intact, Anoth-Zuul can utilize its ambient magic to take lair actions.

Lair Actions

On initiative count 20 (losing initiative ties), Anoth-Zuul can take one lair action to cause one of the following effects:

- A **mummy** bursts through the ground and attacks any enemy it can see. It acts on initiative 20.
- Until initiative count 20 on the next round, any non-undead creature that tries to cast a spell of 6th level or lower in Anoth-Zuul's lair is wracked with pain. The creature can choose another action, but if it tries to cast the spell, it must make a DC 16 Constitution saving throw. On a failed save, it takes (1d6) necrotic damage per level of the spell, and the spell has no effect and is wasted.
- An invisible *wall of force* springs into existence at a point of Anoth-Zuul's choice within range.

Anoth-Zuul can't repeat an effect until they have all been used, and she can't use the same effect two rounds in a row.

ANOTH-ZUUL, MUMMIFIED DRAGON QUEEN

Gargantuan dragon, lawful evil, undead

Armor Class 20 (natural armor)
Hit Points 492 (24d20 + 240)
Speed 20 ft., fly 60 ft.

STR	DEX	CON	INT	WIS	CHA
28 (+9)	11 (+0)	30 (+10)	24 (+7)	24 (+7)	16 (+3)

Saving Throws Dex +7, Con +17, Wis +14, Cha +10
Skills Arcana +21
Damage Resistances fire
Damage Immunities bludgeoning, piercing and slashing from nonmagical attacks, necrotic, poison
Condition Immunities charmed, exhaustion, frightened, paralyzed, poisoned
Senses blindsight 30 ft., darkvision 120 ft., passive Perception 17
Languages Common, Draconic
Challenge 24 (62,000 XP)

Fire Resistance. Anoth-Zuul is protected from fire. All fire damage she receives is reduced by half.

Innate Spellcasting. Anoth-Zuul can cast the following spells without need for components. Her spellcasting modifier is Wisdom (+13, DC 21).

  At will: chill touch (17th level)
  1/Long rest: animate dead (5th level)
  2/Long rest: finger of death, vampiric touch (8th level)

Aura of Exultation. The cultists and undead who worship Anoth-Zuul are empowered by her presence. Any cultist or undead that starts their turn within 60 feet of Anoth-Zuul gains 10 temporary hit points at the start of their turn and while in this aura makes all attacks with advantage.

Legendary Resistance (3/Long rest). If Anoth-Zuul fails a saving throw, she can choose to succeed instead.

Magic Resistance. Anoth-Zuul has advantage on saving throws against spells and other magical effects.

Rejuvenation. If killed or destroyed, Anoth-Zuul gains a new body in 24 hours if her dual heart is intact, regaining all her hit points and becoming active again. The new body appears within 5 feet of her dual heart.

Vessel of Hearts. Anoth-Zuul's dual heart is contained within a large urn. Those in possession of this urn can control Anoth-Zuul's actions. If the urn and dual heart are destroyed, Anoth-Zuul's hit points are reduced by half. The urn has an AC of 20 and 40 hp.

ACTIONS

Multiattack. Anoth-Zuul can use her Frightful Presence. She then makes three attacks: one with her bite and two with her claws.

Breath of Harm (Recharge 5–6). Anoth-Zuul unleashes a torrent of plague-bringing breath in a 60-foot cone. Each creature in the cone must make a Constitution saving throw. On a failed save, it takes 49 (14d6) necrotic damage or half as much damage on a success. The damage can't reduce the target's hit points below 1. If the target fails the saving throw, its hit point maximum is reduced for one hour by an amount equal to the necrotic damage it took. Any effect that removes a disease allows a creature's hit point maximum to return to normal before that time passes.

Rotten Bite. Melee Weapon Attack: +15 to hit, reach 15 ft., one target. *Hit:* 19 (2d10 + 8) piercing damage plus 9 (2d8) necrotic damage. If the target is a creature, it must succeed on a DC 16 Constitution saving throw or be cursed with mummy rot. The cursed target can't regain hit points, and its hit point maximum decreases by 10 (3d6) for every 24 hours that elapse. If the curse reduces the target's hit point maximum to 0, the target dies, and its body turns to dust. The curse lasts until removed by the spell or other magic.

Rotten Claw. Melee Weapon Attack: +16 to hit, reach 10 ft., one target. *Hit:* 16 (2d6 + 9) necrotic damage. If the target is a creature, it must succeed on a DC 16 Constitution saving throw or be cursed with mummy rot. The cursed target can't regain hit points, and its hit point maximum decreases by 10 (3d6) for every 24 hours that elapse. If the curse reduces the target's hit point maximum to 0, the target dies, and its body turns to dust. The curse lasts until removed by the spell or other magic.

Frightful Presence. Any creature within 120 feet of Anoth-Zuul and aware of her presence must succeed on a DC 19 Wisdom saving throw or become frightened for one minute. A creature can repeat the saving throw at the end of each of its turns, ending the effect on itself on a success. If a creature's saving throw is successful or the effect ends, the creature is immune to Anoth-Zuul's Frightful Presence for the next 24 hours.

Tail. Melee Weapon Attack: +15 to hit, reach 20 ft., one target. *Hit:* 17 (2d8 + 8) bludgeoning damage.

LEGENDARY ACTIONS

Anoth-Zuul can take three legendary actions, choosing from the options below. Only one legendary action option can be used at a time and only at the end of another creature's turn. Anoth-Zuul regains spent legendary actions at the start of her turn.

Detect. Anoth-Zuul makes a Wisdom (Perception) check.

Glare of the Ancients. Anoth-Zuul targets one creature she can see within 60 feet. If the target can see Anoth-Zuul, it must succeed on a DC 18 Wisdom saving throw against this magic or become stunned until the end of Anoth-Zuul's next turn. If the target fails the saving throw by 5 or more, it is also paralyzed for the same duration. A target that succeeds on the saving throw is immune to this glare as well as the Dreadful Glare of all mummies and mummy lords for the next 24 hours.

Tail Attack. Anoth-Zuul makes a tail attack.

Wingstorm (Costs 2 Actions). Anoth-Zuul beats her massive wings as blinding dust and sand swirls magically around her. Each creature within 15 feet of Anoth-Zuul must succeed on a DC 16 Constitution saving throw or be blinded until the end of the creature's next turn. Anoth-Zuul can then move up to her fly speed without provoking opportunity attacks.

AUFGEBEN, THE DARK CLOUD

Aufgeben is a grotesque undead abomination. Unlike other dragonkin, he is not a hunter, a predator or an apex beast but a scavenger who consumes rotten flesh, empowered by fear and death. Immune to all diseases, he smells of rot and is almost always preceded by a hail of buzzing flies and vermin as well as rumors of defeat.

In many ways, Aufgeben is an omen. He is the manifestation of fear among a gathered army—he grows stronger when its odds of victory are bleak. As the individual fears of each soldier grow Aufgeben manifests into a terrifying physical form that longs to feast on their bodies once they fall victim to an invading force. As he feeds, he grows stronger, spreading fear and disaster in equal measure.

Few people have witnessed Aufgeben and stories of him are rare. Those who have come in contact with the beast rarely survive. Victims' corpses are never found, their deaths attributed to fey, ghosts, swamp creatures, undead or the other horrors that stalk the battle-torn lands between encamped forces. Aufgeben is a timeless beast and his ruin has been felt around the world, whether or not people know his name. Should anyone have a story about the Dark Cloud—a bard or bartender, for instance—it is often told through parable and myth, as though the story was born of a child's fantasies and fears.

Each time the tale is recounted, the details vary, but one superstitious aspect is consistent. All good generals know fear of losing a battle can manifest into the swarming body of Aufgeben in an instant. A great many field marshals arrive to battle with hairs on their necks standing upright, unable to push down the fear that they will lose the day. Acknowledging such a fear to their soldiers is enough to summon Aufgeben to the fight, his sole purpose to feed on ensuing failure, to relish the taste of defeat.

Aufgeben is the manifestation of sorrow at the end of life, brought forth into horrible form by so many accursed gods. If there is a fate I would not bestow on the lowliest of foes, it would be Aufgeben.

*—Cyrus the Elder,
Sage of Galewind Tower*

Hook

Aufgeben exists wherever there is death—battlefields, graveyards, plague-riddled lands and the like. As such, the beast is likely to be spotted by peasants and travelers, with rumors of his location quick to follow. Though heroes are unlikely to have encountered Aufgeben face to face, anyone with a soldier's background would at least have heard the rumors of a decaying dragon that moves like a murmuration, eating the dead like a carrion beast—and it sounds like something similar is heading for the frontlines. If not, the great dragon can always eat the dead from a sacred cemetery, which will certainly draw the ire of any who fight to cleanse the world of evil. Other hooks could include:

- The party are messengers sent out to tell a general to stand down his army, but they'll need to get there before Aufgeben does.
- The party stumble upon the two-day-old remnants of a battlefield. The stench is unbearable, but the spoils of war have been left behind. Armor, swords and the like lie in puddles of gore, free for the taking. The buzzing of flies that heralds a rotting dragon is heard in the distance.
- The party are part of a large army that remains a little too long after the fight, only to witness Aufgeben land among the carnage and begin feasting on friend and foe alike. In their weakened state, the party are not a threat to the dragon, who has already deemed the dead its spoils of war...

Encounter Conditions

The smell of decay abounds. Aufgeben is most often found in abattoirs, battlefields and graveyards. He has no true lair. He nests wherever there are dead bodies, piles of bones and rotting carcasses.

Encounter

Encounters with Aufgeben are bound to be lengthy. In the open—on a battlefield for instance—he will see the party coming a long way off. He will have time to prepare and to fly away if necessary. Being undead, he does not sleep, so attacking at him at night is unlikely. If possible, Aufgeben would be found atop a pile of bones and corpses to give himself a better view of the surrounding area.

Tactics

Aufgeben is a scavenger and knows the value of killing the weakest thing first, like a vulture waiting for a lamb to die in the hot sun. Whenever possible, Aufgeben uses his Consume Corpse legendary action. Beyond that, he makes sure to use his lair actions in whatever manner will harm the (perceivably) weakest enemy.

Despite being impervious to many attacks, Aufgeben does not think like a traditional dragon. He is a scavenger and eater of the dead. He does not approach anything he cannot kill easily or that is not already dead. Fighting toe-to-toe with the party is not his style and he keeps them at bay with numerous ranged attacks or by dispersing into smaller forms and flying away. Since he is rarely—if ever—encountered underground, Aufgeben flees at the sight of a strong force and only attacks with his breath weapon at a distance. He will never stand toe-to-toe with fighter types.

Even while airborne, Aufgeben can use his lair actions on the party on the ground. When the party approaches a body pile that the dragon is near, Aufgeben immediately takes flight and targets the party from the air, leaving them to deal with the effect of his presence.

Given that there may be several body pile lairs within a few miles of each other, some lairs may be empty or inactive. This is a prime opportunity for some body piles to be decoys. Game masters can surprise the party with a lair action or two to spring as a trap.

Treasure

Aufgeben has no use for treasure. His stomach consumes everything he eats, and only the strongest of magic could survive his psuedo-intestines. The true prize of defeating Aufgeben is his decaying flesh, which could be studied by a powerful wizard, should they reach the corpse in time.

Aufgeben's Lair

Aufgeben is likely nesting somewhere near a recent and cataclysmic battle, his lair a mound of corpses he collected over several weeks. Aufgeben may have several lairs spread out across the lands.

Lair Actions

On initiative count 20 (losing initiative ties), Aufgeben can take one lair action to cause one of the following effects:

- A pocket of rotten flesh gives way beneath one creature of Aufgeben's choosing. That creature must succeed on a DC 18 Dexterity saving throw or suffer 21 (6d6) acid damage as they slip into a pool of collected stomach acid and fetid blood.
- The rotten corpses piled about in this lair shift in a 15-foot area of Aufgeben's choice. Any creature in this area must succeed on a DC 18 Dexterity saving throw or become buried in corpses. Escaping requires a successful DC 18 Strength (Athletics) saving throw.
- Maggots writhing in the corpses in this area surge upward at Aufgeben's command. The ground in a 20-foot radius centered on a point of Aufgeben's choosing becomes difficult terrain for the next round. When a creature moves into or within the area, it takes 5 (2d4) piercing damage for every 5 feet it travels, as the maggots gnaw at the creature's flesh.

Aufgeben can't repeat an effect until they have all been used, and he can't use the same effect two rounds in a row.

Aufgeben, The Dark Cloud

Gargantuan dragon, chaotic evil, undead

Armor Class 24 (natural armor)
Hit Points 471 (23d20 + 230)
Speed 40 ft., fly 80 ft., burrow 40 ft.

STR	DEX	CON	INT	WIS	CHA
27 (+8)	18 (+4)	30 (+10)	14 (+2)	16 (+3)	8 (-1)

Saving Throws Str +15, Dex +11, Con +17, Wis +10, Cha +6
Skills Investigation +16, Nature +16, Perception +17, Stealth +11
Damage Resistances cold, fire, bludgeoning, piercing and slashing from nonmagical attacks
Damage Immunities necrotic, poison
Condition Immunities blinded, charmed, exhaustion, frightened, grappled, paralyzed, petrified, poisoned, prone
Senses blindsight 120 ft., darkvision 120 ft., tremorsense 30 ft., passive Perception 27
Languages Common, Draconic
Challenge 23 (50,000 XP)

Dark Cloud. Any defending army aware of the presence of Aufgeben within 100 miles of a battlefield, at GM discretion, is demoralized. A DC 18 Charisma (Persuasion) check is required to convince 1d100 percent of the force from deserting.

Divide and Devour (1/day). Aufgeben can choose to exist as a fully formed dragon or as multiple smaller versions of himself on a whim. As an action, Aufgeben can disperse into six individual creatures for one minute. These creatures have the statistics of a **young black dragon** but divide Aufgeben's hit points at the time of dispersal equally among them. When the separated creatures lose half their hit points, they reform into one collective creature and regenerate 22 (4d10) hit points.

Flyby. Aufgeben doesn't provoke opportunity attacks when he flies out of an enemy's reach.

Legendary Resistance (3/Day). If Aufgeben fails a saving throw, he can choose to succeed instead.

Turn Defiance (3/day). Aufgeben and any undead within 60 feet of him are immune to the effects of turn undead.

Stench of Death. Aufgeben reeks of the rotten corpses upon which he feeds. Any creature that starts its turn within 10 feet of Aufgeben must succeed on a DC 15 Constitution saving throw or be poisoned until the start of the creature's next turn. On a successful saving throw, the creature is immune to Aufgeben's stench of death until the end of its next turn.

Actions

Multiattack. Aufgeben can use his Frightful Presence. He then makes three attacks: one with his bite and two with his claws.

Bite (single form). Melee Weapon Attack: +15 to hit, reach 15 ft., one target. *Hit*: 19 (2d10 + 8) piercing damage plus 9 (2d8) poison damage. The target must succeed on a DC 21 Constitution saving throw or become poisoned.

Claw (single form). Melee Weapon Attack: +15 to hit, reach 10 ft., one target. *Hit*: 15 (2d6 + 8) slashing damage. If the target is a creature other than undead, it must succeed on a DC 21 Constitution saving throw or be paralyzed for one minute. The target can repeat the saving throw at the end of its turn, ending the effect on itself on a success.

Rotten Breath (Recharge 5–6). Aufgeben exhales acid and rotten flesh in a 90-foot line that is 10 feet wide. Each creature in that line must make a DC 22 Dexterity saving throw, taking 67 (15d8) acid damage on a failed save or half as much damage on a success. Additionally, each creature in the area of effect must succeed on a DC 18 Constitution saving throw or be poisoned until the end of their next turn.

Tail. Melee Weapon Attack: +15 to hit, reach 20 ft ., one target. *Hit*: 17 (2d8 + 8) bludgeoning damage.

Frightful Presence. Each creature of Aufgeben's choice within 120 feet of Aufgeben and aware of it must succeed on a DC 19 Wisdom saving throw or become frightened for one minute. A creature can repeat the saving throw at the end of each of its turns, ending the effect on itself on a success. If a creature's saving throw is successful or the effect ends for it, the creature is immune to Aufgeben's Frightful Presence for the next 24 hours.

Legendary Actions

Aufgeben can take three legendary actions, choosing from the options below. Only one legendary action option can be used at a time and only at the end of another creature's turn. Aufgeben regains spent legendary actions at the start of his turn.

Detect. Aufgeben makes a Wisdom (Perception) check.

Bite Attack. Aufgeben makes a bite attack.

Consume corpse (Costs 3 Actions). Aufgeben devours a dead body, swallowing it whole. Aufgeben can roll hit dice as if taking a short rest, and his breath weapon is automatically recharged.

Wing Attack (Costs 2 Actions). Aufgeben beats his wings. Each creature within 15 feet of Aufgeben must succeed on a DC 23 Dexterity saving throw or take 15 (2d6 + 8) bludgeoning damage and be knocked prone. Aufgeben can then fly up to half his flying speed.

BALAUR, BEAST OF WAR

Balaur was once a proud dragon. He soared over a vast woodland territory filled with a multitude of creatures that cowered before him. Then came the adventurers. For their wizard, it was not enough to just defeat a dragon. Balaur was captured alive and became the subject of this wizard's dark fascination.

Like many proud wizards before him, Balaur's captor became increasingly obsessed with expanding his knowledge. Eventually, this growing curiosity drove the wizard to madness, and he began to vivisect Balaur, prying arcane secrets from the dragon at the ends of cruel implements. Finally, the dragon snapped.

Though the wizard was dead and Balaur's belly full, the dragon was still imprisoned within the bowels of a remote tower. As luck would have it, this tower had long been coveted by a band of duergar marauders. Without the wizard's magic to protect it, these duergar finally captured the fortification, only to discover a dragon kept within.

Balaur had been stripped of all his scales by the time the duergar found him. His hide was scarred beyond all comprehension; he hardly looked like a dragon. The duergar could have killed him, but instead saw an opportunity—though it may have been Balaur that planted the seeds of this idea. The duergar offered to rehabilitate him, forge a new set of scales for him and in return, he would march with their army and bring down the walls of their enemies.

An alliance was formed, towns were plundered and thus the Sunless Horde were born. The dragon-backed duergar march with a deliberate pace; the drums that herald their arrival beat in sync with the almost mechanical steps of their weapon of war. The first sacked cities had enough time to send messages to allies beyond their borders, but the warnings were of little use. One by one, every settlement in the path of this growing army and their seemingly unstoppable siege weapon fell to its overwhelming might or surrendered before the mighty dragon bellowed their buildings into cinders.

The march continues, ever onward, the Horde's desire for more riches driving them to march a bit farther each day. Balaur understands his role, and is grateful for this second chance at life. But he tires of toppling capitals and crushing the weak. There's no challenge. No spark. No worthy warriors willing to stare him down and test his mettle (and, of course, his metal). As the Sunless Horde marches ever onward, perhaps this fact will change.

Hear the drums and feel the thrum—
the dragon comes for thee.
And if you have a lick-a sense
you'll yield yer territree.
His hide is formed of finest plate
his breath a wicked flame.
"On Balaur, Balaur, Balaur on!"
for Balaur is his name.

—From "On Balaur," a 39-stanza poem by Shade Slateslicker of the Sunless Horde

Hook

Balaur is a credible threat to almost any kingdom or nation. In campaigns looking to blend armed conflict with the intrigues of national politics, Balaur unifies those styles. The party will likely be asked to assist one or more nations as they prepare for the coming conflict with the duergar force. Skirmishes with this advancing army will be frequent.

Perhaps the duergar are just beginning to assemble their armies. Should Balaur, the weapon that their clans have rallied behind, be slain, the cohesion among their ranks will crumble and they'll likely disband.

Maybe Balaur has already crippled a kingdom. With the first castle fallen, nearby rulers are in a panic.

Or, it could be that Balaur has begun to balk at the commands of his latest captors. He has already started to look for opportunities to regain his freedom.

However he is introduced, Balaur works exceptionally well in campaigns that involve the continual drama of war. It might only be a threat, at least at first, but a mighty dragon aiding the duergar presents the potential to reshape nations that are not strong or resourceful enough to stand against such a mighty enemy.

Encounter Conditions

On a battlefield amongst the Sunless Horde, an army of duergar.

Encounter

Balaur is not permitted to move without the Sunless Horde following. This force of duergar warriors also contains numerous arcanists and priests of dark gods. They soften up targets before Balaur wades into battle. It is his task to penetrate more fortified defenses, namely city or castle walls.

Confronting Balaur directly often requires raising an army to oppose the duergar that protect him. On the battlefield, the lower-ranking duergar take orders from Balaur, and he uses them to keep enemies at bay. He will eagerly send these troops against his foes, sometimes to the detriment of the greater conflict. These lives are little more than currency to spend to ensure his survival.

Tactics

Balaur does not fight without cause and never without a legion of duergar at his back. Before conflict has a chance to deplete their numbers, they are his most impressive attack. With a terrible roar, he can call down a rain of javelins and crossbow bolts. While his armor weighs him down enough to slow his flight, he remains quite agile on the ground. Should he need to retreat, he often uses his fiery breath to ignite obstacles and feels no remorse in allowing the duergar to stand in the way of his pursuers as well.

In extreme circumstances, Balaur might permit a duergar mage or warpriest to ride upon his back.

Their spells complement his brutality and sometimes they assist him with healing or protection. Balaur's confidence in the durability of his armor is perhaps his only vulnerability. Taking away that advantage makes him much easier to vanquish.

Wealth for War

Balaur's only love is the din of battle. His treasure hoard is full of the implements with which creatures wage war. Such things require tremendous resources to create and maintain, as does the massive suit of adamantine armor he wears. His hoard therefore also contains immense wealth—not just gold and jewels, but caches of iron ore and rare timber.

Balaur's Lair

Balaur's lair is not a permanent structure. Instead, his lair is amid the Sunless Horde, an army of duergar that support him and keep him captive. Dozens of armed duergar and the cooks, blacksmiths and servants that assist them follow Balaur like a shadow. Sometimes commanders give him orders and other times he makes requests of them.

The Sunless Horde travels old routes in the world below, avoiding the painful glare of the sun. The few dwarven settlements deep beneath the surface fell to the duergar long ago and are used by the Sunless Horde to conceal Balaur from their enemies.

Lair Actions

On initiative count 20 (losing initiative ties), Balaur takes a lair action to cause one of the following effects. He can't use the same effect two rounds in a row.

- Balaur chooses up to six allies or siege weapons that he can see within 100 feet of him. These targets can move up to their speed as a reaction.
- Balaur chooses one siege weapon he can see within 60 feet. That siege weapon can make an attack against an object as a reaction. If this attack hits, it deals an additional 20 points of damage.
- Balaur's presence grants advantage to any of its allies and siege weapons in the area for one round.

Regional Effects

Balaur's draconic presence amplifies the impact that the duergar army has upon the world, which often creates one or more of the following effects:

- Fires within 6 miles of the lair burn brighter and hotter than usual and give off a thick, black smoke that has a vaguely metallic scent.
- Creatures within 1 mile of the lair feel a lingering unease. Birds remain silent, horses spook and most of the common folk suffer from poor nights of sleep.

If Balaur dies, conditions of the area surrounding the lair return to normal over 1d10 days.

BALAUR, BEAST OF WAR

Gargantuan dragon, lawful evil

Armor Class 24 (adamantine plate armor)
Hit Points 507 (26d20 + 234)
Speed 40 ft., fly 40 ft. (fly 30 ft. with adamantine armor)

STR	DEX	CON	INT	WIS	CHA
30 (+10)	10 (+0)	29 (+9)	15 (+2)	18 (+4)	22 (+6)

Saving Throws Dex +7, Con +16, Wis +11, Cha +13
Skills Athletics +17, Perception +11, Stealth +7
Damage Immunities none, special (see abilities)
Condition Immunities charmed
Senses blindsight 60 ft., darkvision 120 ft., passive Perception 21
Languages Abyssal, Common, Draconic, Infernal
Challenge 21 (33,000 XP)

Adamantine Armor. Balaur wears a suit of adamantine armor that provides resistance to damage from any attack and grants advantage on saving throws against spells. The armor has a Damage Threshold of 15 and is immune to fire, poison and psychic damage.

While wearing this armor, Balaur's flying speed is reduced to 30 feet, and he must end his movement on a solid surface, or he will fall.

Legendary Resistance (3/Day). If Balaur fails a saving throw, he can choose to succeed instead.

Pounce. If Balaur moves at least 20 feet straight toward a target and then hits it with a claw attack on the same turn, the target takes an extra 9 (2d8) slashing damage. If the target is a creature, it must succeed on a DC 15 Dexterity saving throw or be knocked prone. If the target is prone, Balaur can make a bite attack against it as a bonus action.

Siege Monster. Balaur deals double damage to objects and structures.

ACTIONS

Multiattack. Balaur can use his Frightful Presence. He then makes three attacks: one with his bite and two with his claws.

Bite. Melee Weapon Attack: +17 to hit, reach 15 ft., one target. *Hit:* 21 (2d10 + 10) piercing + 13 (3d8) fire damage.

Claw. Melee Weapon Attack: +17 to hit, reach 10 ft., one target. *Hit:* 17 (2d6 + 10) slashing damage.

Tail. Melee Weapon Attack: +17 to hit, reach 20 ft., one target. *Hit:* 19 (2d8 + 10) bludgeoning damage.

Battle Roar. Any allied creatures that can see and hear Balaur can use their reaction to make a weapon attack. Each creature within 60 feet of Balaur must make a DC 20 Constitution saving throw or become deafened until the end of their next turn.

Frightful Presence. Each creature of Balaur's choice that is within 120 feet of him and aware of him must succeed on a DC 21 Wisdom saving throw or become frightened for one minute. A creature can repeat the saving throw at the end of each of its turns, ending the effect on itself on a success. If a creature's saving throw is successful or the effect ends for it, the creature is immune to Balaur's Frightful Presence for the next 24 hours.

Burning Breath (Recharge 5–6). Balaur exhales fire in a 90-foot cone. Each creature in that area must make a DC 24 Dexterity saving throw, taking 91 (26d6) fire damage on a failed save or half as much damage on a successful one. Objects in the area take the full damage, and flammable objects that aren't being worn or carried are ignited.

LEGENDARY ACTIONS

Balaur can take three legendary actions, choosing from the options below. Only one legendary action option can be used at a time and only at the end of another creature's turn. Balaur regains spent legendary actions at the start of his turn.

Detect. Balaur makes a Wisdom (Perception) check.

Tail Attack. Balaur makes a tail attack.

Overrun (Costs 2 Actions). Balaur moves up to his speed. During this movement, he can move through the spaces of any Large or smaller creatures. When he moves through a space occupied by a creature, that creature must make a DC 22 Strength saving throw or be knocked prone.

Siege Support (Costs 2 Actions). Balaur chooses two siege weapons that he can see and directs them to make attacks against his choice of target. The siege weapons have advantage on this attack.

BALLEG,
THE RAVAGED WYRM

No one utters Balleg's name lightly. Children who use it as a curse word are disciplined, quickly and severely. It is not a name used in jest or spoken without some understanding of why you said it.

Some believe simply whispering its name can summon Balleg.

There are many dragons in the world. No one knows for sure how many. But those who live here understand there's a routine, a balance, and that reality carries with it a few expectations. Red dragons are bad news, but you know what you're in for. Gold dragons are generally good, and they wear their heart on their scales.

But Balleg...Balleg is another story entirely. Balleg redefined evil. Born with tattered wings and plucked from the Void—where all magic is born—Balleg was summoned by a powerful necromancer, Gjorn the Illborn. Looking to avoid detection from any and all powerful things, the wizard squeezed the newborn dragon through the tiniest pinhole in the Void. Upon this "birth," Balleg was thrust into this world and imprisoned by Gjorn.

Impossibly, the beast's flesh continues to surge with arcane possibility in spite of its necrotic state. I intend to reach further into the Void tomorrow. This dragon will serve as my portal to forever life and unlimited power. Lichhood awaits!

—Gjorn the Illborn,
Notes From a Necromancer, Vol. 39

And as unbelievable as it sounds, Balleg somehow became even worse.

For two decades, Balleg was the subject of every cruel experiment Gjorn could fathom. Using Balleg's body as a magical focus, Gjorn carved away at the dragon's flesh, utilizing every piece he could to study the extremities of magic. The experiments were excruciating, and Balleg's body was ripped apart.

Gjorn realized Balleg would not survive at that rate of experimentation pace. And since the magic expended summoning Balleg was far too great to attempt again, he knew this was the only living subject he'd ever have. Gjorn turned his attention to extending Balleg's "life."

His plan was simple: turn the dragon undead.

Using a complicated ritual, Gjorn placed Balleg into a force cage and scorched its body with magic. Hours turned to days, as the necromancer summoned every ounce of magic he knew to transform the dragon into unliving flesh. But Gjorn failed to understand the Void. It does not obey the laws of magic the way other elements do. Instead of weakening, Balleg grew in power. The dragon became something otherworldly.

The necro-dragon's flesh is half-missing. In its place is a spectral image of what Balleg believes it should look like. In this form, Balleg is half-dragon and half-ethereal beast, but all undead. Its flesh is just a tool for navigating the physical world, its shape, an apparatus for striking fear into the weak-willed and superstitious masses. Balleg is not subtle. Balleg is walking destruction.

Balleg wants the world to pay for what has happened to it. Now that nothing remains of the necromancer who brought this state upon it, Balleg's vengeance knows no specific target.

Despite the destruction it has brought to these lands, none will speak its name.

Their fear is justified.

Hook

Balleg's story belongs in any campaign. GMs are encouraged to write rumors of a twisted, malevolent half-dragon into their campaigns long before the party ever encounters Balleg. When they do, it should already have entire regions of the world under its thumb. Balleg easily has the power to control a town or small city. Or even a shire. The stories leading up to its control are up to the GM to devise. But just looking at Balleg should be enough to convince players the average footman is no match against a flying dragon that is only visible half the time.

Encounter

Balleg lacks subtlety. Balleg seeks out those that wish it harm and destroys everything in its path to reach them. There, Balleg will use its power to dismantle the offending hero. For those Balleg does not know, it will simply break them and throw the remains to the wolves.

Tactics

Balleg is especially hateful of spellcasters. Its first action is to burn them to the ground, regardless of who else is there. Its tactics are not dim or wild, but they aren't precise or smart like a field marshal, either. If an opportunity presents itself, even if an average person would know it's a trap, Balleg strikes.

Balleg does not give hardy-looking adventurers the chance to surprise it or catch it in a cave like a hibernating bear. It can also keep its distance from the party, using Enervating Breath on spellcasters. Balleg uses Legendary Resistance wisely. It is well aware of what constitutes powerful magic and reserves this ability for top tier spells.

Outdoors, Balleg attacks the party from a distance, keeping them guessing with aerial moves and magical spells—*earthquake* (500-foot range) and *chain lightning* (150-foot range) are used early, while its Incorporeal Movement and *black tentacles* (90 feet) are used as a surprise attack against an unwitting foe (a spellcaster perhaps) after several rounds of fighting. If a wizard gets within 60 feet of Balleg, it casts *telekinesis* immediately, lifting the wizard in the air and keeping them in its grip.

Underground, Balleg fights tooth and nail. While surrounded, it uses its Ghostly Surge. It alternates its lair actions to summon more minions to its aid. Balleg uses its Incorporeal Movement to get behind the enemies or maneuver when surrounded. It fights like a caged animal, but it has the mind of a wizard, which means it's not going to let anyone get the best of it.

Just when the party thinks they have the advantage, it uses a Legendary Action or its Incorporeal Movement to get away. Or it taps into power they didn't know it had.

Regardless of where Balleg encounters the party, it knows the advantage of keeping itself at a distance from adventurers. It has plenty of minions to throw at the party to occupy them until it can get in close.

Wealth for War

Balleg's previous master owned powerful magic items that survived the dragon's wrath. Spellbooks, necromantic theory and a map to the largest hidden graveyard in the world make up the lion's share of the treasure. Balleg's tormentor also left behind an indestructible iron coffin. Its true purpose is unknown.

Balleg's Lair

Balleg's lair is claustrophobic and cramped. The route to Balleg's final lair is constrained, while the final resting place is just big enough for Balleg to rest in.

Lair Actions

On initiative count 20 (losing initiative ties), Balleg takes a lair action to cause one of the following effects. Balleg can't use the same effect two rounds in a row.

- Four **wights** rise, appearing in unoccupied spaces that Balleg can see within 100 feet. They act immediately and on initiative count 20 in subsequent rounds and obey Balleg's telepathic commands. They remain until Balleg uses this action again. If Balleg dies, the wights become free-willed creatures.
- A wall of moaning, thrashing corpses springs into existence on a solid surface within 120 feet of Balleg. The wall is up to 60 feet long, 10 feet high and 5 feet thick, and it blocks the line of sight. When the wall appears, each creature in its area must make a DC 15 Dexterity saving throw. A creature that fails the save takes 18 (4d8) bludgeoning damage and is pushed 5 feet out of the wall's space, appearing on whichever side of the wall it wants. A creature that ends its turn within 5 feet of the wall must make a DC 15 Dexterity saving throw or take 18 (4d8) bludgeoning damage on a failed save or half as much damage on a successful one.

  Each 10-foot section of wall has AC 5, 15 hit points, resistance to piercing and bludgeoning damage and immunity to necrotic, poison and psychic damage. The wall sinks back into the ground when Balleg uses this lair action again or when Balleg dies.

Regional Effects

The region containing Balleg's lair is warped by its magic, which creates one or more of the following effects:

- Thick clouds shroud the area within 1 mile of the lair. Storms are common, and even during the day the ambient light is dim at best.
- Scavengers and carrion birds are common and aggressive toward creatures within 5 miles of the lair.
- Creatures who take a long rest within 1 mile of the lair must succeed on a DC 10 Wisdom saving throw or suffer madness at GM discretion.

If Balleg dies, these effects end in 1d10 days.

Balleg, The Ravaged Wyrm

Huge undead dragon, chaotic evil

Armor Class 19 (natural armor)
Hit Points 272 (32d12 + 64)
Speed 40 ft., fly 80 ft. (hover)

STR	DEX	CON	INT	WIS	CHA
19 (+4)	21 (+5)	14 (+2)	20 (+5)	18 (+4)	15 (+2)

Saving Throws Dex +11, Con +8, Wis +10, Cha +8
Skills Arcana +11, Perception +10, Stealth +11
Damage Resistances acid, cold, fire, lightning, thunder; bludgeoning, piercing and slashing from nonmagical attacks
Damage Immunities necrotic, poison
Condition Immunities charmed, exhaustion, frightened, paralyzed, poisoned
Senses blindsight 60 ft., darkvision 120 ft., passive Perception 20
Languages Common, Draconic
Challenge 17 (18,000 XP)

Incorporeal Movement. Balleg can move through other creatures and objects as if they are difficult terrain. It takes 5 (1d10) force damage if it ends its turn inside an object.

Innate Spellcasting. Balleg's spellcasting ability is Charisma (spell save DC 16, +8 to hit with spell attacks). Balleg can innately cast the following spells, requiring no material components:

> *Inside lair (1/day each): blight, cloudkill, finger of death, vampiric touch*
> *Outside lair (1/day each): black tentacles, chain lightning, earthquake, telekinesis*

Legendary Resistance (5/Day). If Balleg fails a saving throw, it can choose to succeed instead.

Turning Defiance. Balleg and any other undead within 30 feet of Balleg have advantage on saving throws against any effect that turns undead.

Undead Nature. Balleg doesn't require air, food, drink or sleep.

Actions

Multiattack. Balleg uses its Frightful Presence. It then makes three attacks: one with its bite and two with its claws.

Bite. Melee Weapon Attack: +10 to hit, reach 10 ft., one target. *Hit:* 15 (2d10 + 4) piercing damage plus 7 (2d6) necrotic damage.

Claw. Melee Weapon Attack: +10 to hit, reach 5 ft., one target. *Hit:* 11 (2d6 + 4) slashing damage.

Tail. Melee Weapon Attack: +10 to hit, reach 15 ft., one target. *Hit:* 13 (2d8 + 4) bludgeoning damage.

Balleg's Frightful Presence. Each creature of Balleg's choice that is within 120 feet of Balleg and aware of it must succeed on a DC 17 Wisdom saving throw or become frightened for one minute. A creature can repeat the saving throw at the end of each of its turns, ending the effect on itself on a success. If a creature's saving throw is successful or the effect ends for it, the creature is immune to Balleg's Frightful Presence for the next 24 hours. A creature has disadvantage on saving throws made against this ability.

Enervating Breath (Recharge 5–6). Balleg exhales waves of necrotic energy in a 60-foot cone. Each creature in that area must make a DC 19 Dexterity saving throw, taking 49 (14d6) necrotic damage, and is weakened for one minute, suffering disadvantage on attack rolls, ability checks and saving throws based on Strength on a failed save. On a success, it suffers half as much damage and isn't weakened. A weakened creature can repeat the save at the end of its turn, ending the effect on itself on a success. *Lesser restoration* or similar magic also removes the weakness at GM discretion.

Legendary Actions

Balleg can take three legendary actions, choosing from the options below. Only one legendary action option can be used at a time and only at the end of another creature's turn. Balleg regains spent legendary actions at the start of its turn.

Death Sight (Costs 3 Actions). Balleg targets a single creature that it can see. The targeted creature must succeed on a DC 16 Dexterity saving throw or take 30 (6d10) necrotic damage. The target dies if this damage reduces it to 0 hit points.

Ghostly Surge (Costs 2 Actions). Balleg releases a surge of necrotic energy. Each creature within 10 feet of Balleg must succeed on a DC 18 Dexterity saving throw or take 12 (2d6 + 5) necrotic damage and be knocked prone. Balleg can then fly up to half its flying speed.

Tail Attack. Balleg makes a tail attack.

FURY, DRAGON QUEEN OF HELL

Somewhere in hell's great lake of fire is a hidden island made of pure gold. An ever-growing mountain of gold coins, chalices, idols and other glimmering finery rises from the flames and at its top is a majestic golden throne. Atop that throne rests a dragon—but although Feth'razaal is known as Fury, the Dragon Queen of Hell, she rarely assumes draconic shape. Those who dare to gaze upon her majesty see a woman of unbelievable strength and beauty. Seven feet tall, she is draped in an ash-black dress that crackles with tiny flames like smoldering coals. Her skin is tanned and patches of golden scales burst seemingly at random across her face, arms and slender, powerful legs. An unruly mane of crimson hair cascades down her back, a pair of onyx horns curl from her brow and wings of smoke and flame emerge from her back.

The King of Hell, Asmodeus, admired Feth'razaal's vast bounty of souls and sought her hand in marriage, kneeling and offering her a band of hell-forged gold. Although Feth'razaal knew that the King of Hell could not be trusted and that his proposal was a selfish gesture prodigiously stuffed with false humility, she was flattered despite her better judgment and accepted. She took the pleasing shape of one of hell's greatest warriors, the mighty erinyes, and wedded Asmodeus in his great citadel. She vowed silently to match her treacherous new husband scheme for scheme and wrest power from him just as he sought to undo hers.

But the game grew wearisome after centuries of play. The artifice of love and loyalty wore thin for both Asmodeus and his queen. Feth'razaal's disgust for the selfish, arrogant and oft-distant King of Hell grew boundless, and one day she confronted him on his iron throne. She took his ring from her talon, popped it in her mouth like a sweet and spat the molten gold—melted by her dragonflame—in Asmodeus's face, then departed, vowing one day to claim hell as her own and rule it as its rightful queen. Asmodeus was stunned for only an instant before he rose in fury and demanded his wife's head on a platter, but in that instant, Feth'razaal had already gathered her numerous allies within the courts of hell and flown from her old palace.

Feth'razaal discarded her old name—one that had been tainted by centuries of false love—when she broke her vow with the King of Hell and took on a new title that encompassed her boundless ambition and wrath: Fury. In the intervening eons, Fury carved out a mighty domain within the inferno and named herself an archdevil. Many of the souls she claimed as a mortal dragon millennia ago now loyally serve her as fiendish warriors, preferring the devil they know over the tyrannical rule of Asmodeus. Others take mortal form and venture into the world of the living to steal and pillage gold or souls to deliver as tribute to their queen—just as they did in life. Someday, Fury knows she and her armies will grow powerful enough to dethrone Asmodeus once and for all. Until then, she is content to bide her time and live in luxury as Fury, Dragon Queen of Hell.

Her love for the Lord of the Ninth was almost as strong as her lust for power. Almost, but not quite. And soon, after spending full centuries at his side, she expressed her desires by making her intentions clear: Nothing less than the ultimate crown will sate her.

—An Accounting of Devils, ch. 9: "Desires of the Dragon Queen"

HOOK

The party may first learn of Fury's plot to overthrow Asmodeus from a patron, possibly a celestial or even a deity seeking to capitalize on an infernal coup d'état. They are encouraged to investigate. Of course, by the time the characters are strong enough to journey into hell on a whim, they may have already made allies or enemies within the infernal hierarchy. The characters may be approached by an emissary of an archdevil they have aided or opposed in the past who then offers them a mighty bounty if they save their king from a potential usurper—or they may secretly wish to see the King of Hell deposed, and provide the characters an excellent reward if they aid Fury's cause.

ENCOUNTER CONDITIONS

Fury may be encountered scheming within her lair in hell's deepest fiery circle or elsewhere in the Multiverse as she hunts for allies in her battle against Asmodeus.

Outside of her lair, Fury rarely picks a fight herself. Centuries of navigating the courts of hell have taught her that lies, subterfuge and charm are her greatest assets. She maintains her attractive fiendish form at all times when outside of hell, except when she is forced to fight for her life or when she must assume draconic form to fly from plane to plane.

ENCOUNTER

Fury plays the long game. She aims to make allies of all beings that could aid her in her quest to destroy Asmodeus, and even those who refuse to serve her are often simply cast aside unharmed. But Fury remembers every soul that denied her, and when she decides to take vengeance, her retribution is swift. Whenever she needs souls to bolster her army of devils, she appears from thin air—in fiendish form if her targets are within civilization or in draconic form if they are not—and attacks without pretense.

If approached within her infernal lair, Fury heaps on praise for the party's resourcefulness and skill for reaching the hottest depths of hell. She aims to keep their aggression at bay until she can ascertain their opinion toward Asmodeus and their willingness to join her in her quest. If she thinks they could be worthy allies, she politely requests their allegiance. If they refuse, or if she determines they are of no use to her, she attacks without warning, declaring that if they cannot serve her in life, their souls will serve her for eternity. When encountered in her lair, Fury is joined by an honor guard of two **pit fiends**.

TACTICS

Fury's arrogance may be her undoing. Even as a mortal dragon, she saw humanoid beings as little more than insects. Now, as an archdevil, Fury's hubris has only grown. She begins all combat in her fiendish form unless circumstances require her to fight into a dragon.

At the beginning of combat, Fury spreads damage as widely as she can, demonstrating her power to as many creatures as possible. If she is forced to assume draconic form, Fury realizes that her opponents are not as weak as she suspected and focuses her fire on a single creature to kill it as fast as possible, then raise its soul as a devil using her Lair Action. Even in this state, she fights without care, for she knows she will soon be reborn in hell if she is killed outside the inferno. If she finds herself in any danger of defeat within hell's borders, Fury *plane shifts* away to her old lair on the Material Plane to recuperate. She seethes with anger at not just her wounded pride, but also the loss of her mighty treasure and of such a critical disruption in her war against Asmodeus. Any adventurers who force Fury to retreat in such an undignified manner rise to the top of her list of nemeses.

Fury has sworn to dethrone Asmodeus and has chosen weapons and developed a breath weapon specifically designed to destroy fiends—and to slaughter celestials—in case the gods of the upper planes decide that her quest to kill the King of Hell is a threat to the cosmic balance. Curiously, the magic Asmodeus used to transform Feth'razaal into a devil still lingers in Fury's draconic form, and any creature that she bites may begin to turn into a devil itself. This suits Fury well enough, as it lets her tear through mortal opponents as if they were Asmodeus's servants.

WEALTH

Fury rests upon a treasure hoard befitting an archdevil. The vast bulk of the hoard is an island made entirely of coins from across the millennia, including 10d10 × 100,000 pp, 20d10 × 200,000 gp, 30d10 × 300,000 sp and 50d10 × 500,000 cp. Atop this island of coins are chalices, statues and other objets d'art worth a total of 5d10 × 200 gp.

Also hidden amid the treasure are six wondrous items, which a character can find by spending 10 minutes searching and then making a successful DC 18 Intelligence (Investigation) check. These magic items are: a *mithral plate of fire resistance*, a *nine lives stealer*, a *rod of rulership*, a *staff of striking*, an *Ioun stone of mastery* and a *portable hole*. The portable hole appears to be a piece of heavy black fabric tied into a knot. Untying it and shaking it out causes an additional 5d10 × 1,000 gp to fall out.

Fury's wealth is practically beyond measure, but adventurers who defeat her must then figure out how to return it safely to their home.

Fury, Dragon Queen of Hell

Medium fiend (shapeshifter), lawful evil

Armor Class 18 fiendish form (natural armor), 22 draconic form
Hit Points 405 (30d8 + 270)
Speed 30 ft., fly 60 ft. in fiendish form, fly 80 ft. in dragon form, swim 40 ft. in draconic form

---

STR	DEX	CON	INT	WIS	CHA
21 (+5)	28 (+9)	19 (+4)	16 (+3)	16 (+3)	30 (+10)

Saving Throws Dex +13, Con +17, Wis +11, Cha +17
Skills Insight +11, Intimidation +17, Perception +19, **Persuasion** +17
Damage Immunities acid, cold, lightning
Condition Immunities charmed, exhaustion, frightened, poisoned
Senses truesight 120 ft., passive Perception 29
Languages all, telepathy 120 ft.
Challenge 25 (75,000 XP)

Change Form. Fury can use her action to magically polymorph into her true draconic form. In this form, she is considered a dragon as well as a fiend, and she can use her action to transform back into her fiendish form. Her statistics are the same in each form, except as listed, and except for her size, which increases to Gargantuan in draconic form. Any equipment she is wearing or carrying when she transforms is absorbed or borne by her new form.

If Fury transforms while grappled by another creature, she can attempt to escape the grapple as a reaction. She has advantage on Strength (Athletics) and Dexterity (Acrobatics) checks made in this way.

While Fury is in her fiendish form and she is reduced to half her maximum hit points or takes damage while below her maximum hit points, she can choose to instantly polymorph into her draconic form and gain 150 temporary hit points. After doing so, she cannot transform back into a fiend until she completes a long rest.

Cord of Hellish Restraint. Fury possesses a rope of entanglement that gains additional power while she is attuned to it. Only Fury can attune to this magic item. The DC of the cord's effects is increased to 22, its AC is increased to 25 and its hit points are increased to 50. If the cord is destroyed by an attack that is not silvered, it instantly reforms in Fury's hand with full hit points at the start of her next turn. Fiends and celestials have disadvantage on ability checks and saving throws against the cord's power.

Legendary Resistance (3/Day). If Fury fails a saving throw, she can choose to succeed instead.

Magic Resistance. Fury has advantage on saving throws against spells and other magical effects.

Magic Weapons. Fury's weapon attacks in both fiendish and draconic forms are magical.

Plane Shift. If she flies 80 feet in a straight line in a single turn, Fury can cast *plane shift* as an action before the end of that turn.

Actions

Multiattack. In her humanoid form, Fury makes three attacks. In her draconic form, Fury can use her Damning Presence and then makes one attack with her bite and two with her claws.

Longsword of Planar Disruption (Fiendish Form only). Melee Weapon Attack: +18 to hit, reach 5 ft., one target. *Hit:* 14 (1d8 + 10) slashing damage plus 33 (6d10) force damage if the target is on its home plane.

Cords of Hellish Restraint (Fiendish Form only). Melee Weapon Attack: +18 to hit, reach 10 ft., one target. *Hit:* 12 (1d4 + 10) slashing damage and the target is restrained. A creature restrained by the cords is considered to be on its home plane and takes 11 (2d10) force damage at the start of each of its turns. A creature can make a DC 22 Dexterity saving throw at the end of each of its turns, breaking free and ending the effect on a success. Fiends and celestials have disadvantage on this saving throw.

Longbow of Planar Recall (Fiendish Form only). Ranged Weapon Attack: +13 to hit, range 150/600 ft., one target. *Hit:* 9 (1d8 + 5) piercing damage plus 33 (6d10) force damage if the target is not on its home plane. If this attack reduces a creature to 0 hit points, it is banished to its home plane.

Bite (Draconic Form only). Melee Weapon Attack: +18 to hit, reach 15 ft., one target. *Hit:* 21 (2d10 + 10) piercing damage. If the target is a living creature, it must succeed on a DC 22 Charisma saving throw or take 22 (4d10) radiant damage and gain the fiend type in addition to its original type.

Claw (Draconic Form only). Melee Weapon Attack: +18 to hit, reach 10 ft., one target. *Hit:* 19 (2d8 + 10) slashing damage plus 22 (4d10) necrotic damage if the target is a fiend or celestial.

Tail (Draconic Form only). Melee Weapon Attack: +18 to hit, reach 20 ft., one target. *Hit:* 19 (2d8 + 10) bludgeoning damage.

Damning Presence (Draconic Form only). Each humanoid creature of Fury's choice that is within 120 feet of her and is aware of her must succeed on a DC 22 Charisma saving throw or be charmed by her for one minute. All creatures charmed in this way gain the fiend type in addition to their original type. An affected creature must repeat this save at the end of each of its turns, ending the effect on itself on a success. If the creature is reduced to 0 hit points while charmed in this way, or if it fails this save three times before succeeding once, it is permanently transformed into a **lemure** under Fury's control. The creature can no longer be resurrected until the devil it was transformed into is killed and its soul is repaired by a wish. If a creature's saving throw is successful or the effect ends for it, the creature is immune to Fury's Damning Presence for the next 24 hours.

Breath of Vengeance (Recharge 5–6; Draconic Form only). Fury exhales prismatic fire in a 90-foot cone. Each creature in that area must make a DC 22 Dexterity saving throw, taking 44 (8d10) radiant damage and 44 (8d10) necrotic damage on a failed save or half as much damage on a success. Fiends and celestials have disadvantage on this saving throw.

Legendary Actions

Fury can take three legendary actions, choosing from the options below. Only one legendary action option can be used at a time and only at the end of another creature's turn. Fury regains spent legendary actions at the start of her turn.

Detect. Fury makes a Wisdom (Perception) check.

Attack. Fury makes an attack with her tail or her longsword of planar disruption.

Wing Attack (Costs 2 Actions). Fury beats her wings. Each creature within 15 feet of her must succeed on a DC 23 Dexterity saving throw or take 17 (2d6 + 10) bludgeoning damage and be knocked prone. Fury can then fly up to half her flying speed.

FURY'S LAIR

Fury may be encountered scheming within her lair in hell's deepest fiery circle, or elsewhere in the multiverse as she hunts for allies in her battle against Asmodeus.

Outside of her lair, Fury rarely picks a fight herself. Centuries of navigating the courts of the lower planes have taught her that lies, subterfuge and charm are her greatest assets. She maintains her attractive, fiendish form at all times when outside of hell, except when she is forced to fight for her life, or when she must assume draconic form to fly from plane to plane.

Within her lair, Fury lounges in her fiendish form upon her burning throne. This seat of fiery gold stands atop a mountain of treasure that forms an island with a 120-foot radius in an infernal sea of crackling flames. A creature takes 5 (1d10) fire damage if it begins its turn on this island of red-hot metal.

LAIR ACTIONS

On initiative count 20 (losing initiative ties), Fury takes a lair action to cause one of the following effects. Fury can't use the same effect two rounds in a row.

- Fury causes a jet of molten gold to burst from the ground at a point she can see within 120 feet of her. The gold fills a cylinder that is 50 feet tall with a 10-foot radius, centered on that point. Each creature in that area must succeed on a DC 22 Dexterity saving throw, taking 28 (8d6) fire damage on a failed save or half as much damage on a successful one. On a failed save, a creature is also encased in solid gold, granting it total cover, and is restrained until the casing is broken. The casing has AC 18, 50 hp and is immune to poison and psychic damage. The casing shatters when Fury uses another lair action.
- Fury's eyes flash gold, and all creatures that can see her must succeed on a DC 22 Wisdom saving throw or be charmed by her until she uses another lair action. An affected creature can repeat this save at the end of each of its turns, ending the effect on itself on a success.
- Fury chooses the corpse of a creature that she can see who died within the last minute. Its soul materializes as a **lemure**; at this point, the creature cannot be resurrected until the devil it was transformed into is killed and its soul is repaired by a *wish*.
- Fury promotes a lemure she can see into a more powerful devil. Roll 1d6 on the table below to see what kind of devil the lemure transforms into:

1d6	Devil
1	an **imp**
2	a **spined devil**
3	a **bearded devil**
4	a **barbed devil**
5	a **chain devil**
6	a **bone devil**

REGIONAL EFFECTS

Fury's lair is within the hells, and any party interested in facing her there does so at their peril. Should Fury choose to leave her lair within the hells and take refuge somewhere on the prime material plane (or another location at GM discretion) for an extended period, the power she commands would inevitably shift the landscape around her through proximity. The regional effects below presume Fury has built a lair beyond the hells in the prime material. Adjust at your discretion.

- Any flammable material within 10 miles of the lair would erupt in flame and burn to cinders without arcane intervention. The resulting blaze would leave behind an ashen, smoldering landscape that deals 1d6 fire damage to any creature that ends its turn in contact with it.
- Arcane flame is more powerful within 5 miles of Fury's lair. Any creature that casts a spell that deals fire damage can add an extra damage dice when calculating damage.
- Any fiends within 10 miles of the lair feel the pull of Fury's presence. They must succeed on a DC 22 Wisdom saving throw or fall under her sway, making their way to her lair to be pacted into her service on this plane. A creature can repeat this saving throw following a long rest. If a creature enters into a pact with Fury, this saving throw is no longer necessary— they will serve her whether they want to or not.

If Fury dies, conditions of the area surrounding the lair return to normal after 1d10 days.

GALLOMARG, DISEASE-RIDDEN SERPENT OF THE MAW

Covered in sores and pox-riddled pustules that crack and ooze, Gallomarg is cursed by a great many diseases, none of which seem to affect it, but instead plague those around it. It lives in a state of perpetual agony yet never dies from its own canvas of pain. If it could, it would die, but the great beast continues to lumber on in continual misery, restored by the wasting disease that exponentially replicates within its host.

Gallomarg's unique disease, something the locals have started to call "walking pestilence," works in concord with the dragon while most likely controlling a small part of its instincts. The virus cannot survive if the host dies, and Gallomarg seems the only creature hardy enough to have lived for centuries with this accursed affliction. Other creatures, particularly humans, who are exposed to walking pestilence never gain the regenerative powers that Gallomarg possesses and instead wither into husks of their former selves before rotting away, their bodies a sea of sores and seeping wounds that follow their vein lines as if their blood is boiling.

Gallomarg lives in solitude at the edge of a chasm where a hot sulfur spring disguises its putrid, decaying scent and keeps it safe from those who would do it harm. Gallomarg feeds on whatever it can find among the rubble and detritus of its lair, leaving only when necessary for livestock and easy prey. Devoid of kinship with other dragons, it has begun to devolve into an almost feral state, though shades of the charismatic creature that it was for so long occasionally pierce through the feverish snarls. While Gallomarg wants an escape from its unending torment, dying at the hands of humans seems too great an indignity to bear. Yet, paradoxically, the beast's chosen solitude helps prevent spreading its disease to humanity, suggesting an altruistic streak in spite of its pride.

But the strain that continues to corrupt the host has other aims, if not ideas, and has continued to iterate and evolve, adapting to this altogether uninhabitable cavern. It may have already found a way to spread itself through the water. Or the earth. Or the air.

It may not need its host much longer.

Our children are dying. Our entire council is rife with disease. Even as I write to you, my fingers weep from sores forming in between them. I don't think our hamlet can hold out. And I can't let anyone leave. Something has cursed us.

—Hatcher Halloway,
Oathmaker of Keen Ridge

HOOK

Gallomarg is best left alone. But some adventurers can't take a hint, and surely Gallomarg's head or scales would make an excellent trophy. Or something to be studied. Gallomarg is best used as a unique dragon in a short campaign, mentioned for several sessions in the background as something that eventually needs to be dealt with. Talk of "walking pestilence" and "a great plague" begin to reach the party's ears, though no one knows the source of this cursed illness. A great dragon with horrible sores is known to live in the mountains above the valley near a small farming village, but no one is brave enough to fight it and low-level adventurers should know they will die facing it. As the campaign continues, things grow worse. Local waters turn putrid and undrinkable. Crops have started to fail and walking pestilence is rampant. People develop an advanced and more painful version of the initial illness. They become riddled with pus and sores grow on the insides of their mouths. Their skin turns blotchy and red. Death will be imminent and the rest of the kingdom will share this fate if something isn't done. A wild-eyed alchemist is certain the disease is being caused by the water supply, and the waters all flow from the mountains in the distance.

ENCOUNTER

Gallomarg wants to be left alone, and should any party come looking for it, it will take to higher ground. Its last refuge is to retreat to the sulfur-like conditions of the chasm it calls home.

Gallomarg is neither foolish nor brave. It does not put itself in harm's way and would not engage anything it doesn't need to. Its solitude has taught it that survival is predicated on never being cornered.

Although mostly passive, the beast fights like a demon when enemies approach, delivering scalding attacks on those too stupid to leave it alone, more akin to a badger in this regard.

In its lair, the temperature is nearly unbearable for creatures unprepared for such intense heat. Sulfur fills the air, and the beast's own body smells of decay. Even high-level parties would struggle to stay inside a cavern alongside Gallomarg for too long.

Clever game masters may want to flip the script on this encounter, making it more metaphysical than real. Instead of fighting Gallomarg, the party must overcome the disease that fuels it. In such an encounter, they are dealing with an unseen enemy that can't be negotiated, reasoned or bargained with.

TACTICS

Every square foot of Gallomarg's frame is covered in weeping sores and pustules. No other creature in the known world is capable of delivering so much disease at once. These scabs can explode in a fury of acid that damages everything around Gallomarg. Its breath weapon is another source of disease that cannot be dismissed.

If encountered in its lair, Gallomarg keeps everyone at a distance, using ranged attacks before resorting to its claws as a last resort in an effort to keep the disease within it from spreading. But the walking pestilence has other ideas and might force Gallomarg to engage any hosts who seem hearty enough to carry the disease beyond this cave.

Gallomarg's ability to impart fever dreams is a side effect of the numerous diseases that emanate from its scales and sores. When a party member gets too close to Gallomarg, consider using this power reflexively, as though Gallomarg has no control over it.

Gallomarg is not afraid of death, but it is still an animal with a survival instinct. Nine times out of 10, it will attempt to flee when things turn against it. But should the party near a killing blow against Gallomarg—and it is aware enough of its impending doom to appreciate this fate—it stops putting up a fight, allowing a worthy foe to deliver a coup de grâce.

Whether it remains dead is another question entirely.

TREASURE

Gallomarg's lair is littered with items that can survive the scalding heat of the chasm. Metal weapons warp and gold melts. But Gallomarg does not collect these items: These are all that remains of previous adventurers who came to claim its head as a prize.

GALLOMARG'S LAIR

Gallomarg has taken refuge in a sulfurous chasm marked by hot springs, which have now been corrupted by the disease Gallomarg carries.

LAIR ACTIONS

When fighting inside its lair, on initiative count 20 (losing initiative ties), Gallomarg can take one lair action to cause one of the following effects:

• An area of ground infected by Gallomarg erupts and becomes covered with infected waste. The area can be up to 10 feet on a side. The pus grease remains for one hour or until it is burned away with fire. When the pus appears, each creature on it must succeed on a DC 21 Dexterity saving throw or fall prone and slide 10 feet in a random direction determined by a d8 roll. When a creature enters the area for the first time on a turn or ends its turn there, that creature must make the same save. If the pus is set on fire, it burns away after one round. Any creature that starts its turn in the burning pus takes 22 (4d10) fire damage.
• A creature within 60 feet of Gallomarg's lair suddenly feels feverish, their mind a wreck as they fight off infection. The creature must succeed on a DC 18 Wisdom saving throw or fall under the virus's control, as in the *dominate person* spell. The virus will do

GALLOMARG, DISEASE-RIDDEN SERPENT OF THE MAW

Gargantuan dragon, chaotic neutral

Armor Class 26 (natural armor)
Hit Points 451 (22d20 + 220)
Speed 30 ft., fly 60 ft.

STR	DEX	CON	INT	WIS	CHA
30 (+10)	22 (+6)	30 (+10)	18 (+4)	17 (+3)	9 (-1)

Saving Throws Dex +13, Con +17, Wis +10, Cha +6
Skills Insight +17, Nature +11, Perception +17, Survival +17
Damage Resistances acid, fire, lightning
Damage Immunities bludgeoning, piercing and slashing from nonmagical attacks
Condition Immunities charmed, exhaustion, frightened, paralyzed, poisoned
Senses darkvision 120 ft., tremorsense 30 ft., passive Perception 27
Languages Common, Draconic, Primordial
Challenge 22 (41,000 XP)

Keen Sight. Gallomarg has advantage on Wisdom (Perception) checks that rely on sight.

Legendary Resistance (3/Day). If Gallomarg fails a saving throw, it can choose to succeed instead.

Spider Climb. Gallomarg can climb difficult surfaces, including upside down on ceilings, without needing to make an ability check.

Sunlight Sensitivity. While in sunlight, Gallomarg has disadvantage on attack rolls as well as on Wisdom (Perception) checks that rely on sight.

Supported Host. Gallomarg is the source carrier for a horrific wasting disease that sustains its life in hopes of replicating itself further. Provided it is conscious, Gallomarg regains 26 (4d12) hit points at the start of each of its turns.

Walking Pestilence. Gallomarg is covered in weeping sores and bilious gashes. Any creature that starts its turn within 5 feet of Gallomarg takes 22 (4d10) necrotic damage and 7 (2d6) acid damage. A creature can only be affected by walking pestilence once per day.

ACTIONS

Multiattack. The dragon can use its Frightful Presence. It then makes three attacks: one with its bite and two with its claws.

Bite. Melee Weapon Attack: +15 to hit, reach 15 ft., one target. *Hit*: 19 (2d10 + 8) piercing damage plus 9 (2d8) acid damage.

Claw. Melee Weapon Attack: +15 to hit, reach 10 ft., one target. *Hit*: 15 (2d6 + 8) slashing damage. On a hit, the target is infected with walking pestilence. The disease will present itself in 24 hours, at which point the infected's maximum hit points are reduced by half. Any creature they touch suffers 11 (2d10) necrotic damage and is also infected with walking pestilence, which will present in 24 hours.

Feverish Breath (Recharge 5–6). Gallomarg exhales a fiery, vomitous blast in a 90-foot cone. Each creature in that area must make a DC 22 Dexterity saving throw, taking 36 (8d8) fire damage and 36 (8d8) acid damage on a failed save or half as much damage on a successful one.

Tail. Melee Weapon Attack: +15 to hit, reach 20 ft., one target. *Hit*: 17 (2d8 + 8) bludgeoning damage.

Frightful Presence. Each creature of the dragon's choice that is within 120 feet of the dragon and aware of it must succeed on a DC 19 Wisdom saving throw or become frightened for one minute. A creature can repeat the saving throw at the end of each of its turns, ending the effect on itself on a success. If a creature's saving throw is successful or the effect ends for it, the creature is immune to the dragon's Frightful Presence for the next 24 hours.

LEGENDARY ACTIONS

The dragon can take three legendary actions, choosing from the options below. Only one legendary action option can be used at a time and only at the end of another creature's turn. The dragon regains spent legendary actions at the start of its turn.

Bite Attack. Gallomarg makes a bite attack.

Detect. Gallomarg makes a Wisdom (Perception) check.

Wing Attack (Costs 2 Actions). Gallomarg beats its wings. Each creature within 15 feet of Gallomarg must succeed on a DC 23 Dexterity saving throw or take 15 (2d6 + 8) bludgeoning damage and be knocked prone. Gallomarg can then fly up to half its flying speed.

---

anything it can to ensure it continues to replicate within Gallomarg.

• A portion of earth harboring Gallomarg's own viral wasting disease erupts and takes an ooze-like shape. This virulent mass takes on the manner, shape and statistics of a **gray ooze**, but its attacks carry the ability to pass on walking pestilence as outlined within Gallomarg's stat block.

Gallomarg can't repeat an effect until they have all been used, and it can't use the same effect two rounds in a row.

GLITZ, THE RAPSCALLION

The true origins of Glitz the Rapscallion, Purveyor of Ale, have been shrouded by time. The most recently recorded tale takes place outside a small farming village several miles south of an extensive mountain range. On this hot summer day, a young elven girl witnessed a massive bronze dragon land on a large rock formation overlooking her farm. However menacing he was, the girl was not frightened. She moved toward this magnificent wonder, and as she did so, the bronze dragon bowed his head approvingly toward her. Then, with a mighty beat of his wings, he flew off into the sky, disappearing into the clouds above the mountains. Excited by the encounter, the young farm girl returned home to share her story.

The tale of the bronze dragon became one of prophecy and good omen. The young elven farm girl named him Glitz.

Over the next several decades, the village grew more prosperous, as people from all over the region flocked to this small village due to the rumors of its prosperity. The temperate climate and regular flooding of the nearby river created extremely fertile farmland and provided an endless supply of fish. Business owners experienced increased profits. Inventors, scholars, sages and arcane masters were able to learn and develop new and wondrous creations, adding wealth to the beautiful community.

The village transformed into a bustling metropolis. Regional conditions remained the same while the general well-being and prosperity of the people never diminished.

The cause of this phenomenon perplexed scholars, sages and arcanists alike. Their attempt at figuring out this strange regional occurrence became a driving factor for the community's growth, and their research also led to increases in their magical abilities.

The investigators concluded that this region of the world was at the apex of a randomly occurring conflux of arcane energy.

As time passed, the community enjoyed its seemingly unending prosperity. All the while—beneath the city—a strange, exuberant and hardworking dragon remained the unknown reason for all this wonder.

Occasionally, Glitz would take on the form of different humanoid creatures to check in on the world above. He enjoyed mingling with the denizens of the community; they held a special place in his heart. These mortals provided centuries of personal fulfillment for Glitz and he came to view them all as his children.

At some point, Glitz became enamored with the various types of drinks created by these mortals, especially ale. His curiosity turned into an obsession, which finally became his master craft.

Late one night during early winter, while enjoying an ale in one of his disguises at a local tavern, a beautiful elven woman named Var'Alyn strolled into his life. Enthralled by her beauty, Glitz found himself pulled into conversation with her for several hours. Var'Alyn told him of a tale from her childhood about a bronze dragon that had perched on a nearby rock formation overlooking her farm. From this moment on, their relationship developed into something more. For a long time, Glitz kept his true nature secret, never allowing Var'Alyn to discover who he truly was.

Finally, one day, overcome with a sense of guilt, Glitz showed her his brewery, using the opportunity to reveal his true self. Like the little girl from all those years ago, Var'Alyn, unafraid, showed Glitz compassion, love and friendship. From this moment forward, they began their business and unique relationship.

Glitz now had two loves in his life: Var'Alyn and brewing ale.

In time, Var'Alyn became responsible for most of their business transactions within the city. They began by purchasing land for crops to support ingredients for ales, wines and liquors. Eventually, they decided to open an inn and tavern. They named it The Dragon's Inn. Here, they could focus their energy and use it as the hub for all their other business ventures.

With multiple businesses scattered through the city, Glitz and Var'Alyn decided to create a business council that would properly watch over each aspect of their operation, which is currently running smoothly to this day.

GLITZ'S BUSINESSES

The Brewer's Guild An organization of shopkeepers, merchants and purveyors of brewing within the community. The Brewer's Guild does not regulate, tax or enforce anything regarding ale, wine or liquor within the community. Rather, the purpose of the Brewer's Guild is to gather together all those who love the art of crafting alcoholic beverages. Once a month, guild members gather together at the Guild's office to plan the Brewer's Festival, which takes place in the fall.

Brewer's Festival This is a time of celebration. All those who love crafting alcoholic beverages, meats, pastries and any other type of food associated with ales, wines and liquors gather to sell, trade or give away their products.

The Dragon Inn & Tavern Var'Alyn is Glitz's "Associate" and the individual who runs the Inn & Tavern. This three-story building consists of a large ground floor that holds the tavern and two upper floors where patrons can rent rooms. The kitchen is situated in the basement and within is a secret door to Glitz's lair. The secret door is protected by mechanical and arcane locks and shrouded by powerful divination magic to keep it hidden from prying eyes. Var'Alyn carries a key and knows the magical password to access the door.

Var'Alyn is a beautiful wood elf with shoulder-length straw-colored hair, fair skin and piercing green eyes. Her attire consists of earth tone colors, suggesting she prefers comfort over finery. Upon entering the inn and tavern, everyone is greeted with a nod and smile beckoning them to take place in the bustling establishment.

The inn has several of Glitz's concoctions on offer, including Winter Spice, Frosted Froth, Winter's Eve and A Warm Heart.

Andron's Farm Bozlon Andron runs a farm on the outskirts of the community that is responsible for the production of many ingredients for producing the ales sold at The Dragon Inn and Coralyn's Hops & Barley.

Bozlon Andron is a gruff halfling with floppy brown hair and long sideburns, a grand smile and an ear for a good tale. He is always happy to give a tour of his magnificent farm, as there is a vast array of unique ornamentations scattered throughout the property.

Coralyn's Hops & Barley Coralyn Bonnamere has a two-story brewery and bakery in a busy part of the community. Many of the products produced by Glitz and his team are sold here and at The Dragon Inn.

Coralyn is the average height for a dwarf, with long reddish brown hair braided behind her head, draped down over her left shoulder. She is very personable, loves talking about her newest brew and greets everyone with a warm smile, offering them a free pastry upon their entry into her establishment. Coralyn is one of the top brewers in the community, aside from Glitz.

HOOK

The hooks below are meant to introduce Glitz to the party. You are free to modify them as you see fit. Each hook is a broad adventure concept leaving you as much space as possible to make it your own.

Competing Interests Var'Alynn approaches the party to investigate a recent robbery at Coralyn's Hops & Barley. Apparently, a secret recipe was stolen, and she requests their aid and will offer a suitable magic item as a reward.

She asks that they eliminate the threat and return the recipe.

This quest takes the party into a local warehouse occupied by two devil sisters and their minions, who are looking to disrupt the good nature of the community by altering the recipe and corrupting it before its distribution at the Harvest Festival.

The type of devil you choose should be of equal difficulty level to the party to make it a challenging encounter. You could allow for the party to role-play the situation if they desire, striking a deal with the sisters in exchange for the recipe and them leaving town.

Gaining Favor The love of his life has been abducted, and Glitz needs your help!

Belamont Softshoe approaches the party and begs their help to find his boss, Var'Alyn. He explains to the party that she has been missing for two days and has not shown up to work, which is extremely rare for her. Belamont tells the party that when he arrived at The Dragon's Inn early one morning, the door was ajar and the main room was "tossed about." He searched everywhere and discovered the back door broken open.

When the party investigates the room, they discover a trail leading into the nearby forest. Var'Alyn is being held by a coven of hags in a hidden forest grove corrupted by dark magic. The hags are torturing her in an attempt to discover the location of Glitz. If the party rescues Var'Alyn and defeats the coven, Var'Alyn will introduce them to Glitz, who will offer them a favor of their choosing.

ENCOUNTER CONDITIONS

Glitz is a very kind and humble creature, showing respect to everyone. However, sometimes his age, wisdom and intellect get the better of him, manifesting in the form of sarcastic arrogance.

Glitz can sometimes be found in humanoid form roaming the streets in search of anyone willing to share their heroic tales of adventure, many times offering payment in exchange for their story.

ENCOUNTER

Glitz and friends are meant to be sociable individuals within your campaign; however, this does not mean your players cannot infiltrate or conduct nefarious deeds in Glitz's lairs or businesses! Glitz is a good-aligned dragon with some unpredictable tendencies. He has many ties to the world above: his businesses, the woman of his dreams,

GLITZ, THE RAPSCALLION

Large dragon, chaotic good

Armor Class 22 (natural armor)
Hit Points 425 (34d10 + 238)
Speed 40 ft., burrow 40 ft., fly 80 ft.

STR	DEX	CON	INT	WIS	CHA
25 (+7)	15 (+2)	25 (+7)	30 (+10)	27 (+8)	30 (+10)

Saving Throws Dex +10, Con +15, Cha +18, Wis +16
Skills Arcana +18, Deception +18, History +18, Insight +16, Perception +16, Persuasion +18
Damage Immunities fire
Condition Immunities poisoned
Senses blindsight 60 ft., darkvision 120 ft., passive Perception 26
Languages Common, Draconic, Dwarvish, Elvish, Gnomish, Halfling
Challenge 25 (75,000 XP)

Amphibious. Glitz can breathe air and water.

Legendary Resistances (3/Day). If Glitz fails a saving throw, he can choose to succeed instead.

Magic Resistance. Glitz has advantage on saving throws against spells and other magical effects.

Magic Weapons. Glitz's weapon attacks in all forms are magical.

Innate Spellcasting. Glitz is an 18th-level spellcaster. His spellcasting ability is Charisma (spell save DC 25, +18 to hit with spell attacks). Glitz has the following spells prepared:

Cantrips (at will): *mage hand, mending, prestidigitation, shocking grasp*
1st level (4 slots): *charm person, magic missile, detect magic, hideous laughter*
2nd level (3 slots): *detect thoughts, suggestion, arcane lock, arcanist's magic aura*
3rd level (3 slots): *dispel magic, counterspell, slow, hypnotic pattern, sending*
4th level (3 slots): *fire shield, greater invisibility, arcane eye*
5th level (3 slots): *dominate person, arcane hand, modify memory*
6th level (1 slot): *mass suggestion, irresistible dance*
7th level (1 slot): *prismatic spray, sequester*
8th level (1 slot): *maze, mind blank*
9th level (1 slot): *weird*

ACTIONS

Multiattack. Glitz can use his Intoxicating Presence. He then makes three attacks: one with his bite and two with his claws.

Bite. Melee Weapon Attack: +15 to hit, reach 15 ft., one target. *Hit:* +18 (2d10 + 7) piercing damage.

Claw. Melee Weapon Attack: +15 to hit, reach 10 ft., one target. *Hit:* +14 (2d6 + 7) piercing damage.

Tail. Melee Weapon Attack: +15 to hit, reach 20 ft., one target. *Hit:* 16 (2d8 + 7) bludgeoning damage.

Intoxicating Presence. Glitz unleashes a wave of alcoholic mist filling the area around him within 60 feet. Each creature within the affected area must succeed on a DC 21 Constitution saving throw. On a failure, the creature becomes poisoned and their vision is obscured to a range of 15 feet. A creature can repeat the saving throw at the end of each of their turns. If a creature's saving throw is successful or the effect ends for it, the creature is immune to Glitz's Intoxicating Presence for the next 24 hours.

Aura of Overwhelming Magnificence (Recharge 5–6). A wave of prismatic energy erupts outward from Glitz and envelops every creature within 90 feet. Each creature within the affected area must make a DC 22 Charisma saving throw. On a failure, the creature falls under the influence of one of the following effects:

1: The creature falls unconscious.
2-5: The creature takes 42 (12d6) psychic damage and becomes paralyzed until the end of Glitz's next turn.
6-10: The creature takes 35 (10d6) psychic damage and becomes stunned until the end of Glitz's next turn.
11-15: The creature takes 28 (8d6) psychic damage and becomes incapacitated until the end of Glitz's next turn.
16-21: The creature takes 21 (6d6) psychic damage and becomes deafened and blinded until the end of Glitz's next turn.

Creatures that succeed on the saving throw take half damage and suffer no additional effect.

Change Shape. Glitz magically polymorphs into a humanoid or metallic dragon that has a challenge rating no higher than his own. He reverts to his true form if he dies (a small colorful bird-like dragon). Any equipment he is wearing or carrying is absorbed or borne by the new form (Glitz's choice). In a new form, Glitz retains his alignment, hit points, Hit Dice, ability to speak, proficiencies, Legendary Resistance, lair actions and Intelligence, Wisdom and Charisma scores, as well as his action. His statistics and capabilities are otherwise replaced by those of the new form, except any class features or legendary actions of that form.

LEGENDARY ACTIONS

Glitz can take three legendary actions, choosing from the options below. Only one option can be used at a time and only at the end of another creature's turn. Glitz regains spent legendary actions at the start of his turn.

Detect. Glitz makes a Wisdom (Perception) check.

Wand. Glitz can use his **wand of fireballs** or the **rod of absorption**.

Attack. Glitz can make a melee attack against one target within reach.

Drunken Belch (Costs 2 Actions). Glitz belches an alcoholic substance. Each creature within a 30-foot cone must succeed on a DC 22 Dexterity saving throw or take 14 (4d6) poison damage and become poisoned. On a successful saving throw, the creature takes half damage and is not poisoned.

Var'Alyn, and the general well-being of the community.

These attachments open up many opportunities for adventure. Each of Glitz's businesses details an NPC that can be utilized as a quest giver to further a story within your campaign setting.

TACTICS

If Glitz knows he is going to be attacked or raided, he begins combat *polymorphed* as a young dwarven child who is cleaning the brewery, or he will act like a scared elderly man and pretend to be hiding—yet visible to those entering his lair.

Once combat begins, Glitz will use his Aura of Overwhelming Magnificence followed up by a spell or multiattack on the weakest-looking combatant. Glitz is no fool. He understands spellcasters and the differences between armored foes.

WEALTH

Glitz's lair is filled with many tools and objects used to create potions, ales, etc. An adventurer can find multiple tool sets for brewers, blacksmiths and even thieves. In addition to the tools, his lair has a vast wealth of platinum, gold, silver and copper. There are also gems of varying worth scattered throughout his chamber.

Glitz has a *ring of spell storing*, *rod of absorption*, and a *wand of fireballs* on him. His lair also has the following magical items: a *suit of mithril armor*, a *pearl of power*, an *immovable rod* and *a robe of useful items*.

ROLE-PLAYING GLITZ

Glitz is a Legendary Dragon that may take the form of any metallic type dragon. However, he has chosen the Bronze Dragon form for centuries. He is very fond of it, in part because it hides some of his noticeable girth.

Glitz has taken on many forms throughout his life. However, he has cultivated several humanoid personas throughout that time. The characters below are his favorites.

Belamont Softshoe A halfling male of average age and height with floppy, disheveled brown hair, tan skin and brown eyes. He generally wears dark brown or black clothing.

Dorn Stronghammer An elderly dwarven male slightly shorter than average and rounder at the waist. His bald head gleams with sweat, and a long, braided salt and pepper beard hangs over his plump belly. His piercing blue eyes suggest a young, intelligent mind lurks beneath his aging features.

Avalyn Mesiure A young elven female with an athletic build and long platinum hair with strands of black, which hangs loosely over her shoulders. Her pale skin contrasts with her bright blue and yellow clothing. Various types of jewelry adorn her neck, wrists and fingers.

Marland Baertor A middle-aged half-elven male with a muscular build. Short cropped dirty blonde hair is combed tightly against his head. Dark brown eyes peer

through gold-rimmed spectacles that rest comfortably on his nose. A deep blue vest covers his silky long sleeve white shirt, which is tucked into dark blue pantaloons pulled tightly around his soft black leather boots.

Glitz is a Legendary Dragon that may take the form of any metallic type dragon. However, he has chosen the Bronze Dragon form for centuries. He is very fond of it, in part because it hides some of his noticeable girth.

GLITZ'S LAIR

Glitz can be encountered in his vast brew-making lair under The Dragon's Tavern.

The lair can be mistaken for a massive alchemist's hall, built with care and details that only a dwarf can appreciate. Upon closer examination, it becomes clear that all the equipment and areas are filled with dedicated brewing kettles, burners, large spoons, mash containers, clamps, etc. Everything is meticulously maintained and organized. The entire space is well lit, and the aromas of various brews fill the air.

LAIR ACTIONS

On initiative count 20 (losing initiative ties), Glitz takes a lair action to cause one of the following effects. Glitz can't use the same effect two rounds in a row.

- Thick steam fills the lair in a 60-foot radius around Glitz. Other than Glitz or his allies, each creature starting their turn in the steam must succeed on a DC 15 Constitution saving throw or be blinded. Creatures that succeed on their saving throw experience a mild alcoholic buzz. The steam lasts for two rounds and then fades away. This action may not be used again until the steam dissipates.
- Hot liquid begins to pour from kettles, filling the area with boiling hot water. Each creature within a 30-foot radius of Glitz must succeed on a DC 15 Dexterity check, taking 10 (3d6) of damage. Creatures that succeed take half damage.

REGIONAL EFFECTS

The region containing Glitz's lair is blessed with good fortune, creating one or more of the following effects:

- Farmers within 10 miles of the lair receive double the average crop yields.
- Vendors who sell locally grown fruits and vegetables receive 25 percent more revenue compared to other towns.
- Citizens who reside within 10 miles of the lair for more than a week live 2d6 years longer than if living in comparable lands and also benefit from a +1 bonus to their Charisma and Constitution stats, provided they stay within 10 miles of Glitz's lair.

If Glitz dies, conditions of the area surrounding the lair return to normal after 1d10 days.

ILIZINNII, THE HEART EATER

If you ever find yourself traveling in the Jurgalanaan Desert, whether in Gruhili, Ortalr or anywhere in between, you might hear the colloquial greeting of "Ba heash bru stasa!" from the native peoples. If you were to translate this to the common tongue, it means, roughly, "Your stars are bright." This, of course, would seem perfectly innocent to an outsider, but in truth, this saying could more accurately be translated to "Your stars stay bright," which has a much grimmer context and meaning to the locals.

People in Jurgalanaan are taught to keep one eye on the sky at night for any stars that seem to ripple with darkness, blinking off and back on suddenly. This is the first warning sign of their immediate danger, and in most cases is a death omen if they cannot hide quickly enough. Next comes the "Veratinda ga dylosii" or "thunder of death," as a wave of sound like a strange thunderous rain washes over the ground—and those who find themselves caught out in the open will learn it's already too late.

The Heart Eater has found her next meal.

Ilizinnii is driven by pure, simple, overwhelming greed. It was this greed that initially called her to the tower that Nephalal, an elven necromancer, erected in the vast Jurgalanaan Desert to practice his dark magic far from prying eyes. While not quite the grand and imposing wyrm she is today, Ilizinnii was still a powerful and dangerous adversary for the wizard, with spells and magics of her own. Their battle was a fierce one, with each foe's greed and hubris driving them on, not allowing either to concede the tower and its assortment of collected baubles to the other.

Ultimately, Ilizinnii triumphed—but not without a terrible cost—her sight. Nephalal blighted the wyrm's eyes, and since that day, Ilizinnii has lived in pure darkness, an unforgivable sin committed against her by the necromancer. In a fit of literal blind rage, Ilizinnii demolished the tower, wiping out any remnants of Nephalal's legacy before retreating underground to an enormous limestone cavern.

Rage-induced wails reverberated across the dunes of the arid desert for weeks on end, echoing from deep within the subterranean lair as the dragon mourned her loss. As time passed, her disdain for the treacherous magic that stole her sight consumed every passing moment. With only her twisted desire to inflict pain left to comfort her, the dragon sank into both real and metaphysical darkness.

Ever strong of will and forced to accept her lack of vision, she soon discovered that by bristling her enormous scales and slamming them back down in a constant wave of clacks, she could detect objects and movement near to her by listening to the reverberations. And eventually, Ilizinnii's hearing became so acute that the sound of a beating heart would be enough to wake her from a deep slumber—something more than a few foolish wanderers and adventurers have discovered as they suffered their unfortunate fates.

As will any who underestimate her.

Roleplaying and Tactics

Ilizinnii is a raging tyrant—quick tempered and completely unchallenged by anything within her territory. She lives primarily in solitude. However, she allows certain tribes to approach very near to her home with the intent of lowering human sacrifices down into the enormous main entrance shaft of the cave. She will usually wait for night to cover the entirety of the cave in darkness before her hunt—though, in truth, it hardly gives Ilizinnii the pleasure of a real hunt—unless the victims decide to wander into one of the many lightless tunnels away from the scorching heat beating down on the pit's entrance. Ilizinnii does this not for any additional psychological torture to her victim—though that's certainly a bonus—but to absolutely protect herself from any prying eyes from above that might pose a threat in the sunlight.

Ilizinnii has faced a foe that almost killed her, something most dragons, in their arrogance, tucked away in their caves and lairs, wouldn't even believe is a possibility. But for Ilizinnii it was a harsh moment of revelation: She is not as invincible as she thought. Now with the loss of her sight, she has spent much of her life since that moment in preparation and paranoia. While she is not afraid to leave her cave at night to prowl the desert dunes with malicious intent, she is still a cautious combatant.

No stranger to the use of magic and the devastating effects it can wreak, she will almost assuredly attempt to utterly destroy anyone she perceives as using magic or casting spells while engaged with her. If her opponent seems even remotely capable as a mage, her sense of urgency to gravely wound or outright annihilate them is only slightly outweighed by her sense of self-preservation. She will likely retreat to her lair, where she has several safeguards in place, before pressing her luck.

Encounter Conditions

Ilizinnii's lair is one any dragon would be envious of, and it serves as a significant advantage to the great wyrm against any potential threat to her and her hoard.

When first discovering the cave, it appears more like a sinkhole than a true limestone cave, with a vast opening in the desert floor serving as its entrance. But beyond the previously worked, column-like entrance to the 120-foot drop to the bottom, the cave expands into several large tunnels leading in different directions—all of which are able to accommodate Ilizinnii's girth thanks to whomever originally expanded them in the centuries before Ilizinnii made it her home.

For the dragon, it's perfect. Both defensible and comfortable, complete with its own source of water and a few additional surprises for anyone foolhardy enough to think they might claim her mountain of treasures for themselves, the dragon is far more dangerous within its walls. This is primarily due to its inconceivable darkness, which helps Ilizinnii turn her greatest weakness into a prodigious strength.

Perhaps the most magnificent artifact Ilizinnii has ever claimed for her own is a small obsidian antimagic stone. Realizing what it was upon returning to her lair with it, she has since put it to use above the entrance to her hoard room, embedded in one of the many stalactites. With the stone's reach extending through much of the room, it is the perfect defense against magic. A number of unsuspecting wizards have entered her chamber only to have their magical lights snuffed out...and have protective enchantments dispelled at the worst possible time. With a pool of water that must be crossed before reaching her hoard room, most threats will find themselves without a torch or magical means of sight when facing off with the completely blind yet-still-capable dragon. And for many, the only light they will see is the fleeting soft red glow from Ilizinnii's maw before she unleashes a molten hot spew of flame all over them.

Ilizinnii's Lair

Ilizinnii's Lair is within a vast cave system. Some areas appear to be bottomless, but the area she resides in is large enough for her to fly, taking advantage of different views from various cliff edges.

Lair Actions

On initiative count 20 (losing initiative ties), Ilizinnii takes a lair action to cause one of the following effects. Ilizinnii can't use the same effect two rounds in a row.

- 1d4 + 2 motionless **ropers** (disguised as stalactites and stalagmites) spring into action and attack. They act immediately and on initiative count 20 in subsequent rounds and obey Ilizinnii's commands. They remain until Ilizinnii uses this action again. If Ilizinnii dies, the ropers become free-willed creatures.
- 1d4 + 2 **water elementals** attack from a large pool of water located near Ilizinnii's hoard. They act immediately and on initiative count 20 in subsequent rounds and obey Ilizinnii's commands. They remain until Ilizinnii uses this action again. If Ilizinnii dies, the water elementals become free-willed creatures.
- A nonmagical wall of stone springs into existence within 120 feet of Ilizinnii. The effects are the same as the wall of stone spell; however, the wall becomes permanent and requires no concentration.

ILIZINNII, THE HEART EATER

Gargantuan dragon, neutral evil

Armor Class 19 (natural armor)
Hit Points 444 (24d20 + 192)
Speed 40 ft., climb 40 ft., fly 80 ft.

STR	DEX	CON	INT	WIS	CHA
25 (+7)	12 (+1)	27 (+8)	22 (+6)	17 (+3)	21 (+5)

Saving Throws Dex +8, Con +15, Int +13, Wis +10, Cha +12
Skills Insight +10, Intimidation +19, Perception +17, Stealth +3
Damage Immunities cold, fire
Condition Immunities blinded, charmed, exhaustion, frightened, paralyzed, stunned
Senses blindsight 200 ft., tremorsense 120 ft., passive Perception 34 (sound)
Languages Common, Draconic, Dwarvish, Elvish
Challenge 24 (62,000 XP)

Echolocation. Ilizinnii can't use her blindsight while deafened.
Keen Hearing. Ilizinnii has advantage on Wisdom (Perception) checks that rely on hearing.
Legendary Resistance (3/Day). If Ilizinnii fails a saving throw, she can choose to succeed instead.
Innate Spellcasting. Ilizinnii's spellcasting ability is Charisma (spell save DC 20, +12 to hit with spell attacks). She can innately cast the following spells, requiring no material components:

  At will: *control flames* (extinguish only, no sight required)
  4/day each: *alarm*
  3/day each: *darkness* (45-foot radius), *create or destroy water*
  2/day each: *wind wall, counterspell*

ACTIONS

Multiattack. Ilizinnii can use her Frightful Presence. She then makes three attacks: one with her bite and two with her claws.
Bite. Melee Weapon Attack: +14 to hit, reach 15 ft., one target. *Hit:* 18 (2d10 + 7) piercing damage plus 14 (4d6) fire damage.
Claw. Melee Weapon Attack: +14 to hit, reach 10 ft., one target. *Hit:* 14 (2d6 + 7) slashing damage.
Tail. Melee Weapon Attack: +14 to hit, reach 20 ft., one target. *Hit:* 16 (2d8 + 7) bludgeoning damage.
Frightful Presence. Each creature of Ilizinnii's choice that is within 120 feet of her and aware of her must succeed on a DC 21 Wisdom saving throw or become frightened for one minute. A creature can repeat the saving throw at the end of each of its turns, ending the effect on itself on a success. If a creature's saving throw is successful or the effect ends for it, the creature is immune to Ilizinnii's Frightful Presence for the next 24 hours.
Fire Breath (Recharge 5–6). Ilizinnii exhales fire in a 90-foot cone. Each creature in that area must make a DC 22 Dexterity saving throw, taking 91 (26d6) fire damage on a failed save or half as much damage on a successful one.

LEGENDARY ACTIONS

Ilizinnii can take three legendary actions, choosing from the options below. Only one legendary action option can be used at a time and only at the end of another creature's turn. Ilizinnii regains spent legendary actions at the start of her turn.
Detect. Ilizinnii makes a Wisdom (Perception) check.
Tail Attack. Ilizinnii makes a tail attack.
Wing Attack (Costs 2 Actions). Ilizinnii beats her wings. Each creature within 15 feet of Ilizinnii must succeed on a DC 25 Dexterity saving throw or take 14 (2d6 + 7) bludgeoning damage and be knocked prone. Ilizinnii can then fly up to half her flying speed.
Cacophonous Boom (Costs 2 Actions). Ilizinnii slams down her scales in a deafening wave of sound. Each creature within 120 feet must succeed on a DC 18 Constitution saving throw or become deafened for one minute. If this attack is made within an enclosed structure, they have disadvantage. Additionally, if this attack is within an enclosed structure, Ilizinnii must make this saving throw as well, though she does so normally.

REGIONAL EFFECTS

The region containing Ilizinnii's lair is warped by her magic, which creates one or more of the following effects:

• Desert storms shroud the area within 1 mile of her subterranean lair. The storms are common, and even during the day, the ambient light is dim at best.
• Bats are common and aggressive to creatures within 5 miles of the lair.
• Creatures who sleep during a long rest within 1 mile of the lair must succeed on a DC 10 Wisdom saving throw or be unable to see when they awaken. They are blinded for 1d4 hours.

If Ilizinnii dies, conditions of the area surrounding the lair return to normal over the course of 1d10 days.

GM NOTE: ANTIMAGIC STONE

Wondrous item, legendary
This small obsidian stone creates a 30-foot antimagic sphere, as per the *antimagic field* spell. The magic automatically works in darkness. If natural sunlight shines upon the stone, it cracks, turns to dust and is destroyed.

IMMRYG-UMRYSS, THE SNATCHER

Born from the sinister crossbreeding of an ogre mage and a wyvern, Immryg-Umryss is not the prototypical dragon. While it looks everything like a dragon should, the veneer is where its similarity with other dragons ends. Immryg-Umryss is a twisted and malevolent force at times and a complex and kind being at others. This confluence leads to problems, again and again.

Immryg-Umryss (a name composed of the words for ogre and wyvern in a mad wizard's language) is a magical creature, with none of the preternatural aspects of normal dragons. It lacks all of a dragon's typical instincts and has had to learn on its own how to deal with outsiders. It does not hoard gold. It does not burn villages to the ground with fire. It does not gather minions around it to inflate its ego. In fact, Immryg-Umryss has lived outside the ordinary world of dragons for more than 300 years. Alone, aloof and awkward, the great dragon is an outsider in a world of tyrannical beasts. As such, it is very lonely. But it has a solution.

Immryg-Umryss has taken many hostages over the years. It took a bit of trial and error to learn humans are soft and cannot be handled in a rough manner. It took even longer to learn that young humans live longer and make lasting companions. Each hostage served as another learning step in its development. Everything it understands about the world has come through learning from others or through repetitive failure.

There is no happy middle for Immryg-Umryss.

While it is terrifying for anyone to be taken prisoner by a dragon, Immryg-Umryss is a great host to those who do not attempt to escape. It provides everything a person could need, without exception. Immryg-Umryss is inquisitive and philosophical, the perfect companion to those with open minds. The hostages have even learned a great deal living with Immryg-Umryss, though only a few have been able to use this knowledge in the outside world as those held captive are not permitted to leave.

Sweet Mother and Father,
Everything you have hoped for me has
Now come to fruition. I am well-fed
Daily and rarely want for anything.

Had I been able to say goodbye, know
Everything in my being wanted to. But
Love for my host grows each day, and I
Pray you know I am alive and well.

—Anne Underfoot,
Twenty-Year Guest of Immryg-Umryss

HOOK

A friend of the party (or a party member who can't make this week's session) is kidnapped, and the characters have only a few days to save them. The character is, in fact, unharmed. But being taken by a dragon should give them pause. Feel free to drop hints and rumors that this dragon does horrible things to its victims (though this may be accidental).

ENCOUNTER

Immryg-Umryss has made a home for itself in an old abandoned dwarven mine. This is not its first nest, but since taking over the empty mine, other creatures have left Immryg-Umryss alone. There's no gold here.

Immryg-Umryss is never encountered outside its lair unless it is in the process of taking someone hostage (which is rare).

TACTICS

Immryg-Umryss is alone and paranoid. It has spent most of its life without contact with others, except those it has kidnapped. It has built a lair for itself that is hard for other creatures to get in and out of. Its lair rests on a ledge that can only be reached with chains and pulleys or by magic. Once upon this shelf, the party can stare directly into a massive chamber where Immryg-Umryss waits for them.

If a fight starts, it becomes a different creature entirely. The kind and gentle host turns into a horrid beast of power and magic, capable of sundering small armies. It mixes fire-breathing, magic and pure strength to overcome any adversary. Emphasis on "any."

Immryg-Umryss's lair is perfectly formed to match its fighting style. The ledge and lair are too small for anyone to hide or make a getaway (without plummeting hundreds of feet). Its fire-breathing weapon balloons out to fill most of the lair, ensuring everyone fighting is burned to a crisp. If no one is where they need to be for its breath weapon to be effective, Immryg-Umryss casts *controlled teleport* to put them all in one place.

Preferably just outside—at the edge of the lair.

Immryg-Umryss is not above using its captive(s) as a shield. In fact, once a fight starts, it is unlikely any hostage will survive.

During round three or four, Immryg-Umryss summons bats and insects to itself with its Lair Action.

When the great beast is below half its starting hit points, it uses its Wail of Sadness to plunge its enemies into maddening sorrow.

WEALTH

If there is anything of value in Immryg-Umryss's home, the dragon is not aware of it. Some scraps of raw gold and gold powder may exist somewhere, but Immryg-Umryss does not rest on a pile of gold coins. Any treasure comes in the form of leftover clothing, trinkets and perhaps a spell book from those who died in Immryg-Umryss's care.

IMMRYG-UMRYSS'S LAIR

Immryg-Umryss's lair is located at the top of a cliff edge and within an abandoned dwarven mine that was once connected to a vast cave system.

LAIR ACTIONS

On initiative count 20 (losing initiative ties), Immryg-Umryss takes a lair action to cause one of the following effects. Immryg-Umryss can't use the same effect two rounds in a row.

- A **swarm of bats** or a **swarm of insects** is summoned. They act immediately and on initiative count 20 in subsequent rounds and obey Immryg-Umryss's commands. They remain until Immryg-Umryss uses this action again. If Immryg-Umryss dies, the swarm become free-willed creatures.
- 2d6 + 2 **giant spiders** emerge from gaps in the cave walls. They act immediately and on initiative count 20 in subsequent rounds and obey Immryg-Umryss's commands. They remain until Immryg-Umryss uses this action again. If Immryg-Umryss dies, the giant spiders become free-willed creatures.
- The walls of the lair begin to reverberate, creating a harmonic tone. All creatures within 30 feet of the lair that can hear it must make a DC 13 Constitution saving throw. On a failure, a creature becomes Charmed by Immryg-Umryss. On a success, a creature takes 10 (3d6) psychic damage. A creature can repeat the saving throw at the end of each of its turns, ending the Charmed condition on itself on a success.

REGIONAL EFFECTS

The region containing Immryg-Umryss's lair is warped by its magic, which creates one or more of the following effects:

- High winds batter the cliffside, making any climb to the lair treacherous. Large or smaller creatures must make a DC 15 Dexterity check every 50 feet. If a creature fails a check, they fall.
- Stinging insects are common and aggressive toward creatures within 5 miles of the lair.
- Creatures within 1 mile of the lair suffer two levels of exhaustion.

If Immryg-Umryss dies, conditions of the area surrounding the lair return to normal over the course of 1d10 days.

IMMRYG-UMRYSS, THE SNATCHER

Huge dragon, neutral evil

Armor Class 24 (natural armor)
Hit Points 567 (42d12 + 294)
Speed 40 ft., fly 80 ft.

STR	DEX	CON	INT	WIS	CHA
25 (+7)	15 (+2)	25 (+7)	25 (+7)	15 (+2)	21 (+5)

Saving Throws Dex +9, Con +14, Int +14, Wis +9, Cha +12
Skills Arcana +14, Intimidation +19, Perception +16, Stealth +9
Damage Immunities cold, fire, poison
Condition Immunities charmed, exhaustion, frightened, poisoned, stunned
Senses darkvision 120 ft., passive Perception 26
Languages Common, Draconic, Elvish, Dwarvish
Challenge 24 (62,000 XP)

Innate Spellcasting. Immryg-Umryss's spellcasting ability is Charisma (spell save DC 20 + 12 to hit with spell attacks). It can innately cast the following spells, requiring no material components:

    At will: acid splash (4d6), fire bolt (4d10), mage hand
    4/day each: darkness, gust of wind, magic missile, scorching ray
    3/day each: counterspell, lightning bolt, major image
    2/day each: banishment, controlled teleport
    1/day each: fire storm, globe of invulnerability

Legendary Resistance (3/Day). If Immryg-Umryss fails a saving throw, it can choose to succeed instead.

Regeneration. Immryg-Umryss regains 20 hit points at the start of its turn if it has at least 1 hit point.

Wail of Sadness (1/day). Immryg-Umryss releases a mournful wail. This wail has no effect on constructs and undead. All other creatures within 30 feet of it that can hear it must make a DC 13 Constitution saving throw. On a failure, a creature drops to 0 hit points. On a success, a creature takes 21 (6d6) psychic damage.

ACTIONS

Multiattack. Immryg-Umryss can use its Frightful Presence. It then makes three attacks: one with its bite and two with its claws—or one with its bite, one with a claw and one with a stinger.

Bite. Melee Weapon Attack: +14 to hit, reach 15 ft., one target. *Hit:* 18 (2d10 + 7) piercing damage plus 14 (4d6) fire damage.

Claw. Melee Weapon Attack: +14 to hit, reach 10 ft., one target. *Hit:* 14 (2d6 + 7) slashing damage.

Tail Stinger. Melee Weapon Attack: +14 to hit, reach 20 ft., one target. *Hit:* 16 (2d8 + 7) piercing damage. The target must make a DC 19 Constitution saving throw, taking 24 (7d6) poison damage on a failed save or half as much on a successful one.

Frightful Presence. Each creature of Immryg-Umryss's choice that is within 120 feet of it and aware of it must succeed on a DC 21 Wisdom saving throw or become frightened for 1 minute. A creature can repeat the saving throw at the end of each of its turns, ending the effect on itself on a success. If a creature's saving throw is successful or the effect ends for it, the creature is immune to Immryg-Umryss's Frightful Presence for the next 24 hours.

Fire Breath (Recharge 5–6). Immryg-Umryss exhales fire in a 90-foot cone. Each creature in that area must make a DC 22 Dexterity saving throw, taking 91 (26d6) fire damage on a failed save or half as much damage on a successful one.

LEGENDARY ACTIONS

Immryg-Umryss can take three legendary actions, choosing from the options below. Only one legendary action option can be used at a time and only at the end of another creature's turn. Immryg-Umryss regains spent legendary actions at the start of its turn.

Detect. Immryg-Umryss makes a Wisdom (Perception) check.

Tail Stinger. Immryg-Umryss makes a tail stinger attack.

Wing Attack (Costs 2 Actions). Immryg-Umryss beats its wings. Each creature within 15 feet of Immryg-Umryss must succeed on a DC 25 Dexterity saving throw or take 14 (2d6 + 7) bludgeoning damage and be knocked prone. Immryg-Umryss can then fly up to half its flying speed.

Memory Sting (Costs 2 Actions). Immryg-Umryss emits psychic energy in a 90-foot cone. Each creature in that area must succeed on a DC 17 Intelligence saving throw or take 28 (5d8 + 6) psychic damage and be stunned for 1 minute. Creatures that save take no damage. A creature can repeat the saving throw at the end of each of its turns, ending the stunned condition on itself on a success. If a creature fails the Memory Sting save twice in a row, it suffers three levels of exhaustion. All three levels are removed following a long rest.

GM NOTE: CUSTOM SPELL

Controlled Teleport
6th-level conjuration
Casting Time: 1 action
Range: 30 ft.
Components: V, S, M (pieces of eggshell from 2 different creature types)
Select up to five creatures of your choice you can see within range. Unwilling creatures must succeed on a Wisdom saving throw. On a failed save, you teleport each affected creature to an unoccupied space that you can see within 90 feet of you. The space must be on the floor or ground.

JÖRMUNGAND, THE WORLD SERPENT

Residing in the deepest areas of the vast oceans is Jörmungand, the World Serpent, a dragon so large it's said he can encircle the entire world if he chooses. Legend has it that the serpent was cast out by the gods and into the bottomless abyss of the ocean where he grew to an unimaginable size and strength, emerging when the mood strikes.

Jörmungand's head is easily 50 feet wide and his body equally as gargantuan. This dragon has no wings but instead has a body so vast it can encircle the entire world. Jörmungand's body typically remains coiled and within a 10-mile radius of his head, depending on the depth of the water. He may also choose to Earth Glide, which affords him more room if need be. While stretched around the globe, Jörmungand can even grasp his own tail if he wishes to do so. It is foretold that if Jörmungand grasps his tail and releases, it will bring about the beginning of the end of the world.

Hoping for safe passage, sailors make a sacrifice to the Serpent by tossing precious metals and items of magic into the darkest depths of the ocean. One can only speculate at the amount of treasure that may rest at the bottom of these areas, leagues deep and far away from any would-be adventurers. There has never been a time when the tale of Jörmungand was not told, as offerings have been given to him for longer than recorded history.

Some have returned from their sea travels with stories of Jörmungand. They describe a massive head breaching the water's surface to reveal vibrant colored scales, ranging from deep blues to piercing emerald green. As the ocean waters pour off him, more of his face can be seen. His eyes are vibrant orange—as bright and fierce as the heart of the sun—and his maw is as large as the sturdiest seafaring vessels. Only those who have made an offering lived to tell these tales—many come back with fear in their eyes, forever changed, having barely survived the encounter. They are the ones the serpent has allowed to live, and they help spread the word that Jörmungand is more than a legend. He's real.

All us sea dogs tell tales of the depths beyond: the great whale that charged us when we ran out of wind, the kraken that stole my sweetie, the ladies beneath the surface with whirlpool eyes and eel's tails. But some stories we keep to ourselves, knowing that uttering an ounce of what we saw would require sacrificing even more of our sanity.

—First Mate Jackson Tawdry,
Lone Survivor of the Huntsman Disaster

Hook

The most common encounter with Jörmungand is when he takes the form of a large black house cat. He sometimes finds adventurers interesting as they enter a village or city. The party may notice the cat following them using a DC 15 Wisdom (Insight) check.

The party may be in town to investigate another matter and might draw the attention of the cat form of Jörmungand. He will find it particularly interesting if the party purchases an ox to serve as bait when fishing the deep oceans, as the head of an ox generally is used to lure the massive world serpent to the surface. Another tall tale used by merchants? Perhaps. Nonetheless, it shows Jörmungand they are seeking an audience with him.

Encounter

Jörmungand loves games and has made it known to the town leaders that he offers himself as a test of strength and virtue. The elders do not know of the cat's exact origin, but once every few years he will test an adventuring group that he deems worthy. The townsfolk adore the cat, as it is a boon for the businesses that serve the townsfolk attending the testing of strength event.

The black cat form of Jörmungand will observe the party. If they appear to be of sound mind and spirit, a spectacle is made in the center of town. It takes days to set the scene and spread the news that the game will be played once more. There, the cat willingly makes its way to the stage, the crowd parting to give it access. This is clearly a revered and old tradition within the town.

The test is simple: One being attempts to lift the cat off the ground. However, it should be noted that no one has ever succeeded before. Every mighty hero who has tried has failed to lift the curious beast, which is disguised by powerful magic. Its immense weight is only overcome with a Strength score of 25 or higher, and even that only achieves the lifting of a paw.

If any of the party manage to lift only one paw, the crowd gasps and erupts into applause. The cat immediately runs away and hides. If followed, it communicates telepathically to the winner, congratulating them and informing them that they will be granted a wish. Once the wish is granted, the cat disappears, its eyes flashing bright orange.

Tactics

During the test of strength—leading up to and after— the party's intentions will likely become more apparent, and this determines how Jörmungand chooses to interact with them.

If the party were genuine and kind to the cat as well as the spectators and townsfolk over the days spent there, they are rewarded. However, if they are vicious, selfish or unkind, leveraging their power for personal gain—the cat lures them closer to the seaside, away from the town, and dives into the water.

There, he immediately transforms, unfurling his massive body, his tail crashing straight into the water that stretches far off into the horizon, leaving only the head and upper body for the party to attack from land.

The only real hope of defeating Jörmungand is to attack his head and inflict more than 300 hit points of damage in a single round. Jörmungand knows he will manifest again if he is ever defeated, but he still fights enemies with an unrivaled intensity. He will devour any creature in his path without mercy.

Wealth

Jörmungand's wealth is at the bottom of the deepest oceans. Sailors may know of the specific locations, but the real challenge is traveling to the depths where it lies. If a party member manages to make it there by magical or other creative means, they will find an almost infinite number of coins, baubles and family heirlooms. Disturbing the treasures at the bottom may attract the angry attention of Jörmungand miles below the surface.

The real wealth is gained by how they treat the cat form of Jörmungand. He may choose to grant a wish, a useful magic item or a boon, depending on how the party interacted during the celebration—even if they failed to lift him.

Jörmungand's Lair

Jörmungand lair is effectively the entire ocean, and his ability to shape the sea itself makes encounters with him even more perilous. These actions can be incorporated whenever Jörmungand is encountered at least 1 mile off shore.

Lair Actions

On initiative count 20 (losing initiative ties), Jörmungand takes a lair action to cause one of the following effects. Jörmungand can't use the same effect two rounds in a row.

- Jörmungand can cast *control water* without requiring concentration.
- Jörmungand can cast *control weather* without requiring concentration.
- Jörmungand can cast *wind wall* without requiring concentration.

Regional Effects

If Jörmungand chooses, he can impact the region around his head.

- An isolated thunderstorm causes choppy, violent seas.
- The wind in a 15-mile radius triples in intensity or stalls completely, stranding any vessels with sails.
- Whirlpools that drag vessels to the depths appear, at GM discretion.

If Jörmungand dies, these conditions end immediately.

JÖRMUNGAND, THE WORLD SERPENT

Titanic dragon (shapeshifter), neutral

Armor Class 26 (natural armor)
Hit Points head 369 (18d20 + 180), body 615 (30d20 + 300)
Speed 40 ft., burrow 30 ft., swim 90 ft.

STR	DEX	CON	INT	WIS	CHA
30 (+10)	25 (+7)	30 (+10)	17 (+3)	16 (+3)	28 (+9)

Saving Throws Dex +16, Con +19, Int +12, Wis +12, Cha +18
Skills Insight +12, Intimidation +27, Perception +21
Damage Resistances cold, fire
Damage Immunities poison; bludgeoning, piercing and
    slashing damage from nonmagical attack
Condition Immunities blinded, charmed, exhaustion,
    frightened, paralyzed, stunned
Senses truesight 120 ft., passive Perception 31
Languages all, telepathy 120 ft.
Challenge 30 (155,000 XP)

Amphibious. Jörmungand can breathe air or water.

Change Form. Jörmungand can change into the form of an abnormally large black house cat. If he speaks, it is done so telepathically. In cat form, he is immensely heavy and strong with a Strength of 30. Only a single creature with a Strength of 25 or higher can attempt to lift him enough to bring one paw off the ground. If a party member is able to achieve this test of Strength, once per day they receive advantage on all rolls for 1d4 rounds and are granted a single wish.

Jörmungand does not change into dragon form unless he is within 100 feet of a large body of water. When this occurs, all creatures within 20 feet of the cat must make a DC 18 Dexterity saving throw, taking 35 (10d6) bludgeoning damage on a failed save or half as much on a successful one. Creatures who fail are also knocked prone. As Jörmungand's body forms, he targets the water and is seen unfurling into it as far as the horizon.

Legendary Resistance (5/Day). If Jörmungand fails a saving throw, he can choose to succeed instead.

Magic Resistance. Jörmungand has advantage on saving throws against spells and other magical effects.

Magic Weapons. Jörmungand's weapon attacks are magical.

Earth Glide. Jörmungand can burrow through nonmagical, unworked earth and stone. While doing so, Jörmungand does not disturb the material it moves through.

Siege Monster. Jörmungand deals double damage to objects and structures.

Reflective Body. If Jörmungand is targeted by a *magic missile* spell, a line spell or a spell that requires a ranged attack roll, roll a d4. On a 1 to 3, Jörmungand is unaffected. On a 4, Jörmungand is unaffected and the effect is reflected back at the caster as though it originated from Jörmungand, turning the caster into the target.

Regeneration. Jörmungand's head regains all hit points at the start of his next turn. If Jörmungand takes more than 60 hit points of radiant damage, this trait doesn't function at the start of his next turn. Additionally, Jörmungand's body regains 30 hit points at the start of his next turn. If Jörmungand takes radiant damage on his body, this trait doesn't function at the start of his next turn. Jörmungand dies only if he starts his turn with 0 head hit points and doesn't regenerate.

Poison Body. Any melee attack on Jörmungand's body opens a gaping wound that releases poisonous gas in a 30-foot cone. Each creature in that area must make a DC 22 Constitution saving throw, taking 77 (22d6) poison damage on a failed save or half as much on a successful one.

Discorporation. If Jörmungand's head drops to 0 hit points and does not regenerate, his body is destroyed, and he is unable to take physical form for a time.

ACTIONS

Multiattack. Jörmungand can use his Frightful Presence. He then makes three attacks. In his draconic form, Jörmungand can use his claw, and then makes two attacks with his bite. He does not attack in his cat form.

Bite. Melee Weapon Attack: +19 to hit, reach 50 ft., one target. *Hit:* 29 (3d12 + 10) piercing damage. If the target is a living creature, they must succeed on a DC 22 Constitution saving throw or take 22 (4d10) poison damage.

Claw. Melee Weapon Attack: +19 to hit, reach 10 ft., one target. *Hit:* 17 (2d6 + 7) slashing damage.

Tail/Body. Melee Weapon Attack: +19 to hit, reach 30 ft., one target. *Hit:* 19 (2d8 + 10) bludgeoning damage.

Frightful Presence. Each creature of Jörmungand's choice that is within 120 feet of him and aware of him must succeed on a DC 21 Wisdom saving throw or become frightened for one minute. A creature can repeat the saving throw at the end of each of its turns, ending the effect on itself on a success. If a creature's saving throw is successful or the effect ends for it, the creature is immune to Jörmungand's Frightful Presence for the next 24 hours.

Poison Breath (Recharge 3–6). Jörmungand exhales poisonous gas in a 90-foot cone. Each creature in that area must make a DC 22 Constitution saving throw, taking 91 (26d6) poison damage on a failed save or half as much on a successful one.

LEGENDARY ACTIONS

Jörmungand can take three legendary actions, choosing from the options below. Only one legendary action option can be used at a time and only at the end of another creature's turn. Jörmungand regains spent legendary actions at the start of his turn.

Detect. Jörmungand makes a Wisdom (Perception) check.

Bite. Jörmungand makes a Bite attack.

Tail/Body Attack (Costs 2 Actions). Jörmungand makes a Tail/Body attack.

Tail Bite (Costs 3 Actions). Jörmungand bites and releases the tip of his tail. His body is not currently wrapped around the world (causing it to end) in this instance, but the effect is spectacular nonetheless. An *antimagic field* (as per the spell) bursts out in a sphere with a 100-foot radius, lasting 1d4 rounds and requiring no concentration. Additionally, each creature within 100 feet of the burst takes 36 (8d8) thunder damage.

KARNAGGONN, THE MORNING STAR

Arguably the most powerful dragon in the multiverse, Karnaggonn is a spiritual creature eternally tasked with carrying the souls of the judged across the sky. It is completely impartial in this task and has been fulfilling its duty since the dawn of creation. By this measure, it cannot, in any sense, truly die. It has always returned to this task, collecting scattered souls on behalf of the gods. It always will. It is a cosmic force, an inevitability.

Even to other dragons, Karnaggonn is more akin to a celestial—a comet that circles the heavens. It travels continuously, navigating the cosmos over the course of a full year of its time, carrying the souls of the judged in its wake. Until it reaches its destination, the souls lie in rest, waiting for Karnaggonn to collect and guide them across the sky. Should something derail its course, it will always correct it, returning to its duty and starting a new cycle.

Each soul spends a different amount of time in the wake of the great dragon, but eventually all of the judged are deposited into the plane of purgatory.

Here, they'll spend centuries in penance, striving to understand their missteps and hoping to transition back to the world they came from in a new body to restart their spiritual journey. Some never leave.

Those determined to have suffered enough for their transgressions are returned to their homes on the back of a great turtle named Ghavadra. Ghavadra is tasked with a similar role as Karnaggonn, flying across the cosmos to deliver the souls to the starting point of their new journeys. Though they serve similar purposes, these colossal creatures have never met.

In order to complete its sacred task, Karnaggonn has the ability to switch between realms at will. Those willing to assist it can be brought into the ethereal plane with a thought from the great dragon. When threatened, Karnaggonn calls upon restless souls, bringing them forth from purgatory to help it fend off aggressors. Should they fail, Karnaggonn has another card to play. It can summon up the voices of the deceased who have passed from the lives of its attackers. The voices calm and mollify ill intentions and soothe even the most ferocious anger.

If someone is favored by Karnaggonn, Karnaggonn can similarly confer an opportunity for them to speak with the departed.

Some cultures worship Karnaggonn the way one might worship Apollo's chariot hurtling across the sky. These cultures build their morals and values around Karnaggonn and the balance it brings to the cosmos. In effect, their alignment matrix is shifted further toward law than other cultures, honoring the edict that life is precious and doing things that would lead to divine judgment has significant consequences. No one wants to see Karnaggonn collect the soul of a cousin or a clansman. Step kindly, as they say.

A collector, but also a giver. He moves in the night and day at once, traversing the very idea of time to do his duty. Judgment. We know not by whom, only that when your soul is gathered by the great dragon, you will find yourself transported to your fate.

—Elder T'alla Deepwaters,
Night Mage of Mojnil

Hook

Karnaggonn has collected the soul of someone the party does not consider to be appropriately judged. They must find a way to meet with the great ethereal dragon and convince it to spare the soul in question. Conversely, the party finds themselves collected by Karnaggonn. They have some time before it arrives in purgatory and perhaps a few months in its wake to plead a case for their freedom.

Tactics

Fighting Karnaggonn is likely fruitless. It will not attack unless provoked and most attacks cannot harm it. It will most likely subdue the party—or send them to the ethereal plane—rather than kill them in order to continue on its journey. Killing someone who isn't already marked for judgment by the cosmos or damned to eternity is against the ethos of Karnaggonn.

Should the party insist on attacking Karnaggonn, leverage the moving Lair Actions that surround Karnaggonn whenever it is in flight. Karnaggonn rarely, if ever, lands. It can shift a pesky target to the ethereal plane, or summon spirits from that plane to attack.

Karnaggonn's Lair

This gargantuan creature as old as the universe itself does not dwell in a conventional lair. Always on the move as part of its fated traversal of the multiverse, Karnaggonn's presence creates something akin to a lair in the area around it.

Lair Actions

Karnaggonn can invoke ambient magic generated by its purpose to take lair actions. The lair is active when Karnaggonn is in flight, moving with Karnaggonn and with a range of 300 feet. On initiative count 20 (losing initiative ties), Karnaggonn can take one lair action to cause one of the following effects:

- One creature of Karnaggonn's choice must succeed on a DC 26 Wisdom saving throw. On a failed save, the creature is sent to the ethereal plane for one minute. A willing creature can choose to fail this save on purpose.
- A group of souls steps out of the ethereal plane to aid Karnaggonn, dealing 13 (2d12) necrotic damage and 14 (4d6) cold damage, divided among up to five creatures Karnaggonn can see. The souls return to the ethereal plane immediately after they attack.
- Karnaggonn connects one creature of its choice to a voice from that creature's past. If the creature is hostile toward Karnaggonn, the voice from the past would attempt to persuade the creature to stand down, as in the *calm emotions* spell (DC 26). If the creature is friendly toward Karnaggonn, this connection would last for one minute and functions as the *speak with dead* spell, at GM discretion.

Karnaggonn can't repeat an effect until they have all been used, and it can't use the same effect two rounds in a row.

KARNAGGONN, THE MORNING STAR

Gargantuan dragon, lawful neutral

Armor Class 25 (natural armor)
Hit Points 676 (33d20 + 330)
Speed 60 ft., fly 120 ft.

STR	DEX	CON	INT	WIS	CHA
30 (+10)	20 (+5)	30 (+10)	30 (+10)	30 (+10)	30 (+10)

Saving Throws Str +19, Dex +14, Con +19, Int +19, Wis +19, Cha +19
Skills Arcana +28, History +28, Insight +28, Perception +28, Persuasion +19, Religion +28
Damage Immunities cold, fire, poison, psychic, radiant; bludgeoning, piercing and slashing from nonmagical attacks
Condition Immunities blinded, charmed, frightened, grappled, invisible, petrified, poisoned, prone, restrained, stunned, unconscious
Senses blindsight 120 ft., darkvision 120 ft., truesight 120 ft., passive Perception 38
Languages telepathy 120 ft.
Challenge 30 (155,000 XP)

Discorporation. When Karnaggonn drops to 0 hit points, its body is destroyed, and it is unable to take physical form for a time. It will reform itself in 1d100 days.

Inscrutable. Karnaggonn is immune to any effect that would sense its emotions or read its thoughts, as well as any divination spell that it refuses. Wisdom (Insight) checks made to ascertain Karnaggonn's intentions or sincerity have disadvantage.

Legendary Resistance (5/Day). If Karnaggonn fails a saving throw, it can choose to succeed instead.

Spellcasting. Karnaggonn is a 14th-level spellcaster. Its spellcasting ability is Wisdom (spell save DC 26, +18 to hit with spell attacks). It requires no material components to cast its spells. Karnaggonn has the following cleric spells prepared:

Cantrips (at will): *sacred flame, spare the dying, thaumaturgy*
1st level (4 slots): *command, detect evil and good, detect magic*
2nd level (3 slots): *lesser restoration, zone of truth*
3rd level (3 slots): *dispel magic, tongues*
4th level (3 slots): *banishment, freedom of movement*
5th level (2 slots): *flame strike, greater restoration*
6th level (1 slot): *heroes' feast*
7th level (1 slot): *resurrection*

Soul Shepherd. Karnaggonn serves as an instrument of judgment, shifting souls from the prime material pass on to the netherplanes.

Once per long rest, Karnaggonn can summon these souls to its aid. As a bonus action, 5d4 + 5 spectral **berserkers** appear and protect Karnaggonn to the best of their ability. They possess a fly speed equal to their movement and are ethereal and therefore resistant to all damage from weapons that aren't silvered or magical.

ACTIONS

Multiattack. Karnaggonn can use its Frightful Presence. It then makes three attacks: one with its bite and two with its claws.

Bite. Melee Weapon Attack: +17 to hit, reach 15 ft., one target. *Hit:* 21 (2d10 + 10) piercing damage.

Claw. Melee Weapon Attack: +17 to hit, reach 10 ft., one target. *Hit:* 17 (2d6 + 10) slashing damage.

Tail. Melee Weapon Attack: +17 to hit, reach 20 ft., one target. *Hit:* 19 (2d8 + 10) bludgeoning damage.

Breath Weapons (Recharge 5-6). Karnaggonn uses one of the following breath weapons:

Cold Breath. Karnaggonn exhales cold in a 90-foot line that is 10 feet wide. Each creature in that area must make a DC 24 Dexterity saving throw, taking 71 (13d10) cold damage on a failed save or half as much on a successful one.

Sleep Breath. Karnaggonn exhales sleep gas in a 90-foot cone. Each creature in that area must succeed on a DC 24 Constitution saving throw or fall prone for 10 minutes. This effect ends for a creature if the creature takes damage or someone uses an action to wake it.

Etherealness. Karnaggonn magically enters the Ethereal Plane from the Material Plane, or vice versa.

Frightful Presence. Each creature of Karnaggonn's choice that is within 120 feet of Karnaggonn and aware of it must succeed on a DC 24 Wisdom saving throw or become frightened for one minute. A creature can repeat the saving throw at the end of each of its turns, ending the effect on itself on a success. If a creature's saving throw is successful or the effect ends for it, the creature is immune to Karnaggonn's Frightful Presence for the next 24 hours.

LEGENDARY ACTIONS

Karnaggonn can take three legendary actions, choosing from the options below. Only one legendary action option can be used at a time and only at the end of another creature's turn. Karnaggonn regains spent legendary actions at the start of its turn.

Detect. Karnaggonn makes a Wisdom (Perception) check.

Ethereal Jaunt (Costs 2 Actions). Karnaggonn shifts to or from the ethereal plane.

Spellcasting (Costs 1–3 Actions). Karnaggonn can cast a spell of level 3 or lower. The number of actions spent is equal to the level of the spell.

Tail Attack. Karnaggonn makes a tail attack.

Wing Attack (Costs 2 Actions). Karnaggonn beats its wings. Each creature within 15 feet of Karnaggonn must succeed on a DC 26 Dexterity saving throw or take 17 (2d6 + 10) bludgeoning damage and be knocked prone. Karnaggonn can then fly up to half its flying speed.

KIENNAVALYRISS, THE KEEPER OF SECRETS

There are some dragons who hoard gold, some who collect souls and many over whom the artifacts of antiquity hold a particular sway. Kiennavalyriss would not count herself among these draconic entities. She is instead concerned with ensuring the safe-keeping of an archive of archives, the vast Alabaster Halls, a library of forgotten knowledge. Some of the information Kiennavalriyss guards has been otherwise lost to time, while numerous tomes and scrolls hidden away in various corners of the halls are the stuff of whispered legend, unproven hearsay or the stuttered ramblings of spell-soaked wizards on their deathbeds. Kiennavalyriss keeps all this and more to herself, for herself (or those she deems worthy of learning what she knows).

Those who have survived an audience with Kiennavalyriss report that she is elegant and imposing. The scintillating pattern of her opalescent scales is magnified by the intense illumination in the Alabaster Halls, and she bears a celestial heritage that shines in her eyes. Her mother, the Shimmering Queen, is enshrined in myth as the servant and romantic partner of a now-forgotten exarch of the God of Knowledge. When her mother was cruelly slain by a band of malfeasant rat-catchers, the duty of safeguarding the lore of the library fell to Kiennavalyriss.

The divine blood that burns within Kiennavalyriss is slowly consuming her mortal form. Her hearing is not what it used to be, and the shine is starting to leave the scales along her sides. On the rare occasions that she allows anyone to speak with her, she holds her massive wings over the faded patches on her sides and pushes uncomfortably close to the faces of her audience as they converse with one another.

As these signs of her mortality have crept upon her, she has grown more zealous in her mission. She views the library now as her legacy and a potential tool that she is sorely tempted to use to prolong her dwindling lifespan. In the last few years, she has created a network of scholars and archaeologists that collect new pieces for her library. Chief among her requests: dark tomes that reference the transition to dracolichdom. Few of these agents know the true nature of their patron, and she goes to great lengths to maintain her ruse.

I've never seen anything like it. Walls and walls of shelves bathed in an almost heavenly glow, and standing tall among them—blocking my view of the entirety of these alabaster halls—a proud, stately dragon. She seemed happy to see me, but happier that I would soon be leaving.

—Archmage Seamus Sharafirm, Right Wand of the King

HOOK

Kiennavalyriss is both a potential ally and a possible antagonist. All manner of secret knowledge has been collected within her expansive library, but she jealously guards it. Much of it she believes too dangerous to be anywhere other than locked away in her archives. When convinced of a true need, the lore within her halls could be used to solve nearly any quandary facing the party. She has a dim view of adventurers, having crossed paths with many who unearthed forgotten tomes that were better off in her library. It is likely that the party will first encounter her in such a situation, perhaps as they quest to recover a lost book containing the true name of a demon that has been relentless in harassing them.

Or maybe she contacts the party to send them to recover a codex that recorded the dreams of a mad mage that had survived contact with elder god.

Perhaps one of her agents discovers the significance of a book they are sent to recover. Suspecting the duplicity of the one that hired them, they ask the party for aid in unraveling the mystery of Kiennavalyriss's identity.

It might even be possible that the party finds a tome of dread spellcraft that was stolen from her collection. When Kiennavalyriss discovers it in their possession, she assumes this implicates them in the theft of her property.

Regardless of how the party first meet Kiennavalyriss, their interaction with her is most interesting when there is a tension between their search for information and her desire to keep the secrets of her library from being used by those with ill intent. In the best of circumstances, she will coldly refuse the inquiries of the party until they have proven their worth to her. At her worst, she will turn against them to recover secrets she believes they should not have.

ENCOUNTER

Kiennavalyriss makes her home in an expansive library known only to a few. Referred to by those who know of its existence as the Alabaster Halls, this library is a labyrinthine complex. Every wall of its vast interior is filled with shelving that holds untold volumes of books, scrolls and various other mediums upon which someone has written some precious knowledge.

Designed to suit her unique needs, the rooms and corridors of this place are surprisingly narrow given that a dragon dwells within. These close quarters are intended to prevent outsiders from slipping past unnoticed and puts them face-to-face with Kiennavalyriss so that she might study their face, scrutinizing their hidden intent and reading the words that fall from their lips.

The cramped quarters and full shelves also help dampen ambient sound within the library, giving it an unsettling silence most of the time. Kiennavalyriss prefers the lack of distracting noises and insists that groups of visitors speak clearly and without interrupting one another. During meetings like this, a small rodent-like creature that Kiennavalyriss refers to only as "The Scribe" is present—perched upon her shoulder with an inky quill gripped in its prehensile tail, furiously transcribing the conversation.

Kiennavalyriss seldom ventures outside of her library, though she maintains a relationship with a few orders of priests and wizards from whom she sometimes acquires new books. Within her library, Kiennavalyriss is attuned to many warding spells that alert her to intruders and allow her to lock any door she wishes. She also can create areas of supernatural silence any time she desires.

TACTICS

Kiennavalyriss knows that her partial deafness is her greatest liability. Within her lair, she has taken many precautions to reduce the impact of this reality. The rooms and hallways in her library are cramped and narrow to make it more difficult for adventurers and other would-be plunderers from sneaking past her. The entrance to the library, as well as her personal chambers, are warded with a silent alarm that alerts her to visitors and intruders alike. Finally, the library is brightly lit by shimmering motes of arcane energy.

Though loath to engage in a fight, she is prepared to defend the potentially dangerous lore that exists within her library. With the knowledge at her disposal, she is a formidable spellcaster. She uses her lair actions to seal exits, separating her opponents from each other or forcing them into smaller spaces where she can catch more of them in the area of a single spell. She uses her remaining spells to thwart attempts to plunge her surroundings into darkness and to dispel the magic of her enemies.

If the potential threat posed by losing a small number of titles from her collection is not significant or if she feels that she might easily recover them, Kiennavalyriss will flee if her foes begin to get the better of her. Her command of the doors within the library provides an easy and expedient escape. Only when the lore at stake is of grave import will she battle to her last breath.

WEALTH

Unlike many other dragons, Kiennavalyriss does not hoard wealth. Her treasured possessions are the books, scrolls, clay tablets and other assorted writings that she has recovered and collected over her many decades. The secret histories of countless mortal races are written upon them. There are ancient spells, dead languages and the true names of gods hidden upon the shelves of her vast library. This collection also includes written copies of every conversation that Kiennavalyriss has had with visitors to her library.

KIENNAVALYRISS'S LAIR

The exact whereabouts of the Alabaster Halls is not widely known. It is rumored the library is a demiplane of sorts, its entrance meandering through the cosmos.

LAIR ACTIONS

On initiative count 20 (losing initiative ties),

Kiennavalyriss, The Keeper of Secrets

Huge dragon (celestial), lawful neutral

Armor Class 19 (natural armor)
Hit Points 243 (18d12 + 126)
Speed 40 ft., fly 80 ft.

STR	DEX	CON	INT	WIS	CHA
25 (+7)	15 (+2)	25 (+7)	25 (+7)	15 (+2)	21 (+5)

Saving Throws Dex +9, Con +14, Int +14, Wis +9, Cha +12
Skills Arcana +14, Intimidation +19, Perception +16, Stealth +9
Damage Immunities cold, fire, poison
Condition Immunities charmed, exhaustion, frightened, posioned, stunned
Senses darkvision 120 ft., passive Perception 26
Languages Common, Draconic, Elvish, Dwarvish
Challenge 24 (62,000 XP)

Spellcasting. Kiennavalyriss is a 17th-level spellcaster. Her spell-casting ability is Intelligence (spell save DC 22, +14 to hit with spell attacks). She has the following wizard spells prepared:

Cantrips (at will): fire bolt, light, minor illusion, ray of frost
1st level (4 slots): chromatic orb, color spray, magic missile, sleep
2nd level (3 slots): phantasmal force, ray of enfeeblement, scorching ray, shatter
3rd level (3 slots): counterspell, fireball, haste, vampiric touch
4th level (3 slots): banishment, black tentacles, hallucinatory terrain
5th level (2 slots): cloudkill, gas, wall of force
6th level (1 slot): chain lightning, sunbeam
7th level (1 slot): reverse gravity
8th level (1 slot): sunburst
9th level (1 slot): time stop

Legendary Resistance (3/Day). If Kiennavalyriss fails a saving throw, she can choose to succeed instead.

Silent Spells. Kiennavalyriss can ignore the verbal requirements of any spell she casts when she is within an area of magical silence that she has created.

Actions

Multiattack. Kiennavalyriss can use her Frightful Presence. She then makes three attacks: one with her bite and two with her claws.

Bite. Melee Weapon Attack: +14 to hit, reach 15 ft., one target. *Hit:* 18 (2d10 + 8) piercing damage.

Claw. Melee Weapon Attack: +14 to hit, reach 10 ft., one target. *Hit:* 14 (2d6 + 8) slashing damage.

Tail. Melee Weapon Attack: +14 to hit, reach 20 ft., one target. *Hit:* 16 (2d8 + 8) bludgeoning damage.

Frightful Presence. Each creature of Kiennavalyriss's choice that is within 120 feet of her and aware of her must succeed on a DC 18 Wisdom saving throw or become frightened for one minute. A creature can repeat the saving throw at the end of each of its turns, ending the effect on itself on a success. If a creature's saving throw is successful or the effect ends for it, the creature is immune to her Frightful Presence for the next 24 hours.

Breath Weapons (Recharge 5–6). Kiennavalyriss uses one of the following breath weapons:

Blinding Light. Kiennavalyriss exhales a flash of light in a 60-foot cone. Each creature in that area must make a DC 18 Constitution saving throw, taking 58 (13d8) radiant damage, and is blinded until the end of their next turn on a failed save or half as much without being blinded on a successful one.

Fire Breath. Kiennavalyriss exhales a fiery blast in a 60-foot cone. Each creature in that area must succeed on a DC 18 Dexterity saving throw, taking 63 (14d8) fire damage on a failed save or half as much on a successful one.

Legendary Actions

Kiennavalyriss can take three legendary actions, choosing from the options below. Only one legendary action option can be used at a time and only at the end of another creature's turn. She regains spent legendary actions at the start of her turn.

Detect Thoughts. Kiennavalyriss casts detect thoughts without expending a spell slot.

Tail Attack. Kiennavalyriss makes a tail attack.

Cast a Spell (Costs 1–3 Actions). Kiennavalyriss uses a spell slot to cast a 1st, 2nd or 3rd-level spell that she has prepared. Doing so costs one legendary action per level of the spell.

Wing Attack (Costs 2 Actions). Kiennavalyriss beats her wings. Each creature within 15 feet of her must succeed on a DC 21 Dexterity saving throw or take 14 (2d6 + 7) bludgeoning damage and be knocked prone. She can then fly up to half her flying speed.

Kiennavalyriss takes a lair action to cause one of the following effects. She can't use the same effect two rounds in a row.

- Kiennavalyriss casts *silence*, without requiring concentration. The area is quiet until initiative count 20 on the next round.
- Kiennavalyriss chooses one door she can see within 100 feet of her. If the door is shut, it immediately opens even if it had been locked or magically sealed. If the door is open, it slams shut and is sealed as if she had cast *arcane lock*. A door closed this way remains locked for one hour.
- Kiennavalyriss dispels one area of magical darkness within 100 feet of her. This only dispels darkness that was created by a spell of 5th level or lower.

Regional Effects

The region surrounding Kiennavalyriss's lair is altered by magic, creating one or more of the following effects:

- Books within 6 miles of the lair are difficult to open. Their pages stick together, their covers sometimes feel impossibly heavy and occasional gusts of wind slam them shut. Keeping a book open requires a successful Strength or Dexterity ability check against a DC of 10.
- The area within 6 miles of the lair is unnaturally quiet. The DC of any ability check made to listen to or hear anything is increased by 5.
- Divination spells cast within 1 mile of the lair either fail or redirect to the nearest book or parchment containing some form of written communication.

If Kiennavalyriss dies, conditions return to normal.

KUNDAL,
THE RAINBOW DRAGON

Some dragons bring good fortune and blessings. Some only drink from the sea, linking the world to heaven. Hundreds of stories from history books and mythological tales tell of golden and fortunate dragons that bless humanity with their presence, providing a gateway to heaven.

But Kundal, the Rainbow Dragon, is much more. Choosing never to ascend, Kundal has remained among mortals for millennia, serving the great goddess Mazu and guiding those who seek her wisdom. Kundal is the ultimate symbol of wisdom and balance within one's self. Those who serve or worship the great dragon show their dedication through a spindle-shaped dragon tattooed along their spine. Acquiring such a mark requires a process that is painful but reveals one's commitment to the great serpent.

Kundal lives in an unfathomable cycle that defies our understanding of time. He does not move through the ages the way humans do and therefore the nature of his existence cannot be explained to mortals: These cycles must be experienced. The rainbow dragon's task, therefore, is to find one human every cycle to whom he will grant enlightenment. This chosen mortal learns everything Kundal can teach through symbols and visions beyond the linear limitations of living kind. He or she is then returned to the land of mortals to spread the dragon's message across the earth. When this happens, the cycle ends for a short period while Kundal takes a meaningful rest.

These cycles reliably occur, but do not follow any predictable pattern.

The rainbow dragon is sometimes found with Mazu. The goddess rides Kundal as a mount, and some stories indicate it was Kundal who brought her the wisdom with which she rules. Kundal is the master of all primordial forces: movement, stasis and the beat of time. He is the source of nearly all alchemical and thaumaturgic theory, bridging the gap between this world and all of the places magic comes from.

To gaze upon his face is to look past your own understanding of the world. To cross him is to admit you do not value your life.

The Rainbow Dragon is not of this plane or any other. He is the essence of existence, and yet could be said not to exist.

Kundal serves as Mazu's mount because riding the rainbow dragon is the only thing that can bring any element of surprise to the omniscient.

—Se Hyun,
Winking Monk of Mazu

HOOK

An elder has been selected by Kundal to be the next enlightened one, and the party has been asked to escort her to the top of a tall mountain. She cannot make the journey alone. The journey to meet Kundal is fraught with peril, as would be a face-to-face encounter. Particularly if the elder does not wish to be enlightened.

ENCOUNTER CONDITIONS

Kundal lives at the gateway between the mortal world and heaven. He is sometimes encountered in ethereal spirit space, or in the real world, or in the places between. Where Kundal is located dictates the conditions of the encounter. The further removed from the mortal realm, the more powerful Kundal becomes.

ENCOUNTER

Kundal lives atop a mountain spire above the clouds. Those who seek his wisdom must travel hundreds—if not thousands—of miles to find the great dragon.

The journey to reach him should not be easy. But it is not a traditional series of violent encounters: Instead of spirit guardians and mystical warriors blocking gates, the barriers along the way are metaphysical. Those unworthy to pass simply do not. Each "test" reflects another part of a person's soul and whether they merit a visitation with Kundal.

Whomever is determined worthy—not an easy task—becomes immortal, passing from this realm into the next and leaving everything behind.

TACTICS

Kundal is not a dragon the party would ever fight. His power is to calm and subdue those who would threaten him with his mind-awakening gifts. Those who would attack the great rainbow dragon do so at the peril of their own souls.

Should Kundal judge the heroes as unworthy, however, they are likely to be banished, teleported away or reduced to ash. In addition to Kundal's numerous powers, the very heavens would join forces to aid him in destroying the party.

WEALTH

Kundal's treasures are usually spiritual in nature. The blessings of Kundal may vary, but they translate to an increase in Wisdom, boons that will make a character more enlightened or provide a new perspective on the world. Or he may gift magical powers no one has never seen before.

If Kundal's treasure is ever physical in nature, it is hidden inside a box within another box with numerous locks, keys, puzzle combinations and dead ends to find the true treasure at the heart of it all. Each box is unique, as is each treasure.

KUNDAL'S SUMMIT

In lieu of a lair, Kundal would meet the to-be-enlightened at the top of a tall peak. This apex is shrouded in the clouds and benefits from the following area effects:

LAIR EFFECTS

One of the following occurs on initiative count 20. The same event cannot occur twice in a row, and all three effects must be triggered before an effect can be repeated.

- A 120-foot cloud of calming energy settles on an area within Kundal's line of sight. Each creature within this cloud is under the effects of the *calm emotions* spell unless they succeed on a DC 24 Wisdom saving throw.
- Any creatures hostile to Kundal must succeed on a DC 24 Wisdom saving throw before attempting an attack on Kundal, as if they are under the effect of the *sanctuary* spell.
- One creature within 60 feet of Kundal is granted access to a stunning truth about the nature of the cosmos. This information is life-affirming, but also world-shattering, and the creature must succeed on a DC 24 Intelligence saving throw or be paralyzed for one minute.

Kundal,
The Rainbow Dragon

Gargantuan ancient polychromatic dragon, lawful good

Armor Class 22 (natural armor)
Hit Points 546 (28d20 + 252)
Speed 40 ft. (human form), fly 80 ft., swim 50 ft.

STR	DEX	CON	INT	WIS	CHA
30 (+10)	14 (+2)	28 (+9)	20 (+5)	16 (+3)	28 (+9)

Saving Throws Dex +9, Con +16, Wis +10, Cha +16
Skills Insight +10, Perception +10, Persuasion +16
Damage Resistances cold, fire, lightning
Damage Immunities acid, bludgeoning, piercing and slashing damage from nonmagical weapons
Condition Immunities charmed, deafened, exhaustion, frightened, paralyzed, petrified, poisoned
Senses blindsight 60 ft., darkvision 120 ft., passive Perception 20
Languages Common, Draconic, Celestial
Challenge 24 (62,000 XP)

Discorporation. When the Rainbow Dragon drops to 0 hit points or dies, his body is destroyed, and he is unable to take physical form for a time.
Amphibious. The Rainbow Dragon can breathe both air and water.
Legendary Resistance (3/Day). If Kundal fails a saving throw, he can choose to succeed instead.
Magic Weapons. All attacks by the Rainbow Dragon are considered magical.

Actions

Multiattack. The Rainbow Dragon can use his Frightful Presence. He then makes three attacks: one with his bite and two with his claws. If his breath weapon is available, he may attack with it as well.
Bite. Melee Weapon Attack: +17 to hit, reach 15 ft., one target.
Hit: 21 (2d10 + 8) piercing damage
Claw. Melee Weapon Attack: +17 to hit, reach 10 ft., one target.
Hit: 17 (2d6 + 10) slashing damage.
Tail. Melee Weapon Attack: +17 to hit, reach 20 ft., one target.
Hit: 19 (2d8 + 10) bludgeoning damage.
Frightful Presence. Each creature of the Rainbow Dragon's choice that is within 120 feet and aware of him must succeed on a DC 24 Wisdom savings throw or become frightened for one minute. A creature can repeat the saving throw at the end of each of its turns, ending the effect on a success. If a creature's saving throw is successful, or the effect ends, the creature is immune Kundal's Frightful Presence for the next 24 hours.

Breath Weapons (recharge 5–6). The Rainbow Dragon uses one of the following breath weapons:
Acid Breath. The Rainbow Dragon exhales acid in a 60-foot line that is 5 feet wide. Each creature in the line must make a DC 18 Dexterity saving throw, taking 54 (12d8) acid damage or half as much on a successful one.
Fire Breath. Kundal exhales fire in a 90-foot cone. Each creature in the area must make a DC 24 Dexterity saving throw, taking 71 (13d10) fire damage on a failed save or half as much on a successful one.
Lightning Breath. Kundal exhales lightning in a 120-foot line that is 10 feet wide. Each creature in the line must make a DC 24 Dexterity saving throw, taking 88 (16d10) lightning damage on a failed save or half as much on a successful one.
Repulsion Breath. The Rainbow Dragon exhales repulsion energy in a 30-foot cone. Each creature in that area must succeed on a DC 24 Strength saving throw. On a failed save, the creature is pushed 30 feet away from the dragon.
Sleep Breath. Kundal exhales sleep gas in a 90-foot cone. Each creature in that area must succeed on a DC 24 Wisdom saving throw or fall unconscious for 10 minutes. This effect ends for a creature if the creature takes damage or someone uses an action to wake him.
Slowing Breath. The Rainbow Dragon exhales magical gas in a 60-foot cone. Each creature in the area must succeed on a DC 24 Constitution saving throw. On a failed save, the creature can't use reactions, its speed is halved and it can't make more than one attack on its turn. In addition, the creature can use either an action or a bonus action on its turn, but not both. These effects last for one minute. The creature can repeat the saving throw at the end of each of its turns, taking 63 (14d8) cold damage on a failed save or half as much on a successful one.

Legendary Actions

The Rainbow Dragon can take three Legendary actions, choosing from the options below. Only one legendary action can be used at a time and only at the end of another creature's turn. The Rainbow Dragon regains spent legendary actions at the start of his turn.
Detect. The Rainbow Dragon makes a Wisdom(Perception) check.
Tail Attack. Kundal makes a tail attack.
Move. The Rainbow Dragon can make a move action without provoking an attack of opportunity.
Charm Attack (Costs 2 Actions). The Rainbow Dragon uses magical eye rays on a single target he can see within 120 feet. The targeted creature must succeed on a DC 18 Wisdom saving throw or be charmed by the Rainbow Dragon for one hour or until the Rainbow Dragon harms the creature.

Reactions

Limited Magic Immunity. As a reaction, Kundal may choose to be immune to any spell of level 3 or below. The Rainbow Dragon has advantage on saving throws against all other spells and magical effects.

KUR,
THE DRAGON OF THE VOID

Humans always find a way to upend the truth. Before humanity, powerful, ancient, immortal beasts roamed the world. But with humans came gods. And with gods came the desire to push these ancient beasts underground. The rolls of history are filled with tales of these creatures, forced underground by "better thinking" gods.

No story of this behavior is better known than Kur's.

Eons ago, Kur, who some call the First Dragon, emerged from a ceaseless void and freely roamed the planes as a dark and terrible beast. When the gods were granted immortality through humanity's worship, these deities deemed Kur unworthy of the gift they'd been granted, and made him a mortal being. Out of spite or desperation, the great dragon kidnapped the goddess Ishtar, and the ransom was the return of his immortal status. Ishtar agreed to Kur's price, but once she made him immortal, she cast him into the void for eternity. Knowing the goddess could not be trusted, Kur had expected some form of duplicity. As a contingency, Kur left a tiny piece of his flesh behind. This flesh would never decay, and it ensured Kur could leave the void in time and once again return to the land of mortals, using his own body as an anchor to the mortal realm.

This flesh, powerful in its own right, has remained hidden. Numerous cults serving the dragon, wizards seeking to possess the great beast (or worse) and heroes dedicated to the conquest of all evil have sought Kur's flesh. Thankfully none have succeeded. The small fragment of the dragon's immortal body remains hidden somewhere in the world, perhaps even buried deep beneath its mantle. Should the flesh ever be found, it could undo creation, to say nothing of summoning Kur back from the void.

For her part, Ishtar, the goddess of life and death, is locked in perpetual battle with Kur in the void between the land of the living and the land of the dead. In fact, all of Ishtar's contemporaries fight Kur, though none can defeat him—he is immortal by their hand, and will continue the struggle for freedom from his eternal prison. While the full story of Kur has been lost to time, numerous churches and cults have emerged to venerate the great dragon, who is "like unto them a god."

Our undoing will not be the armies that march on our gates or the spies within our midst. We will destroy ourselves, and the world with us. All we require is a bit of flesh.

—Malchior Vee, the Black Sage, Herald of the Coming Doom

HOOK

Kur waits for someone to find the piece of his undying flesh. He is a world-ending adversary. If the game master truly intends to sunder the world with his presence, it is best to sprinkle details about Kur throughout the campaign. Ancient lore appears from time to time, hinting at a great power from beyond time and reason.

Perhaps the party stumbles upon an ancient language no one understands. Or they battle a cult, only to learn its members were devoted to the worship of some great beast no one else has heard of. They might even learn of a cabal of wizards trying to find a piece of a great dragon's flesh that never withers. Such a rumor would certainly worry brave adventurers hell-bent on saving the world.

Since Kur waits inside the great void for someone to find a piece of his undying flesh, he remains trapped until his circumstances change. If the party inadvertently awakens him, the battle—and all they care for—is surely theirs to lose.

If Kur's flesh is ever discovered and used to summon him, the beast will want to exact vengeance on the goddess who trapped him. If the party gets in his way, he'll slaughter them along his path of destruction. If he fails and escapes, he can exact his vengeance in hundreds of ways.

ENCOUNTER

Any encounter with Kur is based on how and where the party finds him. If they are foolish enough to travel into the void to search for him, the encounter is swift and brutal. Kur is an immortal with semi-omnipotence that only has one limit: he cannot roam freely on the mortal plane. Even the god of death cannot destroy him. But an avatar of his former form can travel to the mortal plane if the circumstances are favorable.

Note: The information presented in the stat block on the next page represents Kur's avatar. Even if the avatar is defeated, it is not permanent, as nothing could ever completely destroy him. Were Kur to be encountered inside the void in some attempt to render him mortal, or prevent his avatar from appearing, the ferocity with which he would attack and the pain he would generate would be incalculable.

The most practical encounter is for the party to fight Kur's avatar, instead of the true dragon. Perhaps this plane is one Kur must travel through in order to reach Ishtar in the underworld. This plane, essentially, acts as a buffer between realms. It is Kur's way of reaching the hells and therefore a necessary step of destruction he must undergo to get what he's after.

TACTICS

Kur is a dragon's dragon, a beast of rage and magic. He cannot be reasoned with. There is no logical path to his destruction. He revels in his immortality and fears nothing. Whatever does the most damage is his first combat option. But his ageless intelligence can also be brought to bear on a group of would-be heroes. He has all the time in the world to plan his next move, and though he could generally lay waste to an entire army on his own, he could also consider an approach that leverages subterfuge and careful plotting rather than muscular plodding. Whatever fight the party thinks they are in for, switch it up and deliver something they'd never expect. Make sure to include lots of pain. Miles of suffering. Ages of agony. You know, bad news.

WEALTH

Kur possesses powers beyond imagination. The treasure he is found with is based on many factors. It is impossible to calculate what the party might find—and therefore this aspect of his existence is at GM discretion. Perhaps he has nothing at all, as he would in the void. On the other hand, his avatar could possess a hoard, like any dragon. Most assuredly, he possesses the power of the void in some form or another. A magical void egg would certainly cancel wizard spells (and the like), or could amplify their power to staggering degrees.

KUR'S LAIR

Within the void, the immortal Kur can call upon his ancient power to cast *wish* twice per long rest. For this reason, any group of adventurers hoping to topple him there will almost assuredly fail. His avatar, if utilized to roam the mortal plane, is a slightly less deadly foe, but if the avatar has established a lair in the mortal realm, destroying him there is nearly as difficult.

LAIR ACTIONS

On initiative count 20 (losing initiative ties), Kur takes a lair action to cause one of the following effects. He cannot use the same effect two rounds in a row.

- Kur casts *time stop*.
- A void blade surges outward from a point within 120 feet of Kur in a 120-foot line. The blade then shifts left or right, slashing every creature in its path for 300 feet. Each creature must succeed on a DC 24 Dexterity saving throw or suffer 28 (8d6) necrotic damage, or half as much on a successful save.
- A creature of void energy, a **shadow demon**, emerges from an area within 300 feet of Kur. It rolls its own initiative, and serves Kur's aims to the best of its ability.

Kur can't repeat an effect until they have all been used, and can't use the same effect two rounds in a row.

Kur,
The Dragon of the Void

Gargantuan ancient black dragon, chaotic evil

Armor Class 27 (natural armor)
Hit Points 735 (42d20 + 294)
Speed 60 ft., fly 120 ft., swim 50 ft.

STR	DEX	CON	INT	WIS	CHA
30 (+10)	24 (+7)	25 (+7)	24 (+7)	24 (+6)	27 (+8)

Saving Throws Con +16, Dex +16, Wis +15
Skills Perception +15, Stealth +16
Damage Resistances necrotic
Damage Immunities acid, bludgeoning, piercing and slashing damage from nonmagical weapons
Condition Immunities charmed, deafened, exhaustion, frightened, paralyzed, petrified, poisoned
Senses blindsight 60 ft., darkvision 120 ft., passive Perception 25
Languages Common, Draconic, Celestial
Challenge 30 (155,000 XP)

Amphibious. Kur can breathe both air and water.
Discorporation. When Kur drops to 0 hit points and dies, his body is destroyed, and he is unable to take physical form for a time.
Innate Spellcasting (6/day). Kur may cast *fire storm*. Spell save DC 24. Spell attack modifier +16.
Legendary Resistance (6/Day). If Kur fails a saving throw, he can choose to succeed instead.
Limited Magic Immunity. As a reaction, Kur may choose to be immune to any spell of level 4 or below. Kur has advantage on saving throws against all other spells and magical effects.
Magic Weapons. All attacks by Kur are considered magical.
Regeneration. Kur regains 31 (2d10 + 20) hit points at the start of each of his turns unless he has suffered radiant damage the previous turn.

Actions

Multiattack. Kur can use his Frightful Presence. He then makes three attacks: one with his bite and two with his claws.
Bite. Melee Weapon Attack: +19 to hit, reach 15 ft., one target.
Hit: 21 (2d10 + 10) piercing damage + 9 (2d8) acid damage.
Claw. Melee Weapon Attack: +19 to hit, reach 10 ft., one target.
Hit: 17 (2d6 + 10) slashing damage.
Tail. Melee Weapon Attack: +19 to hit, reach 20 ft., one target.
Hit: 19 (2d8 + 10) bludgeoning damage.
Frightful Presence. Each creature of Kur's choice that is within 120 feet and aware of him, must succeed on a DC 24 Wisdom saving throw or become frightened for one minute. A creature can repeat the saving throw at the end of each of its turns, ending the effect on a success. If a creature's saving throw is successful or the effect ends, the creature is immune Kur's Frightful Presence for the next 24 hours.
Acid Breath (recharge on 3-6). Kur exhales acid in a 120-foot line that is 20 feet wide. Each creature in that line must make a DC 24 Dexterity saving throw, taking 88 (16d10) acid damage on a failed save or half as much damage on a successful one.

Legendary Actions

Kur can take four legendary actions, choosing from the options below. Only one legendary action can be used at a time and only at the end of another creature's turn. Kur regains spent legendary actions at the start of his turn.
Detect. Kur makes a Wisdom (Perception) check.
Bite. Kur makes a bite attack.
Tail Attack. Kur makes a tail attack.
Wing Attack (Costs 2 Actions). Kur beats his wings. Each creature within 20 feet of Kur must succeed on a DC 24 Dexterity saving throw or take 17 (2d6 + 10) bludgeoning damage and be knocked prone. Kur can then fly up to half his flying speed.
Channel the Void (Costs 2 Actions). Kur magically unleashes void energy. A pulsating wave of negative energy washes over everything within range. Creatures within 60 feet of Kur, including those behind any type of barrier and around corners, cannot regain any hit points until the end of Kur's next turn.
Teleportation. Kur can magically teleport himself, or anyone that he can see, along with any equipment being worn or carried, to an unoccupied space within sight.

Regional Effects

The area around the lair created by Kur's avatar would immediately be influenced by his void energy, creating the following effects within 5 miles of the lair:

- Wind rips through the region and sounds like a maddening roar. A creature who can hear this wind must succeed on a DC 15 Wisdom saving throw or suffer one level of madness at GM discretion.
- Beasts near the lair are all subjugated to Kur's will and they carry the stain of the void. Their attacks deal an extra 7 (2d6) psychic damage in addition to their typical damage.
- Spells cast within 5 miles of the lair have a 10 percent chance of failure. When a creature casts a spell, roll 1d10. On a 1, the spell is cast and the spell slot is wasted, but the spell has no effect.

If Kur's avatar is defeated, these effects immediately dissipate.

KUT-ECHINAE,
MOTHER OF MONSTROSITIES

A strange hybrid of a dragon and chasme, Kut-Echinae is unique among draconic creatures. Barely classified as a dragon, the insectoid Kut-Echinae is the mother of a number of strange and esoteric monstrous hybrids. While not the primary producer of all the realm's monsters, one would be forgiven for making the assumption, as she creates unimaginable horrors from eggs, larvae and even her own vomit. A biological anomaly herself, each creature that hatches from one of her clutches is effectively a new species, akin to ankhegs, basilisks, behir, ettercaps, remorhazes or rust monsters but also wholly distinct from those baseline monstrous classifications.

Kut-Echinae nests in dank, moist places where her cocoons, eggs and "honeycombs" can grow and pupate without her presence. This allows her to travel from region to region, planting her grotesque brood in any area that seems habitable. Like a queen bee, Kut-Echinae builds a nest around herself, leaving her children only when she is certain the hive can thrive without her. As she seeks out a new place to nest and begin the cycle again, her brood work their way to the surface, in many cases disrupting the balance of the ecosystem and in each instance wreaking havoc on the population—particularly among humanoids.

She is more animalistic and less clever than most dragons, but that doesn't mean she's a pushover. She will furiously protect her hatchlings, and they, in turn, will die to ensure she survives. Her territory constantly changes and like a yellowjacket, she never returns to the same lair twice. Each spring, she seeks 10 to 20 nesting sites in which to deposit her offspring. It is not uncommon for Kut-Echinae to burrow deep into the earth and lay eggs inside a crypt, where her young can feed on the dead until they are strong enough to survive the world above.

These are no mere monsters—something off about them. Seen centipedes that can conjure flame, and basilisks that won't just turn you to stone...they'll freeze you to death if you get too close. It's baffling. And I fear it's getting worse.

—Hallison Ulnar,
Roaming Swarmkeeper of the Four Isles

Hook

Kut-Echinae is an advanced state of fecundity. Her body molts and lays eggs, and she builds nests all over the world, in what seems like a straight line. Everywhere she goes, the nests get larger and her brood hibernates longer, producing more powerful offspring. The first of these clutches is discovered in a nearby chasm, erupting into a modest threat to the nearby human population. As the party learns more about these creatures and the threat they pose they would be drawn closer toward Kut-Echinae's final nest.

Encounter

Kut-Echinae is like an insect in many ways. She looks for cool, dry places to lay some of her eggs, and moist places for others. Cave systems, canyons, gullies and forests are perfect places to build a nest, lay her eggs and move on. Each nest takes on a unique shape, built around the local terrain, and each nest sprouts unique monsters with special powers. Ankhegs with regenerative properties, ettercaps that can see into the spirit world or chimeric beasts that grow from a tenebrious womb with four heads and multiple segmented forms, to name a few.

Kut-Echinae might be the ultimate focus of an entire campaign for the party, giving them an unpredictable villain, who produces unpredictable offspring.

Tactics

Kut-Echinae is most likely to be encountered in one of her nests and is always surrounded by members of her offspring. Some are mindless or subservient while others are predators that know not to fight to the death. Regardless, each has unique powers the party should not expect—ex: an ankheg that breathes lighting or fire (or both). Kut-Echinae is designed to be part of a draining series of encounters.

Kut-Echinae is powerful on her own, but with her brood surrounding her, she grows exponentially as a threat. The brood does everything it can to protect her in fight, and vice versa. Consider deploying Kut-Echinae's brood to give her a distinct action economy advantage early on. While her brood keeps the party's strikers occupied, the mighty dragon uses her Feeding Nectar and Droning Wings to dispatch any who would dare disturb her nest.

Her powerful exoskeleton makes her nearly invulnerable to both melee and spell attacks, and she'll retreat into a chitinous ball as a way of exhausting her opponents while she replenishes her breath weapon.

Kut-Echinae's Lair

A warm, often secluded space in which she can safely lay her eggs, Kut-Echinae's lair is damp, sticky and swarming with her brood. Any creature attempting to slay her there is in for the fight of their lives.

Lair Actions

When fighting inside her lair, Kut-Echinae can invoke the ambient magic to take lair actions. On initiative count 20 (losing initiative ties), Kut-Echinae can take one lair action to cause one of the following effects:

- 1d4 **ankhegs** rise from the ground, aiming to protect their queen.
- Each creature in a 20-foot cube becomes affected by the *faerie fire* spell (DC 18) as Kut-Echinae's glowworm supplicants attach themselves to other creatures in the area.
- An area in a 20-foot cube becomes affected by a nectar-based version of the *web* spell (DC 18).

Kut-Echinae can't repeat an effect until they have all been used, and can't use the same effect two rounds in a row.

Regional Effects

Kut-Echinae's ambient magic and chaotic energy directly influence the creatures that are born from her nests, creating strange hybrids that defy logic. Roll twice on the table below (rerolling duplicates) to determine which creatures are affecting the nest in the party's area, as well as the bonus effects granted by her essence.

1d6	Creature	Effect
1	**ankhegs**...	...that cast *fireball* twice per short rest.
2	**giant hornets**...	...that can cast *misty step* at will.
3	**giant fire beetles**...	...that have a 100 feet burrow speed.
4	**basilisks**...	...that are resistant to all damage except for psychic.
5	**war drakes** (pg. 132)...	...that automatically grapple a target on a successful melee attack (DC 16).
6	**displacer drakes** (pg. 133)...	...that can cast *greater invisibility* once per short rest.

KUT-ECHINAE, MOTHER OF MONSTROSITIES

Gargantuan dragon, chaotic neutral

Armor Class 22 (natural armor)
Hit Points 507 (26d20 + 234)
Speed 40 ft., burrow 40 ft., fly 90 ft., swim 40 ft.

STR	DEX	CON	INT	WIS	CHA
27 (+8)	17 (+3)	28 (+9)	17 (+3)	20 (+5)	19 (+4)

Saving Throws Str +16, Dex +11, Con +17, Wis +13, Cha +12
Skills Insight +21, Nature +19, Perception +21, Stealth +19, Survival +21
Damage Resistances fire; bludgeoning, piercing and slashing from nonmagical attacks
Damage Immunities acid, lightning
Condition Immunities blinded, charmed, deafened, frightened, paralyzed, poisoned
Senses blindsight 60 ft., darkvision 120 ft., tremorsense 60 ft., passive Perception 31
Languages Common, Draconic, Primordial, Terran, telepathy 30 ft.
Challenge 26 (90,000 XP)

Chitinous Form. As an action, Kut-Echinae can roll up into a large, chitinous ball. When in this form Kut-Echinae has an AC of 26 and is immune to non-magical bludgeoning, slashing and piercing damage. When Kut-Echinae's chitinous form is targeted by a line spell or a spell that requires a ranged attack roll, roll a d6. On a 1 to 5, Kut-Echinae is unaffected. On a 6, Kut-Echinae is unaffected, and the effect is reflected back at the caster as though it originated from Kut-Echinae, turning the caster into the target.

Droning Wings. Kut-Echinae's wings produce a hypnotizing droning sound to which her brood is immune. Any other creature that starts its turn within 30 feet of Kut-Echinae must succeed on a DC 14 Constitution saving throw or fall unconscious for 10 minutes. A creature that can't hear automatically succeeds on the save. The effect on the creature ends if it takes damage. If a creature's saving throw is successful or the effect ends for it, it is immune to the drone for the next 24 hours.

Legendary Resistance (3/Day). If Kut-Echinae fails a saving throw, she can choose to succeed instead.

Petrifying Gaze. If a creature starts its turn within 30 feet of Kut-Echinae and the two of them can see each other, Kut-Echinae can force the creature to make a DC 15 Constitution saving throw (if Kut-Echinae isn't incapacitated). On a failed save, the creature magically begins to turn to stone and is restrained. It must repeat the saving throw at the end of its next turn. On a success, the

effect ends. On a failure, the creature is petrified until freed by the *greater restoration* spell or other magic.

A creature that isn't surprised can avert its eyes to avoid the saving throw at the start of its turn. If it does so, it can't see Kut-Echinae until the start of its next turn, when it can avert its eyes again. If it looks at Kut-Echinae in the meantime, it must immediately make the save.

ACTIONS

Multiattack. Kut-Echinae can use her Frightful Presence. She then makes three attacks: one with her bite and two with her claws.

Bite. Melee Weapon Attack:+ 15 to hit, reach 15 ft., one target. *Hit:* 19 (2d10 + 8) piercing damage plus 9 (2d8) acid damage.

Claw. Melee Weapon Attack: +15 to hit, reach 10 ft., one target. *Hit:* 15 (2d6 + 8) slashing damage.

Tail. Melee Weapon Attack: +15 to hit, reach 20 ft., one target. *Hit:* 17 (2d8 + 8) piercing damage. The target must make a DC 15 Constitution saving throw, taking 24 (7d6) poison damage on a failed save, or half as much damage on a successful one.

Feeding Nectar (Recharge 5-6). Kut-Echinae expels a thick, nourishing nectar that also breaks down proteins for her growing brood. The queen exhales lightning-infused nectar in a 120-foot line that is 10 feet wide. Each creature in that line must make a DC 23 Dexterity saving throw, taking 88 (16d10) lightning damage on a failed save, or half as much damage on a successful one. Any creature that fails this saving throw is grappled by Kut-Echinae's nectar, and can use its action to escape with a successful DC 18 Strength (Athletics) saving throw.

Additionally, any ally in the area of effect of the nectar is immune to its damage and is instead healed 12 (2d6 + 5) hit points.

Frightful Presence. Each creature of Kut-Echinae's choice that is within 120 feet of Kut-Echinae and aware of her must succeed on a DC 19 Wisdom saving throw or become frightened for one minute. A creature can repeat the saving throw at the end of each of its turns, ending the effect on itself on a success. If a creature's saving throw is successful or the effect ends for it, the creature is immune to Kut-Echinae's Frightful Presence for the next 24 hours.

LEGENDARY ACTIONS

Kut-Echinae can take three legendary actions, choosing from the options below. Only one legendary action option can be used at a time and only at the end of another creature's turn. Kut-Echinae regains spent legendary actions at the start of her turn.

Detect. Kut-Echinae makes a Wisdom (Perception) check.

Tail Attack. Kut-Echinae makes a tail attack.

Wing Attack (Costs 2 Actions). Kut-Echinae beats her wings. Each creature within 15 feet of Kut-Echinae must succeed on a DC 23 Dexterity saving throw or take 15 (2d6 + 8) bludgeoning damage and be knocked prone. Kut-Echinae can then fly up to half its flying speed.

Chitinous Form (Costs 3 Actions). Kut-Echinae can fold into her chitinous form.

NAGHI,
THE STONE DRAGON

Centuries ago, Naghi was wounded in a fight with a temperamental basilisk. Though he was able to kill the beast, his injury festered and what little magic he knew was not enough to staunch the petrification that began to slowly radiate outward from his wound. Eventually, his back left leg went numb and then still.

Dragons are smart, but also vain, and in this regard, Naghi's pride was his undoing. Rather than gnaw the limb completely off, Naghi held out hope that he would be able to find a cure for his ailment.

As his mobility began to suffer, Naghi took to more contemplative studies, exploring the arcane as well as the metaphysical, delving into ways the mind can live on with or without the body.

In his meditations and explorations, he began to push past the limitations brought on by his slow-moving petrification as he mastered the power of his mind. Though he could not stop the progression of the infection that was slowly turning him to stone, he was able to uncover the secret to projecting his spirit into the astral plane. He discovered that as he wandered this plane, time stood still for his body—and also his increasingly severe ailment.

In this way he has preserved his life for several centuries, spending increasingly greater lengths of time wandering the astral plane to delay the inevitable. To protect his corporeal form, Naghi relies upon a network of informants he has recruited to infiltrate the halls of scribes and sages across the realm. Most are unaware of his affliction. He meets with them as an illusory version of himself and remains in contact through their dreams. Should the need arise, he can erase their memories to maintain his secrets.

Naghi has sought sages, met with mages and conferred with clerics about his coming end.

He found their solutions to his affliction wanting, and they found his stone exterior resistant to the typical applications of spells like *greater restoration*. Naghi is hopeful that with further research, a larger ring of spies and a deeper knowledge of the weave, he can sustain his existence forever.

He said, "If I told you whom I served you wouldn't believe me, and I wouldn't tell you anyway, because I wish to continue working in his service. Let's just say I had a vision and leave it at that. Now give me all your diamonds."

—Testimony of Carla Darlington, President of Dwarvencore Gemworks

HOOK

Naghi is driven to act mostly out of paranoia. As his affliction has spread, he has lost the use of his back legs, and the rigid muscles in his back prevent him from using his now-withered wings. He will go to any length to make sure that none learn of his lair, using magic to remove the memories of those that have stumbled upon it. When this tactic is not enough, he will bend them to his will or break their minds. It is likely through one of his informants, or through mere happenstance, that the party will first encounter this reclusive dragon.

Or perhaps the party encounters many individuals in a single borough with no recollection of the time they spent exploring the local caverns.

Or maybe Naghi reaches out to recruit the party into his network of spies and informants, ultimately giving them a choice to permit him to erase their memories of his sanctum or face his wrath.

Or it might happen that Naghi is witnessed in the distance during a brief trip to the astral plane.

Regardless of how they first encounter Naghi, he does everything within his power to avoid confronting them. He might offer information or attempt to coerce them into serving him. It is also possible that he is the object of a quest to help a party member or their ally to rid themselves of a painful memory.

ENCOUNTER CONDITIONS

His lair, the Caves of Contemplation.

ENCOUNTER

With part of his body petrified, Naghi does not travel often. Encounters with him will occur randomly within the astral plane, or they will happen at his discretion within his lair. Traveling in the astral plane via the *astral projection* spell, Naghi is not limited by his affliction and makes for a fearsome foe. Confronted elsewhere, he is usually aware of the impending conflict and can make preparations.

Naghi's private sanctum is within the hollow of a massive volcanic geode at the bottom of a deep cavern. Through the use of the *project image* spell, he can keep tabs on his lair and portions of the surrounding environs. It is through this spell that he most often meets with those that desire an audience with him.

TACTICS

Naghi's primary defense is to never let his enemies know where to find him. His spells allow him to wander the tunnels of his cavern as an illusion and to contact his agents while they sleep. Almost no one has actually seen him.

Most of those that have had the misfortune of stumbling into his inmost sanctum have perished under the full ferocity of his intellect. His psionic might is impressive, and he uses it to disorient his enemies and

turn them against each other. This psychic power is so strong that he can manifest it corporeally, creating a mental projection of his psyche, which appears as an adult silver dragon (see Psychic Projection in Naghi's stat block for details).

This psychic entity is a valuable tactical ally for Naghi during combat. He controls this duplicate completely, and the two are fully coordinated during a fight. The projection is as agile as any dragon and Naghi uses it to attack enemies that are resistant to his ability to occlude their minds.

VALUABLE SPIES

Naghi collects informants the way other dragons gather gold and jewels. None of these individuals are present within his lair—they are connected to him through one another and through Naghi's ability to visit them in their dreams. They have the practical effect of connecting him to a world that he cannot wander on his own and serve as a means of warning him of intruders. It is unknown what other purposes he has bent them to in the past and what actions he would consider having them undertake in the future.

NAGHI'S LAIR

Naghi's cavern is deep below ground, part of a network of old magma tunnels from a long-dormant volcano. Strange crystalline deposits litter the caverns. Naghi wanders these Caves of Contemplation as an illusion—his true form sequestered deeper within the recesses of the earth.

LAIR ACTIONS

On initiative count 20 (losing initiative ties), Naghi takes a lair action to cause one of the following effects. He can't use the same effect two rounds in a row.

- Each creature in the lair must make a DC 15 Charisma saving throw or become unable to knowingly tell a lie, as if under the effects of the *zone of truth* spell.
- One creature Naghi can see must make a DC 15 Intelligence saving throw or become stunned. While stunned, the creature stands mouth agape, drooling. A creature has disadvantage on this saving throw if it has taken psychic damage during the previous round.
- One creature Naghi can see must make a DC 15 Wisdom saving throw or succumb to myriad visions that cloud its mind, causing it to behave erratically as if under the effects of the *confusion* spell.

Naghi, The Stone Dragon

Huge dragon, neutral

Armor Class 24 (natural armor)
Hit Points 589 (38d12 + 342)
Speed 20 ft. (special, see immobile)

STR	DEX	CON	INT	WIS	CHA
26 (+8)	10 (+0)	28 (+9)	30 (+10)	18 (+4)	18 (+4)

Saving Throws Dex +7, Con +16, Int +17, Cha +11
Skills Arcana +17, Perception +11
Damage Resistances psychic, bludgeoning, piercing and
   slashing from nonmagical attacks
Condition Immunities charmed, petrified
Senses blindsight 60 ft., darkvision 120 ft., passive Perception 21
Languages common, draconic, telepathy 120 ft.
Challenge 24 (62,000 XP)

Immobile. Naghi's back legs are petrified, leaving him unable to move at normal speed. As an action, he can use his forelegs to drag himself up to his speed. He has disadvantage on Dexterity saving throws, but cannot be moved or knocked prone.

Innate Spellcasting (Psionics). Naghi's innate spellcasting ability is Intelligence (spell save DC 20). He can innately cast the following spells, requiring no material components:

   At will: astral projection (only while within his lair),
      detect thoughts, project image, telekinesis
   3/day each: dominate person, phantasmal killer, wall of force
   1/day each: dream, hypnotic pattern, reverse gravity,
      telepathic bond

Legendary Resistance (3/Day). If Naghi fails a saving throw, he can choose to succeed instead.

Actions

Multiattack. Naghi can use his Frightful Presence. He then makes three attacks: one with his bite and two with his claws.
Bite. Melee Weapon Attack: +15 to hit, reach 15 ft., one target. *Hit:* 19 (2d10 + 8) piercing damage, plus 13 (3d8) force damage.
Claw. Melee Weapon Attack: +15 to hit, reach 10 ft., one target. *Hit:* 17 (2d6 + 8) slashing damage.

Frightful Presence. Each creature of Naghi's choice that is within 120 feet of him and aware of him must succeed on a DC 21 Wisdom saving throw or become frightened for one minute. A creature can repeat the saving throw at the end of each of its turns, ending the effect on itself on a success. If a creature's saving throw is successful or the effect ends for it, the creature is immune to Naghi's Frightful Presence for the next 24 hours.
Breath Weapon (Recharge 5–6). Naghi exhales lightning in a 120-foot line that is 10 feet wide. Each creature in that line must make a DC 23 Dexterity saving throw, taking 88 (16d10) lightning damage on a failed save, or half as much on a successful one.
Rend Thoughts (Recharge 5–6). Naghi magically tears into the mind of a creature using psychic energy. One creature of his choice within 120 feet that he can see must make a DC 20 Intelligence saving throw or take 54 (8d10 + 10) psychic damage and become dazed. A creature that is dazed by this ability can either move or use an action, but not both. While dazed, a creature cannot use bonus actions or reactions and has disadvantage on Dexterity saving throws. At the end of each of its turns, a dazed creature can repeat its Intelligence save, ending the effect of this ability on a successful save.
Psychic Projection. Naghi manifests a duplicate from psionic energy. This psychic projection has the stats of an **adult silver dragon** but does not have a breath weapon or the legendary resistance trait. It shares Naghi's resistances and immunities. When created, the psychic projection rolls initiative and takes actions on its own turn. The projection is dismissed when it reaches 0 hit points or if Naghi is unconscious or reduced to 0 hit points.

Legendary Actions

Naghi can take three legendary actions, choosing from the options below. Only one legendary action option can be used at a time and only at the end of another creature's turn. Naghi regains spent legendary actions at the start of his turn.
Detect. Naghi makes a Wisdom (Perception) check.
Focus. Naghi dismisses his psychic projection and recharges his *rend thoughts* ability.
Coordinated Assault (Costs 2 Actions). Naghi makes a bite or claw attack. His psychic projection can then move up to its speed and make a bite, claw or tail attack.
Psychic Backlash. Naghi lashes out with the power of his mind. One creature within 15 feet of him must succeed on a DC 20 Intelligence saving throw or take 17 (2d6 + 10) psychic damage. This damage increases to 24 (4d6 + 10) if the target has attacked Naghi during this round.

Regional Effects

The region containing Naghi's lair is warped by his powerful psychic presence, which creates one or more of the following effects:

• In the hour just before dawn and right after sunset, creatures within 6 miles of the lair can hear constant, soft whispers when standing within 10 feet of another creature. These sounds are caused by the thoughts of living creatures being amplified by Naghi's psychic presence. The contents of thoughts heard in this way are unintelligible.

• Rocks within 6 miles of the lair, from pebbles to boulders, become geodes. Areas of exposed rock begin to grow clusters of turquoise-colored crystal. Geode and crystal alike carry a slight static charge that causes hair to stand on end when touched.
• Within 1 mile of the lair, mundane beasts sometimes spontaneously develop sentience as though affected by the spell *awaken*.

If Naghi dies, conditions of the area surrounding the lair return to normal after 1d10 days.

PELLIX,
THE STALKER

An old, fierce and white-scaled dragon, Pellix the Stalker hunts down dragonborn and those with draconic ancestry in an attempt to return the "stolen blood" to the progenitor. He serves the Council of Draconic Truth, a collection of dragons that believe all draconic races to be abominable parasites unworthy of the blood that courses through their veins. The council believes the destruction of the draconic races is an absolute necessity for the future of dragonkind. Pellix represents the culmination of their aims, and now that he has been set loose on the dragonborn of the realm, the council's plans are finally coming to fruition. He is methodical, cunning and strikes without warning. He's already decimated one-eighth of the dragonborn population, working across the realm in a way that hasn't yet aroused suspicion.

Pellix is in every way a paladin to this cause. He sees himself as a true lawful good champion of draconic values. Those who stand in opposition to his beliefs are the villains. Anyone who stands on the side of dragonborn clearly does not understand the role of dragons—as apex predators and overlords—in this world, and they too will find their way onto his growing list.

Cults associated with the worship of dragons also draw Pellix's ire. If it were up to Pellix, all links between dragons and humanity would be severed, though that aspect of his crusade will have to wait. His list lengthens by the day. For now, his task is to destroy the abominations that stand as a mockery of draconic nobility. Most dragonborn do not know of Pellix's existence. He would not be good at his job if they did. Recently, however, as the number of Pellix's victims grows, a horrible rumor has spread among the draconic races. These tales told in whispered tones speak of a powerful winged beast that strikes from the clouds and snatches dragonborn into the sky, rending them apart in mere seconds. No dragonborn would ever guess or know that this great stalker is a dragon itself.

Abominations. An insult to our kind. Dragonborn have perverted the name of true dragons for far too long. The instrument of their destruction will be an arm of this council, as well as its wings. He will hunt each dragonborn down until they are an unutterable memory. To all dragonborn and any who would protect them: Pellix knows your name.

—Takreus the Nightbringer, Ancient Blue Dragon, Head of the Council of Draconic Truth

HOOK

A trail of destruction is discovered over the course of several days: tattered gear, a single boot, a blood-soaked shield bearing the sigil of a notable dragonborn family. These small signs grow more overt, as the shredded bodies of dragonborn, kobolds, half dragons and other draconic races are encountered in several nearby areas over the coming few months. Investigating these clues would lead the party to a noble dragonborn family who are growing concerned about the deaths of several members of their race across the realm. While Pellix is not an immediate threat to the party, he soon will be. It's only a matter of time before a draconic member of the party or one of their dragonborn allies finds their name at the top of Pellix's list.

ENCOUNTER CONDITIONS

Harangued. The dragonborn being hunted is certain to feel trapped and exhausted before the final battle.

TACTICS

Pellix is the ultimate hunter. He is never caught off guard and knows exactly where to find the next dragonborn to be eliminated. He uses his ability to shapeshift and silently observe his prey, attacking only when it is most beneficial to him. He would never be caught in the open, or flat-footed, or unaware of his opponents' strengths. He studies his prey for days or weeks before striking, knowing everything they could bring to the fight. This goes for those who walk alongside the dragonborn as well. Pellix knows every weapon of the dwarven fighter or spells of the elven wizard who stand with the dragonborn scum.

In combat, Pellix targets any dragonborn in a party first, only stopping to harm others who would protect the abomination. Once the dragonborn has been destroyed, he sees no further need for combat and flies away.

Pellix carries with him an array of magical powers that he can bring to the fore. He can turn himself invisible and throw opponents into the sky with his mind (telekinesis). In the unlikely event he is ever cornered, he can cast *entangle* on his foes and invoke the powers of his lair.

PELLIX'S LAIR

Never in the same place twice and always in a fortified position nearly impossible to track down, Pellix lairs up when he needs time to plan his next move or rehabilitate in the rare event an attack didn't immediately go his way. Only a fool would attempt to fight Pellix on his home turf. Some people are fools.

LAIR ACTIONS

When fighting inside his lair, Pellix can invoke the ambient magic to take lair actions. On initiative count 20 (losing initiative ties), Pellix can take one lair action to cause one of the following effects:

- A creature of Pellix's choice is marked by his lair and affected by *hunter's mark*. This effect stacks with Pellix's ability to cast the spell.
- Pellix's roar echoes off the walls of his lair. Each hostile creature that can hear Pellix must succeed on a DC 18 Wisdom saving throw or use their reaction to move 10 feet away from Pellix. Creatures who fail this save have disadvantage on all attacks for one round. Creatures that are immune to the frightened effect are not immune to the echoing roar.
- A creature of Pellix's choice must succeed on a DC 18 Charisma saving throw or become charmed by Pellix. They must spend their next turn moving as close as they can to Pellix, then bow in supplication to him, falling prone. The creature can regain their composure at the start of their next turn.

Pellix can't repeat an effect until they have all been used, and he can't use the same effect two rounds in a row.

REGIONAL EFFECTS

The region containing Pellix's lair is warped by the creature's presence, which creates one or more of the following effects:

- Any draconic creature within 5 miles of Pellix's lair suffers one level of exhaustion. If a draconic creature stays for more than one day within that radius they will suffer another level of exhaustion each day following. In addition, Pellix becomes aware of any draconic creatures within this range and can locate them within one minute.

If Pellix dies, the effects fade over the course of 3d10 days.

Pellix, The Stalker

Gargantuan dragon, lawful evil

Armor Class 22 (natural armor)
Hit Points 615 (30d20 + 300)
Speed 40 ft., burrow 40 ft., fly 90 ft., swim 40 ft.

STR	DEX	CON	INT	WIS	CHA
30 (+10)	14 (+2)	30 (+10)	20 (+5)	21 (+5)	22 (+6)

Saving Throws Str +18, Dex +10, Con +18, Int +13, Wis +13, Cha +14
Skills Deception +22, Insight +21, Nature +21, Perception +21, Stealth +18
Damage Resistances acid, cold, fire; bludgeoning, piercing and slashing from nonmagical attacks
Condition Immunities charmed, exhaustion, petrified, poisoned, prone
Senses blindsight 60 ft., darkvision 120 ft., passive Perception 31
Languages Common, Draconic, Elvish
Challenge 28 (120,000 XP)

Amphibious. Pellix can breathe air and water.

Blood Hunter. Pellix can sense the presence of dragon blood in any creature within 5 miles.

Change Shape. Pellix magically polymorphs into a humanoid or beast that has a challenge rating no higher than his own, or back into his true form. He reverts to his true form if he dies. Any equipment he is wearing or carrying is absorbed or borne by the new form of Pellix's choice.

In a new form, Pellix retains his alignment, hit points, Hit Dice, ability to speak, proficiencies, Legendary Resistances, lair actions and Intelligence, Wisdom and Charisma scores, as well as this action. His statistics and capabilities are otherwise replaced by those of the new form, except any class features or legendary actions of that form.

Innate Spellcasting. Pellix can cast spells without the need for material components. His spellcasting ability is Intelligence (DC 26). He can innately cast the following spells:

3/Day: *entangle, pass without trace*
1/Day: *telekinesis*

Legendary Resistance (3/Day). If Pellix fails a saving throw, he can choose to succeed instead.

Ruthless Reputation. Any creature of draconic origin makes attack rolls and saving throws against Pellix with disadvantage, unless immune to the fear condition.

Stalker's Breath. Pellix can choose from the following breath weapons whenever he uses his breath attack: Acid, Cold, Fire or Lightning.

Stalker's Stride. Pellix can move across or climb any surface without needing to make an ability check. Additionally, difficult terrain doesn't cost him extra movement.

Actions

Multiattack. Pellix can use his Frightful Presence. He then makes three attacks: one with his bite and two with his claws.

Bite. Melee Weapon Attack: +14 to hit, reach 15 ft., one target.
Hit: 19 (2d10 + 8) piercing damage plus 9 (2d8) cold damage.

Claw. Melee Weapon Attack: +14 to hit, reach 10 ft., one target.
Hit: 15 (2d6 + 8) slashing damage.

Tail. Melee Weapon Attack: +14 to hit, reach 20 ft., one target.
Hit: 17 (2d8 + 8) bludgeoning damage.

Breath Weapon (Recharge 5–6). Pellix uses one of the following breath weapons:

Acid Breath. Pellix exhales acid in a 90-foot line that is 10 feet wide. Each creature in that line must make a DC 22 Dexterity saving throw, taking 72 (16d8) acid damage on a failed save or half as much on a successful one.

Cold Breath. Pellix exhales an icy blast in a 90-foot cone. Each creature in that area must make a DC 22 Constitution saving throw, taking 72 (16d8) cold damage on a failed save or half as much on a successful one.

Fire Breath. Pellix exhales a fiery blast in a 90-foot cone. Each creature in that area must make a DC 22 Dexterity saving throw, taking 72 (16d8) fire damage on a failed save or half as much on a successful one.

Lightning Breath. Pellix exhales lightning in a 90-foot line that is 10 feet wide. Each creature in that line must make a DC 22 Dexterity saving throw, taking 72 (16d8) lightning damage on a failed save or half as much on a successful one.

Frightful Presence. Each creature of Pellix's choice that is within 120 feet of Pellix and aware of it must succeed on a DC 18 Wisdom saving throw or become frightened for one minute. A creature can repeat the saving throw at the end of each of its turns, ending the effect on itself on a success. If a creature's saving throw is successful or the effect ends for it, the creature is immune to Pellix's Frightful Presence for the next 24 hours.

Legendary Actions

Pellix can take three legendary actions, choosing from the options below. Only one legendary action option can be used at a time and only at the end of another creature's turn. Pellix regains spent legendary actions at the start of his turn.

Detect. Pellix makes a Wisdom (Perception) check.

Hunter's Mark. Pellix can cast *hunter's mark* (at will) on a creature of his choice.

Tail Attack. Pellix makes a tail attack.

Wing Attack (Costs 2 Actions). Pellix beats his wings. Each creature within 15 feet of Pellix must succeed on a DC 22 Dexterity saving throw or take 15 (2d6 + 8) bludgeoning damage and be knocked prone. Pellix can then fly up to half his flying speed.

Bloodbath (Costs 2 Actions). Pellix uses the power of recovered dragonborn blood, consuming it to recharge his breath weapon and use Hit Dice as if benefitting from a short rest. After consuming the blood, Pellix can attack dragonborn with advantage. Hit points taken from dragonborn following a Bloodbath transfer to Pellix at the end of his turn.

SALATHIIR,
SUFFERING MADE FLESH

Blood thick with pain trickles through the cracks of the multiverse, draining into its darkest and most wretched fissures. The hatred and suffering of the multiverse pools in the depths of the Abyss, and there it boils and churns like the primordial draught that first created mortal life.

For eons, a particular type of demon has been spawned from that malefic brew. Salthezau—also known as Torment Demons—spring fully grown from this pool of twisted emotions and fly across the planes in hopes of filling the cosmos with suffering, thus continuing their wretched species. These tiny demons are the size of large bats and have three pairs of flapping wings surrounding a spherical body dominated by a large, toothy mouth. They are sightless but can sense the emotions of living creatures.

Salthezau are easily overcome alone, but become nightmarish, inescapable terrors when encountered in swarms. When a swarm of salthezau hunt, they can doom even the mightiest of creatures. Such was the case for the dragon Aurathiir, a guardian of order and justice at the border between the cosmic realms of chaos and the rest of the planar cosmos. Aurathiir was a benevolent being, often blessing heroes with weapons and armor forged from shards of his fangs or his massive scales. But even heroic dragons are not immune to suffering.

While flying along the edge of the chaotic planes, Aurathiir saw a black cloud looming on the cosmic horizon. Curious, he investigated, only to learn too late that the cloud was a mass of living beings: a swarm of salthezau larger than anything he had ever seen before. Aurathiir fought bravely against the swarm, but even though hundreds of demons smashed futilely against his scales, thousands more found purchase on his flesh beneath. They latched onto him and weighed him down until he could no longer summon the strength to flap his wings.

And so he fell.

Aurathiir and the swarm of salthezau tumbled for what felt like years into the heart of the Abyss and beyond, until the dragon crashed into the pools of primordial torment which spawned the demons that slew him. There, Aurathiir died.

And centuries later, there in the Abyss, he was reborn as Salathiir, the Demon Dragon—suffering made flesh. It is said that during every mortal generation, it rises from its lightless home in the Abyss to urge mortal beings to give in to their darkest instincts and fill the world with pain, hatred and loss. It is the bane of civilization, the scourge of peace and the devourer of hope. And when it has gorged itself on torment, it returns to the pools from whence it came and rests until its wounds are healed and it can once more wreak devastation upon the world.

So long as evil lurks in the hearts of mortal creatures, the Demon Dragon shall never die.

A swarm of unimaginable despair, a plague of torment and swirling toil—I grow weaker at the thought of committing its name to parchment. It is coming. It will consume us all. Best to end things here before it arrives. Goodbye, my love.

*—Able Margaster,
Last Known Heir of the Lost Fortune*

Hook

The Demon Dragon is spoken of in legends. Many power-hungry monarchs and overzealous occultists have attempted to harness its destructive nature for their own ends. The Demon Dragon is chaos given form, and the suffering it wreaks upon its masters' enemies is only a prelude to its inevitable betrayal as Salathiir casts death indiscriminately upon all—especially the beings that dared to call themselves the Demon Dragon's master.

Only one being has ever been able to harness the Demon Dragon's power without losing control. What myths remain suggest the Demon Dragon's master was a plane-walking sorcerer who managed to weave a spell binding Salathiir's will so tightly it could not escape. The sorcerer's reign of terror lasted decades, threatening the multiverse until both sorcerer and Salathiir were slain by a group of heroes. The power of the sorcerer's spell faded with their death. Many would-be tyrants seek the secret of the spell (known as *Salathiir's perfect binding*) and many more have died seeking it.

Encounter Conditions

If Salathiir is encountered outside of the Abyss, it is because its destructive power has been harnessed by a prideful warlord through a spell such as planar binding. In these circumstances, Salathiir destroys all in its path until it manages to break free of its arcane shackles.

Salthezau

Tiny fiend (demon), chaotic evil

Armor Class 12
Hit Points 5 (2d4)
Speed 0 ft., fly 30 ft.

STR	DEX	CON	INT	WIS	CHA
14 (+2)	15 (+2)	10 (+0)	5 (-3)	10 (+0)	6 (-2)

Skills Acrobatics +4
Damage Resistances cold, fire, lightning; bludgeoning, piercing and slashing from nonmagical attacks
Damage Immunities poison
Condition Immunities poisoned
Senses darkvision 120 ft., passive Perception 8
Languages Salthezau understands Abyssal but can't speak it
Challenge 1 (200 XP)

Pack Tactics. The salthezau have advantage on an attack roll against a creature if at least one of its allies is within 5 feet of the creature and the ally isn't incapacitated.

Actions

Bite. Melee Weapon Attack: +4 to hit, reach 5 ft., one target. *Hit*: 4 (1d4 + 2) piercing damage, and the salthezau attaches to the target. While a salthezau is attached to a creature, it takes 2 (1d4) necrotic damage per attached salthezau at the start of each of its turns. While attached, the salthezau doesn't attack, but the target's speed is reduced by 10 feet. A creature is paralyzed if its speed is 0 while at least one salthezau is attached to it.

If the Demon Dragon is encountered within the Abyss, it lurks within the pool of primordial suffering that spawned it. This lightless void is a 1,000-foot-wide cavern of roughly spherical shape, save for a gaping opening at its top. Its bottom half is filled with viscous liquid that shimmers with oily, spectral colors. This defiling lake has no shores, and a living creature that is not a fiend that touches the liquid or starts its turn touching it must make a DC 21 Charisma saving throw. On a failure, the creature is affected by the *confusion* spell. If a creature fails this saving throw again while confused, it gains a form of short-term madness. If it fails this save again while affected by short-term madness, it gains a form of long-term madness. On a failure while affected by long-term madness, it gains a form of indefinite madness.

Each time a creature fails this saving throw, its form warps to become similar to Salathiir. First, its eyes turn crimson, then jet black scales cover its flesh, then its head becomes perfectly spherical and dominated by a gaping mouth of sharp teeth as dozens of flapping bat wings burst from its flesh. These transformations can be cured individually by a *greater restoration* spell. If the creature fails this save while affected by indefinite madness, it is transformed into a salthezau. Its soul cannot be recovered until the demon is killed and the creature is returned to life by a *wish*.

On initiative count 20, two salthezau demons spawn from the surface of this pool and attack the closest creature. These winged monsters try to drag Salathiir's enemies into the pool of suffering, just as they once corrupted Aurathiir.

Encounter

Salathiir seeks only to destroy and defile. In combat, it uses Frightful Presence and its Gaze of Suffering to turn its enemies against one another. Salathiir roars and gnashes its hundreds of teeth in combat, but rarely speaks intelligibly. Only when it is killed does some semblance of its sanity break through the millennia of corruption. The mind of Aurathiir rasps out the following words in its dying breath, "You have won a brief reprieve, but so long as evil lurks in mortals' hearts, the Demon Dragon will be reborn anew."

Salathiir can only be killed permanently if it is killed in the heart of the Abyss where it was born, and a *wish* spell is used to destroy Aurathiir's body and soul, freeing him from his eternal suffering. If Salathiir is killed but not permanently destroyed, even in the Abyss, it reforms in its birthplace after 25 years of agonizing rebirth.

Tactics

Salathiir's tactics are simple: it follows whatever course of action would cause the most suffering in the world. When the Demon Dragon is bound to the will of an evil mortal, it is often forced to create pain by destroying blindly, rending armies and cities asunder, indiscriminate of warrior or civilian, friend or foe.

Salathiir, Suffering Made Flesh

Colossal dragon fiend, chaotic evil

Armor Class 19 (natural armor)
Hit Points 407 (22d20 + 176)
Speed 60 ft., fly 120 ft.

STR	DEX	CON	INT	WIS	CHA
30 (+10)	13 (+1)	27 (+8)	21 (+5)	22 (+6)	15 (+2)

Saving Throws Dex +8, Con +15, Wis +13
Skills Athletics +15, Intimidation +16, Perception +20
Damage Resistances cold, fire, lightning
Damage Immunities necrotic, poison; bludgeoning, piercing and slashing that is nonmagical
Condition Immunities charmed, exhaustion, frightened, poisoned
Senses truesight 120 ft., passive Perception 30
Languages all, telepathy 120 ft.
Challenge 23 (50,000 XP)

Agonizing Spellcasting. Salathiir's spellcasting ability is Wisdom (spell save DC 21). Whenever a creature makes a saving throw against one of Salathiir's agonizing spells, it takes 11 (2d10) necrotic damage, even if it succeeds on the saving throw. Salathiir can innately cast the following spells, requiring no material components:

At will: bestow curse, fear
3/day each: confusion, contagion, counterspell, harm, hold monster
1/day each: teleport, plane shift, power word stun

Aura of Suffering. Whenever a creature starts its turn within 60 feet of Salathiir, it takes 16 (3d10) necrotic damage and must succeed on a DC 21 Wisdom saving throw or have its movement reduced to 0 until the end of its turn.
Legendary Resistance (3/Day). If Salathiir fails a saving throw, it can choose to succeed instead.
Magic Resistance. Salathiir has advantage on saving throws against spells and other magical effects.
Magic Weapons. Salathiir's weapon attacks are magical.

Actions

Multiattack. Salathiir can use its Frightful Presence. It then makes three attacks: one with its bite and two with its claws.
Bite. Melee Weapon Attack: +17 to hit, reach 15 ft., one target. *Hit:* 21 (2d10 + 10) piercing damage plus 14 (4d6) necrotic damage.
Claw. Melee Weapon Attack: +17 to hit, reach 10 ft., one target. *Hit:* 17 (2d6 + 10) slashing damage.
Tail. Melee Weapon Attack: +17 to hit, reach 20 ft., one target. *Hit:* 17 (2d8 + 10) bludgeoning damage.
Frightful Presence. Each creature of Salathiir's choice that is within 120 feet of the dragon and aware of it must succeed on a DC 17 Wisdom saving throw or become frightened for one minute. A creature can repeat the saving throw at the end of each of its turns, ending the effect on itself on a success. If a creature's saving throw is successful or the effect ends for it, the creature is immune to Salathiir's Frightful Presence for the next 24 hours.
Gaze of Suffering (Recharge 5–6). Salathiir's eyes flash, and all creatures it can see in a 120-foot cone must make a DC 21 Constitution saving throw, taking 77 (14d10) necrotic damage on a failed save or half as much on a successful one. After this, if the creature has fewer than 100 hit points, the creature's mind is overwhelmed by pain. A creature can repeat this saving throw at the end of each of its turns, ending the effect on itself on a success. While in pain, the creature's speed is reduced to 0 and it has disadvantage on attack rolls, ability checks and all saving throws except saves to resist this ability. Additionally, the creature must succeed on a DC 21 Constitution saving throw whenever it tries to cast a spell. On a failure, the spell slot is consumed, but the spell fails.

Legendary Actions

Salathiir can take three legendary actions, choosing from the options below. Only one legendary action option can be used at a time and only at the end of another creature's turn. Salathiir regains spent legendary actions at the start of its turn.
Tail Attack. Salathiir makes a tail attack.
Wing Attack (Costs 2 Actions). Salathiir beats its wings. Each creature within 15 feet of Salathiir must succeed on a DC 25 Dexterity saving throw or take 17 (2d6 + 10) bludgeoning damage and be knocked prone. Salathiir can then fly up to half its flying speed.
Tenebrous Blink (Costs 3 Actions). Salathiir blinks its eyes. A 60-foot radius sphere of magical darkness surrounds it until the start of its next turn. Additionally, Salathiir's Gaze of Suffering recharges.

GM NOTE: SALATHIIR'S PERFECT BINDING

The spell *Salathiir's perfect binding* has been forgotten by all and can only be discovered by completing a long and arduous quest, at the GM's discretion. The spell is identical to the spell *planar binding*, with the following modifications:
- The spell is 9th level.
- Its duration is "until dispelled."
- This spell only affects Salathiir.
- Salathiir has disadvantage on the saving throw to resist this spell, and cannot use its Legendary Resistance to resist the effects of this spell.
- Its material component is a perfect 1-foot-diameter sphere of meteoric iron laced with arcane runes, worth 100,000 gp, which the spell consumes.

Despite this, only fools believe the Demon Dragon to be a mindless beast. In truth, Salathiir is cold and calculating when left to its own devices, often passing up causing temporary pain in the name of causing greater suffering in the future. Even when bound to a mortal, Salathiir is accompanied by a cloud of 2d20 salthezau demons that buzz about him like flies about a corpse.

Wealth

Salathiir does not hoard wealth, but its scales are made of a supernaturally powerful material that can only be worked by the most skilled armorers. When destroyed, 3d100 of these scales clatter to the ground, and each is worth 1,000 gp to a master blacksmith. A weapon or piece of armor made from these scales is a +3 adamantine weapon, armor or shield.

TYRNIN,
THE TWO-HEADED DRAGON

There are legends of all kinds about dragons. Eggs that never open, but the hatchling still communicates through magical spells. Dragons that never grow wings but still fly. Gold dragons born evil, that must be put down by a wailing mother. Serpentine dragons born from black eggs, sharing nothing in common with mother or father. The list of abnormalities is endless.

But there is one legend that defies them all. Mostly because it is true.

Among dragons, there is a well-known curse known as a dysik egg. When two eggs merge and never separate,

"Here's an old joke. What's deadlier than a dragon?" Ogre sighed.
"A dragon with two heads?" asked Derk, his eyes wide.
"No...two dragons, you lummox!" snapped Ogre. "A dragon with two heads? That's not funny at all. That's a nightmare."

—From The Travels of Ogre and Derk by Johan Rolo Regal

dragons believe the brood inside will be evil. In Tyrnin's case, a two-headed dragon was growing inside the dysik egg. His parents, knowing full well what kind of evil this was, abandoned the nest to the elements in hopes that the hatchling would freeze to death.

But this would never happen.

Although he was never expected to live, Tyrnin was born strong and hungry, ready to devour everything he could find. To further exacerbate the problem of a young dragon born without parents, Tyrnin was born evil. And with two heads. One, black as night. The other, silver and sleek. Both of them diabolical and capable of destruction undreamt. Tyrnin aged quickly, as well, growing into a powerful beast in half the time of a typical dragon.

But growing twice as strong, twice as fast meant eating twice as much. Tyrnin knew nothing of territories or control. He ate everything he could find, terrorizing human communities, wiping out livestock and driving some cultures and species into extinction. Quickly.

To make matters worse, Tyrnin fought like a savage beast half the time and was a cold and calculating tactician the other. No other dragons his size could stand up to him. The beast quickly found himself alone, keeping company with his own conjoined head.

It has been hundreds of years now, and the dragon keeps his own council, living on the edge of the mapped territories and feeding on any brave enough to venture beyond the frontier.

Hook

Tyrnin is a bully and a fiendish beast. He is beyond reasoning. He is always looking for a fight (that he can win) and loves nothing more than throwing his weight around with average humans, orcs and the like. Eventually, his actions will go too far and the people he terrorizes will hire adventurers to save them.

Sometimes Tyrnin's ability to plan and strategize takes over and the thoughtless beast begins to act rationally. A cleverly planned ambush (if such a thing is possible for a dragon) would seem out of character for a dragon known for being a bully. Drawing the party into a fight—either through false drama or a carefully planned series of events—would place him in the driver's seat of any fight worth having.

Encounter Conditions

Outdoors and overcast.

Encounter

Tyrnin does not have a conventional lair. He sleeps where he wants and never hibernates. One head is always awake. He always comes for the party under the perfect conditions—when it is dark and he is harder to see.

The party can hunt him all they want, but he remains out of range until he wants to be found. Or he taunts them by flying in the clouds just out of reach.

Tactics

Tynin's instincts vacillate from madness to sanity; it turns on and off almost instantly and it is never clear which brain drives the engine. In a fight, he sometimes acts like a hungry, savage animal and other times like an apex predator.

In either mindset, Tyrnin is aware of his natural weapons and breath weapon. And his magic acts randomly, so when he casts a spell, it is never with an intended purpose. He just wants to hurt as many creatures as possible.

Because Tyrnin has six breath weapons that recharge at various rates, he is almost always breathing fire (or gas, or whatever) at the nearest unless flying out of range.

When he is acting strategically, Tyrnin keeps his distance, attacks spellcasters relentlessly until they are dead and then picks off the rest with ease. Fighter types without ranged attacks are easy prey to a mentally stable Tyrnin.

Tyrnin should not be an easy fight. A party used to combat ending after five to 10 rounds should expect this fight to take twice as long. Tyrnin will not be easy or even predictable. His array of offensive options are sure to keep them guessing.

Note to GMs: If you wish to make the encounter with Tyrnin more difficult, consider giving him an additional action each round.

Wealth

Tyrnin has hidden caches of gold and trinkets all over the hills and mountains he considers his domain. None of it matters to him. He lacks the wherewithal to hoard like a typical dragon. There always seems to be two of any item, however—never matching in style or color, as though Tyrnin was competing with himself.

Tyrnin's Lair

The two-headed monstrosity has no need of sleep, but does need to rest his wings from time to time. His lair is less a fortress and more like a makeshift camp in a cavern, though his more cunning half has still fortified it against intrusion.

Lair Actions

On initiative count 20 (losing initiative ties), Tyrnin takes a lair action to cause one of the following effects; Tyrnin can't use the same effect two rounds in a row:

- Tyrnin triggers one of his traps and a cave-in occurs, dropping heavy rubble on an area with a 15-foot radius. Any creature within this area must succeed on a DC 17 Dexterity saving throw or suffer 18 (4d8) bludgeoning damage and be knocked prone. The area becomes difficult terrain for the remainder of the encounter.
- A roar from Tyrnin's more bestial maw echoes off the walls of this lair. Any creature that can hear this roar must succeed on a DC 18 Wisdom saving throw or become paralyzed until the end of their next turn. A creature frightened of Tyrnin automatically fails this save.
- Tyrnin benefits from a cache of supplies stored in case of emergency, rolling up to four of his hit dice to heal.

Regional Effects

The duality of Tyrnin's personality causes disruptions in the area around his lair:

- A drought impacts the area within 10 miles of the lair despite constant hail storms.
- Predatory beasts within 50 miles of the lair refuse to hunt or devour prey in the region, eating only carrion or vegetation, perhaps out of fear of offending the apex predator in their midst.
- Creatures of the sky fly no higher than 20 feet off the ground within 50 miles of the lair out of deference for the two-headed monster that rules the region.

If Tyrnin dies, the area surrounding the lair returns to normal over the course of 1d10 days.

TYRNIN, THE TWO-HEADED DRAGON

Gargantuan dragon, chaotic evil

Armor Class 19 (Natural Armor)
Hit Points 518 (28d20 + 224)
Speed 40 ft., climb 40 ft., fly 80 ft.

STR	DEX	CON	INT	WIS	CHA
27 (+8)	14 (+2)	27 (+8)	20 (+5)	22 (+6)	24 (+7)

Saving Throws Dex +9, Con +15, Int +12, Wis +13, Cha +14
Skills Insight +13, Intimidation +21, Perception +20, Stealth +9
Damage Immunities bludgeoning
Condition Immunities blinded, charmed, exhaustion, frightened, paralyzed, stunned
Senses passive Perception 30 (34 for sound)
Languages Common, Draconic, Dwarvish, Elvish
Challenge 24 (62,000 XP)

Two Heads Are Better Than One. Tyrnin has advantage on Wisdom (Perception) checks and on saving throws against any condition he is not already immune to. This includes deafened, fatigued, grappled, incapacitated, invisible, petrified, poisoned, prone, restrained and unconscious.

Legendary Resistance (3/Day). If Tyrnin fails a saving throw, he can choose to succeed instead.

Magic Resistance. Tyrnin has advantage on saving throws against spells and other magical effects.

Magic Weapons. Tyrnin's weapon attacks are magical.

ACTIONS

Multiattack. Tyrnin can use his Frightful Presence. He then makes three attacks: two with his bite and one with his claws, or two with his bite and one with his tail.

Bite. Melee Weapon Attack: +15 to hit, reach 15 ft., one target. *Hit:* 19 (2d10 + 8) piercing damage plus 14 (4d6) poison damage.

Claw. Melee Weapon Attack: +15 to hit, reach 10 ft., one target. *Hit:* 15 (2d6 + 8) slashing damage.

Tail. Melee Weapon Attack: +15 to hit, reach 20 ft., one target. *Hit:* 17 (2d8 + 8) bludgeoning damage.

Frightful Presence. Each creature of Tyrnin's choice that is within 120 feet and aware of him must succeed on a DC 21 Wisdom saving throw or become frightened for one minute. A creature can repeat the saving throw at the end of each of its turns, ending the effect on itself on a success. If a creature's saving throw is successful or the effect ends for it, the creature is immune to Tyrnin's Frightful Presence for the next 24 hours.

Breath Weapon (Recharge 4-6, see Polymorph Breath). Tyrnin may choose one of the following breath weapons as an Action:

Acid Breath. Tyrnin exhales acid in a 90-foot line that is 10 feet wide. Each creature in that line must succeed on a DC 22 Dexterity saving throw, taking 67 (15d8) acid damage on a failed save or half as much on a successful one.

Cold Breath. Tyrnin exhales an icy blast in a 90-foot cone. Each creature in that area must succeed on a DC 22 Constitution saving throw, taking 72 (16d8) cold damage on a failed save or half as much on a successful one.

Fire Breath. Tyrnin exhales fire in a 90-foot cone. Each creature in that area must make a DC 22 Dexterity saving throw, taking 91 (26d6) fire damage on a failed save or half as much damage on a successful one.

Paralyzing Breath. Tyrnin exhales paralyzing gas in a 90-foot cone. Each creature in that area must succeed on a DC 24 Constitution saving throw or be paralyzed for one minute. A creature can repeat the saving throw at the end of each of its turns, ending the effect on itself on a success.

Poison Breath. Tyrnin exhales poisonous gas in a 90-foot cone. Each creature in that area must succeed on a DC 22 Constitution saving throw, taking 77 (22d6) poison damage on a failed save, or half as much on a successful one.

Polymorph Breath (Recharge 6). Tyrnin exhales magical energy in a 30-foot cone. Each creature in that area must succeed on a DC 22 Wisdom saving throw or be changed into a nonmagical object of Tyrnin's choice. If the creature succeeds on their save, it is not affected. The affected creature transforms, along with whatever it is wearing and carrying, into that form. The creature's statistics become those of the object, and the creature has no memory of time spent in this form. After the effect ends, it returns to its normal form. A creature can repeat their saving throw at the end of each of its turns, ending the effect on itself on a success.

LEGENDARY ACTIONS

Tyrnin can take three legendary actions, choosing from the options below. Only one legendary action option can be used at a time and only at the end of another creature's turn. Tyrnin regains spent legendary actions at the start of his turn.

Detect. Tyrnin makes a Wisdom (Perception) check.

Tail Attack. Tyrnin makes a tail attack.

Wing Attack (Costs 2 Actions). Tyrnin beats his wings. Each creature within 15 feet of Tyrnin must succeed on a DC 25 Dexterity saving throw or take 15 (2d6 + 8) bludgeoning damage and be knocked prone. Tyrnin can then fly up to half his flying speed.

Breath Weapon (Costs 2 Actions). Tyrnin may use one of his breath weapons as long as it is charged.

Random Spell (Costs 3 Actions). Tyrnin can cast one spell from each head. Tyrnin's innate spellcasting ability is Charisma (spell save DC 22, +14 to hit with spell attacks). He can cast the following spells, requiring no material components. Each random spell is determined by rolling 1d10 on the following chart:

1) *black tentacles*	6) *insect plague*
2) *confusion*	7) *greater invisibility*
3) *conjure elemental*	8) *reverse gravity*
4) *disintegrate*	9) *sequester*
5) *eyebite*	10) *teleport*

UMUNAIRU,
SHEPHERD OF STORMS

Umunairu is a dragon of storm and sky. Her slender serpentine form swims through the heavens, borne aloft on delicate wings. Lustrous feathers cover her body, reflecting and refracting the light around her. Those who have seen her describe her as a force of nature—like a flash of lightning in the night sky, the setting sun before a storm, a dancing aurora or a fading rainbow.

When the World Serpent needed an army of celestial champions, Umunairu willingly sacrificed her spirit to birth the couatl. The couatl flourished in the mortal realm, and their existence was a true gift to humanity. The couatl were imbued with a fragment of Umunairu's draconic might and appearance and Umunairu received a gift in return. As long as even one couatl lives, she will never know a natural death.

This boon is not without drawbacks. Over the intervening millennia, the population of couatl has begun to dwindle. Most do not recall the reason for their existence or the nature of their origin. The couatl still serve a sense of divine order, but now do so with less specificity than in their prime, and those that remain often wander the realm in search of a noble purpose. The quests they undertake are dangerous, and those who do not ally themselves with powerful adventurers typically perish in their efforts.

A portion of Umunairu's memory is lost each time one of her children passes from the mortal world, and as time marches slowly forward, the resulting emotions associated with the loss have become more turbulent. When such a death occurs, all Umunairu has is the stinging ache of the absence without a sense of why. The confusion this causes coupled with the sorrow and rage she experiences with the realization of each new loss has left her rash and temperamental. The storms around her reflect this inner turmoil, making much of the landscape surrounding her lair an inhospitable place.

Her children will all save this realm,
her joy will shine and spread.
The path they lay will light the way
upon the road ahead.
So say we now, and say we then,
and say we 'til we reach the end.

—"A Song for Umunairu"
Ancient Folk Tune, Author Unknown

HOOK

Umunairu is not a common adversary. Perched high above civilization, she is content to remain apart. Her interests rarely intersect with the world in such a way that she harms it. The party are most likely to meet her after an encounter with the couatl. She watches as many of her children as she can. When they are threatened, she views this as a personal affront, visiting unrelenting retaliation against those that draw her ire.

Or maybe she needs the help of brave adventurers to save her children. She offers riches from her gemstone hoard to entice reluctant heroes into acting in her interests.

Or maybe she has discovered some great secret of the World Serpent and wishes now to undo his work, knowing that her own life will be forfeit should the couatl be destroyed.

Or maybe Umunairu's mood has soured, and the storms around her home have grown considerably. They unleash torrential rainfall and damaging winds in the area and locals demand a solution for these supernatural disasters.

However she is introduced, Umunairu's presence in a campaign is marked by complex or unclear motives. Working with or against her almost always involves untangling a dense web of conflicting emotions and delicate perspectives. To this end, the study of the storms that surround her lair can help provide context or clues to the contents of her heart and mind.

ENCOUNTER CONDITIONS

Summit of the Stormcrags, a massive mountain range.

ENCOUNTER

Umunairu is protected by the incredible height of the peak where she makes her home. Ascending the steep crags to reach the mountaintop is an incredible challenge. Deadly falls, harsh weather and hungry predators make travel to the summit almost impossible even without the intervention of the dragon's magic.

It can take several days to reach the summit of the Stormcrags. Only the foolhardy and desperate dare to brave the climb. The fierce winds there send oblivious climbers tumbling down to their deaths. A tribe of strange ape-like creatures lives along the snow line of the crags, and starving ghosts haunt the site where a previous expedition made its final encampment. These are but a few of the myriad dangers that await those who seek to confront the dragon.

TACTICS

Umunairu fights like a force of nature. She bears down upon her enemies relentlessly, holding nothing back when the time for conflict arises. The raging storms surrounding her lair provide a significant advantage in battle. She can call down thunderous bolts of lightning to devastate her foes or command the wind to scatter them. Once isolated, Umunairu crushes the life out of weaker opponents and attempts to pull stronger enemies into the sky so that she might shatter them upon the jagged peaks beneath her home.

When faced with an overwhelming invasion, Umunairu will choose to flee. Her lair atop the Stormcrags is not the first she has claimed and is unlikely to be her last. She can take to the skies easily, hiding in the dark storm clouds gathered about her home. The height of the mountain makes it unlikely that any pursuers will be able to keep up with her retreat.

VIBRANT BAUBLES

Umunairu collects colorful things including flowers, dyed garments and even a few coins. Her favorite, though, is gemstones. Rubies, emeralds, sapphires, diamonds and cut stones of every other hue glitter within the dimly lit recesses of her lair.

UMUNAIRU'S LAIR

Beneath magnificent storm clouds is a barren mountain peak, pockmarked with lightning-scorched stone. Umunairu spends much of her time lounging on a flat expanse just outside the cave hiding her hoard. She communes with the storm here, shaping the weather to her whims, without fear of discovery.

LAIR ACTIONS

On initiative count 20 (losing initiative ties), Umunairu takes a lair action to cause one of the following effects. She can't use the same effect two rounds in a row.

- Umunairu causes a line of strong, buffeting wind 60 feet long and 10 feet wide to blow in any direction of her choice, originating from a point anywhere in her lair. Each creature that starts its turn in the line must succeed on a DC 23 Strength saving throw or be pushed 15 feet in a direction following the line. Any creature in the line must spend 2 feet of movement for every 1 feet it moves when moving along the line. The gust disperses gas or vapor, and it extinguishes candles, torches and similar unprotected flames in the area. It causes protected flames, such as those of lanterns, to dance wildly and has a 50 percent chance to extinguish them. The wind ends at the start of Umunairu's next turn.
- Umunairu chooses a point she can see within 100 feet of her in the lair. A booming thunderclap rocks the area, and any creature within 20 feet of that point must succeed on a DC 18 Constitution saving throw

Umunairu, Shepherd of Storms

Colossal dragon, lawful neutral

Armor Class 22 (natural armor)
Hit Points 418 (27d20 + 135)
Speed 40 ft., fly 80 ft., swim 40 ft.

STR	DEX	CON	INT	WIS	CHA
29 (+9)	10 (+0)	21 (+5)	18 (+4)	17 (+3)	27 (+8)

Saving Throws Dex +7, Con +12, Wis +10, Cha +15
Skills Insight +10, Perception +10, Stealth +7
Damage Immunities lightning, thunder
Condition Immunities charmed, deafened, stunned
Senses blindsight 60 ft., darkvision 120 ft., passive Perception 20
Languages Common, Draconic
Challenge 24 (62,000 XP)

Innate Spellcasting. Umunairu's innate spellcasting ability is Charisma (spell save DC 23, +15 to hit with spell attacks). On her turn she can innately cast the following spells, requiring no material components:

> *At will: color spray, dancing lights, thunderwave*
> *1/day each: control weather, lightning bolt, sleet storm*
> *3/day: call lightning, control water, wind wall*

Legendary Resistance (3/Day). If Umunairu fails a saving throw, she can choose to succeed instead.

Actions

Multiattack. Umunairu can use her Frightful Presence. She then makes three attacks, one with her tail and two with her bite, or three bite attacks.

Bite. Melee Weapon Attack: +16 to hit, reach 15 ft., one target. *Hit*: 30 (2d10 + 9) piercing damage.

Constrict. Umunairu crushes a creature that she has grabbed. The creature must succeed on a DC 20 Strength saving throw or take 30 (6d6 + 9) bludgeoning damage.

Tail. Melee Weapon Attack: +16 to hit, reach 20 ft., one target. *Hit*: 18 (2d8 + 9) bludgeoning damage and the target is grappled (escape DC 19). Until this grapple ends, the target is restrained.

Frightful Presence (Recharge 5–6). Each creature of Umunairu's choice that is within 120 feet of her and aware of her must succeed on a DC 21 Wisdom saving throw or become frightened for one minute. A creature can repeat the saving throw at the end of each of its turns, ending the effect on itself on a success. If a creature's saving throw is successful or the effect ends for it, the creature is immune to Umunairu's Frightful Presence for the next 24 hours.

Breath Weapons (Recharge 5–6). Umunairu uses one of the following breath weapons:

> ***Lightning Breath.*** Umunairu exhales lightning in a 120-foot line that is 10 feet wide. Each creature in that line must make a DC 23 Dexterity saving throw, taking 88 (16d10) lightning damage on a failed save or half as much damage on a successful one.
> ***Tempest Breath.*** Umunairu exhales blustery winds in a 60-foot cone. Each creature in that area must succeed on a DC 23 Strength saving throw. On a failed save, the creature is knocked prone and pushed up to 60 feet away.

Legendary Actions

Umunairu can take three legendary actions, choosing from the options below. Only one legendary action option can be used at a time and only at the end of another creature's turn. Umunairu regains spent legendary actions at the start of her turn.

Detect. Umunairu makes a Wisdom (Perception) check.

Tail Attack. Umunairu makes a tail attack.

Constrict (Costs 2 Actions). Umunairu uses her constrict ability against a creature that it has grappled.

Wing Attack (Costs 2 Actions). Umunairu beats her wings. Each creature within 15 feet of her must succeed on a DC 24 Dexterity saving throw or take 16 (2d6 + 9) bludgeoning damage and be knocked prone. She can then fly up to half her flying speed.

---

or take 12 (2d8 + 3) thunder damage and be deafened until the end of its next turn.

• Umunairu calls down a bolt of lightning, choosing a point on the ground anywhere in her lair. Each creature within 5 feet of that point must make a DC 20 Dexterity saving throw, taking 16 (3d10) lightning damage on a failed save or half as much damage on a successful one.

Regional Effects

The region containing Umunairu's lair is warped by her tempestuous magic, which creates one or more of the following effects:

• Auroras, rainbows, sunsets and other colorful natural occurrences are twice as bright and remarkably vibrant within 5 miles of the lair. These lights also tend to twist and distort, bearing a striking resemblance to the visage of Umunairu.

• Storms within 6 miles of the lair are uncommonly strong. Winds scream and roar, lightning blows apart

trees and illuminates the sky like daytime and thunder is loud enough to knock over unsecured objects and deafen creatures standing out in the open.

• Within 1 mile of the lair, storm clouds darken the skies night and day. Brilliant flashes of lightning and peals of thunder are constant. On sunny days, rainbows ring the outer edges of these storms.

If Umunairu dies, conditions of the area surrounding the lair return to normal over the course of 1d10 days.

VANADON-NECROTH, THE SCALED BOOK OF THE DEAD

In ancient times, the dragon scribe Vanadon served the goddess of the dead and protected her endless *Book of the Dead*, a massive tome which, thanks to his diligence, bore the names and final words of all creatures who ever have died, and who ever will die. Vanadon served his goddess dutifully for centuries, but even the servants of the dark lady of death are mortal, and their lives end in time. Unwilling to face the end, Vanadon simply refused to perish. He consumed the endless *Book of the Dead* and took its power into his own body, transforming himself into the Living Book of the Dead.

The queen of death, furious at her rebellious servant, banished Vanadon from her domain, and he hid in shameful isolation for several centuries in a forgotten corner of Elysium, the hallowed fields of the honored dead. Throughout this time, the names and last words of the dead inscribed themselves upon his milky-white scales. When he emerged, with scales covered in endlessly shifting patterns of black scrawling, he became known as Vanadon-Necroth, the Scaled Book of the Dead. Despite the fury of the queen of the dead, Vanadon-Necroth built his lair atop a hill in the gardens of Elysium and became beloved by the undying gardens' heroic inhabitants as a keeper of the memories of the dead.

Though the loremaster Vanadon once kept his library open to all creatures, he has grown paranoid in recent centuries. His archive-lair was once a majestic castle that towered over the eternal gardens of Elysium, but no more than five decades past, Vanadon-Necroth transported his entire archive-lair elsewhere in the planes, leaving only the crumbling, gutted structure of his once-magnificent castle in its wake. The charms that keep Vanadon-Necroth eternally alive also grant him the power of perfect recollection and all information he adds to his infallible intellect is instantly inscribed upon his ivory scales.

Now, the Archives of the Dead drift on the waves of the endless astral plane, tethered to the bones of a dead god of memory, whose name is forgotten to all but Vanadon-Necroth himself. Within this arcane fortress, Vanadon-Necroth stores and maintains all of the physical tomes and scrolls he collected in his many centuries of life—and has since inscribed the details of countless spells from all disciplines of magic upon his scales. Though he no longer needs physical records of his accrued knowledge, he takes pleasure in reading and re-reading his favorite scrolls.

To gaze upon him is to look, albeit briefly, on the collected knowledge of the universe. A living archive with the sharpest teeth you've ever seen.

—Garthon the Meandering, Arcane Storyweaver

Hook

Vanadon-Necroth prefers to be left alone to guard the records of the dead in peace, but every few generations he welcomes powerful mortal travelers to his home. Some come for simple reasons, such as to learn the final words of an ancient ancestor—possibly revealing the location of a hidden treasure or an arcane secret. Others come seeking the names of ancient heroes who have been lost to time so that they might be resurrected to aid them in their quests.

Vanadon-Necroth's archives are a dungeon of twisting passages, filled with traps, undead and construct servitors and arcane wards made to deter all but the most determined knowledge-seekers from reaching his sanctum.

Encounter

Vanadon-Necroth is a reclusive and scholarly dragon that rarely courts conflict. More often, conflict comes to him as powerful planar travelers seek him out to abuse his eons of collected knowledge or to pluck the spell-inscribed scales from his very hide. When beings with noble intentions visit him and seek a particularly powerful piece of knowledge, such as an earth-shaking spell or the secrets of a legendary warrior, he challenges them to a duel to test their ability to wield such power. In these cases, he does not kill his opponents; he merely knocks them unconscious when they are reduced to 0 hit points.

Tactics

Vanadon-Necroth values his own survival over all other things. While his hoard of priceless and irreplaceable treasures means the world to him, all the knowledge that he has gleaned from them live on within his mind and written across his scales. These things cannot be replaced.

He uses *time stop* or *wish* as soon as possible to prevent harm from befalling him. While using *time stop,* Vanadon-Necroth has up to five turns to act with impunity. He tends to first create a *forcecage* around one dangerous target. Then he casts *greater invisibility* upon himself. Then, after making any final preparations, he casts *prismatic spray* upon as many of the intruders as possible.

From here, he uses his invisibility and powers of flight to stay as far from his enemies as possible while still raining death down upon them.

Wealth

The undead dragon scribe's wealth is made up entirely of art objects, historically significant jewelry, ancient books and scrolls and a few rare coins collected from across the eons.

Taken together, Vanadon-Necroth's entire wealth is equivalent to double the value of a challenge 17+ treasure hoard. However, his true wealth is the knowledge

contained on his scales. A creature that studies Vanadon-Necroth's scales finds that they are milky white, but covered with black text, like the pages of a book. A creature can find any spell on Vanadon-Necroth's scales by spending one hour in study and making a successful Intelligence (Investigation) check with a DC equal to 10+ the level of the spell the creature is searching for.

Vanadon-Necroth's Lair

The archive-lair of Vanadon-Necroth floats amidst the islands of planar detritus adrift in the cosmic oceans of the Astral Plane. Its crumbling stone structure is perched atop the skull of a dead god.

The remains of Vanadon's castle are labyrinthine and laden with magical traps, but the dragon himself rarely leaves the archive's heart. This central library is a massive circular chamber, nearly 1,000 feet in diameter and rising over 500 feet up. Its walls are covered from floor to ceiling with bookshelves, each one crammed full of arcane and esoteric texts and relics of bygone ages.

Dozens of galleries curl around the outer walls, each 15 feet above the other, and floating staircases drift idly throughout the library, connecting the different levels of the archive together on a whim. Some stairs spin lazily in midair as if to encourage visitors to defy gravity and climb them upside-down or at an angle perpendicular to the ground.

Vanadon-Necroth has not left his astral domain in the five centuries since he first settled there. He spends his endless days in meditation at the center of his archive.

Lair Actions

On initiative count 20 (losing initiative ties), Vanadon-Necroth takes a lair action to cause one of the following effects. Vanadon-Necroth can't use the same effect two rounds in a row.

- Vanadon-Necroth regains a spell slot of 8th level or lower. Roll a d8 to determine the level of the spell slot regained. If he has no spent slots of a level equal to or lower than the result of the roll, nothing happens.
- Vanadon-Necroth randomly casts a spell from the 20 spells he has prepared. Roll 1d20 and count up from the lowest-level spell he currently has prepared with his Spellcasting feature (starting with his 4th-level spells). Once a spell has been selected he chooses its target or where the spell's area affects. Casting a spell in this way does not consume a spell slot.
- Vanadon-Necroth chooses a bookcase or floating staircase within his lair and telekinetically hurls it at a creature that he can see within 120 feet of him, making a ranged weapon attack with a +12 bonus to hit. On a hit, the creature takes 35 (10d6) bludgeoning damage and must succeed on a DC 25 Strength saving throw or fall prone.

VANADON-NECROTH, THE SCALED BOOK OF THE DEAD

Gargantuan undead dragon, lawful neutral

Armor Class 18 (natural armor)
Hit Points 315 (18d20 + 126)
Speed 40 ft., fly 80 ft.

STR	DEX	CON	INT	WIS	CHA
24 (+7)	9 (-1)	24 (+7)	30 (+10)	17 (+3)	21 (+5)

Saving Throws Dex +6, Con +14, Wis +10, Cha +12
Skills Arcana +17, History +17, Nature +17, Perception +10, Religion +17, Stealth +6
Damage Immunities cold, necrotic, poison; bludgeoning, piercing and slashing that is nonmagical
Condition Immunities charmed, exhaustion, frightened, paralyzed, poisoned
Senses blindsight 60 ft., darkvision 120 ft., passive Perception 20
Languages all
Challenge 22 (41,000 XP)

Legendary Resistance (3/Day). If Vanadon-Necroth fails a saving throw, he can choose to succeed instead.

Magic Resistance. Vanadon-Necroth has advantage on saving throws against spells or other magical effects.

Magic Weapons. Vanadon-Necroth's weapon attacks are magical.

Signature Spellcasting. Vanadon-Necroth is a 20th-level spellcaster. His spellcasting ability is Intelligence (spell save 25, +17 to hit with spell attacks).

He always has the following 1st, 2nd and 3rd-level spells prepared and can cast them at will without expending a spell slot:

1st level (at will): identify, illusory script, magic missile, shield
2nd level (at will): blur, ray of enfeeblement, see invisibility
3rd level (at will): clairvoyance, counterspell, dispel magic

Spellcasting. In addition to the above, Vanadon-Necroth has the following wizard spells prepared:

4th level (3 slots): arcane eye, banishment, black tentacles, blight, greater invisibility, polymorph
5th level (3 slots): animate objects, arcane hand, dominate person, legend lore, mislead, modify memory
6th level (2 slots): chain lightning, flesh to stone, globe of invulnerability
7th level (2 slots): forcecage, prismatic spray
8th level (1 slot): feeblemind
9th level (1 slot): time stop, wish

ACTIONS

Multiattack. Vanadon-Necroth can use his Frightful Presence. He then makes three attacks: one with his bite and two with his claws.

Bite. Melee Weapon Attack: +14 to hit, reach 10 ft., one target. *Hit:* 18 (2d10 + 7) piercing damage.

Claw. Melee Weapon Attack: +14 to hit, reach 5 ft., one target. *Hit:* 14 (2d6 + 7) slashing damage.

Tail. Melee Weapon Attack: +14 to hit, reach 15 ft., one target. *Hit:* 16 (2d8 + 7) bludgeoning damage.

Frightful Presence. Each creature of Vanadon-Necroth's choice that is within 120 feet of the dragon and aware of it must succeed on a DC 20 Wisdom saving throw or become frightened for one minute. A creature can repeat the saving throw at the end of each of its turns, ending the effect on itself on a success. If a creature's saving throw is successful or the effect ends for it, the creature is immune to the dragon's Frightful Presence for the next 24 hours.

Breath Weapons (Recharge 5–6). Vanadon-Necroth uses one of the following breath weapons:

Desiccating Breath. Vanadon-Necroth exhales a blast of super dry air in a 60-foot cone. Each creature in that area must make a DC 20 Constitution saving throw, taking 58 (13d8) necrotic damage on a failed save or half as much damage on a successful one. If this damage reduces a creature to 0 hit points, it must succeed on a DC 20 saving throw or be disintegrated. A disintegrated creature and everything it is wearing and carrying, except magic items, are reduced to a pile of fine gray dust. The creature can be restored to life only by means of a *true resurrection* or a *wish* spell.

Paralyzing Breath. Vanadon-Necroth exhales paralyzing gas in a 60-foot cone. Each creature in that area must succeed on a DC 20 Constitution saving throw or be paralyzed for one minute. A creature can repeat the saving throw at the end of each of its turns, ending the effect on itself on a success.

Change Shape. Vanadon-Necroth magically polymorphs into a humanoid or beast that has a challenge rating no higher than his own or back into his true form. He reverts to his true form if he dies. Any equipment he is wearing or carrying is absorbed or borne by the new form (his choice).

LEGENDARY ACTIONS

Vanadon-Necroth can take three legendary actions, choosing from the options below. Only one legendary action option can be used at a time and only at the end of another creature's turn. He regains spent legendary actions at the start of his turn.

Tail Attack. Vanadon-Necroth makes a tail attack.

Wing Attack (Costs 2 Actions). Vanadon-Necroth beats his wings. Each creature within 15 feet of him must succeed on a DC 20 Dexterity saving throw or take 14 (2d6 + 7) bludgeoning damage and be knocked prone. He can then fly up to half his flying speed.

Unwind Death (Costs 3 Actions). Vanadon-Necroth chooses a creature that died within the last minute that he can see. That creature returns to life, regains 100 hit points and is charmed by Vanadon-Necroth. While charmed in this way, it must obey Vanadon-Necroth's commands to the best of its ability. It can make a DC 20 Wisdom saving throw at the end of each of its turns, ending the charm on itself on a success.

Volthaarius,
The Traveler in Silver Mist

Volthaarius soars through the realm of thought and dreams, borne upon wings of silver and swirling light. A great, sleek form glimpsed in the last hint of twilight above a celestial forest and a deep echoing call above a fiendish battlefield in the lower planes. Few have seen the great dragon that slips between the folds of the multiverse, and fewer still know his name, but for those who learn of his existence, the secrets of all creation await. A few monikers for the planar dragon circulate in occult halls of learning: The Traveler in Silver Mist, The Silver Pilgrim, The Rainbow Sage. In the most secluded of wizards' towers and temple scriptoriums, a few tomes whisper the dragon's name in fading ink—Volthaarius.

To the diligent or obsessed researchers who learn about Volthaarius, the planar dragon, he is a symbol of both knowledge and freedom. The boundaries between worlds are no barrier to his wandering, and he appears without seeming pattern or warning, in any corner of creation. When observed, he rarely stays long. Always on the move, the great silver and multi-hued wyrm is continuously searching. Ancient beyond record, Volthaarius's origins are lost to all but his own memory. He was once a silver dragon much like any other found in the myriad worlds of the material plane.

Like his kin, Volthaarius adored all things historical. And in his wandering youth, he amassed a vast hoard of treasure and knowledge. He collected the histories and trappings of empires and hid them away in his lair deep in the heart of a mountain. Unlike most silver dragons, however, he began to grow selfish. Never cruel, he merely lost his care for the mortals and gods whose stories he collected; instead he dedicated his great lifespan to the collection itself. As the years rolled on, the more relics he gathered and the more esoteric and strange his tastes became. He then turned his sights outward and began searching for truths beyond the material plane and the mortals who dwell there. It was during this obsessive quest that Volthaarius became one with that which he sought. He has a name–or had one–at the very least. Volthaarius is sure of that much. Whatever his name might have been eludes him now. Whispering to him from trinkets and scraps of lore at first, the presence grew louder and more insistent the more he collected. The whisper became a voice both asking and offering. The statues were the final turn of the key that opened the lock. A consciousness vast beyond imagining from beyond the most distant stars slipped into the world, and offered the then-ancient miserly dragon the means to go anywhere, and collect anything if only Volthaarius would agree to bring it along. How could the obsessive old dragon refuse?

This is when the silver dragon fully changed. His body stretched. His mind expanded. His nature became more obscured. His reach clawed between the planes themselves. He slipped into the murky expanse of the astral plane, and there Volthaarius and the presence he carried within his soul became one. They became something unique.

Centuries passed as the planar dragon soared through the astral plane, gathering the silver winds into his soul, moving through color pools to the outer planes and back again. Volthaarius stretched forth his will into the astral plane and re-wove a portion of it deep within the silver clouds for his own use. A single point of space folded on itself again, and again, and formed a realm the dragon now calls Refuge. Within Refuge, Volthaarius can shape substance out of the sky to his whim and needs. All the collected wealth and hoarded knowledge of his previous life now reside in an enormous central spire, carefully cataloged in a manner incomprehensible to any outside observer.

Hook

Adventurers uncover the truth of a tremendous threat beyond anything they've ever known. The remnant of an ancient civilization long destroyed or even forces from a world far removed from their own compel the characters to desperately seek stranger and more forgotten lore in search of a solution. Eventually, a mad scholar has a few scraps of truth that point to the existence of the planar dragon, and his legendary access to that which is hidden.

Encounter Conditions

Chance encounters with the planar dragon can happen absolutely anywhere. He might suddenly appear in a swirling rift of bright color in the sky and lazily soar toward the horizon.

Volthaarius is content to leave lesser creatures be, perhaps giving them the slightest bit of attention in passing without changing course or slowing his travel. Creatures who attack the planar dragon can expect a sudden, powerful lashing out of claws, teeth and tail—or if they're fortunate, a swift magical prison as the dragon merely continues on his way.

Sometimes, the dragon finds himself drawn to other creatures, particularly mortals. The party could experience a chance meeting with a traveler who happens to be in the same region, and Volthaarius might pause to converse, trying to learn all he can of the individual's history. Or, more rarely, the dragon feels drawn to a particular place. He doesn't know where exactly, but he knows the way, and travels through the planes until he finds the creature somehow calling to him across the multiverse.

In any case, Volthaarius might impart a tiny measure of his power to a mortal. Such pacts of power are exceedingly rare, but by virtue of his strange otherworldly essence, the planar dragon can create warlocks through such an investiture.

Encounter

Volthaarius is inquisitive and surprisingly soft-spoken. He prefers to engage in normal speech if possible, and only uses telepathy if the creatures that have caught his interest don't share any common languages with him. His singular drive is to gather knowledge and artifacts. He might even be willing to trade rather than take anything a creature has.

If somehow approached while in his lair, Volthaarius is much more wary. The portals to and from Refuge are hardly common knowledge, so the planar dragon takes all such visitors to his home seriously, and evaluates them for any sort of threat they might pose in the course of a cordial greeting and conversation. If the visitors seem frivolous, he politely, but firmly, asks they leave his home. Creatures that intrigue him or prove to have interesting or new knowledge can expect his hospitality and shrewd negotiations for an exchange of knowledge.

The dragon can become quite obsessive, however, and sometimes loses sight of the fact that mortals interact with time differently than he does. Mortals with fascinating perspectives on a topic might find themselves effectively kept prisoner within Refuge.

If Volthaarius suspects that visitors are there to steal or damage any part of his hoard, may the gods be with them.

Tactics

It might be possible to get the drop on Volthaarius by offering some bit of lore or an artifact he desires, but that's a risky proposition at best.

When accosted outside his lair, Volthaarius usually only feels the need to subdue attackers within a *forcecage* or behind a *wall of force* or to bind them in his dimensional breath. If a single exhalation, spell or even snatching a foe in his claws and teleporting with them hundreds of feet into the air to impress upon them the gravity of their situation can defuse a battle, Volthaarius is content to injure or kill as few foolish creatures as possible before going on his way.

If the creatures persist—or worse, threaten his hoard—Volthaarius attacks without mercy. He makes full use of his superior mobility to remain out of reach of any potential threats while separating them using his force magic. Before moving into melee, he prefers to blanket a group of foes with Dimensional Binding Breath to tip the scales even further in his favor.

If his foes show no ability to fly, he uses his Force Breath to disintegrate the terrain beneath his enemies, especially if he can cause them to fall. Any creature that steals from or threatens Volthaarius's hoard earns his full attention, and he is relentless until he recovers the stolen loot or slays a hapless vandal. Volthaarius is usually willing to accept a surrender, or to allow broken enemies to flee, so long as they leave his precious collections behind.

Wealth

The hoard contained in the Refuge Spire puts entire empires to shame. While the majority of the cache takes the form of collected knowledge, there is substantial physical wealth gathered from across the breadth of the multiverse. The total value of coins, gems, jewelry and assorted objects of art and cultural artifacts exceeds 20 million gp. In addition to monetary and artistic treasures, the trove of lost knowledge is the object of even some lesser deities' envy. Searching and cataloging the knowledge takes years if the scholar is lucky and skilled, or decades if a novice. The sprawling complex within the Spire defies mortal understanding of space, and there is no central index to help plunderers or visitors navigate without Volthaarius's help.

The collected tablets, tomes, scrolls and other more exotic means of recording information cover every conceivable topic obtained from multiple planets on the prime material and all of the planes of the multiverse. If a character can find the correct section, spending 1d4 days in research affords advantage and a +10 bonus on Intelligence checks to learn facts about the covered topic. A single creature can gain these benefits about one topic per week due to the amount of work required to access specific subjects. In addition to roll benefits, the collection contains many specific secrets relevant to events, locations and creatures in the multiverse. Use this as a means to provide plot-critical discoveries or hooks for large scale story arcs.

Tucked away amongst this knowledge are written versions of every wizard spell, dozens of scrolls with a variety of spells, two each of every type of scroll of protection and a collection of magical tomes. The magical tomes include one each of the **manual of bodily health**, **manual of gainful exercise**, **manual of quickness in action**, **tome of clear thought**, **tome of leadership and influence** and **tome of understanding**.

Volthaarius's Lair

Volthaarius's lair is an expansive demiplane called Refuge, nestled within the silver clouds of the Astral Plane. The lair is a sprawling space with an all-around sky of purple, red, blue and pink, dotted with glittering golden stars in continually changing constellations. Silvery clouds drift through the demiplane and solidify into floating silver islands and mountains. Time doesn't pass for creatures in the demiplane, age doesn't touch them and hunger and thirst are distant memories.

Volthaarius's home proper is in a spire of silver and stone in the "center" of the demiplane. The spire hovers in space like a great spindle. The interior holds chambers and tunnels so vast they couldn't possibly fit into the outer dimensions of the spire.

Lair Actions

On initiative count 20 (losing initiative ties), Volthaarius takes a lair action to cause one of the following effects. Volthaarius can't use the same effect two rounds in a row.

• Volthaarius creates a magical Scything Blade Of Silvery Mist at a point within 100 feet The blade lasts for one round. Each creature within 15 feet of that point must succeed on a DC 15 Dexterity saving throw or take 13 (3d8) slashing damage and take 7 (2d6) necrotic damage at the start of its turn from bleeding essence. Any creature can take an action to staunch the wound with a successful DC 15 Wisdom (Medicine) check. The wound also closes if the target receives magical healing.
• Volthaarius suddenly, but momentarily, reinstates the flow of time in a 30-foot cube he can see. Each creature in the area suffers disadvantage on attack rolls until initiative count 20 on the following round from disorientation and must make a DC 15 Wisdom saving throw. On a failed save, a creature takes 11

(2d10) necrotic damage and gains one level of exhaustion. A creature's exhaustion levels can't be increased above 3 by this action.
• Volthaarius forms a wall out of silvery mist within 100 feet of him. The wall is 20 feet high, 60 feet long, and 2 feet thick and has AC 17 and 20 hit points per 5-foot section. The wall is immune to force, psychic and poison damage. A creature in the wall's space when it appears is pushed to one side of its choice. The wall lasts until Volthaarius uses this action again, or dies.

Regional Effects

Volthaarius can create stable gateways from his lair to other planes. It takes Volthaarius eight hours of concentration while within his lair to create a gateway, and he can maintain up to nine gates at a time. If he creates a 10th gate, the oldest gate collapses. Gates are swirling discs of color that range from 5 to 20 feet across. A creature that moves into one side of the gate appears at the other immediately.

The demiplane of Refuge is linked through the astral plane to every corner of the multiverse. A creature in the lair is considered to be on the same plane as any other creature or object in existence. *Sending* spells cast while within the lair have no chance of failing, a succubus can communicate telepathically with a charmed thrall on any other plane, etc.

The region containing Volthaarius's lair is warped by the dragon's magic, which creates one or more of the following effects:

• Creatures in the lair don't age or require food or drink.
• A creature in the lair can move by thought, essentially hovering in any direction with a speed equal to three times its Intelligence score.

If Volthaarius dies, the demiplane collapses in 1d4 hours. Any creatures or objects still in the demiplane at that time are ejected into random locations on the Astral Plane. If Volthaarius returns to life, a new demiplane forms in 1d10 days.

Volthaarius, The Traveler in Silver Mist

Gargantuan dragon, chaotic neutral

Armor Class 23 (natural armor)
Hit Points 585 (30d20 + 270)
Speed 40 ft., fly 80 ft. (hover)

STR	DEX	CON	INT	WIS	CHA
30 (+10)	14 (+2)	29 (+9)	18 (+4)	18 (+4)	28 (+9)

Saving Throws Dex +10, Con +17, Wis +12, Cha +17
Skills Arcana +12, History +12, Insight +12, Perception +12, Persuasion +17, Stealth +10
Damage Immunities cold, fire
Condition Immunities exhaustion
Senses blindsight 60 ft, darkvision 120 ft, passive Perception 22
Languages Celestial, Common, Deep Speech, Draconic, telepathy 120 ft.
Challenge 25 (75,000 XP)

Innate Spellcasting. Volthaarius's innate spellcasting ability is Charisma (spell save DC 25, + 17 to hit with spell attacks). He can innately cast the following spells, requiring no material components:

> At will: *plane shift* (willing creatures only), *sending, wall of force*
> 1/day each: *forcecage, legend lore*

Legendary Resistance (3/Day). If Volthaarius fails a saving throw, he can choose to succeed instead.
Magic Weapons. Volthaarius's weapon attacks are magical.
Sever Silver Cord. If Volthaarius scores a critical hit against a creature traveling through the Astral Plane by means of the *astral projection* spell, he can cut the target's silver cord instead of dealing damage.
Timeless Nature. Volthaarius doesn't require food, drink or sleep.

Actions

Multiattack. Volthaarius can use his Frightful Presence. He then makes three attacks: one with his bite and two with his claws.
Bite. Melee Weapon Attack: +18 to hit, reach 15 ft., one target.
Hit: 21 (2d10 + 10) piercing damage plus 11 (2d10) force damage.
Claw. Melee Weapon Attack: +18 to hit, reach 10 ft., one target.
Hit: 17 (2d6 + 10) slashing damage.

Tail. Melee Weapon Attack: +18 to hit, reach 20 ft., one target.
Hit: 19 (2d8 + 10) bludgeoning damage.
Frightful Presence. Each creature of Volthaarius's choice that is within 120 feet of him and aware of him must succeed on a DC 25 Wisdom saving throw or become frightened for one minute. A creature can repeat the saving throw at the end of each of its turns, ending the effect on itself on a success. If a creature's saving throw is successful or the effect ends for it, the creature is immune to Volthaarius's Frightful Presence for the next 24 hours.
Breath Weapons (Recharge 5–6). Volthaarius uses one of the following breath weapons:

> *Force Breath.* Volthaarius exhales a 90-foot line of crackling, multicolored light. Each creature in that line must make a DC 25 Dexterity saving throw, taking 66 (12d10) force damage on a failed save, or half as much on a successful one. Large or smaller nonmagical objects that aren't being worn or carried are automatically reduced to dust. Huge or larger objects have a 10-foot-by-10-foot space destroyed around the line where the line passes through them. Creations of magical force, such as the wall created by wall of force or a forcecage, are destroyed.
> *Dimensional Binding Breath.* Volthaarius exhales silvery fog in a 90-foot cone. Each creature in the area must make a DC 25 Dexterity saving throw. On a failure, wisps of mist that thicken the fabric of the planes bind the creature. A bound creature is reduced to half speed and has disadvantage on attack rolls. If a bound creature tries to teleport or travel to another plane, it must succeed on a DC 25 Charisma saving throw or fail. A creature can repeat the saving throw at the end of each of its turns, ending the effect on itself on a success.

Teleport. Volthaarius magically teleports, along with any equipment he is wearing or carrying and any creatures he is grappling, up to 120 feet to an unoccupied space he can see.

Legendary Actions

Volthaarius can take three legendary actions, choosing from the options below. Only one legendary action option can be used at a time and only at the end of another creature's turn. Volthaarius regains spent legendary actions at the start of his turn.
Detect. Volthaarius makes a Wisdom (Perception) check.
Tail Attack. Volthaarius makes a tail attack.
Planar Slip (Costs 2 Actions). Each creature within 15 feet of Volthaarius must succeed on a DC 26 Dexterity saving throw or take 10 (3d6) force damage and be knocked prone. Volthaarius then uses his Teleport action.

VYRAETRA, THE WRETCHED WYRM

A farmer pauses in revolted fascination to stare at a blackened stalk of corn—putrid ooze seeping out from beneath a writhing mass of maggots. A young child watches in horror as his sister slowly turns to stone inside the hen house as a lizard-like bird skitters between her feet. A trader on the way to town notices a growing buzzing sound only moments before a swarm of biting flies descends upon him.

Vyraetra has come to this land.

It might have started with a slain godling. It could have been unspeakable treachery or lies that spread discord among beloved brothers. It may have even been the theft of mortal souls. Vyraetra does not speak of the act that began the curse nor of how long it has been cursed to wander the mortal world. Instead, Vyraetra rails against the egotistical gods and their vainglorious supplicants.

Where Vyraetra goes, a great curse follows—rotting the land even as it rots Vyraetra's heart.

Any details of the vile act that earned Vyraetra divine punishment have long since been lost to history.

Accounts that appear to describe Vyraetra and its actions seem to stretch back centuries—though some scholars have argued that stories of the dragon took on elements of older allegories. The similarities shared with the oldest legends are poor evidence for the supposedly unnatural lifespan of this vile beast.

If any of these accounts are to be believed, it's that Vyraetra is unable to sire draconic offspring. On one occasion, an adventuring group that encountered this wretched dragon discovered a brood of cockatrice eggs within its lair. Others describe Vyraetra as being something other than simply male or female. The few reputable sightings of the dragon lack any description of attributes that dragon hunters use to differentiate the gender of dragons.

Instead, they tell of a dragon with dozens of pairs of shortened legs, like some kind of behemoth behir. Vyraetra has wings, but they are said to be noticeably smaller than those of other dragons. Almost too atrophied to support the dragon's weight. Rather than prowl the skies, Vyraetra burrows beneath the earth, spreading its poison across the landscape. It is also said that Vyraetra's maw is deformed, hinged in too many places and filled with entirely too many teeth. This detail might be an embellishment that arises from the dragon's ability to burrow faster than even the oldest purple worms—but it might also be real.

Vyraetra tends not to remain in any one place for very long. Stories claim that the nature of its curse is such that it rots the lands around any area where Vyraetra seeks refuge. As crops spoil and water turns foul, most mortals flee. Drawn by the curse, monsters flock to the ruins left in the wake of such an exodus. Eventually Vyraetra tires of the nuisance caused by these creatures and sets out to claim yet another lair.

I asked you to uncover answers to our current predicament and all you can offer are stories of a cursed dragon? Our people are starving. Determine a way to end this famine. Or eat your last meal.

—Lady Calloway Dawnblower,
Queen of the Arbor Realms

Hook

The spreading taint infecting the lands around Vyraetra's lair makes this dragon an excellent focal point for a campaign. Dealing with the monsters lingering near an area Vyraetra has abandoned can provide hints at the nature of this cursed dragon. When similar phenomena begin to spread in another location, the players might make the connection and be able to confront the dragon armed with some idea of what may happen.

Or, Vyraetra's presence might come as a surprise when the players are sent to cleanse the land of the terrible curse that has befallen the kingdom.

It is also likely that the ruins Vyraetra currently inhabits hold a relic that the players need to address some other impending calamity.

Maybe one or more of the PCs serve one of the gods that cursed Vyraetra and become a target of the dragon's malicious vengeance.

Regardless of how they happen upon Vyraetra, approaching this dragon is anything but predictable. Numerous and unrelated groups of creatures are present as obstacles the players must overcome should they want to confront the dragon. Even the land itself works against the players, becoming progressively more tainted and challenging to navigate the closer they come to whatever ruins Vyraetra has made a lair within.

Encounter Conditions

The Lost City was once the capital of a grand empire. Like countless other cities that have fallen from the taint that Vyraetra's curse brings, it is empty of any civilized creatures. Instead, gnolls, lizardfolk and various other monstrous humanoids have built encampments in the lands around the lair. Some even inhabit the stone husks of ancient buildings that lay closer to the dragon's lair.

Encounter

Approaching Vyraetra's lair is no easy feat. The entire area is teeming with aggressive, monstrous humanoids. These creatures rarely owe any sort of loyalty or allegiance to Vyraetra, but the influence of the curse changes them and makes their behavior more dangerous and unpredictable.

Tactics

Vyraetra is fierce, but cowardly. It will not engage in a fair fight. Instead, Vyraetra uses its incredible burrowing speed to strike without warning and retreat to safety without reprisal. It is also keenly aware of the location of nearby monstrous inhabitants and will lead pursuers toward these places as a distraction.

When a fight to the death appears inevitable, Vyraetra aggressively employs underhanded tactics. It burrows beneath its enemies as often as possible, emerging only to strike out against them and retreat to safety once more.

Wealth of Fallen Empires

Vyraetra wants only an end to the suffering inflicted upon it by the gods and has almost no use for any treasure. It does keep a collection of religious artifacts — most desecrated and worthless. Many bear iconography that does not appear to belong to any of the known gods. They are trophies Vyraetra keeps as a reminder of its slowly unfolding vengeance. In addition to these minor trinkets, its hoard also often contains whatever valuables were abandoned when the original denizens of the Lost City fled. Some of these are works of magical artifice that haven't been witnessed in lifetimes.

Vyraetra's Lair

Vyraetra claims the ruins of a fallen kingdom as its home. Once beautiful lands have withered under the weight of the curse that Vyraetra carries. Blighted crops feed no one and the capital of this forgotten kingdom quickly collapsed. The empty, crumbling city is now home to Vyraetra and its brood.

Unlike many other ruined cities, the forest has not reclaimed this one. Vyraetra's curse holds back the encroaching flora. The stone facades of buildings still crumble, however, and wood rots quickly. Most structures left standing in the open are veritable death traps within. Floors collapse underfoot and stone ceilings fall when the supports are examined. Vyraetra tunnels between such structures, using them as naturally occurring defenses for the den in which they dwell.

Lair Actions

On initiative count 20 (losing initiative ties), Vyraetra takes a lair action to cause one of the following effects. It can't use the same effect two rounds in a row.

- A tremor shakes the lair in a 60-foot radius around Vyraetra. Each creature other than Vyraetra on the ground must succeed on a DC 15 Dexterity saving throw or be knocked prone.
- Vyraetra causes biting insects to temporarily swarm at a point within 100 feet of it, casting *insect plague* as a 5th level spell with a DC of 18. Vyraetra does not need to provide material components to cast this spell. The insects disperse at the end of the round.

VYRAETRA, THE WRETCHED WYRM

Gargantuan dragon, chaotic neutral

Armor Class 22 (natural armor)
Hit Points 367 (21d20 + 147)
Speed 50 ft., fly 40 ft, burrow 80 ft.

STR	DEX	CON	INT	WIS	CHA
27 (+8)	14 (+2)	25 (+7)	16 (+3)	15 (+2)	16 (+3)

Saving Throws Dex +9, Con +14, Wis +9, Cha +10
Skills Perception +16, Stealth +9
Damage Immunities force
Condition Immunities charmed
Senses tremorsense 160 ft., darkvision 120 ft.,
  passive Perception 26
Languages Common, Draconic
Challenge 21 (33,000 XP)

Legendary Resistance (3/Day). If the dragon fails a saving throw, it can choose to succeed instead.

Magic Resistance. Vyraetra has advantage on saving throws against spells or other magical effects.

Magic Weapons. Vyraetra's weapon attacks are magical.

Stench. Any creature that starts its turn within 10 feet of Vyraetra must succeed on a DC 18 Constitution saving throw or be poisoned until the start of its next turn. On a successful saving throw, the creature is immune to Vyraetra's stench for 24 hours.

Tunneler. Vyraetra can burrow through solid rock at half its burrow speed and leaves a 10-foot-diameter tunnel in its wake.

ACTIONS

Multiattack. Vyraetra can use its Frightful Presence. It then makes five attacks: one with its bite and four with its claws.

Bite. Melee Weapon Attack: +15 to hit, reach 15 ft., one target. *Hit*: 19 (2d10 + 8) piercing damage, plus 9 (2d8) poison damage.

Claw. Melee Weapon Attack: +15 to hit, reach 10 ft., one target. *Hit*: 11 (2d6 + 8) slashing damage.

Tail. Melee Weapon Attack: +15 to hit, reach 20 ft., one target. *Hit*: 17 (2d8 + 8) bludgeoning damage.

Frightful Presence (Recharge 5–6). Each creature of Vyraetra's choice that is within 120 feet of the dragon and aware of it must succeed on a DC 19 Wisdom saving throw or become frightened for one minute. A creature can repeat the saving throw at the end of each of its turns, ending the effect on itself on a success. If a creature's saving throw is successful or the effect ends for it, the creature is immune to the dragon's Frightful Presence for the next 24 hours.

Putrid Breath (Recharge 5–6). Vyraetra exhales a cloud of vile ichor in a 90-foot cone. Each creature in that area must make a DC 22 Constitution saving throw, taking 45 (10d8) poison damage and 18 (4d8) necrotic damage or half as much on a successful one. If a creature fails its save against this ability a second time, it contracts a disease as if it were affected by the *contagion* spell.

LEGENDARY ACTIONS

Vyraetra can take three legendary actions, choosing from the options below. Only one legendary action option can be used at a time and only at the end of another creature's turn. Vyraetra regains spent legendary actions at the start of its turn.

Detect. Vyraetra makes a Wisdom (Perception) check.

Tail Attack. Vyraetra makes a tail attack.

Burrow. Vyraetra tunnels into the ground and moves up to half its speed.

Burst (Costs 2 Actions). Vyraetra moves up to half its speed and then bursts from beneath the ground and makes up to four claw attacks against adjacent creatures. If the space Vyraetra emerges into is occupied by a creature of large or smaller size, the creature must succeed on a DC 19 Dexterity save or fall prone in an empty adjacent space. Vyraetra cannot enter the space a creature of Huge size or larger.

REGIONAL EFFECTS

The region containing Vyraetra's lair is plagued by the effects of the curse that follows this wretched dragon, creating one or more of the following effects:

• Chickens, and any other local fowl, lay eggs that hatch only cockatrices.

• The area within 10 miles of the lair stinks of rotting vegetation. Crops that once grew in this area remain as blackened, moldy stalks and no new vegetation grows here. Swarms of biting insects gather in shadedplaces.

• Violent tremors occur sporadically within 6 miles of the lair. These earthquakes happen at random, sometimes as often as five times within a single day.

If Vyraetra dies, conditions of the area surrounding the lair return to normal after 1d10 days.

XAVOUR, THE PLAGUE BRINGER

Centuries have passed since the first telling of his story, which is one of myth and legend passed down through the generations by song and tale. Even though this is an ancient proverb, it is still told among small tribes of humans who live far from any civilization, deep in the wilderness. This is a tale told to young children, teaching them about arrogance, humility and how to properly worship their divine creators. This tale of morality also illustrates the consequences of their actions. This tale is known as the legend of Xavour, the Plague Bringer.

Long ago, a young half-orc boy was born to unfortunate circumstances—his human mother found herself at the mercy of an orc raider. Though she was battered and beaten, she remained proud, showing her people that she could overcome extreme adversity. A trait of her people.

Several months later, she realized she was carrying a child. She was determined to keep it, even though it was the result of her unfortunate encounter. Ta'Kambi was driven to raise her child into something wonderful, beautiful and strong. She would turn her tragedy into a blessing. Unfortunately, during the birth of her son, she suffered greatly, succumbing to the trauma, but not before naming her boy Zakambi.

Now the orphan and outcast was to be cared for by his people, who would not dishonor their beliefs and abandon this child to the world.

As Zakambi grew older, many of his people accepted him for who he was: a dedicated and caring individual. Others saw him as "a half breed," "a plague" or "a black blood."

During his youth, the elders noticed his gift for healing and medicine, so they cultivated his talents, guiding him in the proper direction. Zakambi would continue his tutelage as apprentice to the tribe's shaman. For many years, he followed the teachings of his elders, learning the ways of their healing rituals. Soon, his apprenticeship ended and he ascended to become the tribe's shaman. A leader among his people.

As the tribe's shaman, he was responsible for their rituals regarding the gods, healing and sacrifice and their seasonal rituals and celebrations.

Zakambi grew to prominence, garnering a level of worship among his people. Using the gifts bestowed upon him by their deities, he saved many lives and brought the tribe years of prosperity and good fortune.

During one of their harvest festivals, his tribe began to pay homage to him rather than their deity. Their admiration of him instead of their gods caused Zakambi to become arrogant, lazy and wicked. His cruelty grew along with his arrogance, sacrificing those who "misspoke" or questioned him—shrouding his anger and cruelty as "divine guidance" and the "will of the gods."

One day, while performing a routine healing ritual upon one of the tribal elders, Zakambi's powers vanished and the elder died. This brought great shame upon him and caused his people to doubt his ability. His failed ritual was seen as a sign. He was no longer fit to lead his people. He was shunned, and later banished from his village.

Orphaned yet again.

Cast out, Zakambi made his way into the world beyond, forced to wander the dangerous lands surrounding his home. While wandering, Zakambi pleaded, prayed and begged for his powers to return. Yet there was no answer—no divine response. Only silence.

Powerless, broken and disgraced, Zakambi blamed his people for turning him away. He also blamed his deity for abandoning him at such a crucial moment. Months would pass. His sorrow and despair turned into anger and rage, followed by madness and delusion.

Zakambi whispered into the night, talking to himself—and something else.

One night, while resting near a campfire on the open plains, he cried out in anguish, begging for someone to answer. Several hours passed. The quiet night and whispering discordant voices answered his cry for help.

A shadowy figure emerged from the darkness. The cacophony of indecipherable words diminished, forming a singular voice. They spoke in a deep, raspy, malicious tone:

"My son, now you can become what I meant you to be."

The figure stepped into the dim light of the campfire, shrouded in a long cloak of shadow that clung to its form like waves of roiling smoke. He sat beside Zakambi, and whispered into his ear, offering him a chance at redemption—revenge—and the means to reclaim what was stolen from him. The figure said, "I am Batara Kala. I am the one who made you."

Starving, dehydrated and delusional, Zakambi was oblivious to who this figure actually was, thinking it was a figment of his broken mind. Regardless, Zakambi accepted the gifts, giving in to his anger and hatred.

He rose the next morning with renewed physical and mental strength. His mind was clear. The fog of madness that plagued him had vanished. Yet something was gnawing at him. He decided to travel home to confront those who had cast him out so long ago. There was a hunger within him. However, he had no desire to eat.

His travels became a blur of emotional rage, fueled by his desire for retribution. The dark powers growing within became a driving force for destruction. Power and savageness drove him every passing day. With each act of violence, he only wanted to commit more atrocities.

The continued cycle of violence propelled a greater use of his new powers. It began to twist his spirit even further into an emotional abyss. As he grew dark and more aberrant, his physical form began to morph as well. Zakambi's quest of vengeance caused his limbs to elongate, stretching both flesh and bone and his tolerance for pain. Razor sharp claws grew from his hands and feet. His skin became gray and scaled. His torso tore away from his body, and formed into wings of thick leathery flesh—exposing his ribcage to the elements as a swarm of deadly insects exploded from within. The endless hunger for revenge enlarged his jaw and filled his mouth with large razor-sharp teeth.

Over time, this new power and his madness became all he knew. Eventually, he learned the ability to change into whatever form he desired.

Zakambi returned to his village, causing a great deal of panic among everyone. As they gathered around, questioning the purpose of his return, he unleashed the full fury of his new form upon them. He slaughtered everyone in a fit of rage, leaving a path of gore in his wake. In this act of violence, Zakambi became enthralled with the scent of blood and flesh, devouring both as he went from one soul to the next—drenching himself in the destruction of innocence. Those he did not consume were flayed, staked and left as sacrifices to his real father.

This display of horrific violence corrupted the ground for miles around. All life began to wither and fade. Trees rotted and petrified. Animals died or became abominations of their former selves. What did not flee changed with the land.

His old home was reclaimed. Revenge was his and his reign began. Zakambi threw off the shackles of his former life, calling himself Xavour. He may be an abomination, but he is no longer alone. The voice still speaks.

HOOKS

Relative Safety

A major populated area near where the party has a base of operations or spends most of their time is experiencing some odd circumstances.

Recently, the denizens of this locale have been experiencing vivid dreams resulting in violent outbursts, daytime nightmares and extreme bouts of madness. Upon further investigation, the party discovers a small group of priests has recently moved into an old warehouse, making it their place of worship. These priests have been seen walking the streets late at night, blessing the area, attempting to "aid" the citizens with their ailments. They would share what they know of Xavour and explain he is the likely cause of this torment.

A Noble Cause

A close friend of the party (a noble or political figure) has started to keep odd hours, miss important meetings, and experience a change in personality. This individual seems to be pale, exhausted and constantly irritated with everyone around them.

If the party investigates, they find that their friend has recently discovered an old manuscript written by a long-dead priest from the Disciples of Decay. This text speaks of the teachings of Xavour called the Three Pillars of Decay. If the party are able to get their hands on the text, they find that many of the pages are filled with scrawlings of madness and delusion. Among these are vague references of where to find Xavour and how to contact the remaining Disciples of Decay, Xavour's cult of death clerics.

With Great Power

The party has heard rumors of townsfolk going on a pilgrimage into a section of land that is extremely dangerous.

Wild rumors of salvation, power, forgiveness and even immortality have spread throughout the town. Families have lost husbands, wives, sons and daughters. The town is experiencing official problems as well. Figures in positions of power have also left or have gone missing entirely.

If the party investigates the matter further, they discover that a small chapter of the Disciples of Decay has infiltrated a local priesthood in town. These priests have been instructing individuals that if they travel through the poisonous swampland (near Xavour's lair) they will find ultimate salvation.

Unwanted Attention

The party has risen in status over their time as adventurers, attracting the attention of many deadly adversaries. One of them just so happens to be Xavour and he has turned his full attention on them!

Xavour plans to extinguish the growing power of the party as he views them as a challenge to his reign. Utilizing the many resources of the Disciples of Decay, Xavour has a disciple dispatch several degenerates into the town where the party resides to stir up trouble.

When the local authorities seem to have the situation under control, violent and destructive forces will enter the town again. Meanwhile, a few of Xavour's priests spend their nights plaguing the dreams of the sleeping citizenry. They wake in violent fits of rage and madness and overwhelm the local authorities. Once the town has suffered enough, the party receives a message stating that if they wish to see the town's problems end, they must face Xavour within his corrupted village, deep in the wilds.

Weapon of Power

The party learns that Xavour has a dangerous and powerful weapon in his possession.

Through research or word of mouth, the party discovers that a powerful entity living in a hazardous region of the world is utilizing a great weapon of power that has been devastating the lands surrounding him, slowly turning the area into wretched swampland. Upon further investigation, the party finds information that leads them to Xavour's lair.

ENCOUNTER CONDITIONS

Xavour's original village has become his current home. It is deep within a wilderness that is corrupted and has almost withered away into a swamp of rot and decay. Swarms of insects buzz around the dank terrain. Every creature found wandering here is an undead version of its prior form.

TACTICS

Xavour calls to his followers to attack and destroy villages prior to his arrival. Accompanying his priests are undead minions that swarm villagers and animals as the priests take prisoners for sacrifice.

Once a town is secured by his followers, Xavour moves in. He sometimes transforms into his original half-orc form or chooses to remain in dragon form. If there is resistance, he transforms into his dragonform.

Xavour will cast *dominate person*, instructing victims to kill other members of their village. Once there is enough chaos and destruction, he will move in and join the fray.

WEALTH

Xavour wields his magical Morningstar of Malady. Treasure may be scattered throughout the lair. It may only take time to find it. Whatever treasure you wish to put into Xavour's lair is your choice. It could be magical loot from past adventurers, mundane items, coins or gems.

THE CULT OF DECAY

Xavour has built up a following of supplicants eager to exploit the trappings of power wielded in the name of violence. They call themselves the Cult of Decay, and their aims are simple: to stoke horror and serve their master. To learn more about the Cult of Decay, turn to pg. 152.

XAVOUR'S LAIR

A wretched swamp teeming with undead and biting flies, Xavour's lair is centered near his ancestral home, not far from where his birth mother was buried. At GM discretion, the area within 300 feet of the lair is difficult terrain, as outlined in Regional Effects.

LAIR ACTIONS

On initiative count 20 (losing initiative ties), Xavour takes a lair action to cause one of the following effects. He can't use the same effect two rounds in a row.

- The thick mud around the lair seizes in a region with a 30-foot radius. Any creature within this region must succeed on a DC 18 Strength (Athletics) check at the start of its turn or is considered grappled. A creature that fails this check can reattempt it as an action at the start of subsequent turns. This effect fades when this lair action is used again.
- The flies that swarm this lair create a thick cloud that's difficult to see through centered on a point of Xavour's choosing. Any creature within 20 feet of the cloud's center is blinded until the cloud is dispersed. The cloud of flies dissipates when this lair action is used again.
- An undead **owlbear** rises from the muddy earth at a point of Xavour's choosing.

REGIONAL EFFECTS

The region containing Xavour's lair is steeped in evil and corrupts the life around it, delivering the following effects at GM discretion:

- The area within 5 miles of the lair is dense, thick mud and is difficult terrain.
- No trees or other plants are alive within 10 miles of the lair, and any beast that can be found within this range is undead.
- Any creature that takes a long rest within 10 miles of the lair must succeed on a DC 18 Wisdom saving throw. On a failed save, the creature does not benefit from a long rest, as their sleep is disrupted by horrific nightmares.

If Xavour dies, conditions of the area surrounding the lair return to normal after 1d10 days.

Xavour, The Plague Bringer

Gargantuan undead dragon, chaotic evil

Armor Class 21 (natural armor)
Hit Points 492 (24d20 + 240)
Speed 45 ft., climb 40 ft., fly 80 ft.

STR	DEX	CON	INT	WIS	CHA
25 (+7)	18 (+4)	30 (+10)	30 (+10)	20 (+5)	10 (+0)

Saving Throws Str +14, Con +17, Wis +12, Int +17
Skills Arcana +17, History +17, Insight +12, Perception +12
Damage Resistances cold, slashing, piercing and bludgeoning damage from nonmagical weapons.
Damage Immunities poison, necrotic
Condition Immunities blinded, charmed, exhaustion, frightened, grappled (while in dragon form), paralyzed, petrified, poisoned, prone
Sense Blindsight 120 ft., Darkvision 120 ft., passive Perception 22
Languages Common, Draconic, Abyssal, Orcish
Challenge 24 (62,000 XP)

Aura of Dread (dragon form only). Each creature that is within 120 feet of Xavour and aware of him must succeed on a DC 21 Wisdom saving throw or become frightened for one minute. A creature who rolls a 10 or below becomes paralyzed until the end of Xavour's next turn. A creature can repeat the saving throw at the end of its turns, ending the effect on itself on a success. If a creature's saving throw is successful, the creature is immune to Xavour's Aura of Dread for the next 24 hours.

Innate Spellcasting. Xavour's spellcasting ability is Intelligence (spell save DC 25, +17 to hit with spell attacks). Xavour can innately cast the following spells, requiring no material components:

> At will: *chill touch, friends, shocking grasp, mage hand, true strike*
> 4/day each: *charm person, detect magic, magic missile, shield*
> 3/day each: *animate dead, blight, blur, cloudkill, counterspell, crown of madness, detect thoughts, dispel magic, dominate person, greater invisibility, slow, suggestion, vampiric touch*
> 1/day each: *antipathy/sympathy, circle of death, create undead, feeblemind, finger of death, rot (pg. 179), power word kill*

Legendary Resistances (3/Day). If Xavour fails a saving throw, he may choose to succeed instead.

Magic Resistance. Xavour has advantage on saving throws against spells and other magical effects.

Magic Weapons. Xavour's weapon attacks in all forms are magical.

Shape Change. Xavour can spend his action to change into his original half-orc form. He can revert back to his dragon by spending his action again. Any equipment he is wearing or carrying is absorbed by the new form (Xavour's choice).

In his humanoid form, Xavour retains all of his spell-casting abilities, alignment, hit points, Hit Dice, ability to speak in his known languages, proficiencies, Legendary Resistance and lair actions and his ability scores remain the same. His damage resistances remain unchanged. His statistics and capabilities are otherwise replaced by those of the new form, except any class features or legendary actions of his new form.

Aura of Putrescence. Any creature within 15 feet of Xavour is suddenly overwhelmed with the smell of decay and rotting flesh. The creature must make a DC 18 Constitution saving throw. On a failure, the creature takes 11 (3d6) poison damage.

If the creature's saving throw is 10 or below they become poisoned, and for the next week, the creature has disadvantage on all Wisdom (Perception) checks requiring smell, as the smell of rotting flesh remains with them.

If a creature's saving throw is successful, the creature is immune to the effects of Xavour's Aura of Putrescence for the next 24 hours. A creature can repeat the saving throw at the end of each of its turns, ending the poisoned effect on a success. However, the smell remains.

Actions

Multiattack. Xavour can make three attacks in his humanoid form with the Morningstar of Malady. In his dragon form, he can make two claw attacks and one with his bite or tail.

Bite (dragon form only). Melee Weapon Attack: +14 to hit, reach 15 ft., one target. *Hit*: 18 (2d10 + 7) piercing damage, plus 10 (3d6) poison damage. The target must succeed on a DC 21 Constitution saving throw or become poisoned.

Claw (dragon form only). Melee Weapon Attack: +14 to hit, reach 10 ft., one target. *Hit*: 21 (4d6 + 7) slashing damage, plus 14 (4d6) necrotic damage.

Morningstar of Malady (half-orc form only). Melee Weapon Attack: +14 to hit, reach 5 ft., one target. *Hit*: 11 (1d8 +7) bludgeoning damage, plus 10 (3d6) poison damage. The target must make a DC 18 Constitution saving throw. On a failed save, the target's flesh begins to wither and rot. The target becomes vulnerable to bludgeoning damage and is afflicted with the effects of the *contagion* spell.

Plague Swarm (Recharge 5-6; dragon form only). A swarm of undead biting insects bursts from within his ribcage. Each creature within 15 feet of Xavour must succeed on a DC 21 Constitution saving throw, taking 63 (18d6) necrotic damage on a failed save or half as much on successful one.

Spiked Tail (dragon form only). Melee Weapon Attack: +14 to hit, reach 20 ft., one target. *Hit*: 16 (2d8 + 7) piercing and bludgeoning damage, plus 14 (4d6) poison damage.

Legendary Actions

Xavour can take three legendary actions, choosing from the options below. Only one legendary action option can be used at a time and only at the end of another creature's turn. Xavour regains spent legendary actions at the start of his turn.

Melee Attack. Xavour makes a tail, claw or bite attack.

Cast Spell (Costs 2 Actions). Xavour may cast one spell, even if the daily usage of that spell has been expended.

Shape Change (Costs 2 Actions). Xavour may shape change to his dragon or half-orc form.

Plague Swarm (Costs 3 Actions). Xavour may use his Plague Swarm ability, even if it has not recharged.

XYLAARION,
THE SHACKLED QUEEN

Take a moment and imagine the world's most terrifying dragons. Red dragons. Black dragons. Demonic beings from ancient myths have come and gone...and yet the dragons remain. Take them all together and fold them into a single beast. Imagine that dragon, filled with anger and spite and rage and a mother's unquenchable guilt. Imagine a dragon so terrifying she birthed all other dragons, was punished for it, shackled into a realm of titans and erased from all histories.

Every single one.

Xylaarion is the Shackled Queen and the godmother of all evil that has ever been willed into the world. Other goddesses may claim they invented evil or control evil or lord over the realms of evil. But those deities are lying. Or confused.

Or just plain wrong.

Xylaarion is the first and only evil world ever knew. When someone prays to an evil god, they are actually worshipping Xylaarion.

Before the words to describe such a creature existed, she was there. Though why anyone would want to describe the essence—nay, mother—of all evil is beyond me. Beyond all of us.

—Garth the Guiltless,
Alemaster of the Silver Tap

Before there was light, there was Xylaarion. Before there was even a void, there was Xylaarion. She is alpha and omega. The great divide between hope and eternity. She can shatter mountains and undo all living things with a thought. She is so powerful, in fact, that she was once worshipped by the titans themselves. The stories of her power are countless and span all cultures.

Or they used to.

For millennia, Xylaarion ruled the known planes. All of them. Even while she rested, she remained the Queen of Eternity and the Empress of Fate. Her reign of terror was so great, even when she slept, the stars trembled from the sound of her breath.

Then came the "Day of the Collar," when Xylaarion slept and the titans gathered en masse around her body. Unable to kill the Queen, the titans did the only thing they could. Having fashioned a great and unbreakable collar and a series of magical shackles, the titans held her down and quickly imprisoned the great dragon.

Xylaarion struggled, and many titans perished, but the collar was on her. It rendered her voice incapable of speech so no one would hear her bellows, and the shackles cut off her rage so no more would suffer her might. Her soul and body were thus transported to the realm of Tartarus, imprisoned for eternity.

Afterward, the titans began the arduous work of removing her name from history, breaking the languages apart so the name Xylaarion could not be pronounced, or memorized...or even remembered. The world went from a single-faith monoculture to the hundred-fold nations we now know. All to remove Xylaarion's name from their tongues. Should the shackles ever come off, Xylaarion cannot be destroyed—only once again subdued.

Hook

Building encounters around Xylaarion is not easy. She is not meant to be known or found. She is meant to build legends and campaigns around, as cultists still whisper her name, and ancient texts mention an unpronounceable goddess of fire and destruction no one should ever unchain. She could end every world and plane, so certainly a creature to be handled with care.

Encounter Conditions

Within Tarturus, a hellish prison of fire and oppression.

The Shackled Queen cannot be found through ordinary means. She exists inside the void, at the end of an eternal plane of torment and imprisonment, buried under a mountain and surrounded by titans. Here she has languished, for millenia.

But there are those cults and esoteric and hermetic wizards who have learned the name Xylaarion, through some ill-fortunate means. Some wish to summon her to this world. Some wish to join her in oblivion.

Xylaarion's prison cannot be understood or fathomed by mortal minds. To enter her domain is folly. To witness her is to look into the eyes of eternal evil. If any should survive this moment of trespass, then madness surely follows.

But for intrepid adventurers, this is just the beginning...

Tactics

Note: If Xylaarion were unshackled, she could kill one creature per round with a thought. The following tactics are for the shackled version of Xylaarion.

Each round, Xylaarion uses her lair action to summon spikes or fill the air with the sound of wailing voices.

Xylaarion almost always uses her breath weapons first, before anything else. Breath of Despair ensures the PCs will fail most of their die rolls for the foreseeable future while Disrupting Force pushes everyone away from her. Disrupting Force is best in the first round, as she follows up with No Friend Of Mine.

On the second round of combat, Xylaarion uses No Friend Of Mine to direct the most towering warrior to attack the smallest spell-caster (whenever possible), often with malicious results.

She uses *forcecage*, *resilient sphere* and *wall of force* to impose her will on others (and torment them as she has been tormented), especially magic-users. She uses *confusion* and *maze* on the stupidest foes she encounters. Those who get too close suffer from *disintegrate*, *feeblemind*, *reverse gravity* and *telekinesis*. And if that does not send the message to leave her alone, Xylaarion uses her breath weapons again.

If, for some reason, the PCs are able to withstand the fight against Xylaarion, she resorts to fighting hand to hand, which is a deadly multiattack onslaught.

Wealth

Xylaarion possesses no wealth. Nothing of value to anyone. She is a prisoner and as such the only thing she possesses are her shackles, made from an indestructible material no human has ever encountered.

Xylaarion's Lair

It's possible that with all the time she's spent in Tarturus, Xylaarion has subverted the power of the collar that binds her to make herself feel more at home. If you feel your party needs even more of a challenge, the lair actions and regional effects listed could be utilized as part of an encounter in Tarturus.

Lair Actions

On initiative count 20 (losing initiative ties), Xylaarion takes a lair action to cause one of the following effects. She can't use the same effect two rounds in a row.

• Xylaarion summons spikes from out of the darkness. Each creature must succeed on a DC 21 Dexterity saving throw or be spiked to the floor, suffering 35 (10d6) piercing damage. A spiked creature has a movement of 0. As an action, a creature can make a DC 20 Strength (Athletics) check to free itself, causing 2d6 additional piercing damage. The metal spikes are forged in Tarturus and are considered magical weapons. They have an AC 18 with 60 hit points and are immune to psychic and poison damage. The spikes last until Xylaarion uses this lair action again or until she dies, after which they turn to dust.

• Xylaarion chooses a point she can see within 100 feet of her in the lair. The area within 30 feet of that point fills with the sound of a thousand voices wailing in despair. Each creature other than Xylaarion in the area must succeed on a DC 21 Wisdom saving throw or lose one adventuring level and suffer a level of exhaustion. Xylaarion can repeat this action when it is available, causing the party to lose additional levels and suffer another level of exhaustion.

Xylaarion,
The Shackled Queen

Gargantuan dragon (titan), neutral evil

Armor Class 24 (natural armor)
Hit Points 546 (28d20 + 252)
Speed 40 ft., fly 80 ft. (chains limit movement to 100 ft.)

STR	DEX	CON	INT	WIS	CHA
30 (+10)	10 (+0)	29 (+9)	15 (+2)	18 (+4)	22 (+6)

Saving Throws Dex +8, Con +17, Wis +12, Cha +14
Skills Perception +12, Stealth +8
Damage Immunities force
Condition Immunities charmed
Senses blindsight 60 ft., darkvision 120 ft., passive Perception 28
Languages Abyssal, Common, Draconic, Infernal
Challenge 24 (62,000 XP)

Discorporation. When Xylaarion drops to 0 hit points or dies, her body is destroyed, and she is unable to take physical form for a time. When she reappears, she remains shackled.

Innate Spellcasting. Xylaarion's innate spellcasting ability is Charisma (spell save DC 22, +14 to hit with spell attacks). She can innately cast the following spells, requiring no material components:

> *3/day each: arcane hand* (appears as spectral chains), *confusion, disintegrate, earthquake, eyebite, feeblemind, forcecage, globe of invulnerability, hold monster, maze, resilient sphere, reverse gravity, telekinesis, wall of fire, wall of force, wall of stone.*

Legendary Resistance (3/Day). If Xylaarion fails a saving throw, she can choose to succeed instead.

No Friend of Mine. Xylaarion chooses a single target she can see. A character must succeed on a DC 21 Wisdom saving throw or be compelled to attack the closest ally. A creature can repeat the saving throw at the end of each of its turns, ending the effect on itself on a success.

Actions

Multiattack. Xylaarion can use her Frightful Presence. She then makes three attacks: one with her bite and two with her claws.

Bite. Melee Weapon Attack: +18 to hit, reach 15 ft., one target.
Hit: 21 (2d10 + 10) piercing damage, plus 13 (3d8) force damage.
Claw. Melee Weapon Attack: +18 to hit, reach 10 ft., one target.
Hit: 17 (2d6 + 10) slashing damage.
Tail. Melee Weapon Attack: +18 to hit, reach 20 ft., one target.
Hit: 19 (2d8 + 10) bludgeoning damage.

Frightful Presence. Each creature of Xylaarion's choice that is within 120 feet of her and aware of her must succeed on a DC 21 Wisdom saving throw or become frightened for one minute. A creature can repeat the saving throw at the end of each of its turns, ending the effect on itself on a success. If a creature's saving throw is successful or the effect ends for it, the creature is immune to Xylaarion's Frightful Presence for the next 24 hours.

Breath Weapons (Recharge 4–6). Xylaarion uses one of the following breath weapons:

> *Disrupting Force.* Xylaarion exhales disruptive force in a 90-foot line that is 10 feet wide. Each creature in that line must make a DC 24 Dexterity saving throw, taking 63 (14d8) force damage, and is pushed 15 feet away from her and knocked prone on a failed save or receives half as much damage and isn't pushed or prone on a successful one.
> *Breath of Despair.* Xylaarion exhales gas in a 90-foot cone. Each creature in that area must succeed on a DC 24 Wisdom saving throw or have disadvantage on attack rolls, ability checks and saving throws for one minute. A creature can repeat the saving throw at the end of each of its turns, ending the effect on itself on a success. A creature that can't be charmed is immune to this effect.

Legendary Actions

Xylaarion can take three legendary actions, choosing from the options below. Only one legendary action option can be used at a time and only at the end of another creature's turn. Xylaarion regains spent legendary actions at the start of her turn.

Detect. Xylaarion makes a Wisdom (Perception) check.

Tail Attack. Xylaarion makes a tail attack.

Snatch (Costs 2 Actions). Xylaarion makes a claw attack. If the attack hits a creature that is Large or smaller, the creature is grappled (escape DC 25). Until this grapple ends the target is restrained. Xylaarion has two claws, each of which can grapple only one target.

Wing Attack (Costs 2 Actions). Xylaarion beats her wings. Each creature within 15 feet of her must succeed on a DC 25 Dexterity saving throw or take 17 (2d6 + 10) bludgeoning damage and be knocked prone. She can then fly up to half her flying speed.

Regional Effects

The region containing Xylaarion's lair is warped by her magic, which creates one or more of the following effects:

- All creatures within 1 mile of Xylaarion's lair suffer Level 1 exhaustion.
- The area within 6 miles of the lair is full of damp, dreary mist. The area within the mist is lightly obscured.
- Creatures within 1 mile of the lair that are bound, restrained or caged suffer without end. Such creatures age slowly, physically aging one year for every 10 years that pass. Additionally, creatures in the area with four or more levels of exhaustion no longer require food or drink.

If Xylaarion dies, conditions of the area surrounding the lair return to normal—as "normal" as Tartarus can be—over the course of 1d10 days.

ZUTH,
THE ETERNAL

Crisp evening descends as a furtive group of druids converges upon a weathered stone dais. As the druids chant in unison, a quarreling flock of birds falls silent and takes to the sky, fleeing a terrible threat yet unseen. An expectant hush builds as if the forest itself holds its breath until a deep and vibrant thrumming beats from the heart of the earth. A tumultuous crash rattles the boiling sky and screaming lightning rips an ancient tree in twane. Nearby, an inert hill heaves with life as a sleeping giant wakes and rises towards the angry clouds above and rooted trees cling as if desperate to hang onto its broad back. It lets out a thunderous roar that's heard for leagues. Earth and stone, mud and gravel, moss and silt slough from the giant in massive slopping heaps while it moves forth with languid ease. Lumbering and heavy, its height seemingly unlimited, and the earth itself sighs while cracking beneath its weight.

And now the maddened and feverish worshipers exclaim, "Arise, Zuth, arise!"

Laws of nature are unavoidable, absolute and eternal. What is born surely dies. For every balmy, warm summer, there is a chilling, cruel winter. Day invariably gives way to night. Just as above has below and black has white, all that is good has an opposite and equal reflection in evil. In short, each thing that exists has its direct counterpoint, a reversed mirror image that balances its place, and indeed its meaning, in the whole of existence.

All natural things have their respective opposites, except Zuth. Zuth is the personification of this harmonious force of balance and opposites. Zuth is ancient; it is enormous and it is the ultimate expression of nature's absolute and impersonal will.

Legend tells that Zuth was created from all elements. The supra-personal Will of Nature drew from itself a powerful being to act as a counter to the presence of dragons. After all, being that they are creatures of magic, dragons are outside the bounds of natural order. Zuth rises from its deep slumber when it senses the call to restore symmetry between all dragons: good or evil, gold or black, fire or ice.

If there are too many green dragons in the world, Zuth corrects this dysfunction. If there's a surplus of bronze dragons, Zuth restores the average.

Zuth is forever. Even if destroyed, it is always birthed again in time. When Zuth sheds one of its scales, that scale works its way deep into the earth like an oak seed. There, within a cradle of dirt and stone and throughout several centuries, the scale forms an exact duplicate of Zuth. Therefore, even if one version of Zuth is defeated, another will always return to take its place in order to restore nature's order.

Zuth possesses non-verbal intelligence. It thinks only in images and only has the base emotions of an animal. Its communication is telepathic, expressing its will with imagery and emotional impressions. Often it is difficult to determine its exact motives and aims, as the images often have no context, leaving the guesswork entirely in the hands of those who receive the impressions.

The presence of Zuth has fueled many speculations as to why it exists in the world, and some druids have come to revere this mighty creature, lending to it a status of a demi-god or a potent spirit of nature itself.

Zuth awakens when the stars align in a particular formation once in a century. Additionally, once every thousand years, a purge occurs. In this purge, Zuth rises to destroy dragons indiscriminately. Other dragons of all types seem to sense each upcoming cleansing. The world sees far more dragon activity as they collectively panic in the months before a forthcoming purge. Zuth destroys all the unlucky dragons that are in its path. During such purging events, the dragon population is culled without any logical pattern, and the events last until Zuth is destroyed.

A great mystery lies in Zuth's designless cullings. How can there be any balance in absolute destruction? It is a question that none but nature itself can answer.

Hook

The party is approached by a gold dragon who has been pursued by Zuth for many weeks. They are encouraged to assist the dragon upon the promise of riches, prestige or for future aid from the dragon. Upon their investigation, the group discovers a druidic cult that has grown up around the stories of Zuth. Its members will interfere with the party's plans and try to thwart them at all passes. If the group gets too close to Zuth, the cult will assemble in full force and attack. Should the group prevail, the final encounter with Zuth is imminent. If successful, the gold dragon will reward the group appropriately.

Encounter Conditions

Tracking or following Zuth is relatively easy, given the potential trail of destruction it may leave. However, if Zuth is below ground, the only indicator of its movement are the occasional tremors of the earth. Zuth is fully capable of emerging anywhere on the planet. Consider utilizing the vast scope of Zuth's domain when determining where to create your encounter—the edge of a dense forest or within the ridges and canyons of a mighty mountain range.

Tactics

Zuth's main tactic is surprise, leveraging its ability to Earth Glide 120 feet. It will use this to his advantage when stalking any prey, and it usually ambushes dragons within their lairs. If any encounter starts to become a challenge, Zuth will simply burrow down and emerge at a more strategic location. Essentially, rather than soaring the skies, Zuth "flies" underground.

Wealth

Tracking Zuth reveals precious metals, gems and random items that may have stuck to its body over time. Such items were picked up as it burrowed through veins of gold and ancient geode pockets deep within the earth. The finds are quite random, but PCs may collect the equivalent of a small goldmine's worth of treasure by following its trail above the surface and picking up what has fallen off its body.

Zuth's Lair

Because Zuth lies dormant until summoned, it does not have a conventional lair. It can, however, bring its will to bear on its immediate environment. If seeking an additional challenge, use the following Lair Actions in area within 300 feet of Zuth.

Lair Actions

On initiative count 20 (losing initiative ties), Zuth takes a lair action to cause one of the following effects. Zuth can't use the same effect two rounds in a row.

- A tremor shakes the area in a 60-foot radius around Zuth. Each creature on the ground must succeed on a DC 18 Dexterity saving throw or be knocked prone.
- Zuth summons 1d4 **treants** to his aid. These creatures act on their own initiative according to Zuth's will but become free creatures in the event of his death.
- Any creature with a direct tie to the natural order at GM discretion (nature clerics, oath of the ancients paladins or druids in general) must succeed on a DC 20 Wisdom saving throw or fall under Zuth's sway until the start of the next round per initiative. Their actions are at GM discretion and must serve the larger purpose Zuth was summoned to pursue.

ZUTH, THE ETERNAL

Titanic dragon, neutral

Armor Class 27 (natural armor)
Hit Points 738 (36d20 +360)
Speed 40 ft., burrow 120 ft., swim 40 ft.

STR	DEX	CON	INT	WIS	CHA
30 (+10)	18 (+4)	30 (+10)	10 (+0)	10 (+0)	10 (+0)

Saving Throws Dex +13, Con +19, Int +9, Wis +9, Cha +9
Skills Insight +10, Intimidation +18, Perception +18
Damage Resistances cold, fire
Damage Immunities poison; bludgeoning, piercing and slashing damage from nonmagical attacks
Condition Immunities blinded, charmed, exhaustion, frightened, paralyzed, stunned
Senses truesight 120 ft., passive Perception 28
Languages draconic, telepathy 120 ft.
Challenge 30 (155,000 XP)

Amphibious. Zuth can breathe air or water.
Discorporation. When Zuth drops to 0 hit points, its body is destroyed, and it is unable to take physical form for a time.
Dragon Sense. Zuth may use the *scrying* spell as a natural ability. Zuth uses this ability to target dragons only.
Earth Glide. Zuth can burrow through nonmagical, unworked earth and stone. While doing so, Zuth does not disturb the material it moves through.
False Appearance. While Zuth remains motionless, it is indistinguishable from a hillside or mountainside.
Legendary Resistance (6/Day). If Zuth fails a saving throw, it can choose to succeed instead.
Magic Resistance. Zuth has advantage on saving throws against spells and other magical effects.
Magic Weapons. Zuth's weapon attacks are magical.
Reflective Body. If Zuth is targeted by a magic missile spell, a line spell, a spell that requires a ranged attack roll or any breath weapon, roll a d4. On a 1 to 3, Zuth is unaffected. On a 4, Zuth is unaffected and the magic effect or breath weapon is reflected and targets the caster as though the spell or effect originated from Zuth.
Regeneration. Zuth regains 30 hit points at the start of its turn. If Zuth takes radiant damage on its body, this trait doesn't function at the start of its next turn. Zuth dies only if it starts its turn with 0 hit points and doesn't regenerate.
Siege Monster. Zuth deals double damage to objects and structures.

ACTIONS

Multiattack. Zuth can use its Frightful Presence. It then makes three attacks. Zuth can use its bite, then makes two attacks with its claws.
Bite. Melee Weapon Attack: +19 to hit, reach 50 ft., one target. *Hit:* 29 (3d12 + 10) piercing damage. If the target is a living creature, it must succeed on a DC 22 Constitution saving throw or take 22 (4d10) poison damage.
Claw. Melee Weapon Attack: +19 to hit, reach 10 ft., one target. *Hit:* 17 (2d6 + 10) slashing damage.
Tail. Melee Weapon Attack: +19 to hit, reach 30 ft., one target. *Hit:* 17 (2d8 + 10) bludgeoning damage.
Rock. Ranged Weapon Attack: +19 to hit, range 60/240 ft., one target. *Hit:* 36 (4d12 +10) bludgeoning damage.
Frightful Presence. Each creature of Zuth's choice that is within 120 feet of it and aware of it must succeed on a DC 21 Wisdom saving throw or become frightened for one minute. A creature can repeat the saving throw at the end of each of its turns, ending the effect on itself on a success. If a creature's saving throw is successful or the effect ends for it, the creature is immune to Zuth's Frightful Presence for the next 24 hours.
Poison Breath (Recharge 3–6). Zuth exhales poisonous gas in a 90-foot cone. Each creature in that area must make a DC 22 Constitution saving throw, taking 91 (26d6) poison damage on a failed save or half as much on a successful one.

If the creature is a dragon, Zuth's poison breath bypasses any natural or magical poison resistances and immunities. A dragon must first save against the poison breath. A dragon must then make a DC 22 Constitution saving throw. On a failed save, it takes an additional 75 (10d6 + 40) force damage or half as much on a successful one. If the damage reduces the dragon to 0 hit points, it is disintegrated.

A disintegrated dragon and everything it is wearing and carrying, except magic items, are reduced to a pile of fine gray dust. The dragon can be restored to life only by means of a true resurrection or a wish spell.

LEGENDARY ACTIONS

Zuth can take three legendary actions, choosing from the options below. Only one legendary action option can be used at a time and only at the end of another creature's turn. Zuth regains spent legendary actions at the start of his turn.
Bite. Zuth makes a Bite attack.
Burrow. Zuth is able to move, burrowing into the earth, without provoking an attack of opportunity.
Detect. Zuth makes a Wisdom (Perception) check.
Rock. Zuth makes a Rock attack.
Tail Attack. Zuth makes a tail attack.
Summon Lightning (Costs 2 Actions). Zuth summons lightning from a nearby storm cloud. The point of origin is within 500 feet of Zuth. The bolt strikes a 10-foot area that Zuth can see. Any creature within 10 feet of that point must make a DC 17 Dexterity saving throw, taking 54 (12d8) lightning damage on a failed save or half as much on a successful one. Any lightning immunity becomes a resistance instead. Any resistances to lighting is considered full damage.

A REALM OF DRAGONS

DRACONIC CREATURES HAVE A WIDE-RANGING IMPACT ON THE WORLD AROUND THEM, SHAPING ECONOMIES, FOSTERING CULTS AND SHIFTING THE ARCANE.

DRAGON RIDERS

A PLAYABLE CLASS FOR 5E ADVENTURES

The bond formed between rider and mount has long been viewed as something which transcends the common bond between beast and humanoid. Trust must be developed; a relationship built. It is incredibly difficult for a rider to form a relationship with a beast whose intelligence and power may surpass even their own, yet the Dragon Riders of Mésanffor broke this boundary long ago. Their tradition spread, their techniques adopted and adapted in small corners of the realm by brave warriors with the will to fight and the courage to fly. The bond between dragon and rider is unique to their pairing, meaning that though riders may share similar styles in various parts of the realm, the execution is as diverse as dragons themselves.

ISOLATED TRADITION

The method of breeding and domesticating dragons began in a city isolated by the elements. Flanked on one side by a wide, rushing river and steep, treacherous mountains on the other, the Elven city of Sinfarel was naturally sheltered from outside interference. The mountain range, the Tenggers, was also a breeding ground for drakes of all colors, shapes and sizes. Wyverns and dragons were a regular sight in the air over Sinfarel, and reports of wyrms just outside the city limits were commonplace. Needless to say, this did not create a welcoming atmosphere for outsiders.

For many years, skilled citizens of Sinfarel began taking advantage of their precarious situation and formulated a method of domesticating the dragons of the Tengger Mountains. Traditions of training alongside their dragon companions, once a necessity born of proximity, became the focus of their practice. Rather than preparing themselves to fight these creatures, they began to fight alongside them, endearing themselves to the dragons in their midst.

A POWERFUL BOND

The most curious and—at the same time—crucial aspect of dragon riding was found to be the bond formed between the rider and their companion. From a very young age, the dragons would connect to their rider on a spiritual level. Their minds linked, and as they both grew, this bond would begin to show arcane promise.

This fact became the centerpiece of the methods and techniques developed by the early dragon riders. Together, the Dragon Rider and Dragon Companion could become an unbreakable unit with strategies and maneuvers unique to their partnership. The path of the Dragon Rider is solitary, but the rider is never alone.

CREATING A DRAGON RIDER

When creating a Dragon Rider character, consider the relationship with their Dragon Companion as an integral part of their story. Have they always wanted to be a Dragon Rider, or was this something thrust upon them unexpectedly? What was the process of receiving or choosing the Companion? Discuss with your GM the role Dragon Riders play in the world; how common they are, what organizations they may be a part of, etc. Refer to the Dragon Companion section for more information on choosing your Rider's Companion.

QUICK BUILD

You may make a Dragon Rider quickly using these suggestions. First, put your highest ability score in either Strength or Dexterity depending on the weapon(s) you plan to use. Put your next highest score in Constitution. Second, choose the Folk Hero background.

DRAGON RIDER

Level	Proficiency Bonus	Features	Maneuvers Known	Maneuver Points
1st	+2	Novice Rider, Draconic Vein	–	–
2nd	+2	Fighting Style	–	–
3rd	+2	Dragon Trainee, Dragon Maneuvers, Draconic Vein Feature	3	3
4th	+2	Ability Score Increase	3	4
5th	+3	Extra Attack	3	5
6th	+3	Adept Rider	4	6
7th	+3	Draconic Vein Feature	4	7
8th	+3	Ability Score Increase	4	8
9th	+4	Draconic Awareness	4	9
10th	+4	Improved Saddle, Signature Maneuver	5	10
11th	+4	Draconic Vein Feature	5	11
12th	+4	Ability Score Increase	5	12
13th	+5	Bond of Scales	5	13
14th	+5	Expert Rider	6	14
15th	+5	Draconic Vein Feature	6	15
16th	+5	Ability Score Increase	6	16
17th	+6	Isolated Prey	6	17
18th	+6	Perfected Maneuvers	7	18
19th	+6	Draconic Vein Feature, Ability Score Increase	7	19
20th	+6	Master Rider	7	20

CLASS FEATURES

As a Dragon Rider, you gain the following class features.

HIT POINTS

Hit Dice: 1d8 per Dragon Rider level
Hit Points at 1st level: 8 + your Constitution modifier
Hit Points at higher levels: 1d8 (or 5) plus your Constitution modifier per level after 1st

PROFICIENCIES

Armor: Light armor, medium armor, shields
Weapons: Simple weapons, martial weapons
Tools: Leatherworker's tools
Saving Throws: Strength, Wisdom
Skills: Choose two from Athletics, Acrobatics, Stealth, Nature, Animal Handling, Perception and Intimidation

DRAGON RIDER EQUIPMENT

You may start with the following equipment plus any equipment granted by your background:

- One martial weapon
- Any two simple weapons
- (a) Leather armor or (b) scale mail
- Leatherworker's tools and an explorer's pack

If you forgo this equipment, you start with 5d4 x 10 gp to buy your equipment.

NOVICE RIDER

At 1st level, you are granted a Dragon Companion. The stats, abilities and rules for this Companion are in the Dragon Companion section. You may communicate telepathically with your Companion while they are within 1 mile of you.

DRACONIC VEINS

Also at 1st level, you choose one of two Draconic Veins: Dragon Knight or Dragon Outrider.

FIGHTING STYLE

At 2nd level, you adopt a fighting style as your specialty. Choose one of the following options. You can't take a fighting style more than once, even if you later get to choose again.
Archery. You gain a +2 bonus to attack rolls made with a ranged weapon.
Great Weapon Fighting. When you roll a 1 or 2 on a damage die for an attack you make with a melee weapon that you are wielding with two hands, you can reroll the die and must use the new roll—even if the new roll is a 1 or a 2. The weapon must have the two-handed or versatile property for you to gain this benefit.
Dueling. When you are wielding a melee weapon in one hand and no other weapons, you gain a +2 bonus

to damage rolls with that weapon.
Two-Weapon Fighting. When you engage in two-weapon fighting, you can add your ability modifier to the damage of the second attack.

DRAGON TRAINEE

At 3rd level, you have begun to train extensively with your dragon. You can buy or use 10 gp worth of leather and spend eight hours creating a saddle for your dragon companion, and gain the ability to ride the dragon while it is walking.

DRAGON MANEUVERS

Starting at 3rd level, you gain three Maneuver Points and may choose three Dragon Maneuvers from the Dragon Maneuvers section. If the Maneuver requires a target creature to make a saving throw, the DC equals 8 + your companion's Strength Modifier + your proficiency bonus, unless specified otherwise. You learn an additional maneuver at 6th level and again at 10th, 14th and 18th level. You gain one additional Maneuver point each time you gain another level of Dragon Rider.

These Maneuver points recharge after a short or long rest.

ABILITY SCORE INCREASE

When you reach 4th level—and again at 8th, 12th, 16th and 19th level—you can increase one ability score of your choice by 2, or two ability scores of your choice by 1, up to a maximum of 20.

Using the optional feats rule, you can forgo taking this feature to take a feat of your choice instead.

EXTRA ATTACK

At 5th level, you may attack twice when taking the attack action.

ADEPT RIDER

At 6th Level, you have become extremely comfortable on the back of your Dragon Companion and may now ride it while it flies. In addition, each of your attacks deals +1 damage while mounted.

DRACONIC AWARENESS

At 9th level, you gain advantage on Initiative checks.

IMPROVED SADDLE

At 10th level, you may spend 8 hours and 25 gp worth of leather to craft an improved saddle. With this saddle, it only costs 5 feet of movement to mount and dismount, and you can no longer be involuntarily dismounted.

SIGNATURE MANEUVER

Also at 10th level, you may choose one Tier 1 Dragon Maneuver you have already learned to be your Signature Maneuver. The Signature Maneuver may be performed once between a short or long rest without expending any Maneuver points. The Dragon Maneuver you learn at 10th level may be selected as your Signature Maneuver.

BOND OF SCALE

At 13th level, you may use a short rest to mend the wounds of your Dragon Companion. Any Hit Dice you expend during a Short Rest also heal the dragon for that same amount.

EXPERT RIDER

At 14th level, you have nearly perfected aerial combat. While mounted, each of your attacks deals +3 additional damage, and you score a critical hit on a 19 or higher d20 attack roll.

ISOLATED PREY

At 17th level, you may use a bonus action to target a creature you can see, and your Dragon Companion becomes fixated on that target. While a creature is targeted in this way, all attacks made by you and your Companion have advantage and deal an additional weapon die damage. In addition, opportunity attacks against the creature no longer require a reaction but are still limited to only one attack. Isolated Prey lasts for one minute or until the creature is killed.

PERFECTED MANEUVERS

At 18th level, your previously chosen Signature Maneuver is perfected and no longer costs Maneuver points. In addition, you select a maneuver from any tier to be your second Signature Maneuver, including the Dragon Maneuver gained at this level.

MASTER RIDER

At 20th level, your bond with your Companion becomes unbreakable. While mounted, you and your Companion have advantage on all saving throws. Your telepathic bond persists as long as you are on the same plane. In addition, if you have 0 Maneuver points upon rolling initiative, you start your turn with 5.

ADDITIONAL DRAGON MANEUVERS

Consult with your GM to create and balance your own personalized Maneuvers. Every Dragon Rider should feel distinct and have their own strengths and weaknesses. When creating Dragon Maneuvers, think of the risks involved and how big the pay-off for taking that risk. The higher the risk—the higher the reward.

DRACONIC VEINS

Dragon Riders may choose one of two Veins with their companions at 1st level. You may bolster your defenses and physical prowess as a Dragon Knight or flit effortlessly through the sky as a Dragon Outrider.

DRAGON KNIGHT

If you choose Dragon Knight at 1st level, your bond with your Companion bolsters your fortitude. You gain proficiency in Heavy Armor.

SCALED HIDE

At 3rd level, you gain +3 Max hp and +1 additional Max hp for each level you gain in Dragon Rider.

TOOTH AND CLAW

At 7th level, when you deal damage to a creature, you may deal additional damage equal to your Dragon Rider level. Tooth and Claw recharges at a short or long rest.

DRACONIC ABILITY

At 11th level, your bond with your Companion enhances your fortitude beyond natural capabilities. Choose either Strength or Constitution. That ability's maximum is increased to 22.

STRENGTH OF SCALE

At 15th level, whenever you roll a Strength check or Strength saving throw, you may add a d6 to the total.

AURA OF DOMINANCE

At 19th level, you become a bulwark of Draconic power. You may use an action to gain resistance to all types of damage for one minute. During that time, all of your weapon attacks deal an additional weapon die of the damage type appropriate to your dragon companion. Aura of Dominance recharges after a short rest.

DRAGON OUTRIDER

If you choose Dragon Outrider at 1st level, your bond with your Companion sharpens your senses. You gain proficiency in Perception. If you already have proficiency in Perception, you gain expertise.

MOONLIGHT HUNTER

At 3rd level, you and your Companion gain darkvision out to a range of 120 feet.

SUPPLE WINGS

At 7th level, your Companion gains the ability to Dash as a bonus action, and any stealth checks made while mounted gain advantage.

Draconic Ability

At 11th level, your bond with your companion enhances your scouting abilities beyond natural capacity. Choose either Dexterity or Wisdom. That ability's maximum is increased to 22.

Take Aim

At 15th level, your bond with your companion enhances your accuracy. Once per turn, the Dragon Outrider may choose to reroll one attack that misses.

Aura of Agility

At 19th level, you may use an action to massively enhance your quickness and accuracy. For one minute, the movement speed of you and your companion is doubled and you may make an additional attack per attack action. Aura of Agility may be used once per long rest.

Multiclassing

Multiclassing Prerequisite
• Dragon Rider: Strength 13 or Dexterity 13

When choosing Dragon Rider as a multiclass option, consider how your character may have been introduced to this rare lifestyle. Perhaps they met another Dragon Rider who connects them to a trainer. They may also have stumbled upon a young dragon and instantly felt a connection form between them. A true Dragon Rider is a rarity and requires either the strength or agility to maintain control while your companion performs dangerous maneuvers through the air.

Dragon Companion

At 1st level, you choose a Dragon Companion (pg. 128) to grow, level, explore and fight by your side. This dragon grows like any other, but shares your alignment. Its growth is stunted by the process of domestication.

Your Companion operates on your initiative and shares your action. On your turn, you may command them to move, take the Dash, Dodge or Disengage actions without sacrificing any movement or action of your own. For your Companion to attack, you must sacrifice one of your attacks for each attack they take. Your Companion may be knocked unconscious, but their magical bond with you prevents them from being permanently killed unless you are also killed. Your Companion regains health as usual. The Dragon Companion Chart dictates what Proficiency Bonuses and additional Hit Dice your Companion gains upon leveling up. Dragon types available to serve as your Companion are presented on the following page.

Dragon Companion

Level	Proficiency Bonus	Hit Dice	Features
1st	+2	1d12	Darkvision
2nd	+2	2d12	Breath Attack
3rd	+2	3d12	Size Increase, Natural Armor
4th	+2	3d12	Ability Score Increase
5th	+3	4d12	Shape Change
6th	+3	5d12	Fly Speed Increase, Breath Attack Range Increase
7th	+3	6d12	Natural Armor
8th	+3	6d12	Ability Score Increase
9th	+4	7d12	Advanced Darkvision
10th	+4	8d12	Breath Attack Range Increase
11th	+4	9d12	Fly Speed Increase
12th	+4	9d12	Ability Score Increase
13th	+5	10d12	Natural Armor
14th	+5	11d12	Breath Attack Range Increase
15th	+5	12d12	Size Increase
16th	+5	12d12	Ability Score Increase
17th	+6	13d12	Natural Armor
18th	+6	14d12	Breath Attack Range Increase
19th	+6	15d12	Fly Speed Increase
20th	+6	15d12	Ability Score Increase 7

Ruby Dragon

This dragon's scales are a bright red color at a young age, eventually progressing towards a darker crimson later in life. Their breath is released in a fiery cone of intense heat, easily incinerating anything in its path. The ruby dragon's breath attack requires a Dexterity saving throw.

Sapphire Dragon

This dragon's scales begin as the color of the sky; soft blue, with flecks of cloudy white. As they age, the scales shift into a deep oceanic blue. Their breath manifests as a line of electrical energy, eventually gaining enough power to stop the heart of any living creature caught in its fury. The sapphire dragon's breath attack requires a Dexterity saving throw.

Emerald Dragon

This dragon's scales begin as a light, grassy green, then age into the verdant green color of an untouched forest. Their breath is released in a toxic cone of poisonous gas, poisonous enough to leave even the most potent enemies retching and gasping for air. The emerald dragon's breath attack requires a Constitution saving throw.

Opal Dragon

This dragon's scales begin as a gleaming white, sometimes having phosphorescent flecks of light reds and greens. As they age, those phosphorescent flecks disappear and are replaced with gray, ashy undertones. The opal dragon's breath is a cone of ice so frigid that it freezes the very air inside it, and any living thing in the area may shatter from the sheer cold. The opal dragon's breath attack requires a Constitution saving throw.

Obsidian Dragon

This dragon's scales appear almost dark gray at birth, eventually growing into scales as black as night. The obsidian dragon's breath is a heaving line of virulent acid, destructive enough at young ages to melt flesh and bone. At older ages, this acid is rumored to be able to melt stone, even metal. The obsidian dragon's breath attack requires a Dexterity saving throw.

Darkvision

At 1st level, the Dragon Companion gains Darkvision out to a range of 60 feet. At 9th level, this range increases to 90 feet.

Breath Attack

At 2nd level, you may use an Action to command your Dragon Companion to expel its Breath Attack. Any creature caught in its range must succeed on a Saving throw (DC 8 + proficiency + Dragon's Constitution Modifier) appropriate to the type of dragon. On a failure, they take 2d6 damage of the appropriate type or half on a success. This damage increases by a 1d6 each level after the 2nd. The dragon's breath attack recharges during a short or a long rest. Ruby, emerald and opal dragons' breath attacks begin as a 15-foot cone. Sapphire and obsidian dragons' breath attacks begin as a 30-foot line.

Size Increase

At 3rd level, the Dragon's size increases from Medium to Large, its walking speed increases by 5 feet and its fly speed increases by 10 feet. In addition, the damage die for its Bite, Tail and Claw attacks increase by one die size (d4 to d6, d6 to d8, etc.). At 15th level, its size increases from Large to Huge and it gains the same additions to its walk and fly speed, and its damage die increase an additional size.

Natural Armor

Also at 3rd level, the Dragon Companion's AC increases by 1 point. This increase happens again at 7th, 11th and 17th level.

Hatchling Dragon Companion

Medium dragon, same alignment as rider

Armor Class 15 (natural armor)
Hit Points 14 (1d12+2)
Speed 20 ft., fly 20 ft.

STR	DEX	CON	INT	WIS	CHA
16 (+3)	12 (+1)	14 (+2)	10 (-0)	10 (+0)	11 (+0)

Saving Throws Str +5, Con +4, Wis +2, Cha +2
Skills Perception +2, Stealth +3
Damage Resistances (Breath Attack damage type)
Senses Darkvision 60 ft., Passive Perception 12
Languages Common, Draconic

Actions

Multiattack. Once the Rider has gained access to Extra Attack, the Dragon Companion may use any of the following attacks once per turn, following the rules of attacking as a Dragon Companion.
Bite. Melee Weapon Attack: +5 to hit, one target.
Hit: 7(1d6+3) piercing damage plus 3 (1d4) damage of the appropriate type.
Tail. Melee Weapon Attack: +5 to hit, one target.
Hit: 8(1d8+3) bludgeoning damage.
Claw. Melee Weapon Attack: +5 to hit, one target.
Hit: 6 (1d4+3) slashing damage.
Breath Attack (1/rest). The Dragon releases its breath in a 15/30-ft. cone/line. Each creature caught in its range must succeed on a DC 12 saving throw appropriate to the Dragon's type or take 2d6 damage of the appropriate type or half on a success.
Dragon Maneuvers. If the target of a Dragon Maneuver is forced to make a saving throw against the Dragon's Save DC, the DC is 8 + Dragon's Strength Modifier + Dragon's Proficiency.

ABILITY SCORE INCREASE

At 4th level and again at 8th, 12th, 16th and 19th level, the player may choose to increase one of the Dragon's ability scores by 2, or two of the Dragon's ability scores by 1, to a maximum of 20.

SHAPE CHANGE

At 5th level, the Dragon Companion gains the ability to change its form into a medium humanoid as an action. The player chooses this form, and the Dragon may only assume this same form each time. In this form your companion may use its Claw and Breath attack, loses its fly speed, and its walking speed is 30 feet. Its stats otherwise remain the same.

FLY SPEED INCREASE

At 6th level, the Dragon Companion's flying speed increases by 10 feet. This increase happens again at 11th and 19th level.

BREATH ATTACK RANGE INCREASE

Also at 6th level, the range of the Dragon's Breath Attack increases by 10 feet. This increase happens again at 10th, 14th and 18th level.

DRAGON MANEUVERS

At 3rd level, you may choose three Dragon Maneuvers from the following list, if you fulfill the prerequisites.

TIER 1 (1 POINT)

Charging Strike (*Dragon Form Only*)
As an action and while mounted, your Dragon Companion charges forward, and you make a Melee weapon attack. If the Dragon moves at least 10 feet in a straight line towards a target and the attack hits, the strike does an additional 2d8 damage. If it hits, that creature must also make a Strength saving throw against the Dragon's save DC or fall prone.

Coordinated Flank
As a bonus action while unmounted, you and your dragon flank a single opponent. If you and your Dragon are within 5 feet of the same creature, all of your attacks on that creature have advantage until the beginning of your next turn.

Swipe the Leg (*Dragon Form Only*)
As a bonus action, you may command your Dragon Companion to make a tail attack against a large or smaller creature. If it hits, the creature takes damage from the tail attack and must make a Strength Save against the Dragon's save DC. On a failure, they are knocked prone.

Take the Hit

As a reaction when hit by an attack, you can command your Dragon to take the hit for you, or you can take the hit for your Companion instead. Your Dragon Companion must be within 5 feet of you to use this Maneuver.

Evasive Maneuvers (*Dragon Form Only*)

As a Bonus Action and while riding your Dragon, you may take the Dodge action. This applies to both you and your Dragon Companion.

Create an Opening (*Dragon Form Only*)

You may create an opening for your allies to escape by commanding your Companion to create a massive gust of wind with their wings. Using your reaction, Create an Opening allows allies within 20 feet of your Dragon Companion to move away from an enemy without incurring attacks of opportunity.

Bolstered Defense (*Knight only*)

Your bond with your Companion enhances your natural defenses. As a bonus action, you may bolster your defenses, increasing your AC by an amount equal to your Dragon's Constitution modifier until the beginning of your next turn.

Scan the Perimeter (*Outrider only*)

You may use a bonus action to scan the area. Any invisible or hidden creatures within 60 feet are revealed only to you until the beginning of your next turn.

TIER 2 (2 POINTS, REQUIRES LEVEL 5)

Drag 'n' Drop (*Dragon Form Only*)

If your Companion makes a bite attack against a medium or smaller creature and the attack hits, you may use Drag 'n' Drop to attempt to trap the creature in your Companion's mouth. The creature must succeed on a Strength saving throw against the Dragon's Save DC or it is grappled and restrained. The Dragon may move at half movement speed with the creature in its mouth and may use a bonus action to release it. The grappled creature must use an Action and succeed on a Strength saving throw to free itself.

Channeled Breath

Your connection to your Dragon companion allows them to channel their breath attack through your weapon. As an action, you may make all creatures in a 15-foot cone in front of you make a saving throw against your Dragon's breath attack. On a failure, they take 4d8 damage of that type or half damage on a success. You may spend additional maneuver points to increase this damage by an additional 1d8 per 2 Maneuver Points spent.

Fury Strikes (*Dragon Form Only*)

As an action, your Dragon Companion unleashes a bite and two claw attacks in a flurry. If all three attacks hit, regain one Maneuver point.

Diving Strike (*Dragon Form Only*)

As an action, you may dismount your companion midair and make an attack with advantage against an opponent in your path to the ground. If the attack hits, it deals normal damage and an additional amount of damage equal to the fall damage you would typically take from the fall (1d6 bludgeoning damage for every 10 feet, maximum of 20d6). When you land, you must make a Dexterity saving throw. On a success, you take no damage from the fall. On a failure, you take half damage. Save DC 15, increases +1 for every 10 feet above 50 feet.

Manifestation (*Knight Only*)

Your draconic connection allows you to manifest the physical form of the dragon on your body. As a bonus action, you may strike out with the manifestation of a draconic claw, dealing 1d10 + your Strength modifier slashing damage and an additional 1d8 of your Dragon Companion's respective elemental damage. You may spend additional Maneuver Points to increase the elemental damage dealt by an additional 1d8 per 2 maneuver points spent.

Manifestation (*Outrider Only*)

Your draconic connection allows you to manifest the physical form of the dragon on your own body. As a bonus action, draconic wings burst from your back. You gain a fly speed equal to that of your Companion for one minute.

TIER 3 (5 POINTS, REQUIRES LEVEL 10)

Ravage (*Dragon Form Only*)

If your companion makes a Bite attack at a creature and the attack hits, you may use Ravage to force the creature to make a Strength saving throw against your Companion's Save DC. On a failure, they take the Bite damage and an additional 10d6 slashing damage as your Companion spins viciously and tears flesh from bone.

Recharge

You may use an action to funnel energy into your Companion to immediately recharge their Breath Attack.

Unleash

As an Action, you release the bond which connects you to your Dragon Companion, causing your Companion to enter a primal draconic fury. Roll a new initiative for your Companion. For one minute, the Companion operates on that initiative and may make two attacks per attack action. In addition, your Companion's attacks deal an additional weapon die of damage. For the duration, the Companion's Breath Attack recharges on a 5 or higher d6 roll. At the end of the minute, the Companion's Breath Attack may not be used again until a short or long rest, and you must make a DC 12 Animal Handling check. On a failure, the Companion becomes hostile towards you and your allies until you use an action to succeed on the Animal Handling check.

War Drake

War drakes are bred for conflict and often used on the front lines for significant battles. War drakes can be dispatched in combat or serve as mounts. They are distinctive from other drakes due to their size, musculature and large horns.

A favored mount by hobgoblins and orcs, war drakes strike fear in enemies due to their unusual size and strength. They also are found protecting the lairs of dragons. Five or more war drakes are more than enough to protect most lairs.

A war drake's primary motivation is based around its belly. They become very loyal when they are cared for. These drakes will never be found in the wild and are highly sought after, with values reflecting how specialized they have become in war and as superior guardians. When conflicts happen, their benefits increase exponentially.

Tactics

While it lacks a breath weapon, in combat, the war drake's gore and charge ability certainly make up for it.

Their primary purpose is serving as mounts for the leaders of armies, but make no mistake: this is an up-close and personal attacker that can take a hit. On their own, the drake may be considered reckless, with little planning or strategy. But, as a mount, they thrive, serving their riders with gory efficiency.

Generals utilizing war drakes know that to attack at night will give the drake an advantage, leveraging their darkvision of 60 feet and postponing an attack until an enemy can be charged effectively. When multiple war drakes are utilized, they attack from the sides as well as the frontlines.

A war drake is fierce and will lock on to a single target until it is defeated. Only when a war drake is reduced to near death will it break its focus and flee for survival.

War Drake
Large dragon, unaligned

Armor Class 18 (natural armor)
Hit Points 136 (16d10 + 48)
Speed 40 ft.

STR	DEX	CON	INT	WIS	CHA
19 (+4)	14 (+1)	18 (+3)	6 (-2)	9 (+0)	8 (-1)

Skills Perception +2
Senses darkvision 60 ft., passive Perception 12
Languages understands Draconic but can't speak it
Challenge 5 (1,800 XP)

Siege Monster. The war drake deals double damage to objects and structures.
Keen Senses. The drake has advantage on Wisdom (Perception) checks that rely on sight or smell.
Charge. If the drake moves at least 10 feet straight toward a target and then hits it with a gore attack on the same turn, the target takes an extra 9 (2d8) piercing damage. If the target is a creature, it must succeed on a DC 14 Strength saving throw or be pushed up to 10 feet away and be knocked prone.

Actions
Multiattack. The drake attacks twice, once with its bite and once with its tail, or once with gore and once with bite.
Bite. Melee Weapon Attack: +5 to hit, reach 5 ft., one target.
Hit: 8 (1d8 + 4) piercing damage.
Gore. Melee Weapon Attack: +6 to hit, reach 5 ft., one target.
Hit: 13 (2d8 + 4) piercing damage.
Tail. Melee Weapon Attack: +5 to hit, reach 5 ft., one target.
Hit: 7 (1d6 + 4) bludgeoning damage.

Drake of Displacement

Fey drakes were brought back from the Feywild to serve as guardians. Their unique defensive abilities make them a formidable obstacle for any creatures choosing to force their way past. They can be trained and are loyal if they are cared for and well fed with a steady supply of meat.

The drake's unique ability to displace light gives it the illusion of being in two places at the same time, causing confusion in its enemies and making it more difficult to attack.

Similar in appearance to normal drakes, what sets a drake of displacement apart are the unusual, curved tentacled limbs that sprout from its back. Each tentacle ends with cup-like pads that have spikes within.

These unique drakes serve masters ranging from humanoids to ancient dragons. Their ability to frustrate any would-be treasure seeker is their primary task. The drake's ability to use its repulsion breath weapon can push an enemy away from an entrance or give it space to use its tentacle attack.

Tactics

The drake's repulsion breath (when available) can provide it space to move. Skilled tacticians take advantage of the drake's tentacle reach of 10 feet. A drake of displacement will seek out the smallest, or "weakest" opponent first—and if any are isolated, even better.

If its enemies are able to hit and disrupt the displacement, it will disengage so it can move out of range until the end of its next turn. The drake's reach and ability to cause attacks to have disadvantage on it make it a more mobile threat.

Drake of Displacement (Fey Drake)

Medium dragon, unaligned

Armor Class 16 (natural armor)
Hit Points 75 (10d8 + 30)
Speed 40 ft.

STR	DEX	CON	INT	WIS	CHA
18 (+4)	12 (+1)	16 (+3)	6 (-2)	10 (+0)	8 (-1)

Skills Perception +2
Senses darkvision 60 ft., passive Perception 12
Languages understands Draconic but can't speak it
Challenge 4 (1,100 XP)

Avoidance. If the drake is subjected to an effect that allows it to make a saving throw to take half damage, it instead takes no damage if it succeeds on the saving throw and only half damage if it fails.

Displacement. The drake projects a magical illusion that makes it appear to be standing near its actual location, causing attack rolls against it to have disadvantage. If it is hit by an attack, this trait is disrupted until the end of its next turn. This trait is also disrupted while the drake is incapacitated or has a speed of 0.

Actions

Multiattack. The drake makes three attacks, one with its bite, one with its tail and one with its tentacles.

Bite. Melee Weapon Attack: +5 to hit, reach 5 ft., one target. *Hit:* 8 (1d8 + 4) piercing damage.

Tail. Melee Weapon Attack: +5 to hit, reach 5 ft., one target. *Hit:* 7 (1d6 + 4) bludgeoning damage.

Tentacle. Melee Weapon Attack: +6 to hit, reach 10 ft., one target. *Hit:* 7 (1d6 + 4) bludgeoning damage plus 3 (1d6) piercing damage.

Repulsion Breath (Recharge 5-6). The drake exhales repulsion energy in a 15-foot cone. Each creature in that area must succeed on a DC 12 Strength saving throw. On a failed save, the creature is pushed 15 feet away from the drake.

PUGGON

It is an inarguable fact that the Elves of Sinfarel are master dragon breeders. Not only have they created various dragonoids with which they can bond and ride upon, but they have also created many different breeds of dragons—including the puggon. First conceived as companions to children, these adorable creatures soon became highly sought-out status symbols in the rest of the realm.

Eventually, some puggons made their way into the world outside Sinfarel by trade and even through theft. Once loosed upon the outside world, animal breeders soon created their own versions of this unique dragon. They bred new types of puggons, many times smaller and more charming than their original counterparts. Soon, they were sold as pets to the wealthy and as lifetime companions to noble children.

Generally, wealthy females often keep puggons as pets or status symbols, for they are as exotic as they are cuddly. They are a fashionable accessory as much as they are a companion, often carried beneath an arm or in a special box with a shoulder strap.

The bearer of a puggon receives a bonus to their Charisma, as the critters are quite appealing to any who behold them. Usually when a person sets eyes upon this cute and cuddly dragon, they will have a hard time resisting the urge to pet it.

PUGGON

Small dragon, same alignment as owner

Armor Class 11 (Natural Armor)
Hit Points 5 (1d8 +1)
Speed 30 ft., fly 10 ft.

STR	DEX	CON	INT	WIS	CHA
10 (+0)	14 (+2)	12 (+1)	4 (-3)	12 (+1)	12 (+1)

Skills Perception +3
Senses passive Perception 13
Languages understands basic common but can't speak it.
Challenge 1/8 (25 XP)

Adorable. If a puggon is within 10 feet of its owner, it provides them with +2 bonus to Charisma (Persuasion) checks.
Compelled Petting. Any non-evil humanoid with an Intelligence of 5 or more that is within 20 feet of a puggon and can see it, must make a DC 13 Wisdom save or be compelled to pet it.

ACTIONS

Bite. Melee Weapon Attack: +3 to hit, one target.
Hit: 2 (1d4+ 1) piercing damage.

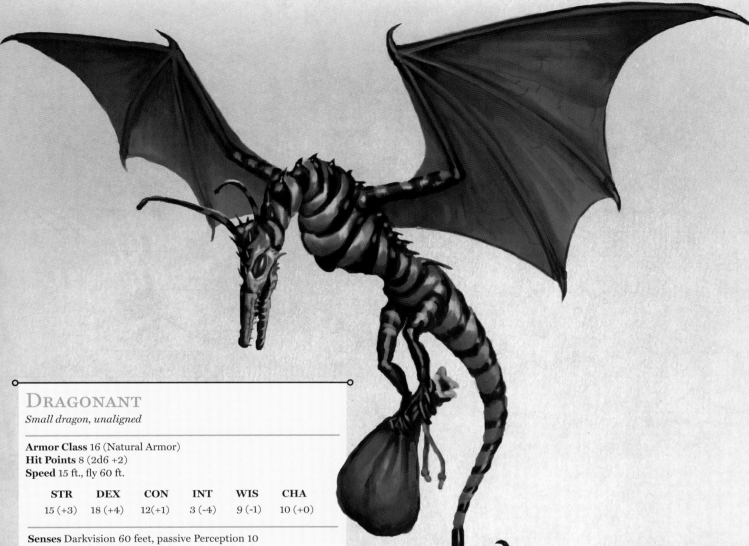

DRAGONANT
Small dragon, unaligned

Armor Class 16 (Natural Armor)
Hit Points 8 (2d6 +2)
Speed 15 ft., fly 60 ft.

STR	DEX	CON	INT	WIS	CHA
15 (+3)	18 (+4)	12(+1)	3 (-4)	9 (-1)	10 (+0)

Senses Darkvision 60 feet, passive Perception 10
Languages --
Challenge 2

Gold Sense. A dragonant can smell gold, precious metals and gems within 60 feet. Only valuables that are buried 5 feet deep or more or stored within a magical container are immune to the dragonant's Gold Sense. Once a dragonant discovers a cache of valuables, it telepathically communicates the location to other dragonants within range.

Hivemind. A dragonant communicates telepathically with others of its hive within a 10-mile radius. This is a natural ability. If a dragonant is harmed or attacked, it will summon the rest of its hive. A large swarm forms in 4d4 minutes. When a swarm manifests, it gains a breath weapon as a legendary action.

ACTIONS

The dragonant may attack once per round. Use one of the following actions:

Bite. Melee Weapon Attack: +4 to hit, reach 5 ft., one target.
Hit: 6 (1d4 + 4) piercing damage.

Claw. Melee Weapon Attack: +4 to hit, reach 5 ft., one target.
Hit: 11 (2d8 + 4) slashing damage.

Stinger. Melee Weapon Attack: +4 to hit, reach 5 ft., one creature.
Hit: 2 (1d4) piercing damage. The target must make a DC 10 Constitution saving throw, taking 7 (2d6) poison damage on a failed save or half as much damage on a successful one.

DRAGONANT

Ask any venerable dwarven miner about the pesky creatures called dragonants, or ask a town's elder, whose domicile lies in the shadows of any high, jagged mountains and you will be told the same story: the dragonant is more than a menace. It's a formidable, fearsome curse. Great care must be taken with the handling of precious metals and gemstones when there is a hive of these greedy pests nearby, for their sole purpose is the mindless hoarding of any treasures they find.

Their hand-shaped hives can be found high upon the windswept peaks of any jagged mountain chain. Every single "finger" of this hive rivals the length and breadth of a great wyrm's mighty tail. Upon closer observation, innumerous, minuscule beasts zip in and out of long mud structures that resemble the nests of wasps. Each creature carries in a single small gem or coin or any trinket of value the size and weight of an apple or smaller. They work day

Dragonant Swarm
Large dragon, unaligned

Armor Class 18 (natural armor + swarm bonus)
Hit Points 127 (15d10 + 45)
Speed fly 60 ft.

STR	DEX	CON	INT	WIS	CHA
18 (+4)	18 (+4)	17 (+3)	6 (-2)	13 (+1)	10 (+0)

Saving Throws Dex +6, Con +5, Wis +3, Cha +2
Skills Perception +5, Stealth +6
Damage Immunities acid
Senses Darkvision 120 ft., passive Perception 15
Languages --
Challenge 8 (3,900 xp)

Gold Sense. A dragonant swarm can smell gold, precious metals, and gems within 90 feet. Only valuables that are buried 5 feet deep or more or stored within a magical container are immune to the dragonant's gold sense.

Swarm. The swarm can occupy another creature's space and vice versa, and the swarm can move through any opening large enough for a small creature. The swarm can't regain hit points or gain temporary hit points. When the swarm is reduced to half its hit points, it dissipates and will not reform until 1d4 hours have passed.

Hive Power. The dragonant swarm distorts itself and moves together to form a single dragon-like shape. It is ever moving, making it difficult to target. The swarm receives bonuses to its Armor Class and stats when compared to a single drone. Unlike a single dragonant, the hivemind of the swarm can strategize, thinking as one, and respond to threats effectively—even choosing targets when using Frightful Presence.

Frightful Presence. Each creature of the swarm's choice that is within 120 feet of it and aware of it must succeed on a DC 14 Wisdom saving throw or become frightened for one minute. A creature can repeat the saving throw at the end of each of its turns, ending the effect on itself on a success. If a creature's saving throw is successful or the effect ends for it, the creature is immune to the dragonant's Frightful Presence for the next 24 hours.

Actions

Multiattack. The dragonant swarm makes three attacks: one with its bite and two with its claws, or one with its stinger and twice with its claws.

Bite. Melee Weapon Attack: +7 to hit, reach 10 ft., one target. *Hit*: 15 (2d10 + 4) piercing damage.

Claw. Melee Weapon Attack: +7 to hit, reach 5 ft., one target. *Hit*: 11 (2d6 + 4) slashing damage.

Hive Sting. Melee Weapon Attack: +7 to hit, reach 10 ft., one creature. *Hit*: 11 (2d6 + 4) piercing damage. The target must make a DC 15 Constitution saving throw, taking 24 (7d6) poison damage on a failed save, or half as much damage on a successful one.

Smother. Melee Weapon Attack: +7 to hit, reach 5 ft., medium or smaller creature. *Hit*: 11 (2d6 + 4) bludgeoning damage. On a hit, The creature is grappled by numerous dragonants (escape DC 15). Until this grapple ends, the target is restrained, blinded, and at risk of suffocating, and the dragonants can't smother another target. At the start of each of the target's turns while smothered, the target takes 15 (3d6 + 3) bludgeoning damage.

Legendary Actions

The dragonant swarm can take one legendary action, choosing from the options below. Only one legendary action option can be used at a time and only at the end of another creature's turn. The dragonant swarm regains spent legendary actions at the start of their turn.

Detect. The swarm makes a Wisdom (Perception) check.

Smother Attack. The swarm makes a smother attack.

Acid Breath (Recharge 5-6). The swarm exhales acid in a 30-foot cone. Each creature in the area must make a DC 14 Dexterity saving throw, taking 49 (11d8) acid damage on a failed save or half as much on a successful one.

or night while depositing these valuables into their nest, and when one pipe is filled to the brim, they seal it off and begin anew on filling another, endlessly, until the side of a mountain collapses from the sheer weight of their greed, or the swarm is destroyed and the valuables recovered.

Miners have often encountered them in singles or pairs, and they always warn of disturbing these sour beings. They appear to have a hive mind, no matter the distance, and they communicate with the swarm seemingly instantly. If a single dragonant is disturbed or killed while it investigates an area containing valuables, the rest of the hive will attack within minutes. While the hive is on full attack, it will leave a few soldiers behind to protect the nest. Once provoked, the dragonant swarm attacks mercilessly until the offending targets are killed. There is no reasoning with these creatures, as they run on pure instinct. Many seasoned veterans of the wilds will say to give one a single coin should you encounter it, but be gone from the area with haste, mainly when a large amount of valuables is in one place.

Sometimes, a single dragonant drone can be found in a town, searching and sniffing out prized assets. If they should sniff out anything of value that is any precious metal or gemstone, they will seek it out doggedly, determined to take it back to their nest. Once a drone encounters a larger store of valuable items (200 gp total value or higher), the drone will signal its hive. Within 1d4 hours, the town or mine becomes overrun with a whole swarm of them, numbering into the thousands. They investigate every crack and fissure, and the only real solution to keeping valuables safe is to bury them at least 5 feet beneath the ground or evacuate them from the area before the swarm's arrival. Once found, valuables are picked clean from a town or mine in a matter of hours, as they leave no corner unexplored, scouring the area for anything precious. If the group moves their valuables more than a mile away before the hive arrives, the swarm cannot find them.

TACTICS

Dragonants are not particularly bright, but their sense of self-preservation is strong, and they know they are more powerful in a swarm than they would be on their own. If encountering a situation where it feels its life is in danger, a lone dragonant would signal to others of its kind, then hide and wait for the swarm to form. Though they can bite, claw and sting potential threats (and will, if cornered) they know they're better off waiting for reinforcements. And when the swarm arrives, it's usually angry and aggressive. It can be an overwhelming force, and should be approached with caution. Because dragonants innately understand the power of strength in numbers, their strategy in a fight or flight situation is to divide and conquer—especially if the smell of riches is in the air. The swarm's breath weapon can blast an entire area, after which the gathered cloud of dragonants would swoop in to overwhelm a lone target with its Smother or Hive Sting.

The swarm would also have the collective experience required to know that some creatures possess the ability to target numerous foes at once, and as such would direct their attacks at spellcasters the moment they are revealed to the swarm. They are relentless creatures who will give everything to protect the swarm, but should it seem as though their numbers are rapidly dwindling during a combat encounter, they are also sensible enough to retreat. Should a swarm suffer losses that take its size down to a third of where it started (having taken by roughly 95 hit points) it will consider its options and work to gather the valuables it can before departing swiftly for the hive.

HAND OF THE DRAGON

ORIGINS & CREATION

Deep in the ground, where kobolds build their lairs, among their vast network of dens and caverns there are large hatcheries filled with kobold eggs. In a few of these kobold lairs lie individual chambers set aside to create more powerful kobolds. These specific hatcheries are used for breeding kobolds chosen to become members of the Hand of the Dragon, an elite infiltration team tasked with various missions on behalf of their patron.

This is the highest honor any kobold can be chosen for.

Long before they hatch, some of the eggs are separated from the general population and brought to the Hatchery of Sorting, where they are inspected by an individual known as the Overseer who, decides which eggs will be placed. Once an egg is selected for placement, it is brought into one of three other hatcheries. Each of these hatcheries has its own team who watch over, protect and maintain the general treatment of the hatchery. There is one individual among each team, bearing the title of Curator, who is responsible for infusing the eggs with powerful magic specific to their assigned roles, each of which were designated by the Overseer.

THE HATCHERIES

The first hatchery is known as the Hatchery of Scoundrels. These kobolds are infused with magic that increases their nimbleness, creating a more dexterous creature both in and out of combat. These kobolds have the ability to move through darkness without making a sound, making them excellent assassins.

The second hatchery is known as the Hatchery of Schemers. Here, kobolds are infused with magic that grants the ability to wield arcane power and use wondrous enchanted items. Their overall intellect and wisdom is enhanced as well so that their ability to retain important information; make quick, intelligent decisions; and lead missions for their patron have a higher chance of success.

The third and final hatchery is the Hatchery of

Brutality. These kobolds are infused with magic that increases their strength, endurance, combat prowess and reflexes. Once hatched and trained, their duties are to protect their team members at all costs, ensuring everyone survives and that mission routes are adequately secured. The kobolds that survive this process are hearty with muscular builds, capable of delivering or taking punches that would likely fell their uninfluenced kin.

Once these magically infused kobolds hatch, they are placed into another wing of their respective hatcheries where their training truly begins. All three hatcheries focus on combat and physical fitness. Once their training is complete, they move on to drills and routines specific to their roles. Scoundrels focus on the intricate workings of traps, locks, stealth techniques and quick, deadly combat maneuvers. Schemers focus on the manipulation of arcane, planning missions and team-leading exercises. Brutes focus on mission security, enhanced combat training with various weapons and route planning.

Once each team member has completed their rigorous programming, they are assigned teams and begin training together. They are given practice missions to complete and participate in sparring matches against other teams. Finally, when an entity known only as the Warden decides they are ready for their first mission, they graduate, enjoy a massive feast and are handed their first mission. Some ship out for duty the same night.

GM NOTE: KOBOLD ABOMINATIONS

Infusing kobolds with powerful magic does not always work out as the Curators planned; occasionally, some of them hatch as Abominations and are seen as disgusting wretches tossed aside for lesser purposes. These kobolds are generally used as frontline fodder in direct assaults or are unleashed into the taller humanoid populations to act as a diversion for Infiltrator teams or (in rare cases) for general chaotic enjoyment. Until the need arises, these cast-outs are kept in a separate Hatchery wing—the Crypt—a large, lightless cavern where they are fed by metal chutes and trap doors used to drop in whatever food is available.

TEAM MAKEUP

The Warden ensures the creation of a seamless unit with a balance of skills, typically comprising one Schemer, two Brutes and two Scoundrels. This five-member team is referred to as a Hand. A Hand never exceeds more than five members but is not limited to a specific makeup (as an example, a Hand comprising a Schemer and four Brutes is called a Fist). There is never more than one Schemer per Hand, though Schemers from separate teams occasionally compare strategies on a combined mission. The smallest strike teams allowed by the Warden is a team of three—a Schemer, Brute and Scoundrel—and is called a Probe, typically only utilized for intelligence gathering missions.

CAMPAIGN & STORY ADVICE

A Hand of the Dragon team is used to infiltrate various types of settlements; everything from small camps of bandits to sprawling urban environments. Their mission and approach to achieving it are heavily contingent on the context of the mission itself, and is at GM discretion. The team's skills cover a wide range, from assassination to arson, kidnapping or sabotage—the list is as long as your imagination.

TEAM MENTALITY

Once a Hand is tasked with a goal, they meet up to discuss their mission. The Schemer lays out the overall basic concepts of the plan as well as the direct orders given to them by their patron; the Schemer expects each team member to handle their own responsibilities. The Brute is responsible for the safety and security of the team, before, during and after the mission. The Scoundrel is accountable for any of the more covert aspects of the mission and is often the only team member that may attempt aspects of a given assignment alone.

FIGHTING TACTICS

When the Hand of the Dragon actually engages in combat, which they generally try to avoid, they work as a close quarters fighting team. Their general approach is baiting their enemy by feigning weakness so other members of the team (usually Scoundrels) can gain a tactical advantage.

SPECIFIC TEAM MEMBER DUTIES

The Brute. The enforcer of the team, the Brute brings the strength and combat prowess necessary for a small group to operate in dicey situations. The Brute is responsible for the security of the team, ensuring it can handle any dangerous encounters before, during or after their mission.

KOBOLD BRUTE

Small humanoid (kobold), lawful evil

Armor Class 17 (chain shirt, shield)
Hit Points 52 (8d6 +24)
Speed 30 ft.

STR	DEX	CON	INT	WIS	CHA
16 (+3)	16 (+3)	16 (+3)	10 (-0)	10 (+0)	8 (-1)

Skills Athletics +6, Perception +3, Stealth +6, Survival +3
Senses Darkvision 60 ft., passive Perception 13
Languages Common, Draconic, Thieves' Cant
Challenge 5 (1,800 XP)

Magic Resistance. The Brute has advantage on saving throws against spells and other magical effects.
Pack Tactics. The Brute has advantage on an attack roll against a creature if at least one of its allies is within 5 feet of the creature and the ally isn't incapacitated.
Sunlight Sensitivity. While in sunlight, the Brute has disadvantage on attack rolls, as well as on Wisdom (Perception) checks that rely on sight.

ACTIONS

Multiattack. The Brute makes two attacks: one with its mallet and one with its shield.
Hand Crossbow. Ranged Weapon Attack: +4 to hit, range 30/120 ft., one target. *Hit*: 6 (1d6 + 3) piercing damage.
Mallet of Repeated Offense (pg. 177). Melee Weapon Attack: +7 to hit, reach 5 ft., one target. *Hit*: 6 (1d6 + 4) bludgeoning damage.
Shield Bash. Melee Weapon Attack: +6 to hit, reach 5 ft., one target. *Hit*: 6 (1d6 + 3) bludgeoning damage. If the attack roll critically hits, the target must make a DC 15 Constitution saving throw or become stunned until the end of the Brute's next turn.

The Schemer. The Schemer is the leader of the group. They communicate directly or indirectly with their patron and are held accountable when things do not go as planned. The Schemer is also responsible for designing the plans, their overall tactics and anything else necessary for achieving their goals. After receiving orders, they gather the required team members and put the plan into motion. It's also possible they are too smart for their own good. Because all members of the Hand of the Dragon are bred for success in their specific field, Schemers are the only Hatchery sect that possess the sense of autonomy required to change or defy orders, leading to conflict with their patrons when they don't succeed.

KOBOLD SCHEMER

Small humanoid (kobold), lawful evil

Armor Class 12 (*mage armor* 16)
Hit Points 14 (4d6)
Speed 30 ft.

STR	DEX	CON	INT	WIS	CHA
7 (-2)	16 (+3)	10 (+0)	16 (+3)	16 (+3)	8 (-1)

Skills Arcana +6, Investigation +6, Perception +6, Stealth +6
Senses Darkvision 60 ft., passive Perception 16
Languages Common, Draconic, Thieves' Cant
Challenge 5 (1,800 XP)

Equipment. The Schemer carries the following equipment at all times: **burglar's pack, chime of opening, potion of healing, wand of secrets**

Magic Resistance. The Schemer has advantage on saving throws against spells and other magical effects.

Pack Tactics. The Schemer has advantage on an attack roll against a creature if at least one of the kobold's allies is within 5 feet of the creature and the ally isn't incapacitated.

Spellcasting. The Schemer is a 5th-level spellcaster. Its spellcasting ability is Intelligence (spell save DC 14, +6 to hit with spell attacks). The Schemer has the following wizard spells prepared:

> *Cantrips (at will):* light, friends, message, mage hand
> *1st level (4 slots):* magic missile, mage armor, detect magic, expeditious retreat
> *2nd level (3 slots):* hold person, locate object
> *3rd level (2 slots):* dispel magic, gaseous form

Sunlight Sensitivity. While in sunlight, the Schemer has disadvantage on attack rolls, as well as on Wisdom (Perception) checks that rely on sight.

ACTIONS

Dagger. Melee Weapon Attack: +6 to hit, reach 5 ft., one target. *Hit*: 1 (1d4 - 2) piercing damage.
Sling. Ranged Weapon Attack: +6 to hit, range 30/120 ft., one target. *Hit*: 5 (1d4 + 3) bludgeoning damage.

REACTIONS

Direct. The Schemer can use its reaction to give one team member another action on that team member's turn.

KOBOLD SCOUNDREL
Small humanoid (kobold), lawful evil

Armor Class 15 (studded leather)
Hit Points 22 (5d6 + 5)
Speed 30 ft.

STR	DEX	CON	INT	WIS	CHA
7 (-2)	16 (+3)	12 (+1)	16 (+3)	16 (+3)	8 (-1)

Skills Investigation +9, Perception +6, Sleight of
    Hand +6, Stealth +9
Senses Darkvision 60 ft., passive Perception 16
Languages Common, Draconic, Thieves' Cant
Challenge 5 (1,800 XP)

Cunning Action. On each of its turns, the Scoundrel can use a
bonus action to take the Dash, Disengage or Hide action.
Equipment. **potion of healing, burglar's pack, Thieves' tools,
lock picks of thievery** (pg. 177)
Magic Resistance. The Scoundrel has advantage on saving throws
against spells and other magical effects.
Pack Tactics. The Scoundrel has advantage on an attack roll
against a creature if at least one of the kobold's allies is within 5
feet of the creature and the ally isn't incapacitated.
Shroud (3/Day). The Scoundrel can call upon the shadows to
envelop him and those within a 10-foot. radius. If activated during
the day, it creates shadows as if it were dim light. If activated at
night, it is considered nonmagical darkness. Creatures shrouded
by this effect have advantage on Dexterity (stealth) checks and
Wisdom (Perception) checks made to see through the shrouded
area have disadvantage.
Sneak Attack (1/Turn). The Scoundrel deals an extra 7 (2d6)
damage when it hits a target with a weapon attack and has
advantage on the attack roll or when the target is within 5 feet of
an ally of the Scoundrel that isn't incapacitated and doesn't have
disadvantage on the attack roll.
Sunlight Sensitivity. While in sunlight, the Scoundrel has
disadvantage on attack rolls, as well as on Wisdom (Perception)
checks that rely on sight.

ACTIONS
Multiattack. The Scoundrel makes two attacks: one with its
shortsword and one with its dagger.
Shortsword. Melee Weapon Attack: +6 to hit, reach 5 ft., one
target. *Hit*: 6 (1d6 + 3) piercing damage.
Dagger. Melee Weapon Attack: +6 to hit, reach 5 ft., one target.
Hit: 5 (1d4 + 3) piercing damage.

The Scoundrel. Thief, pickpocket and general
cutthroat, this wily kobold uses their capabilities to
guide the team in and out of the area without being
noticed. The Scoundrel works with the Brute on their
points of entry and exit, ensuring everything is in place.
They are also responsible for finding and disarming
traps, opening locked doors, as well as finding hidden
compartments, entrances and more.

KOBOLD ABOMINATION

Medium aberration (kobold), lawful evil

Armor Class 14 (natural armor)
Hit Points 60 (8d8 +24)
Speed 40 ft.

STR	DEX	CON	INT	WIS	CHA
16 (+3)	12 (+1)	16 (+3)	5 (-3)	7 (-2)	5 (-3)

Saving Throws Str + 6, Con +6
Damage Resistances Bludgeoning, piercing and slashing damage from nonmagical weapons
Damage Immunities poison
Condition Immunities charmed, poisoned, exhaustion
Senses Blindsight 60 ft., passive Perception 8
Languages Common and Draconic, but cannot speak
Challenge 2 (450XP)

Charge. If the Abomination moves at least 10 feet straight forward toward a target and then hits with its headbutt attack on the same turn, the target takes an extra 7 (2d6) bludgeoning damage. If the target is a creature, it must succeed on a DC 13 Strength saving throw or be knocked prone. If the target fails its saving throw, the kobold abomination can use its bonus action to make a headbutt attack.

Pack Tactics. The Abomination has advantage on an attack roll against a creature if at least one of the kobold's allies is within 5 feet of the creature and the ally isn't incapacitated.

Sunlight Sensitivity. While in sunlight, the Abomination has disadvantage on attack rolls, as well as on Wisdom (Perception) checks that rely on sight.

ACTIONS

Multiattack. The Abomination makes two slam attacks and one headbutt.

Slam. Melee Weapon Attack: +6 to hit, reach 5 ft., one target. *Hit:* 10 (2d6 + 3) bludgeoning damage.

Headbutt. Melee Weapon Attack: +6 to hit, reach 5 ft., one target. *Hit:* 6 (1d6 +3) bludgeoning damage.

ENCOUNTER POSSIBILITIES

A strike force from the Hand of the Dragon is an elite team that should not be underestimated, and when utilized in a way that plays to their strengths, can cause all sorts of problems for adventurers who are aligned against them. Below are just a few ideas for incorporating the Hand of the Dragon into your ongoing campaign. Change any of the details to account for party composition or specifics within your campaign at GM discretion.

1d6	The party encounters...
1	...a Hand strike force (1 Schemer, 2 Scoundrels and 2 Brutes) attempting to break into a tavern well after hours. Beneath the tavern's floor is a hidden vault hiding an artifact belonging to a rival dragon cult.
2	...a Fist (1 Schemer, 4 Brutes) interfering with a merchant's wagon. The brutes have flipped the wagon on its side and are battering their way through the undercarriage where the Schemer knows the driver keeps his cache of gold.
3	...a Hand strike force (1 Schemer, 2 Scoundrels and 2 Brutes) that have been tracking the party for weeks, having been hired to infiltrate the party's camp when they are at their most vulnerable and kidnap one of them for a forced face-to-face with their patron.
4	...a pair of Abominations that has been let loose in a town nearby. A Probe (1 Schemer, 1 Scoundrel and 1 Brute) have been tasked with observing them from afar to see how many members of this town are willing to fight to protect themselves.
5	...rumors of an ailing dragon in the nearby hills. If they attempt to slay this dragon, they will find the lair is empty, part of a word-of-mouth trap set by two Hand strike forces (2 Schemers, 4 Scoundrels and 4 Brutes) on a mission to eradicate any would-be dragon slayers from the region.
6	...a Fist (1 Schemer, 4 Brutes) hunting down a rogue Schemer, currently on the run following a disagreement with her patron about the best way to topple a siege tower.

Dräken

A playable race for the 5e system.

Born With Dragon Magic

Some great dragons affect the region around them so much that many children in the womb are altered by their magic and take on characteristics of whichever dragon was near. Sometimes these regional effects linger for decades, even after a dragon is no longer present.

Random dragon-like mutations can appear in children. In some cases it's clear a child is affected when they are born, with easily identifiable eyes, horns or skin that are similar to dragons. Some children do not show any variance from their own race until they mature into adulthood. The effects are not limited to certain races; any within the affected area could be mutated by the dragon's regional magic.

Dräken Traits

The dragon's magical traits will manifest in numerous ways. No two dräkens are alike. Some show very little physical change, while others are incredibly exotic — even demonstrating amazing dragon-like abilities.

Ability Score Increase. Pick a dragon type and adjust the character's ability scores on the mutation tables below. Other dragon types and their associated Ability Score increases are at GM discretion.

CHROMATIC
Black Dragon: Str +1, Con +1, Cha +1
Blue Dragon: Str +1, Con +1
Green Dragon: Str +1, Con +1
Red Dragon: Str +2, Con +1
White Dragon: Str +1, Con +1, Int +1

METALLIC
Brass Dragon: Str +1, Con +1
Bronze Dragon: Str +1, Con +1
Copper Dragon: Str +1, Con +1
Gold Dragon: Str +1, Con +1, Cha +1
Silver Dragon: Str +1, Con +1, Cha +1

Age. A dräken can start to enter adulthood faster than a normal human, elf, orc, etc.—typically a year or two faster, as the magic that builds within begins to manifest at an increasing rate. Most live 50 percent longer than what is usual for their base race.

Alignment. Dräkens are as varied as their natural race is. Most dräkens lean towards neutral to good but depending on the alignment of the dragon that affected the region, it may have a significant impact upon the outlook of a dräken.

Size. Dräkens are usually 10–20 percent taller and more muscular than most humanoids, but it can vary, depending on the level of mutation from the dragon that affected the area.

Speed. A dräken's base speed is 30 feet.

Draconic Magic. A dräken has draconic magic flowing through their veins. Choose the powers that manifest from the mutation tables that follow. There are 4 levels of mutations, ranging from cosmetic to draconic powers.

Breath Weapon. Consult the mutation table to see if a breath weapon becomes a mutation. If so, use the table at right.

Dragon Type	Damage Type	Breath Weapon
Black Dragon	Acid	5 x 30-ft. line (Dex save)
Blue Dragon	Lightning	5 x 30-ft. line (Dex save)
Green Dragon	Poison	15-ft. cone (Con save)
Red Dragon	Fire	15-ft. cone (Dex save)
White Dragon	Cold	15-ft. cone (Dex save)
Brass Dragon	Fire	15-ft. cone (Dex save)
Bronze Dragon	Lightning	5 x 30-ft. line (Dex save)
Copper Dragon	Acid	5 x 30-ft. line (Dex save)
Gold Dragon	Fire	15-ft. cone (Dex save)
Silver Dragon	Cold	15-ft. cone (Dex save)

A dräken with a breath weapon mutation may use their breath weapon as an action. Each creature in the area must make a saving throw. The DC for the saving throw equals 8 + your Constitution modifier + your proficiency bonus. A creature takes 2d6 damage on a failed save and half as much on a successful one. Damage increases to 3d6 at 6th level, 4d6 at 11th level and 5d6 at 16th level.

After you use your breath weapon, it cannot be used again until you've completed a short or long rest.

Damage Resistances. You have resistances based on the dragon type that affected the region. This may vary, depending on the mutation.

Languages. You speak, read and write Common. You understand Draconic as you come of age, but must train to speak it and write it.

TRAITS BASED ON DRAGON TYPE

CHROMATIC DRAGONS

Black Dragon. Bad temper, cruelty, disdain for weakness, cruel, sense of entitlement. Attracted to swamplands and ruins.

Blue Dragon. Vain, easily insulted, arrogant, territorial. Attracted to desert regions and shiny gems.

Green Dragon. Tricksters, bad-tempered, aggressive, power hungry. Attracted to forests, manipulating humanoids.

Red Dragon. Exceptionally vain and arrogant, greedy, quick to rage, isolationist, competitive. Attracted to mountainous regions, plus any wealth and the documenting of it.

White Dragon. Animalistic, cruel, greedy, vicious, relying more on survival instincts, easily offended. Attracted to cold regions and ivory.

METALLIC DRAGONS

Brass Dragon. Conversational, jovial, talkative, demanding attention. Attracted to hot/dry climates and magic items that would make for a stimulating conversation.

Bronze Dragon. Observant, strategic, interested in warfare and water vessels. Attracted to coastal areas and books of military history.

Copper Dragon. Jokers, humorous, enjoy riddles, tend to be thrifty/conservative. Attracted to hilltops and metal treasures.

Gold Dragon. Majestic, wise, reserved, private. Attracted to beautiful locations such as rivers, lakes and waterfalls. Favors pearls and gemstones.

Silver Dragon. Friendly and social. Morally driven, with an emphasis on good deeds. Attracted to high mountain peaks that are secluded and the occasional abandoned citadel located high among the clouds.

DRÄKENS IN THE WORLD

Dräkens are rare. Most PCs would be meeting a dräken for the first time. While accepted in most areas of the world, their widely varying mutations and personality oftentimes give others pause. ("What 'kind' of dräken are you?") When dräkens meet new people, they are usually met with comments on their unique appearance and hesitancy about their intentions—not unlike meeting new people of any race in some respects.

Dräkens are not limited in any way when it comes to exploring the world. They are as varied as the humanoid beings who birthed them. Their connection to their draconic cousins makes them fascinating to some and an abomination to others. They are humanoid representations of the magical powers of dragons and will be treated very differently depending on where they are in the world and who they are dealing with.

DRÄKEN MUTATIONS

At 1st level, roll 1d4 to see how many mutations a dräken has. Re-roll duplicate mutations. To determine which mutation chart to use, take the number (1-4) rolled and make as many percentile rolls (1-100). On a roll of 1-50, use the Level 1 chart; 51-85, use the Level 2 chart; 86-94, use the level 3 chart; 95-100, use the level 4 chart.

Roll mutations again at 4th, 8th, 12th, 16th and 20th level.

DRÄKEN MUTATION CHART
Level 1: Cosmetic
Roll percentile (1-100)

Roll	Mutation
1	Arms: muscular and sinewy
2	Arms: extra long
3	Arms: forearms have small winglets
4	Arms: scaled forearms
5	Arms: bat wing-like skin
6	Build: always slender
7	Build: beautiful proportions
8	Build: graceful
9	Build: unusually light
10	Build: muscular
11	Digits: long
12	Digits: metallic nails
13	Digits: one more or one fewer
14	Digits: shining talons
15	Digits: colorful nails
16	Dragon-colored ears
17	Scaled ears
18	Pointed ears
19	Ears can pivot
20	No ears
21	Dragon/catlike eyes
22	Glowing eyes
23	Iridescent eyes
24	Jewel-like eyes
25	Multicolored eyes
26	Face never ages and is youthful
27	Metallic dragon-colored lips
28	Perfect facial symmetry
29	Beautiful facial features
30	Metallic facial scar
31	Hair always moves
32	Hair colored like exotic bird feathers
33	Hair is short and very fine
34	Hair is metallic-colored
35	Hands always cool to the touch
36	Hands always warm to the touch
37	Scaled hands
38	Palms have scales
39	Hands slightly blur when moved
40	No fingerprints
41	Head: aggressive features
42	Head: bald
43	Head: draconic features
44	Head: deep-set eyes
45	Head: elongated shape
46	Legs: clawed feet
47	Legs: extra long
48	Legs: chromatic dragon-colored shins
49	Legs: metallic dragon-colored shins
50	Legs: unnaturally long feet
51	Your shadow animates on its own
52	Your shadow has a tail
53	Your shadow is dark and metallic
54	Your shadow is prismatic
55	Your shadow has wings
56	Ashen-colored skin
57	Scaled skin
58	Chromatic dragon-colored skin
59	Metallic dragon-colored skin
60	Glowing skin
61	Iridescent skin
62	Shadowy skin
63	Metallic sheen skin
64	Prismatic scaled skin
65	Shimmering hue skin
66	Voice has no echo
67	Voice has a musical quality
68	Voice is unusually high
69	Voice is unusually low
70	Draconic whispers heard within 100 feet
71	Wings: leathery
72	Wings: small, decorative on back
73	Wings: light
74	Wings: large chromatic dragon-colored
75	Wings: prismatic
76	Always looks clean
77	Always well-lit
78	Androgynous
79	Breathing sounds deep
80	Clothing billows with no wind
81	Chromatic dragon-colored freckles
82	Does not sweat
83	Metallic-scented breath
84	Dragon tail

Roll	
85	Melodic laugh
86	Tears are metallic dragon-colored
87	Wind whips up when entering room
88	Smooth skin/no body hair
89	Sharp teeth
90	All birds become quiet within 50 feet
91	Dragon-related birthmark
92	Steamy breath
93	Body has metallic scent
94	Food and drink all taste sweet
95	Lucid sleeping
96	Horns
97	Footprints are dragon-like
98	Body temperature of 99 or higher
99	Roll twice, ignore result 99 or higher
100	Roll 3 times, ignore result 99 or higher

Level 2: Abilities
Roll percentile (1-100)

Roll	Mutation
1	3/long rest, as an action, you can heal 1d6 hit points.
2	As an action, use *cure wounds* 3/long rest as a spell-like ability.
3	As an action, you can cast *light* as a spell-like ability.
4	Once per day, you can drink a flask of water containing 1 gp of gold dust to heal 1d6 hit points.
5	You gain advantage on Wisdom (Survival) checks.
6	You possess taloned fingers that act as natural weapons. They deal 1d4 points of damage on a successful hit and are considered magical weapons.
7	You gain advantage on Wisdom (Insight) checks.
8	Use Charisma instead of Constitution to determine how many minutes you can hold your breath. 1 + your Charisma modifier (minimum of 30 seconds).
9	Add +2 to Strength score.
10	You may live entirely on a meat diet.
11	You do not suffer from altitude sickness.
12	Your swim speed is naturally 20 feet.
13	You have advantage on attacks on good-aligned creatures
14	As an action, you can cast *animal friendship* as a spell-like ability once per day.
15	1/long rest: If you reach 0 hit points, you may take one more round of actions before falling unconscious.
16	You have advantage on Dexterity (Acrobatics) checks.
17	3/long rest, as an action you may use *breath weapon* (pg. 145) as a spell-like ability.
18	You have advantage on saving throws against poison.
19	As an adult, you do not physically age. However, you live as long as your base race + 50 percent.
20	Add +2 to Dexterity score.
21	Any armor you wear appears as silver or gold. This illusion applies as long as you wear any armor.
22	You have advantage on any Wisdom (Insight) saving throws.
23	3/long rest, as an action, you can cast *create water* as a spell-like ability.
24	You have resistance to thunder damage.
25	You have resistance to damage from attacks of opportunity.
26	1/long rest you have a burst of speed for one minute. Your speed is doubled. You gain a +2 bonus to AC. You have advantage on Dexterity saving throws, and you gain an additional action on each of your turns. That action can be used only to take an Attack (one weapon Attack only), Dash, Disengage, Hide, or Use an Object action.
27	1/long rest you may use the spell *identify* as a spell-like ability.
28	1/long rest you may use the spell *tongues* as a spell-like ability.
29	2/long rest you have advantage on initiative rolls.
30	1/long rest you have advantage on grappling check.
31	You have advantage against enchantment spells
32	1/long rest you can cast *shield* as a spell-like ability.
33	Coins become clean and shiny if you handle them. Values increase by 10 percent.
34	1/long rest, you gain +2 to AC for one minute when you take the Dodge action.
35	1/long rest you can cast *aid* as a spell-like ability.
36	You have immunity to non-magical insect bites or stings.
37	2/long rest you gain advantage on any Charisma check.
38	1/long rest, you emanate a 10-foot healing aura as a spell-like ability. The aura lasts for one minute. While the aura is active, any creature you choose within the aura that drops to 0 hit points regains 1 hp at the start of their next turn. A creature can only benefit from this aura once.

39	You can mimic the sound of any animal.
40	Add +2 to Intelligence.
41	1/long rest any willing creature within 10 feet of you is immune to the effects of the *scrying* spell.
42	1/long rest you may grant one extra bonus action to a single friendly creature within 20 feet. This includes an offhand attack, casting a spell or a class feature.
43	You have advantage on any saves against fear effects.
44	If you are within 300 feet of a dragon in the area, you can meditate for 10 minutes to learn its name.
45	You have exceptional hearing and advantage on Wisdom (Perception) checks involving hearing.
46	Breath weapon. As an action you can use your breath weapon based on the dragon traits detailed on pg. 145.
47	You have immunity to a dragon's Frightful Presence.
48	3/long rest, as an action, you can cast *spiritual weapon* as a spell-like ability. The spell takes the shape of a small spectral dragon with sharp claws.
49	You gain advantage on Dexterity saving throws.
50	Add +2 to Wisdom.
51	1/long rest 50 gp can be turned into a wholesome meal that heals 1d4 creatures to full health. This is considered a short rest.
52	1/long rest, as an action, you can cast *comprehend languages* as a spell-like ability.
53	+2 added to Charisma.
54	You gain advantage to attacks against evil-aligned creatures.
55	1/long rest, as an action, you can cast *augury* as a spell-like ability.
56	1/long rest, as an action, you can cast *zone of truth* as a spell-like ability.
57	You gain advantage on Death saving throws.
58	Any creature that causes harm to you must roll a DC14 Constitution save, or suffer 1d4 points of acid damage.
59	Choose any ability score and increase it by 2.
60	You always know where true north is.
61	When rolling a d20, treat a 19 as a 20.
62	Regeneration. You regain 1 hit point each round. Fire or acid damage disrupts regeneration, requiring normal or magical healing. Once fully healed, the regeneration resets.
63	+3 AC bonus against any creature that has a charge attack.
64	Frightful Presence. 1/day, each creature of your choice within 20 feet and aware of you must succeed on a DC 15 Wisdom saving throw or become frightened for three rounds. A creature can repeat the saving throw at the end of each of its turns, ending the effect on itself on a success. If successful, a creature is immune to your Frightful Presence for 24 hours.
65	1/year, summon a **pseudodragon**. A telepathic bond exists as long as the pseudodragon is within 1 mile. If the pseudodragon is within 10 feet, the bonded pair share its Magic Resistance trait.
66	You gain advantage on attacks against undead.
67	If a creature is within 10 feet, you always know if they are speaking the truth or lying.
68	1/long rest, as an action, you may cast *gust of wind* as a spell-like ability.
69	1/long rest, as an action, you may cast *mass cure wounds* as a spell-like ability.
70	+2 added to Constitution.
71	3/long rest, holding 5 gp or more for 10 minutes heals 2d8 hp of damage.
72	1/long rest you are resistant to 3rd-level spells or below.
73	If your dead body is laid upon a treasure hoard or pile of gold valued at 10,000 gp or more, you are returned to life as if by the *raise dead* spell. This ability works 1d4 times in your lifetime.
74	1/long rest you may touch any willing creature to reduce their level of exhaustion down to 1.
75	You know the alignment of any creature within 10 feet.
76	1/week, as an action, you may cast *remove curse* as a spell-like ability.
77	1/year, as an action, you may cast *contact other plane* as a spell-like ability.
78	1/day, you may determine the value of any item.
79	You know the positions of the stars and can navigate anywhere without getting lost.
80	You have resistance to fire.
81	Any willing creature within 10 feet of you heals 1d6 additional Hit Points when taking a short rest.
82	1/long rest, as an action, you may cast *mending* as a spell-like ability.
83	You have advantage on all ability checks if you are within 100 feet of an evil-aligned dragon.
84	You have resistance to cold.
85	Any healing effects upon you are doubled.
86	You and friendly creatures within 10 feet of you can't be Frightened while you are conscious.
87	You gain advantage on Wisdom (Animal Handling) checks.
88	All weapon attacks are magical.

Roll	Mutation
89	You have immunity against disease.
90	You have resistance to acid.
91	1/long rest you can fly for 2d4 rounds at a speed of 40 feet.
92	3/long rest you can choose to go first on initiative.
93	1/long rest, as an action, you can cast *enlarge/reduce* as a spell-like ability.
94	1/week, as an action, you can *shapechange* as a spell-like ability.
95	You gain advantage on Charisma (Persuasion) checks.
96	3/long rest you can re-roll a 1.
97	1/long rest if you fail a saving throw, you can choose to succeed instead.
98	1/long rest you have resistance to any dragon breath weapon.
99	You cannot be surprised.
100	Roll on this table twice, ignoring rolls of 100.

Level 3: Abilities and Drawbacks
Roll a d20 (1-20)

Roll	Mutation
1	2/long rest, for 1 minute, you have advantage on attacks against good-aligned creatures. However, evil-aligned creatures have advantage against you until the end of your next turn.
2	Add +2 to Strength score. Subtract 1 from Intelligence score.
3	2/long rest, for one minute, you gain advantage on any Charisma check, but have disadvantage on all Dexterity checks.
4	2/long rest you may choose to go first on initiative, but gain 1 level of exhaustion.
5	3/long rest you have advantage on a saving throw, but take 1d6 psychic damage for each unsuccessful save.
6	1/long rest, as an action, you cast *lightning bolt* as a spell-like ability. The spell shocks you as well and you take 1d4 lighting damage.
7	3/long rest you gain advantage on a melee attack. However, a single enemy within range takes an attack of opportunity against you.
8	Any willing creature within 10 feet of you heals 2d6 additional hit points when taking a short rest. However, you take 1d6 points of necrotic damage.
9	Add +2 to Intelligence score. Subtract 1 from Charisma score.
10	You have resistance to fire, but have vulnerability to cold damage.
11	1/week you can *shapechange* as a spell-like ability. If outside, the new form attracts unwanted attention from insects, obscuring the area for 10 minutes.
12	1/long rest you can cast *haste* upon yourself as a spell-like ability. However, no other spell-like abilities can be used until you take a short rest.
13	Gain +1 to any ability score. Your skin becomes pearlescent white and you have sunlight sensitivity.
14	2/long rest you may roll an extra d6 on an attack damage roll, but reduce your maximum hp by 1d4 until you take a long rest.
15	1/long rest if you fail a saving throw, you can choose to succeed instead. The effect causes you to be stunned for 1d4 rounds.
16	1/long rest you cannot be surprised. However, you are forced to go last on initiative.
17	1/long rest any gold you spend is considered double its value, but your Wisdom score is reduced by 2 points until you take a short rest.
18	2/long rest, for one minute, you have advantage to attacks against evil-aligned creatures. However, good-aligned creatures have advantage against you until the end of your next turn.
19	You have advantage on all ability checks if you are within 100 feet of a dragon. However, the dragon becomes keenly aware of your location as if using the *scrying* spell, with the equivalent knowledge of a body part, lock of hair, bit of nail or the like.
20	Add +2 to your AC as natural armor. Choose one ability score and reduce the number by 1.

Level 4: Drawbacks
Roll a d20 (1-20)

Roll	Mutation
1	Your eyes are blighted and you have sunlight sensitivity.
2	-1 to Strength score.
3	-1 to Dexterity score.
4	-1 to Constitution score.
5	You must eat twice as much as a normal creature. Each day that passes without eating five meals will result in a level of exhaustion.
6	You extinguish any natural light source within 10 feet.
7	Any friendly creature you touch is slowed for 1d4 rounds per initiative. An affected creature's speed is halved, it takes a −2 penalty to AC and Dexterity saving throws, and it can't use reactions.
8	You are obsessed with collecting gold and valuables and have disadvantage when negotiating the price of anything of value.
9	When talking, there is a one in four chance of only speaking draconic. Roll 1d4. On roll of 1, the condition occurs and lasts one minute.
10	Dogs within 20 feet that can see you begin barking.
11	You are wracked with paranoia in a city. Any Charisma checks are at a disadvantage in towns, villages or cities.
12	When speaking to any commoner, roll a d10. If the result is a 1, the commoner must succeed on a DC 15 Wisdom saving throw or be frightened.
13	In moonlight, all ability scores under 13 are reduced to 8.
14	Spell-like abilities have a 1 in 10 chance of failure (1 on d10).
15	If you roll a 1 on any Death saving throw, you automatically die.
16	You always go last on initiative.
17	-1 Intelligence score.
18	-1 Wisdom score.
19	-1 Charisma score.
20	You have thunder susceptibility. Take 1d4 extra bludgeoning damage on every thunder-based attack against you.

DRAGON CULTS

When you've lived as long as some of the dragons in this book, you're going to attract a bit of attention. May as well turn it into something useful—like a small army that will follow your every command.

THE DISCIPLES OF DECAY

Hierarchy: Vicar of Decay, Lifeless, Degenerates

Racial Makeup: The Disciples of Decay cult worships Xavour, the Plague Bringer, and is mainly comprised of half-orcs, orcs and humans. Half-orcs account for most of the cult members, however, as Xavour was a half-orc prior to his transformation into a dragon. The belief is that since half-orcs are closer to his original form, Xavour will bestow greater favors upon those followers.

Origin Story and Organization: The Disciples of Decay initially formed shortly after Xavour's rise to prominence. When Xavour traveled the land and left a wake of desolation, certain persons were attracted to his power. These individuals sought him out and begged to follow him, and Xavour allowed their worship. Xavour is by no means a patron that actually bestows magical powers upon those who worship him. However, there is one half-orc whom he has chosen to lead this ragtag group: Ja-ah'Or. This individual is known as the Vicar of Decay, and he is the only one who has received magical assistance from Xavour. Ja-ah'Or (Ja-a-oar) was the strongest and first to offer his life up to Xavour. Ja-ah'Or uses his abilities to gather others to the cause of sacrifice, consumption and death. These are the Three Pillars of Decay, and each one symbolizes an important aspect of their beliefs.

As the cult grew, Ja-ah'Or came to require subordinates to manage its followers. To that end, he created a leadership class known as the Lifeless, upon whose members he bestowed magical abilities. Their job is to break down the cult's vast following into smaller, more manageable groups, direct day-to-day operations and oversee recruitment efforts. Those responsible for performing these tasks are known as Degenerates, the lowest in the cult and the most plentiful.

Recruitment, Mission & Goals: The Disciples of Decay seek to spread Xavour's teachings. They use the Three Pillars of Decay to guide themselves in their practices, rituals and recruitment. When the Lifeless, often followed by a company of Degenerates, travel to populated areas, they disguise who they are and speak kindly to strangers. Their one identifying mark is a tattoo of an X in a circle clutched by a dragon's claw. Though this tattoo is most often found upon a cult member's left forearm, it sometimes appears in the form of a talisman hanging around their neck.

The Disciples of Decay seek out the homeless and the outcast. They spend their time in seedy inns, rough-and-tumble taverns and dimly lit alleys corrupting the weak, infirmed and depressed, offering them a chance at power, redemption and greatness. Most of the time, these unfortunate people are used in the cult's sacrificial rituals. Some are found worthy of being accepted into the ranks of the Degenerates.

Tactics: In the more civilized areas of the world, the Disciples of Decay use scrolls of magical power to cause chaos within cities, spurring interest in their teachings. They whisper into the dreams of sleeping victims and cause nightmares. They create panic with disease, blindness and madness.

When they have caused enough desperation within a town, they enter and offer a solution to the problem they created. They accept the panicked citizens into their ranks, with most of them earmarked to be sacrificed in the name of a patron that most likely does not care.

The world is an unforgiving place. So are the Disciples of Decay. They keep a long list of enemies in their *Book of Heretics*. The cult members populate the book with the names of people they interact with during their time in "civilized" cultures. This book is used for all manner of evil purposes, from blackmail to murder.

JA-AH'OR, THE VICAR OF DECAY
Large half-orc, lawful evil

Armor Class 13 (chain shirt)
Hit Points 88 (13d8 + 30)
Speed 30 ft.

STR	DEX	CON	INT	WIS	CHA
18 (+4)	10 (+0)	16 (+3)	13 (+1)	16 (+3)	13 (+1)

Skills Intimidation +6, Medicine +8, Religion +6
Senses passive Perception 14
Languages Common, Draconic
Challenge 8 (3,900 XP)

Dark Favor. As a bonus action, Ja-ah'Or can expend a spell slot to cause his melee weapon attacks to deal an extra 10 (3d6) necrotic damage to a target on a hit. This benefit lasts until the end of the turn. If Ja-ah'Or expends a spell slot of 2nd level or higher, the extra damage increases by 1d6 for each level above 1st.

Spellcasting. Ja-ah'Or is a 13th-level spellcaster. His spellcasting ability is Wisdom (spell save DC 16, +8 to hit with spell attacks). He has the following cleric spells prepared:

Cantrips (at will): light, sacred flame, thaumaturgy
1st level (4 slots): inflict wounds, guiding bolt, sanctuary
2nd level (3 slots): lesser restoration, spiritual weapon
3rd level (3 slots): spirit guardians, vampiric touch
4th level (2 slots): blight, death ward
5th level (1 slot): cloudkill

ACTIONS
Mage's Multiattack. Ja-ah'Or can make two attacks with his Heavy Mace or make one attack and cast a spell.
Heavy Mace. Melee Weapon Attack: +9 to hit, reach 10 ft., one target. *Hit*: 8 (1d8 + 4) bludgeoning damage.

Adventure Hooks

1. A small village is experiencing a widespread onset of nightmares. Residents of all ages claim a great calamity is going to strike their town. Some have vanished in the night. The locals believe they have fled, yet none of their belongings were taken. Their homes are just empty.

2. Recently, children of a town have started to go blind. Their parents have brought them to the local priest, who heals the children, only for them to return the next day, blind again. Either these priests are innocent to the cause, or they are Disciples of Decay who have taken the place of resident priests and are waiting for the right time to strike.

3. The local taverns have started to lose their regulars. At first, some thought these folks had found another watering hole. But one day, a local huntsman was out looking for game and came upon a gruesome scene: a shrine constructed with the bloodless, dismembered bodies of the missing regulars.

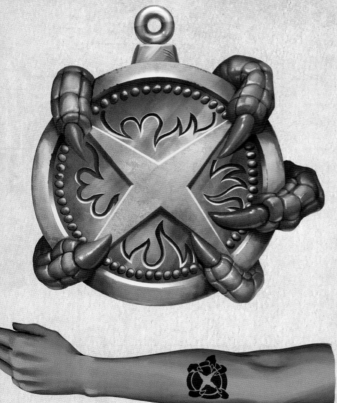

Lifeless Cult Fanatic

Medium humanoid (any race), lawful evil

Armor Class 13 (leather armor)
Hit Points 33 (6d8 + 6)
Speed 30 ft.

STR	DEX	CON	INT	WIS	CHA
11 (+0)	14 (+2)	12 (+1)	10 (+0)	13 (+1)	14 (+2)

Skills Deception +4, Persuasion +4, Religion +2
Senses passive Perception 11
Languages Common, Draconic
Challenge 2 (450 XP)

Dark Devotion. The Lifeless has advantage on saving throws against being charmed or frightened.

Sickening Death. When the Lifeless dies, its body explodes, spreading poisonous bile. Any creature within 30 feet of the Lifeless when it dies must succeed on a DC 15 Constitution saving throw or suffer 14 (4d6) poison damage.

Spellcasting. The Lifeless is a 4th-level spellcaster. Its spellcasting ability is Wisdom (spell save DC 11, +3 to hit with spell attacks). It has the following cleric spells prepared:

Cantrips (at will): light, sacred flame, thaumaturgy
1st level (4 slots): command, inflict wounds, shield of faith
2nd level (3 slots): hold person, spiritual weapon

Actions

Multiattack. The Lifeless makes two melee attacks.

Dagger. Melee or Ranged Weapon Attack: +4 to hit, reach 5 ft. or range 20/60 ft., one creature. *Hit:* 4 (1d4 + 2) piercing damage.

Degenerates

Medium humanoid (any race), any non-good alignment

Armor Class 13 (leather armor)
Hit Points 9 (2d8)
Speed 30 ft.

STR	DEX	CON	INT	WIS	CHA
18 (+4)	14 (+2)	10 (+0)	10 (+0)	11 (+0)	10 (+0)

Skills Deception +2, Religion +2
Senses passive Perception 10
Languages Common, Draconic
Challenge 1/2 (100 XP)

Dark Devotion. The Degenerate has advantage on saving throws against being charmed or frightened.

Brutal Efficiency. If the Degenerate succeeds on a melee attack, it can make two additional attacks as a bonus action.

Actions

Long Spear. Melee Weapon Attack: +7 to hit, reach 10 ft., one creature. *Hit:* 7 (1d6 + 4) piercing damage.

Long Spear. Ranged Weapon Attack: +5 to hit, 20/60 ft., one creature. *Hit:* 5 (1d6 + 2) piercing damage.

The Cult of Zuth

Hierarchy: High Priest, Diviner, Acolyte

Racial Makeup: The cult is mainly made up of humans, half-elves and a smattering of elves.

Background: These druidic worshipers revere the great dragon Zuth, honoring the beast as a living, breathing deity. The druids see in Zuth all the contradictory principles of harmony and chaos expressed in a single being.

The cult of Zuth exists to predict and document Zuth's arrivals, to give warning to those in its path and to obstruct all efforts to prevent Zuth's rampages of destruction. They are well aware of the contradictions in their stated purposes, but they are contradictions that imitate the being they worship. In their minds, Zuth is a necessary component of Nature, and Nature is a force beyond all mortal comprehension. They take this dichotomy at face value, and their convictions are firmly grounded in Zuth being an unyielding truth of the universe.

The cult has utilized the arts of astronomy and divination to predict each of Zuth's arrivals for thousands of years. Their history states that they have made all predictions of Zuth's appearances without flaw. Each time Zuth appears, they record the event with great diligence, tallying the fatalities of dragons and coldly documenting the collateral damage that results from Zuth's hunts.

Their indifference to suffering has caused many to hate the cult, driving them beyond the edges of civilization. As a result, the cult's numbers have dwindled over the centuries, from thousands to barely a hundred. It is the opinion of the cult's members that their motives are sorely misunderstood; their intentions are to help not harm, and to keep others from interfering in Zuth's necessary work. Many people reject this narrative, and some nations have outright banned the practice of worshiping Zuth. Others kill cult members on sight, seeing them as protectors of a brutal force that begets great suffering.

Regardless of the perils, cultists will often arrive months or even years before a Great Purge to warn the realm of its arrival. Some listen, but this is rare. Zuth only comes around every hundred years—and thousands of years pass between Great Purges—so Zuth's existence is usually in question by cult outsiders. Most mortal beings regard the stories of Zuth as complete fiction concocted by fanatics.

A New Vision

Recently, a charismatic human member of the cult, Erdonan Haverth, has risen up through the ranks to sit at the head of the cult. By careful and clever manipulations and assistance from a powerful magic artifact, he has charmed the members into believing that he is the personification of Zuth and that he should be worshiped as such. At first, the cult was skeptical, but Erdonan persevered in his clever deceptions, using tactics like information control (milieu control), gaslighting, mystical manipulation and various magical mind control techniques to grasp and maintain power.

Erdonan began his cult membership as an honest and devoted disciple. However, in his travels and adventures, he came across an amulet that granted him power over the minds of others. This power had a price, and that was paid in full with his sanity. An evil spirit resides within this amulet, placed there by a mad warlock long since dead. This evil spirit has transformed the once honest Erdonan into a tool for its domination of life. Erdonan himself is unaware of the changes in his personality, as they have taken place over years and years. Those immune to the forces of the evil spirit have seen this change in the once mild-mannered cult member and secretly work to usurp him.

Adventure Hooks

1. Several skeptical members of the cult approach the party and request assistance with removing Erdonan from the cult's leadership. They are quite distraught, having seen their fellow members succumb to such obvious trickery. They are definitely in the minority, however, hence their desperate plea of help to an outside group. They have gathered a meager fortune as a reward.

2. Have a zealot influence a nearby town, resulting in the cult's influence growing to the point where most are converted. As above, a small minority within the town appeals to the traveling group for help with expunging the evil influence, as lately there have been human sacrifices to bring about Zuth's next arrival. This is, in fact, a lie spread by Erdonan. The evil spirit that possesses him craves blood, misery and suffering, and so it uses Erdonan as a vessel to achieve these ends. The group may also try to thwart one of these sacrifices and find themselves amid an angry crowd and have to escape, only to find that the execution went on as scheduled as soon as they were driven away. If the group manages to kill Erdonan or remove his amulet, the townspeople will awake from their hypnotic trance in horror. Their attitude will be grateful yet mournful of a bittersweet end to their captivity. Reward the group as appropriate to their level with a moderate cache of gems, silver and gold. Once the elders of the town discover the amulet was the source of their misery, they will demand its destruction.

Erdonan, Archdruid of Zuth

Medium human, chaotic evil

Armor Class 16 (hide armor, shield)
Hit Points 93 (17d8 + 17)
Speed 30 ft.

STR	DEX	CON	INT	WIS	CHA
10 (+0)	14 (+2)	12 (+1)	12 (+1)	20 (+5)	18 (+4)

Saving Throws Int +5, Wis +9
Skills Nature +5, Perception +9, Persuasion +8
Senses passive Perception 19
Languages Common, Draconic, Druidic
Challenge 10 (5,900 XP)

Amulet of Amongar. This amulet contains the spirit of Amongar, a dark presence working to corrupt the mortal plane. Any creature wearing the amulet must succeed on a DC 30 Wisdom saving throw at the start of each dawn or must spend the day doing Amongar's bidding.

Spellcasting. Erdonan is a 13th-level spellcaster. His spellcasting ability is Wisdom (spell save DC 17, +9 to hit with spell attacks). He has the following druid spells prepared:

Cantrips (at will): *druidcraft, mending, poison spray, produce flame*
1st level (4 slots): *cure wounds, entangle, faerie fire, peak with animals*
2nd level (3 slots): *animal messenger, beast sense, hold person*
3rd level (3 slots): *conjure animals, meld into stone, water breathing*
4th level (3 slots): *dominate beast, locate creature, stoneskin, wall of fire*
5th level (3 slots): *commune with nature, mass cure wounds, tree stride*
6th level (1 slot): *heal, heroes' feast, sunbeam*
7th level (1 slot): *fire storm*

ACTIONS

Shillelagh. Melee Weapon Attack: +10 to hit, reach 5 ft., one target. *Hit*: 8 (1d6 + 5) bludgeoning damage.

Change Shape (2/Day). Erdonan magically polymorphs into a beast or elemental with a challenge rating of 6 or less and can remain in this form for up to 9 hours. Erdonan can choose whether his equipment falls to the ground, melds with his new form or is worn by the new form. Erdonan reverts to his true form if he dies or falls unconscious. Erdonan can revert to his true form using a bonus action on his turn.

While in a new form, Erdonan retains his game statistics and ability to speak, but his AC, movement modes, Strength and Dexterity are replaced by those of the new form, and he gains any special senses, proficiencies, traits, actions and reactions (except class features, legendary actions, and lair actions) that the new form has but that he lacks. He can cast his spells with verbal or somatic components in his new form.

The new form's attacks count as magical for the purpose of overcoming resistances and immunity to nonmagical attacks.

Purge Cultists

Medium humanoid (any race), chaotic neutral

Armor Class 14 (hide armor)
Hit Points 90 (12d8 + 36)
Speed 30 ft.

STR	DEX	CON	INT	WIS	CHA
11 (+0)	15 (+2)	16 (+3)	10 (+0)	20 (+5)	14 (+2)

Saving Throws Dex +5, Con +6, Wis +8
Skills Animal Handling +8 Nature +3, Perception +8
Senses passive Perception 18
Languages Common, Druidic
Challenge 4 (1,100 XP)

Beast Wardens. Any beast controlled or commanded by the Purge Cultist rolls twice the usual damage dice when rolling for damage.

Spellcasting. The purge cultist is a 7th-level spellcaster. Its spellcasting ability is Wisdom (spell save DC 14, +6 to hit with spell attacks). It has the following druid spells prepared:

Cantrips (at will): *druidcraft, produce flame, resistance, thorn whip*
1st level (4 slots): *cure wounds, faerie fire, thunderwave*
2nd level (3 slots): *beast sense, flame blade, pass without trace*
3rd level (3 slots): *conjure animals, plant growth*
4th level (1 slot): *dominate beast*

ACTIONS

Quarterstaff. Melee Weapon Attack: +3 to hit, reach 5 ft., one target. *Hit*: 3 (1d6) bludgeoning damage or 4 (1d8) bludgeoning damage if used with two hands.

Dragon Hunting

The formal practice of hunting and killing dragons specifically for resources harvested from their corpses was declared illegal more than 250 years ago. The practice was banned due to the many dangers involved with hunting dragons—the most important being the destruction hunted dragons often wrought upon society.

Towns and communities that prospered for a time, their growth spurred by the wealth trade in dragon parts could foster, faced the wrath of dragons who sought vengeance for their kin, laying waste to the cities that profited from the slaughter and harvesting of their dragonkind. Dragons took special care to destroy towns that hosted dragon hunters. So thorough was their quest for vengeance that mere rumors of a dragon hunter having passed through made a community a target.

In a rare time of solidarity, leaders across the lands made it known that dragon hunting was an offense punishable by death. All flying ships were grounded and dismantled. Harvesting dragon organs was never allowed again.

This, of course, was a problem for those who profited from hunting dragons. Many dragon hunters went underground, and their trade is only whispered of today. There is a black market for buying and selling dragon organs away from any villages or towns. Community leaders dare not take the risk of hosting dragon hunters, no matter how profitable it may be.

Dragon Hunters in Society

Most dragon hunters encountered today are considered boisterous and lower class, lacking any self-awareness or knowledge of history. Entire villages were destroyed and families wiped out as the dragons took their vengeance. Anyone claiming to have a romantic or sympathetic idea about dragon hunting is usually considered controversial. Those that claim the title of "dragon hunter" are often looked at with disgust—or at the very least, suspicion—as it is usually only associated with bringing destruction to otherwise peaceful communities.

Some dragon hunters see themselves as logical or rational business types, supplying what the market needs. Others see themselves as heroes, ridding the world of dragons and various monsters that have no regard for the lives of most humanoids. Whatever the reason, the trade of dragon-related goods remains incredibly profitable, but comes with a hefty price: It's easily the most dangerous job in the realm.

Dragon Hunting Today

Recently, a book of magic was discovered (ironically found in a long-abandoned dragon hoard) that could put the 250 years of peace with dragonkind at risk. Inside, it is rumored that there are many spells specifically designed to utilize the organs from dragons. These spells were lost to history, but have since resurfaced, as the book's contents have been copied and shared in mage's circles throughout the realm. While this spellbook and its copies are not widely available, it brings attention (many would say unwanted attention) back to dragon hunting and to the black market economy that exists around it. Whatever small market there may have been for dragon-related trophies, this discovery has since driven prices up, as the harvested organs, scales and bones are now considered a rare commodity.

Worse still for the market (though some may argue it's a positive), the effectiveness of these spells helps push back the ever-increasing rise of monstrous activity. For decades, there has been an increase in violence toward peaceful communities from nearby orc tribes, goblin hordes and various other monsters that would claim the world as their own. Whether the humans, elves, dwarves and halflings would admit it, the magic generated from using dragon-enhanced spells is actually beneficial. As such, the black market for dragon parts has grown considerably. Dragon hunters remain in demand, despite their outlaw status. Some leaders, including royalty, employ dragon hunters in off-the-books arrangements as part of their territory's arcane defense programs.

A Dwarf Remembers

Only the oldest dwarves and elves (who choose to acknowledge it) recall the times that dragon hunting was an open profession. One dwarf in particular speaks fondly of his days as the captain of a dragon hunting ship called the *Golden Talon*—a heavily armored, 20-ton airship that saw 58 documented air battles. Rynden Aethedorn was the last airship captain to struggle for air supremacy at the young (by dwarven standards) age of 65. He hasn't forgotten the thrill of the hunt or the danger it carries alongside it.

Rynden Aethedorn has been openly critical of the politics that have been in place for 200+ years. It's abundantly clear he yearns to once again do battle with the most fearsome creatures of the sky. He is as passionate as he is possessed, with a dangerous look every time he speaks—enough to penetrate any soul. It's obvious why anyone would follow him onto his ship, as his tales of conquest over deadly draconic beasts could stir even the most conservative adventurer's heart. Clearly, he knows what he's doing, despite there being a touch of madness associated with his passion and charisma.

Rynden is beyond wealthy, having obtained all his riches hunting dragons centuries ago. Yet, he is not driven by the pursuit of wealth. That is a foolish reason to him ("Only a fool chases coin"). He is driven only by the hunt and the reward of keeping the world safe —despite never receiving credit for it. He has no love for politicians that seek to vilify him for being "out of touch" and for being a fossil of a time long past. While he admires dragons (a few have left their permanent scars upon him), they are simply an objective to overcome. A means to an end. A commodity that is...necessary for progress.

If the party were to seek him out, Rynden would prove he walks the walk even as he talks by furiously pointing to any area of a map and stating with a mad look in his eye, "The world needs me. Though they won't know it until their city is overrun with orcs. They might not like it, but what I do is necessary for survival. I've seen the slow creep of filth edging our borders. You humans don't see it because your flame burns out quickly. Time is your enemy. I see it with my ancient eyes, I do. It's happening, and I'll die before we get overrun by those damned monsters. Where did the real heroes go? It's time we turn the tide again."

He would then turn to face the group with a smile, "What's the worst that will happen? Death? Hahaha! Life is the hunt. Life is the reward you get by hunting the beast in the sky. That is when you know you are alive!" If they are interested, Rynden would invite any party members to join his band of dragon hunters. He can sniff out a snitch and would know a genuine interest when it presents itself. The life of a dragon hunter is not easy by any stretch, but it could prove immensely profitable, or at least rewarding. It could also land them in prison.

BECOMING A DRAGON HUNTER

Any PC may become a dragon hunter, provided they meet the following prerequisites:

- Strength 13, Wisdom 15, Charisma 15
- No outstanding warrants or bounties

Half of all wealth obtained is dedicated to a chosen dragon hunting faction. A PC who fails to pay them is stripped of all their benefits. A PC declares themselves to a faction, and it is a well-guarded secret. At GM discretion, the practice of dragon hunting is illegal. Therefore, it is never discussed openly.

After a declaration ceremony to their faction, a PC gains the following benefits:

- Advantage on Frightful Presence saving throws.
- Advantage on Breath Weapon saving throws.
- At 10th level, a PC can choose to be resistant to one damage type: Acid, Cold, Lightning or Fire. These resistances do not stack with any other similar effects.
- At 11th level, once per long rest, a dragon hunter may cast *true strike* as a bonus action.
- Immediate attunement to **dragon tools** (pg. 177).

DRAGON HUNTING FACTIONS

All dragon hunting factions are underground operations. There are several layers of protection in place to ensure only those worthy of hiring dragon hunters can do so. Speaking openly about dragon hunting may land the party in jail, depending on what a town's history with dragons may be. As such, these factions are more likely to seek the party out rather than be discovered at random.

THE DRAGON SWORDS

The Dragon Swords is the oldest and most infamous of the dragon hunting factions. A clandestine operation, its name is spoken only in hushed tones. This faction often has members spread out into various cities, hidden in plain sight. Their well-constructed buildings rarely show activity, but they remain standing to this day. Any symbolism on the outside has been removed and replaced with city sigils and iconography. Its current leader is a dwarf named Rynden Aethedorn.

It is rumored that the Dragon Swords (members call themselves *the Swords*) have one of the last remaining dragon hunting ships in the world. If true, no one has seen it fly in hundreds of years.

THE LIGHTS OF GOLDEN TRIUMPH

Nearly forgotten, and perhaps only remaining in stories, the Lights of Golden Triumph were the last documented faction to hunt dragons openly—some would say defiantly. Their members were all arrested after continuing the practice. Most were executed as a harsh reminder of the devastation the practice of dragon hunting brought upon local villages.

Rumors suggest some members still meet in secret, but it is unclear if the faction truly functions now. In its day, they wore fine garments of black and gold with a sigil of a severed dragon claw.

THE GREEN SWORDS

The Green Swords is a spin-off and a rival faction of the Dragon Swords. Rynden Aethedorn and an elf called Bellanus Yanorin argued over how to run the faction "properly" centuries ago. This led to the creation of the Green Swords, but due to the outlawed practice of dragon hunting, this splinter group went underground, deep within the forests. It is unclear if the faction still meets or has members, but in its time, due to the skill of their crews and the wealth they created, the Green Swords were considered the greatest dragon hunting faction the world had ever known.

DRAGON PARTS ECONOMY

Everything, allegedly, has a price. Dragon parts are no different. What follows is a list of dragon organs and price associated for each dragon type, as well as how those parts can be utilized in spellcasting. Specific dragon organs are used for magic item creation, healing and rituals. Others are explicitly used for spell casting. Unique dragons that are harvested may provide more rare ingredients and their effects at GM discretion.

Determine which dragon parts will be useful after a dragon is killed. A fierce battle may render many of the parts listed below as damaged or useless. Depending on how the battle went, you may determine whether or not harvesting a particular part is more challenging.

DRAGON SIZES

A dragon's body will typically last up to three days before completely spoiling. Depending on the size of the dragon, consider how it will be transported. Field dressing a dragon body may be the best or only option.

Size	Length	Weight
Wyrmling	4-8 ft.	20-40 lb
Young	16-30 ft.	320-2000 lb
Adult	30-55 ft.	2000-20,000 lb
Ancient	55-85 ft.	20,000-160,000 lb
Great Wyrm	85-120 ft.	160,000-1,250,000 lb

UNDERSTANDING THE TABLE

Part. The useful dragon part that may be harvested.
Usage. Typical usage of the part. These may be components for magic spells, adornments for armor or improvements to arms or simply trophies for collectors.
GP Value. The typical market value of a part sold. Merchants will offer 50-75 percent of the GP Value when buying dragon parts.
DC. The difficulty level of handling or field dressing any dragon part. A creature must roll a Wisdom (Survival) check against this DC to properly handle a dragon part. Failure by 5 or more results in a damaged and useless part that has no value.
DC Fail Result. The result of a failed DC check.
Spoilage. How many days a dragon part will last before spoiling.

> • *What is a* **Draconis Fundamentum?**
> An organ found only inside dragons relating to the dragon's breath weapon, the *draconis fundamentum* is a gland that helps metabolize and transform whatever the dragon eats into fuel for its breath weapon.

Dragon Parts Economy: Wyrmling and Young

Dragon Age	Part	Usage	GP Value	DC	DC Fail Result	Spoilage
Wyrmling	Blood (10 vials)	Component	175	15	–	.5
Wyrmling	Claws (each)	Component	100	5	–	–
Wyrmling	Draconis Fundamentum	Component	1,000	20	2d10 breath weapon damage*	3
Wyrmling	Egg	–	–	–	–	–
Wyrmling	Eyes	Component	100	10	–	2
Wyrmling	Gizzard	Component	80	18	2d6 breath weapon damage*	3
Wyrmling	Heart	Component	2,000	15	–	2
Wyrmling	Horn/Bones	Component/Trophy/Armor	500	5	–	–
Wyrmling	Liver	Component	100	10	–	2
Wyrmling	Scales (each)	Component/Trophy/Armor	10	15	–	–
Wyrmling	Skull	Trophy/Armor	1,000	5	–	–
Wyrmling	Tooth	Component/Trophy	50	5	–	–
Wyrmling	Tongue	Component	50	5	–	3
Wyrmling	Wings	Component	2,000	10	–	–
Young	Blood (10 vials)	Component	200	15	–	.5
Young	Claws (each)	Component	150	5	–	–
Young	Draconis Fundamentum	Component	1,500	20	3d10 breath weapon damage*	3
Young	Egg	–	–	–	–	–
Young	Eyes	Component	150	10	–	2
Young	Gizzard	Component	100	18	3d6 breath weapon damage*	3
Young	Heart	Component	3,000	15	–	2
Young	Horn/Bones	Component/Trophy/Armor	600	5	–	–
Young	Liver	Component	200	10	–	2
Young	Scales (each)	Component/Trophy/Armor	15	15	–	–
Young	Skull	Trophy/Armor	1,500	5	–	–
Young	Tooth	Component/Trophy	75	5	–	–
Young	Tongue	Component	75	5	–	3
Young	Wings	Component	2,000	10	–	–

*Breath weapon damages are: Acid, Cold, Fire, Lightning and Poison. Damage depends on the type of dragon being harvested. Proceed with caution!

Dragon Parts Economy: Adult and Ancient

Dragon Age	Part	Usage	GP Value	DC	DC Fail Result	Spoilage
Adult	Blood (10 vials)	Component	250	15	–	.5
Adult	Claws (each)	Component	200	5	–	–
Adult	Draconis Fundamentum	Component	2,000	20	4d10 breath weapon damage*	3
Adult	Egg	Component/Trophy	10,000	20	–	–
Adult	Eyes	Component	200	10	–	2
Adult	Gizzard	Component	120	18	4d6 breath weapon damage*	3
Adult	Heart	Component	4,000	15	–	2
Adult	Horn/Bones	Component/Trophy/Armor	1,000	5	–	–
Adult	Liver	Component	500	10	–	2
Adult	Scales (each)	Component/Trophy/Armor	30	15	–	–
Adult	Skull	Trophy/Armor	2,000	5	–	–
Adult	Tooth	Component/Trophy	100	5	–	–
Adult	Tongue	Component	100	5	–	3
Adult	Wings	Component	3,000	10	–	–
Ancient	Blood (10 vials)	Component	500	15	–	.5
Ancient	Claws (each)	Component	200	5	–	–
Ancient	Draconis Fundamentum	Component	2,000	20	6d10 breath weapon damage*	3
Ancient	Egg	Component/Trophy	20,000	–	–	–
Ancient	Eyes	Component	400	10	–	2
Ancient	Gizzard	Component	240	18	6d6 breath weapon damage*	3
Ancient	Heart	Component	8,000	15	–	2
Ancient	Horn/Bones	Component/Trophy/Armor	1,500	5	–	–
Ancient	Liver	Component	700	10	–	2
Ancient	Scales (each)	Component/Trophy/Armor	50	15	–	–
Ancient	Skull	Trophy/Armor	3,000	5	–	–
Ancient	Tooth	Component/Trophy	125	5	–	–
Ancient	Tongue	Component	200	5	–	3
Ancient	Wings	Component	6,000	10	–	–

Dragon Part Weights

Part	Age	Weight
Claws	Wyrmling	30 lb
Draconis Fundamentum	Wyrmling	80 lb
Egg	Wyrmling	–
Eyes	Wyrmling	5 lb
Gizzard	Wyrmling	80 lb
Heart	Wyrmling	200 lb
Horn/Bones	Wyrmling	5-10 lb
Liver	Wyrmling	50 lb
Scales	Wyrmling	–
Skull	Wyrmling	200 lb
Tooth	Wyrmling	.5 lb
Tongue	Wyrmling	30 lb
Wings	Wyrmling	100 lb

Part	Age	Weight
Claws	Adult	80 lb
Draconis Fundamentum	Adult	150 lb
Egg	Adult	50 lb
Eyes	Adult	20 lb
Gizzard	Adult	150 lb
Heart	Adult	500 lb
Horn/Bones	Adult	20-30 lb
Liver	Adult	100 lb
Scales	Adult	–
Skull	Adult	700 lb
Tooth	Adult	1 lb
Tongue	Adult	80 lb
Wings	Adult	500 lb

Part	Age	Weight
Claws	Young	60 lb
Draconis Fundamentum	Young	125 lb
Egg	Young	–
Eyes	Young	10 lb
Gizzard	Young	125 lb
Heart	Young	400 lb
Horn/Bones	Young	10-20 lb
Liver	Young	80 lb
Scales	Young	–
Skull	Young	500 lb
Tooth	Young	1 lb
Tongue	Young	60 lb
Wings	Young	250 lb

Part	Age	Weight
Claws	Ancient	100 lb
Draconis Fundamentum	Ancient	200 lb
Egg	Ancient	50 lb
Eyes	Ancient	25 lb
Gizzard	Ancient	200 lb
Heart	Ancient	600 lb
Horn/Bones	Ancient	30-40 lb
Liver	Ancient	150 lb
Scales	Ancient	–
Skull	Ancient	800 lb
Tooth	Ancient	1 lb
Tongue	Ancient	100 lb
Wings	Ancient	1000 lb

Miscellaneous dragon part uses: Work with your players to imagine useful and creative ways to implement dragon parts into your game. Dragons are very magical creatures, so the possibilities are endless. Examples include.
• Dragon horn shards: Used for healing, adding resistances, overall general health and stamina.
• Armor upgrades using scales and bones.
• Dragon blood: Potions of Strength or Constitution, vitality, cures, etc.
• Weapon upgrades created by using portions of the *draconis fundamentum* in a forge.
• Some areas of the world may value dragon parts more than precious metals. The exchange rate may be well worth traveling to these regions.

ENHANCED SPELLS
USING DRAGON COMPONENTS

Listed below are spells that use material components. Each of them have been enhanced by the addition of parts harvested from dragons. Their magical nature can increase the potency or allow for added effects to occur.

Spell Name	Level	Material Component	Components Consumed?
Acid Arrow	2	Powdered rhubarb leaf and an adder's stomach *Black dragon horn shavings: damage increase of 1d4*	No
Aid	2	A tiny strip of white cloth *Silver dragon tooth: add an additional target*	No
Alarm	1	A tiny bell and a piece of fine silver wire *Silver dragon scales: range increase of 10 feet*	No
Animal Friendship	1	A morsel of food *Gold dragon scale: imposes disadvantage on the save*	Yes
Animal Messenger	2	A morsel of food *Brass dragon tooth: grants the beast resistance to all damage*	Yes
Animate Dead	3	Drop of blood, piece of flesh and pinch of bone dust *Piece of dragon liver: 1 additional undead*	Yes
Antimagic Field	8	Pinch of powdered iron or iron filings *Metallic dragon horn shavings: range increase of 10 feet*	Yes
Antipathy/Sympathy	8	Lump of alum soaked in vinegar for antipathy effect, or a drop of honey for the sympathy effect *3 different dragon scales: duration of 5 additional days*	No
Arcane Eye	4	A bit of bat fur *Dragon scales: range increase of 10 feet*	No
Arcane Hand	5	Eggshell and a snakeskin glove *Dragon claw: the hand gains resistance to non-magical damage*	No
Arcane Lock	2	Gold dust worth at least 25 gp *Dragon egg shell: the DC increases by 5 (15 total)*	Yes
Arcane Sword	7	Miniature platinum sword with a grip and pommel of copper and zinc, worth 250 gp *Dragon tooth: add 1d10 force damage*	No
Arcanist's Magic Aura	2	Small square of silk *Dragon tongue: the aura cannot be dispelled*	No
Astral Projection	9	One jacinth (gemstone) for each creature affected. Each must have a worth 1,000 gp. Also 1 ornately carved bar of silver worth 100 gp *4 silver dragon scales: the silvery cord is immune to damage*	Yes
Augury	2	Specially marked sticks, bones or similar tokens worth at least 25 gp *Dragon eye: one additional question*	No
Awaken	5	An agate worth at least 1,000 gp *Dragon claw: reduces casting time by 4 hours*	Yes
Bane	1	A drop of blood *Portion of a dragon heart: target one additional creature*	No
Banishment	4	An item distasteful to the target *Dragon tooth: target 1 additional creature*	No
Barkskin	2	A handful of oak bark *2 different dragon scales: target's AC is not less than 17*	No
Black Tentacles	4	A piece of tentacle from a giant octopus or a giant squid *Portion of a dragon tongue: add 1d6 bludgeoning damage*	No
Bless	1	A sprinkling of holy water *A brass dragon's eggshell: die becomes 1d6*	No

Spell Name	Level	Material Component	Components Consumed?
Clone	8	Diamond worth 1,000 gp and at least 1 cubic inch of flesh of the creature to be cloned. Vessel worth at least 2,000 gp that has a sealable lid and large enough to hold a Medium-sized creature (urn, coffin, mud-filled cyst in the ground or crystal container filled with salt water) *Dragon liver: reduces casting time by half*	No
Color Spray	1	Pinch of powder or sand that is colored red, yellow and blue *Dragon's tooth: double the total hit points rolled*	No
Commune	5	Incense and a vial of holy or unholy water *Dragon skull shard: ask an additional question*	No
Comprehend Languages	1	Pinch of soot and salt *Dragon tongue: additional target can benefit from casting*	No
Cone of Cold	5	Small crystal or glass cone *White dragon scale: additional damage die*	No
Confusion	4	3 nutshells *Dragon bone shard: save is made with disadvantage*	No
Conjure Elemental	3	Burning incense for air, soft clay for earth, sulfur and phosphorus for fire or water and sand for water *Portion of a dragon gizzard: increase challenge rating by 1*	No
Conjure Woodland Being	6	1 holly berry per creature summoned *Dragon scale: increase challege rating by 1*	Yes
Contingency	6	Statuette of yourself carved from ivory and decorated with gems worth at least 1,500 gp *Dragon eye: raises contingent spell limit to level 6*	No
Continual Flame	2	Ruby dust worth 50 gp *Red dragon claw piece (5 lbs): flame creates heat and deals 1d6 fire damage until dispelled*	Yes
Control Water	4	Drop of water and a pinch of dust *Dragon bone focus: spell doesn't require concentration*	No
Control Weather	8	Burning incense and bits of earth and wood mixed in water *Dragon skull: increases duration of spell to 24 hours*	No
Create or Destroy Water	1	Drop of water if creating water or a few grains of sand if destroying it *Portion of a dragon heart: additional 10 gallons of water*	No
Create Undead	6	1 clay pot filled with grave dirt, 1 clay pot filled with brackish water and a 150 gp black onyx stone for each corpse *Blue dragon eye: undead rise with 10 temporary hit points*	No
Creation	5	Tiny piece of matter of the same type of the item you plan to create *Green dragon scale: double the duration of item created*	No
Darkness	2	Bat fur and a drop of pitch, or piece of coal *Ancient red dragon eye: caster can see through darkness*	No
Darkvision	2	Either a pinch of dried carrot or an agate (ornamental stone) *Portion of a dragon eye: effect lasts until after a long rest*	No
Delayed Blast Fireball	7	Tiny ball of bat guano and sulfur *Red dragon scales: add additional 2d6 fire damage*	No
Detect Poison and Disease	1	A yew leaf *Dragon heart portion: doubles spell's range to 60 feet*	No
Detect Thoughts	2	A copper piece *Brass dragon skull sliver: saving throw is made at disadvantage*	No

Spell Name	Level	Material Component	Components Consumed?
Disintegrate	6	A lodestone and a pinch of dust *Portion of a draconis fundamentum:* *add additional 3d6 force damage*	No
Dispel Evil and Good	5	Holy water or powdered silver and iron *Gold dragon's tooth: the spell doesn't require concentration*	No
Divination	4	Incense and a sacrificial offering appropriate to your religion, together worth at least 25 gp *Metallic dragon scale: the event divined can fall within 14 days*	No
Dream	5	A handful of sand, a dab of ink and a writing quill plucked from a sleeping bird *Chromatic dragon scales (2): any psychic damage is doubled*	Yes
Earthquake	8	Pinch of dirt, piece of rock and lump of clay *A blue dragon's toe: the caster gains a burrow speed equal to* *their walking speed for the duration of the spell*	No
Enhance Ability	2	Fur or feather from a beast *Dragon scales: target 1 additional creature*	No
Enlarge/Reduce	2	Pinch of powdered iron *Dragon horn: range increased to 50 feet*	No
Faithful Hound	4	A tiny silver whistle, a piece of bone and a thread *Two dragon's teeth: attack deals additional 2d8 piercing damage*	No
False Life	1	Small amount of alcohol or distilled spirits *Two different dragons' scales: 10 additional temporary* *hit points*	No
Fear	3	A white feather or the heart of a hen *Portion of a dragon skull: range is a 50-foot cone*	No
Feather Fall	1	A small feather or a piece of down *Sliver of dragon wing: the caster can levitate for 2d4 rounds*	No
Feeblemind	8	Handful of clay, crystal, glass or mineral spheres *A bit of dragon brain matter: heal no longer reverses this spell*	No
Find Familiar	1	10 gp worth of charcoal, incense and herbs that must be consumed by fire in a brass brazier *The eye of a red dragon: the familiar is a* **psuedodragon**	Yes
Find the Path	6	Set of divinatory tools—such as bones, ivory sticks, cards, teeth or carved runes—worth 100 gp and an object from the location you wish to find *Dragon bone shard: path will lead you through nearby riches*	No
Fireball	3	Tiny ball of bat guano and sulfur *Red dragon scales: add additional 3d6 fire damage*	No
Fire Shield	4	A bit of phosphorous or a firefly *Red dragon and white dragon scales: additional 1d8 damage*	No
Flame Blade	2	Leaf of sumac *Portion of a red dragon liver: add additional 1d6 fire damage*	No
Flame Strike	5	Pinch of sulfur *Portion of a red dragon liver: add additional 2d6 fire damage*	No
Flaming Sphere	2	A bit of tallow (rendered form of beef or mutton fat), a pinch of brimstone and a dusting of powdered iron *Portion of a red dragon liver: add additional 1d6 fire damage*	No
Flesh to Stone	6	Pinch of lime, water and earth *A black dragon's tooth: spell can target an additional creature*	No
Floating Disk	1	A drop of mercury *Dragon bone shard: the disc can support 1,000 lbs*	No
Fly	3	A wing feather from any bird; *Portion of a dragon heart: target 1 additional creature*	No
Gate	9	Diamond worth at least 5,000 gp *Dragon skull: the spell no longer requires concentration*	No
Gentle Response	2	A pinch of salt and 1 copper piece placed on each of the corpse's eyes, which must remain for the duration *Four unique dragons' scales: the spell's duration doubles*	No

Spell Name	Level	Material Component	Components Consumed?
Gentle Response	2	A pinch of salt and 1 copper piece placed on each of the corpse's eyes, which must remain for the duration *Four unique dragons' scales: the spell's duration doubles*	No
Globe of Invulnerability	6	Glass or crystal bead that shatters when the spell ends *Piece of dragon bone: the globe extends to a 15-foot radius*	Yes
Glyph of Warding	3	Incense and powdered diamond worth at least 200 gp *Dragon tooth: the DC to discover the glyph increases by 1*	Yes
Goodberry	1	Sprig of mistletoe *2 dragon scales: add additional 1d6 berries*	No
Grease	1	Bit of pork rind or butter *Sliver of dragon liver: the square increases to 20 feet*	No
Greater Restoration	5	Diamond dust worth at least 100 gp *A dragon's eyelid: the target gains 20 temporary hit points*	Yes
Guards and Wards	6	Burning incense, a small measure of brimstone and oil, a knotted string, a small amount of blood from a dark-dwelling monstrosity and a small silver rod worth at least 10 gp *A dragon's claw: reduces casting time to 1 minute*	No
Gust of Wind	2	Legume seed *A piece of dragon's wing: extends gust to 90 feet*	No
Hallow	5	Herbs, oils and incense worth at least 1,000 gp *A pound of dragon flesh: extends area of effect to 120 feet*	Yes
Hallucinatory Terrain	4	A stone, a twig and a bit of green plant *A green dragon's eye: area of effect is a 300-foot cube*	No
Haste	3	Shaving of licorice root *Portion of a dragon heart* *Side effects removed after spell ends*	No
Heat Metal	2	Piece of iron and a flame *Red dragon scales: add additional 1d8 fire damage*	No
Heroes' Feast	6	A gem-encrusted bowl worth at least 1,000 gp *A gold dargon scale: hit point increase becomes 4d10*	Yes
Hideous Laughter	1	Tiny tarts and a feather that is waved in the air *Dragon's toenail: following a save, deals 1d10 fire damage*	No
Hold Monster	5	A small, straight piece of iron *Dragon bone fragment: target 1 additional creature*	No
Hold Person	2	A small, straight piece of iron *Dragon bone fragment: target 1 additional humanoid*	No
Holy Aura	8	A tiny reliquary worth at least 1,000 gp containing a sacred relic, such as a scrap of cloth from a saint's robe or a piece of parchment from a religious text *Dragon gizzard: aura creates a fear effect, as in the* fear *spell*	No
Hypnotic Pattern	3	A glowing stick of incense or a crystal filled with phosphorus material *A gold dragon's eye: save is made at disadvantage*	No
Ice Storm	4	A pinch of dust and a few drops of water *White dragon horn: additional 4d6 cold damage*	No
Identify	1	A pearl worth at least 100 gp and an owl feather *A dragon's tongue: ritual casting time reduced to 1 minute*	No
Illusory Script	1	A lead-based ink worth at least 10 gp *A drop of dragon's blood: requires a level 5 spell to dispel*	No
Imprisonment	9	A vellum depiction or a carved statuette in the likeness of the target and a special component that varies according to the version of the spell you choose, worth at least 500 gp per Hit Die of target *A dragon's claw: a successful save does not grant immunity*	Yes
Insect Plague	5	A few grains of sugar, some kernels of grain and a smear of fat *Dragon tooth: additional 2d10 piercing damage*	No

Spell Name	Level	Material Component	Components Consumed?
Locate Animals or Plants	2	A bit of fur from a bloodhound *A green dragon's eye: spell extends to 10 miles*	No
Locate Creature	4	A bit of fur from a bloodhound *A blue dragon's eye: spell extends to 2,000 feet*	No
Locate Object	2	A forked twig *A red dragon's eye: spell extends to 2,000 feet*	No
Longstrider	1	A pinch of dirt *Portion of dragon liver: 1 additional target*	No
Mage Armor	1	A piece of cured leather *3 different dragon scales: target's base AC becomes 16+ its Dexterity modifier*	No
Magic Circle	3	Holy water or powdered silver and iron worth at least 100 gp *A gold dragon's claw: spell radius becomes 30 feet*	Yes
Magic Jar	6	A gem, crystal, reliquary or some other ornamental container worth at least 500 gp *A black dragon heart: spell extends to monstrosities*	No
Magic Mouth	2	A small bit of honeycomb and jade dust worth at least 10 gp *One pound of dragon tongue: message can be 50 words*	Yes
Magnificent Mansion	7	A miniature portal carved from ivory, a small piece of polished marble and a tiny silver spoon, each worth at least 5 gp *A bronze dragon's scales: duration is 48 hours*	No
Major Image	3	A bit of fleece *4 scales from 4 metallic dragons: duration is 1 hour*	No
Mass Suggestion	6	A snake's tongue and either a bit of honeycomb or a drop of sweet oil *A dragon tongue: save is made at disadvantage*	No
Moonbeam	2	Several seeds of any moonseed plant and a piece of opalescent feldspar *Metallic dragon scales: additional 1d10 of radiant damage*	No
Move Earth	6	An iron blade and a small bag containing a mixture of soils: clay, loam and sand *A dragon's claw: caster gains a burrow speed of 30 feet*	No
Nondetection	3	A pinch of diamond dust worth 25 gp sprinkled over the target *Three metallic dragon's teeth: spell duration is 12 hours*	Yes
Pass Without Trace	2	Ashes from a burned leaf of mistletoe and a sprig of spruce *A portion of dragon's wing: stealth rolls have advantage*	No
Passwall	5	A pinch of sesame seeds *A Draconis Fundamentum: when the spell ends it creates a level 3* fireball *in its place*	No
Planar Binding	5	A jewel worth at least 1,000 gp *A dragon's skull: the save is made at disadvantage*	Yes
Plane Shift	7	A forked metal rod worth at least 250 gp, attuned to a particular plane of existence *A silver dragon's scale: can transport an additional 4 creatures if traveling to a different plane*	No
Polymorph	4	A caterpillar cocoon *A dragon's claw: the polymorphed creature can make a melee attack as a bonus action (2d6 slashing) damage*	No
Private Sanctum	4	A thin sheet of lead, a piece of opaque glass, a wad of cotton and powdered chrysolite *12 ounces of dragon bone dust: spell becomes permanent in half the time if cast with dragon bone dust each time*	No

Spell Name	Level	Material Component	Components Consumed?
Programmed Illusion	6	A bit of fleece and jade dust worth at least 25 gp *A dragon eye: checks to investigate are at disadvantage*	No
Project Image	7	A small replica of you made from materials worth at least 5 gp *A dragon eye: checks to investigate are at disadvantage*	No
Rope Trick	2	A powdered corn extract and a twisted loop of parchment *A dragon scale: space can hold up to 12 Medium or smaller creatures*	No
Silent Image	1	A bit of fleece *A dragon eye: checks to investigate are at disadvantage*	No
Simulacrum	7	Enough snow or ice to make a life-sized copy of the duplicated creature; hair, fingernails or other pieces of the creature's body placed inside; and powdered ruby worth 1,500 gp, sprinkled over the duplicate *A crushed dragon tooth: if damaged, duplicate regains 5 hit points per long rest*	Yes
Sleep	1	A pinch of fine sand, rose petals or a cricket *A dragon skull shard: add additional 1d8*	No
Sleet Storm	3	A pinch of dust and a few drops of water *White dragon scale: area of effect has a 60-foot radius*	No
Slow	3	A drop of molasses *A bronze dragon scale: target an additional creature*	No
Speak With Dead	3	Burning incense *A portion of dragon's tongue: ask additional question*	No
Spider Climb	2	A drop of bitumen (oil sand) and a spider *2 different chromatic dragon scales: no concentration needed*	No
Spike Growth	2	7 sharp thorns or small twigs, each sharpened to a point *A dragon's tooth: deals additional 1d4 damage*	No
Spirit Guardians	3	Holy symbol *At least 1 chromatic dragon scale for evil or 1 metallic dragon scale for good/neutral: damage increase by 2d8*	No
Stinking Cloud	3	Rotten egg or several skunk cabbage leaves *A pound of dragon flesh: radius becomes 30 feet*	No
Stone Shape	4	Soft clay, which must be worked into roughly the desired shape of the stone object *A dragon scale: can affect up to 10 feet of stone*	No
Stoneskin	4	Diamond dust worth at least 100 gp *1 chromatic dragon scale and 1 metallic dragon scale: no concentration needed*	Yes
Suggestion	2	A snake's tongue and either a bit of honeycomb or a drop of sweet oil *A portion of dragon's tongue: save is at disadvantage*	No
Sunbeam	6	Magnifying glass *Portion of a dragon heart: additional 3d8 radiant damage*	No
Sunburst	8	Fire and a piece of sunstone *A Draconis Fundamentum: spell causes a fear effect as in the fear spell*	No
Symbol	7	Mercury, phosphorus, powdered diamond and opal with a total value of at least 1,000 gp *A portion of dragon heart: moving the object the glyph is placed on does not cause the spell to fail*	Yes
Telepathic Bond	5	Pieces of eggshell from 2 different kinds of creatures *A dragon scale: target an additional four creatures*	No

Spell Name	Level	Material Component	Components Consumed?
Teleportation Circle	5	Rare chalks and inks infused with precious gems worth at least 50 gp *12 ounces of dragon bone dust: casting the spell with dragon bone every day decreases the time required to make the spell permanent by half*	Yes
Tiny Hut	3	Small crystal bead *A portion of dragon heart: radius of hut is 15 feet*	No
Tongues	3	Small clay model of a ziggurat *A dragon's tongue: the target learns draconic permanently*	No
True Polymorph	9	A drop of mercury, a dollop of gum arabic and a wisp of smoke *Portion of a dragon liver: no concentration needed*	No
True Resurrection	9	A sprinkle of holy water and diamonds with at least 25,000 gp *12 silver dragon scales: reduces diamond cost by half*	Yes
True Seeing	6	An ointment for the eyes that costs 25 gp, is made from mushroom powder, saffron and fat *Portion of a dragon eye: duration becomes 2 hours*	Yes
Unseen Servant	1	A piece of string and a bit of wood *A dragon's claw: servant can make a claw attack (2d6 slashing) as an action*	No
Wall of Fire	4	A small piece of phosphorus *Red dragon scales: add additional 3d6 fire damage*	No
Wall of Force	5	A pinch of powder made by crushing a clear gemstone *A bronze dragon tongue: panels need not be contiguous*	No
Wall of Ice	5	A small piece of quartz *White dragon scales: add additional 4d6 cold damage*	No
Wall of Stone	5	Small block of granite *Dragon bone dust: the wall's AC is 17*	No
Wall of Thorns	6	Handful of thorns *A dragon's tooth: damage types increase by 1d4*	No
Warding Bond	2	Pair of platinum rings worth at least 50 gp each. You and the target must wear them for the duration. *Dragon blood filigree: target's AC increases by 2*	No
Water Breathing	3	A short reed or piece of straw *4 black dragon scales: targets gain a swim speed of 20 feet*	No
Water Walk	3	A piece of cork *A black dragon wing sliver: duration is two hours*	No
Web	2	A bit of spider web *A vial of dragon blood: web can fill a 30-foot cube*	No
Wind Walk	6	Fire and holy water *A silver dragon scale: time to shift forms is reduced by half*	No
Wind Wall	3	A tiny fan and an exotic feather *A white dragon scale: wall deals cold damage instead of bludgeoning*	No

AERIAL COMBAT & AIRSHIP OPTIONS

I t's hard to know which came first, the dragon attacks or the dragon hunting, but it's easy to state which side of the conflict had the advantage from the outset. With their natural ability to fly (to say nothing of their incredible strength and the devastation they can conjure with a single bellowing breath), dragons always had the upper claw on creatures bound by gravity. On the rare occasion a conflict wasn't going its way, a dragon could simply take to the skies, soaring for miles with no regard for difficult terrain or territorial borders and causing general frustration for even the most skilled dragon hunters. But necessity is the mother of invention, and in this case, would-be hunters knew they'd need to find a way to pursue their quarry into the air. Arcanists and artificers attempted various means of granting flight to the flightless, but the length of a typical dragon hunt (as well as the concentration required to maintain them) made simple *fly* spells impractical, and though the sharpest minds were able to model machinery after birds of the air as well as the dragons themselves, they had a difficult time creating materials light enough to soar but still sturdy enough to withstand a dragon's breath weapon. When the breakthrough finally arrived, its inspiration was not from the air, but the sea: with the proper arcane boosts, great vessels utilized in the pursuit of gargantuan aquatic beasts could serve as floating fortresses. Within a few decades, this revelation led to the birth of an airborne armada.

Today, airships utilized for dragon hunting have as much variety in size and shape as the dragons they pursue. Some are more equipped than others, and many are centuries old, considered objects of antiquity representing a controversial past. All dragon hunting airships are outlawed worldwide, as their appearance typically provokes dragon attacks on nearby towns. Airship launches must be done in remote areas, preferably under cover of night. Dragon hunting airships manned by magic users who can disguise the ship are much more effective in their pursuit of the most dangerous prey. Airships are extremely rare and have attributes that set them apart from a standard seaworthy ship. Bound air elementals and fire elementals are sometimes used to propel the vessel and eliminate the need for giant inflated balloons that are extremely susceptible to damage from dragons or other beasts blessed with the ability to fly.

Scrolls and tomes detailing the dragon hunters' heyday cite the need for a well-rounded crew that includes warriors operating high powered ballistas and mages who can cast offensive and defensive spells or quickly repair any catastrophic damages. And of course, a fearless captain—one who knows how to rally a crew and convince them to fly directly toward certain death.

GM NOTE: BOUND ELEMENTALS
Airships utilizing a bound elemental (or several) are fast and powerful, but theses boons come at a cost. Bound elementals experience a state of limbo while being bound. They do not suffer damage or age or understand their surroundings. Their freedom is jarring. If a bound elemental is set free, it may lash out at any creature within 100 feet of it.

PILOTING THE AIRSHIP

Only a Captain has the ability to control bound elementals. Captains are attuned to the magic of the airship or its elemental engine.

Captain Maneuvers. Roll opposing Charisma checks between the Captain and elementals whenever a ship maneuver is made, such as taking off, landing, turning, increasing or decreasing speed, etc.

Fire and air elementals are -2 on Charisma checks. Ties go to the Captain. On a success, the airship obeys. On a failure, the ship continues on the previous course or will slow to a stop and hover. The ship will obey on the next successful Charisma check from the Captain. If this check fails three times in a row, the elementals may start to escape their bindings, at GM discretion.

If a Captain is knocked unconscious or dies, there will be no way to control the elementals. The ship will either continue its current course or eventually come to a stop and hover (movement 0) or, at GM discretion, begin to return to the ground.

GM NOTE: A LITTLE HELP

Any spells or magic items provided by the crew or other passengers (including the party) on the ship can help increase the Captain's Charisma roll.

TURNING

An airship must reduce speed to half its normal elemental engine speed to turn.

An airship will travel a minimum of the hull length before it can fully turn left, right, up or down. Once it has finished turning, it can resume normal speed or take the Dash action on the next round.

Example: If an airship is 100 feet long, it may turn 100 feet at a time at half speed. Once it is traveling in the desired direction, speed returns to normal on the following round.

AIRSHIP OBSTACLES

High Winds and Storms. Inclement weather can prove problematic and poses disadvantage on Captain Maneuvers. Airship speed is reduced by 15 feet.

LARGE WEAPONS

Airship Cannon (firing iron balls). *Ranged Weapon Attack:* Range 300/500 ft., one target. *Hit:* 44 (8d10) bludgeoning damage.

It takes one action to load a cannon, and one action to aim and fire.

Loading a Large Weapon. A creature must succeed on a DC 10 Strength (Athletics) check to insert an iron ball into the cannon.

Airship Ballista. *Ranged Weapon Attack:* Range 300/600 ft., one target. *Hit:* 28 (8d6) piercing damage. If the target is a creature who is Medium size or smaller, they must succeed on a DC 12 Strength saving throw or be pushed back 10 feet. An airship ballista has advantage on attack rolls against a Medium or smaller target within 100 feet.

It takes one action to load an airship ballista, and one action to aim and fire.

Loading a Large Weapon. A creature must succeed on a DC 10 Strength (Athletics) check to wind the ballista.

(Optional) Airship Ballista With Alchemist Fire.
Ranged Weapon Attack: Range 150/300 ft., one target. *Hit*: 14 (4d6) fire and bludgeoning damage. Any creature within 10 feet of the target area must make a DC 15 Dexterity saving throw or catch on fire (wooden objects automatically catch on fire). On a hit, the target takes 2 (1d4) fire damage at the start of each of its turns. A creature can end this damage by using its action to make a DC 10 Dexterity check to extinguish the flames.

The fire spreads around corners. It ignites flammable objects in the area that aren't being worn or carried. Similar to incoming fire from a standard ballista, if the target is a creature who is Medium size or smaller, they must succeed on a DC 12 Strength saving throw or be pushed back 10 feet.

An airship ballista has advantage on attack rolls against a Medium or smaller target within 100 feet.

SHIP TO SHIP ENGAGEMENT

Piercing Damage. Dragon hunting ships are resistant to piercing damage.

Cover. Any crew member on a ship being attacked has three-quarter cover. During an incoming surprise attack, the crew has half cover for the surprise round and three-quarter cover for subsequent rounds.

A target with half cover has a +2 bonus to AC and Dexterity saving throws. A target has half cover if an obstacle blocks at least half of its body.

A target with three-quarter cover has a +5 bonus to AC and Dexterity saving throws. A target has three-quarter cover if roughly three-quarters of it is covered by an obstacle.

BOARDING

Airships equipped with grappling hooks may attempt to board another airship.

Boarding. Boarding may occur following a Ram Legendary Action or 2d4 successful Captain maneuvers to position the airship within 30 feet of another airship.

A Captain must declare a Boarding once they are within 100 feet of another airship. Once the Captain has made 2d4 successful Captain's Maneuvers to position the ship alongside the ship they are hoping to board, the airship will be in the proper position to grapple. Any failure or disruption of a Captain's Maneuver will force the Captain to start over.

Grappling Hooks. Once an airship is within 30 feet of another ship, a crew member or PC may attempt to throw grappling hooks. A minimum of two hooks attached to a ship is required to attempt to board.

Throwing a grapple requires a DC 15 Strength (Athletics) check. A crew member or PC may attempt to throw a grapple once per round.

Once grappled, a ship may be pulled closer, requiring a group Strength (Athletics) check of DC 55. On a success, the ships are pulled 20 feet closer to one another.

Jumping. A crew member or PC may jump to the other ship when they are close enough. A crew member or PC can jump a distance equal to their Strength score with a 10-foot running start. As part of this leap, the creature must succeed on a DC 10 Strength (Athletics) check to clear the opposing airship's hull. Otherwise, they hit it, requiring a resolution on the following turn—a DC 10 Strength (Athletics) check to climb over the hull. On a failed save, the creature falls from the side of the ship.

If a creature clears the hull they must succeed on a DC 10 Dexterity (Acrobatics) check to land on their feet. On a failed check, the creature falls prone.

Cover. Crew members or PCs attempting to grapple or board another airship benefit from half rather than three-quarter cover.

Crew Members. Boarding another ship is a risky proposition. Each airship has a minimum crew requirement. If the boarding party's absence reduces an airship's crew below this threshold, the airship can no longer benefit from its maneuvers and will simply hover with a speed of 0. This fact holds true if a boarding party manages to incapacitate enough members of the crew of the ship they are attempting to board.

Grappled Speed. If a ship has grappled another airship, its speed is reduced to half the speed of the grappled airship. Once a ship is grappled, it may not take the Dash action until it is free of the grapple.

Removing Grapples. The crew aboard any ship that is grappled may attempt to remove the grappling hooks before (or during) a boarding attempt.

A hempen rope has AC 15 and 2 hit points and can be ripped apart with a successful DC 17 Strength (Athletics) check. Some airship captains equip their airships with magical ropes that have AC 20 and 20 hit points. These ropes regenerate 1 hit point every round as long as they have at least 1 hit point. These ropes cannot be damaged using a Strength check, and are resistant to all damage from nonmagical weapons.

PC ACTIONS ON AN AIRSHIP

Because the party is unlikely to sit back as passive passengers when danger arrives, the following guidelines are useful when determining their role (as well as their actions) aboard an airship.

• Treat PCs as Crew Members.

• When calculating movement, an airship is considered normal terrain. In high winds or dangerous storms, the surface is considered difficult terrain.

• PCs can help fill roles usually held by crew members. One PC counts as one crew member, unless the PC's background or proficiencies might offer a reason for them acting as two crew members. As an example, an individual with the Sailor background who is proficient in Navigator's Tools could serve a dual role as a ballista-firing navigator.

• A PC may follow Captain commands to pilot the ship. They must be able to understand the Captain or they will be unable to utilize the airship helm controls.

• Use a PC's Dexterity score to position the ship controls properly. A Captain must make a Charisma check against the Elementals to make a maneuver, but if the Captain is away from the airship controls, a PC may take their place instead.

The airship controls are DC 13 and must be made for each maneuver. On a failure, the ship continues on the previous course or will slow to a stop. The ship will obey on the next successful Dexterity check from the PC.

• A PC may fire a Large Weapon (airship cannon or ballista). These are treated as Ranged Weapon Attacks, using the Weapon's attack modifier. PCs roll to attack and to calculate roll damage. A Large Weapon may be used once per round.

HIGH ALTITUDES

Airships can travel at 50 feet (fire elemental) or 90 feet (air elemental), depending on the type of elementals providing thrust, suffering no ill effects of high altitude.

The crew will need to spend five days or more acclimating to the environment if the airship flies above 10,000 feet. PCs that have not acclimated to high altitudes will need to take double the amount of short rests per day for every eight hours they are subjected to high altitudes. If PCs are unable to take two short rests within eight hours, they will suffer two levels of exhaustion. A long rest removes one level of exhaustion.

BOUND ELEMENTALS

Bound elementals are summoned within a magical containment device that propels an airship. The device is generally constructed and attuned to the ship itself. An elemental is unaware of the fact that it has been summoned and doesn't know it is being used to fly an airship—only becoming fully aware after the containment device fails or is damaged. A bound elemental is not harmed while being contained, will not age, and will not require food or water to survive. Some elementals have been known to be bound for hundreds of years, depending on the quality of materials used for the containment device.

AIRSHIP REPAIR

Captains, PCs and crew members may repair an airship. In many ways, an airship can be seen as a type of creature or construct. It varies from ship to ship, but basic repairs can be done when the airship is hovering or even moving at normal speeds. Standard repairs restore 1d10 hp per day to an airship and can be completed under normal conditions. Spells that repair items, such as mending, can restore 1d6 + 2 hp at a time, even in combat.

AIRSHIP POINTS OF INTEREST

Every ship is different, but most dragon hunting airships feature the following:

• Topdeck
• Bound elemental engine
• Captain controls
• Crew quarters
• Captain quarters
• Storage
• Galley
• Latrine

FALLING

Much like sailors know they may end up in the drink while managing the duties their ship requires, any member of an airship's crew knows they could take a tumble over the side of their vessel at any time—it's a hazard of the job. Only in the case of an airship, there's no water to catch their fall (well, there could be, but it's usually a long way down). A creature falls roughly 500 feet per round, at GM discretion. If contacting a surface without intervention, a creature takes 1d6 bludgeoning damage for every 10 feet it falls, to a maximum of 20d6. The creature lands prone, unless it avoids taking damage from the fall.

CREATING CAPTAINS AND AIRSHIPS

Much like crafting a custom monster or NPC for your adventures, the abilities and personalities of a dragon hunting captain and the capabilities of the ship at their command are entirely at your discretion. As you seek to build a memorable NPC and their ship, consider the following:

Motivation. Given that dragon hunting is both illegal and highly dangerous, why does your captain engage in it? Perhaps they are driven by coin, or the thrill of the hunt. Or maybe they are bent on revenge, barely able to rest as they doggedly pursue the ancient winged creature that still haunts their dreams. Whatever their reasons for pursuing dragon hunting as a livelihood, every captain has at least one. Determining what it is is the fastest way to establish who they are.

Personality. Once you know your captain's motivation, think about how it might affect or inform their personality. Do they embrace the inherent danger of their profession with gallows humor or does the fact that death could come at any moment imbue them with a bit more solemnity? If they are in it for the coin, perhaps they strut around in the finest trappings or maybe they are saving every copper they can in order to pay off an enormous debt. Because dragon hunting airships require crews of varying sizes, most captains carry themselves with a fair amount of charisma, but they are also generally intelligent and skilled enough with martial weaponry to protect themselves in a scrap. Not every captain is ruthless, but some are legendarily so. Not every captain insists on skinning a felled dragon with their own hands, but some do. Not every captain knows their own weakness, but most have a few—some hide them better than others. Regardless of their differences, every dragon hunting captain has one thing in common: a love for their ship.

Special Features. Like other humanoid NPCs, a captain may have special abilities or arcane skills. Some have acquired the most advanced airships money can buy while others have struggled to gather a modest crew. Your captain's station, wealth and personality should be reflected in the ship and crew they command.

SAMPLE CAPTAIN: GARTH MONTANA

GARTH MONTANA

Small halfling, chaotic good

Armor Class 17 (magical blue dragon leather coat)
Hit Points 144 (17d10 + 51)
Speed 30 ft.

STR	DEX	CON	INT	WIS	CHA
14 (+2)	14 (+2)	17 (+3)	18 (+4)	16 (+3)	20 (+5)

Saving Throws Str +7, Con +8
Skills Acrobatics +7, Animal Handling +8, Perception +8, Persuasion +10, Sleight of Hand +7
Resistances fire
Senses passive Perception 18
Languages Common, Draconic, Halfling, Elvish
Challenge 16 (15,000 XP)

Brave. Garth has advantage on saving throws against being frightened.
Breath Weapon Absorption (2/Long Rest). If Garth fails a saving throw against a dragon's breath weapon, he can absorb half the damage and store it to be unleashed with his next melee attack.

Magic Resistance. Garth has advantage on saving throws against spells and other magical effects.
Parry. Garth adds 2 to his AC against one melee attack that would hit him. To do so, the captain must see the attacker and be wielding a melee weapon.
Lucky. Garth can reroll any 1 rolled on a D20, but must use the result of the second roll.
Blue Dragon Coat. Magical leather coat. Provides base AC of 17.
Ring of Dragon Armor (blue). This ring provides Garth with damage reduction of 10 on any lightning breath weapon attack.
Ring of Flying. Garth can use this ring to cast *fly* on himself three times per long rest.

ACTIONS

Multiattack. Garth makes two melee attacks or uses Motivational Speech.
Longsword. Melee Weapon Attack: +7 to hit, reach 5 ft., one target. *Hit:* 6 (1d8 + 2) slashing damage or 7 (1d10 + 2) slashing damage if used with two hands.
Heavy Crossbow. Ranged Weapon Attack: +7 to hit, range 100/400 ft., one target. *Hit:* 7 (1d10 + 2) piercing damage.
Motivational Speech. Garth gives a rousing speech that imbues any creature of his choice that can hear him with the resolve to get the job done. Affected creatures gain advantage on their next attack roll or saving throw and gain 1d10 + 5 temporary hit points.

SAMPLE AIRSHIP: *The Golden Talon*

THE GOLDEN TALON, DRAGON HUNTING AIRSHIP

Gargantuan Vehicle (120 ft. by 30 ft.)

Creature Capacity 8 crew minimum, 16 maximum
Travel Pace 12 miles per hour (230 miles per day)

STR	DEX	CON	INT	WIS	CHA
24 (+7)	14 (+2)	20 (+5)	0 (+0)	0 (+0)	0 (+0)

Damage Immunities poison, psychic
Condition Immunities blinded, charmed, deafened, exhaustion, frightened, incapacitated, paralyzed, petrified, poisoned, prone, stunned, unconscious

Legendary Resistance (1/Day). If the Captain of the airship fails a saving throw, they may choose to succeed instead.
Magic Weapons. The airship's weapon attacks are magical.
Ship Damage Resistance. The ship has immunity to all damage equal to or less than 20 hit points.

ACTIONS

Multiattack. On its turn, the airship can take three actions. The airship acts on initiative count 20. The airship can make two ranged attacks with its Airship Ballistas. These may be fired by the crew or by PCs.
Crew. The airship crew takes their own actions. These are PC actions and not airship actions.
Move. The airship makes a maneuver. Requires a Captain Maneuver.

HULL

Armor Class 16
Hit Points 500 (damage threshold 20)
Carrying Capacity 68,000 lb
Ram Yes

CONTROL: HELM

Armor Class 18
Hit Points 75 (damage threshold 20)
The helm is where the captain uses Captain Maneuvers. If the helm is reduced to 0 hit points, all Captain Maneuvers are made at disadvantage until it is repaired.

MOVEMENT: ELEMENTAL ENGINE (2)

Armor Class 18
Hit Points 100 each (damage threshold 20); If reduced to 0 hit points, the elemental containment is lost, and the elemental will attack the nearest target within 100 feet. If both engines are reduced to 0 hit points, the ship speed is reduced to 0 and it begins to fall. If one engine is reduced to 0, speed is halved until it is repaired.
Heavy or medium load A medium to heavy load is considered half or more of the Carrying Capacity (Hull) weight (speed 45 with a heavy or medium load).
Locomotion (air) elemental power, speed 90 ft. Normal speed (Travel Pace) can be sustained indefinitely.

A ship can Dash and increase speed by using one of its three actions. A ship must be at normal speed to maneuver.
The airship can Dash in a straight line and up to five rounds before suffering one level of exhaustion. The airship will slow to 0 and hover once exhaustion reaches level 5. The airship may return to normal speed after finishing a short rest.

WEAPONS: AIRSHIP BALLISTAS (3)

Armor Class 15
Hit Points 50 each (damage threshold 20)
Airship Ballista. *Ranged Weapon Attack:* Range 300/600 ft., one target. *Hit*: 28 (8d6) piercing damage. If the target is a creature of Medium size or smaller, it must succeed on a DC 12 Strength saving throw or be pushed back 10 feet. An airship ballista has advantage on attack rolls against a Medium or smaller target within 100 feet.

LEGENDARY ACTIONS

Due to the highly magical nature of the airship, it provides two legendary actions, choosing from the options below. Only one legendary action option can be used at a time and only at the end of another creature's turn. The airship regains spent actions at the end of its turn.
Ram (Recharge 5-6). The airship may ram another airship or creature. The airship must be traveling in a straight line for 120 feet or more prior to attacking. The ship or creature takes 70 (12d10 + 10) bludgeoning damage on a successful ram hit. Any creatures that are not secured aboard the rammed ship must make a successful dexterity check or be knocked prone.
Detect. The Captain of the airship may make a Wisdom (Perception) check.
Airship Ballista. A crew member or PC can make an Airship Ballista attack.

Magic Items

Draconic Items

Artifacts and weaponry can be influenced by the components utilized in their creation, and items crafted from dragon parts are no exception—in fact, they are often exceptional. The skill required to work with components harvested from dragons is such that it's almost guaranteed the end result will be one of high quality, as master craftsmen spend years refining their skills before attempting to work with such rare ingredients. These items are fine examples of the form, and should inspire you to incorporate pieces of draconic origin into your own custom creations.

CLOAK OF THE DRAGON

Wondrous item, very rare (requires attunement)

While wearing this cloak, you reduce the damage of any dragon's breath weapon attack by 10 hit points each time you are hit. If you are reduced to 0 hit points by a dragon's breath weapon attack, you immediately are brought to 1 hit point instead. This ability can only be used once per long rest. In addition to these features, you gain a +1 bonus to AC and all saving throws as long as you are wearing this cloak.

DEATH SHROUD

Robe, very rare (requires attunement)

This deep black hooded robe is tattered and worn and generally resembles an ordinary traveler's robe except for the small wisps of shadow which emanate from its edges during the night.

While attuned and wearing this robe, you have resistance to necrotic damage. Additionally, when you make a saving throw to avoid necrotic damage, you may expend a Hit Die and add the number rolled to your saving throw. You must decide to roll the Hit Die before you roll your saving throw. You may do this a number of times equal to your current usable Hit Dice.

DRAGON STAFF

Staff, very rare (requires attunement by a spellcaster)

This ornate staff features a floating dragon head with its mouth open at the top. The head rotates to position a breath weapon attack. The staff has three charges. Expending a charge releases one of five breath weapon type, caster's choice. The type of save and the spread of the weapon is determined by its type, detailed below. Expended charges reset following a long rest.

Acid. 45-foot line, 5 feet wide. DC 17 Dexterity saving throw for half damage.
Cold. 45-foot cone. DC 17 Dexterity saving throw for half damage.
Fire. 45-foot cone. DC 17 Dexterity saving throw for half damage.
Lightning. 60-foot line, 5 feet wide. DC 17 Dexterity save for half damage.
Poison. 45-foot cone. DC 17 Constitution saving throw for half damage.

DRAGON TOOLS

Tools, rare (requires proficiency in Survival)

These tools are specifically designed to field dress a dragon. Using these after a dragon is hunted and killed provides the user advantage on all Wisdom (Survival) skill checks made to dress and portion the dragon.

Included as a set are the following:
bailer, blubber fork, blubber pike, boarding knife, bone saw, bone spade, butcher's glaive, carving blade, cutting spade, fire pike, gaff, head spade, hide hooks, mincing knife, skimmer, skinning knife, skinning pole, stirring pole.

In total, the tools weigh 100 pounds.

LOCK PICKS OF THIEVERY

Tools, rare (requires attunement by someone proficient in Sleight of Hand)

These dull gray iron tools look old and worn to the untrained eye. However, upon further examination through magical means, it is discovered that there are magical properties imbued upon them, as they were crafted using a bit of dragon bone.

These lock picks have six charges. While holding them, you can use an action to expend one charge to gain advantage on a Dexterity (Sleight of Hand) check when attempting to pick a lock.

The lock picks regain 1d4 expended charges daily at dawn. If you expend the lock pick's last charge the magic fades from the lock picks and they become a mundane set of tools.

MALLET OF REPEATED OFFENSE

Mace, rare (requires attunement)

This simple mallet crafted from a dragon's tooth has various holes and knots throughout its haft and head, resembling a broken tree branch.

You gain a +1 bonus to attack and damage rolls made with this mallet. When you roll a 15 or higher on your attack roll with this weapon, you automatically make another attack roll at disadvantage.

MORNINGSTAR OF MALADY

Morningstar, artifact (requires attunement and proficiency with Martial Melee Weapons)

This weapon is made of one solid piece of black metal studded with dark bronze material on the head, lacquered in the blood of a felled bronze dragon. It was originally wielded by the chief elder of Xavour's tribe. After his return, he slew the elder, took his weapon and began his rampage of destruction. Once his village was decimated, he began venturing out into the surrounding regions to seek revenge on others.

Every life he took left a piece of their soul inside the weapon, corrupting it, and eventually the morningstar transformed into a perverted form of its original purpose. The golden weapon that used to be a holy relic of his tribe became the twisted, abyssal weapon it now is. Fully transformed into a weapon of destruction, its powers cause flesh and bone to rot upon contact, making his victims more vulnerable to his attacks.

Rumors of the weapon's original powers are unknown, but there is some speculation that if it causes this much destruction, maybe it could be cleansed and brought back to its original nature—and be turned into a weapon for good.

You gain a +3 bonus to attack and damage rolls made with this magic weapon, plus 10 (3d6) poison damage. It scores a critical hit on a roll of 19 or 20.

While attuned to this artifact, and you attack a creature with this weapon and deal damage, the creature must make a DC 18 Constitution saving throw. On a failure, the target's flesh begins to wither and rot. The target becomes vulnerable to bludgeoning damage and is afflicted with the *contagion* spell.

Random Properties

A weapon of true chaos, the Morningstar of Malady has the following random properties, which reset any time a creature attunes to it:

- 2 minor beneficial properties
- 1 major beneficial property
- 2 minor detrimental properties
- 1 major detrimental property

MINOR BENEFICIAL PROPERTIES

01-20	While attuned to this artifact, you have resistance to cold damage.
21-30	While attuned to this artifact, you have resistance to necrotic damage.
31-40	While attuned to this artifact, you can use an action to cast the *bane* spell.
41-50	While attuned to this artifact, you have resistance to poison damage.
51-60	While attuned to this artifact, you gain proficiency with the Deception skill. If you already have it, you gain expertise in it.
61-70	While attuned to this artifact, you cannot be frightened.
71-80	While attuned to this artifact, you gain the ability to cast *disguise self* once per long rest.
81-90	While attuned to this artifact, you cannot be charmed.
91-100	While attuned to this artifact, you gain a +1 bonus to Armor Class.

MAJOR BENEFICIAL PROPERTIES

01-20	While attuned to this artifact, one of your ability scores increases by 1, to a maximum of 25.
21-30	While attuned to this artifact, your walking speed increases by 10 feet.
31-40	While attuned to this artifact, you gain advantage on saving throws against poison.
41-50	While attuned to this artifact, you can't be blinded.
51-60	While attuned to this artifact, you can use an action to cast the *rot** spell.
61-70	While attuned to this artifact, you gain an additional 3d10 + 10 hit points to your maximum.
71-80	While attuned to this artifact, you have advantage on Constitution saving throws.
81-90	While attuned to this artifact, you gain darkvision out to 60 feet. If you already have darkvision, your vision extends to 90 feet.
91-100	Roll twice. You cannot gain the same benefit twice.

MINOR DETRIMENTAL PROPERTIES

01-20	While attuned to this artifact, every time you take a long rest, all plant and animal life within 10 feet of you begins to wither and rot. This effect lasts for 1d6 + 2 days.
21-30	While attuned to this artifact, your skin turns pale and scaly. This effect lasts until you are no longer attuned, then fades after 1d6 + 4 days.
31-40	While attuned to this artifact, a slight odor of death follows you. This effect lasts for 1d8 + 2 days.
41-50	While attuned to this artifact, your eyes turn a milky white with yellow pupils. This effect lasts until you are no longer attuned, then fades after 1d10 + 2 days.
51-60	While attuned to this artifact, your fingernails grow long black and become razor sharp. They cause 1 point of damage to any creature you "accidentally" strike with them. This effect lasts until you are no longer attuned, then fades after 1d4 + 2 days.
61-70	While attuned to this artifact, you gain another flaw determined by the GM, which is amplified, and can emerge during play at any time. This effect is permanent.
71-80	When you first attune to the artifact, you gain one of the following phobias for one month, determined by the GM: Ablutophobia, Agliophobia, Batophobia, Chionophobia, Decidophobia, Eosophobia. This effect lasts until you are no longer attuned, then fades after 2d10 + 5 days.
81-90	When you first attune to this weapon, the magical nature of the weapon drains you. Your Strength ability score decreases by 2 for 1d4 days. You also gain one level of exhaustion for 1d6 days.
91-100	Roll again, and that effect becomes permanent.

MAJOR DETRIMENTAL PROPERTIES

01-20	While attuned to this artifact, you have disadvantage on Charisma (Persuasion) checks.
21-30	While attuned to this artifact, you become paranoid by anyone who asks you more than two questions and become instantly hostile toward them.
31-40	While attuned to this artifact, your paranoia increases and you become hostile toward anyone who seems untrustworthy toward you or your allies. To determine this, make a Wisdom (Insight) check with disadvantage. On a failure, the target's intentions seem untrustworthy.
41-50	When you attune to this artifact, you take 33 (6d10) necrotic damage.
51-60	While attuned to this artifact, you attract creatures with evil or malicious intentions. For example, criminals, demons, devils, etc. They seek you out for assistance with their evil plans. The type and intention of this creature is to be determined by the GM at any time during play.
61-70	When you first attune to this artifact, you age for 2d10 + 10 years.
71-80	When you first attune to this artifact, you gain an evil familiar with a CR equal to your Charisma modifier. The familiar is determined by the DM.
81-90	While attuned to this artifact, and you reduce a creature to 0 hit points, there is a 15 percent chance (roll percentage) you become attracted to the smell of flesh and begin eating the flesh of your victim even if you are in the middle of combat.
91-100	Once attuned to this artifact, you attract the attention of a powerful god, who will send a planetar to claim it from you. The arrival of this angel of reckoning is at GM discretion.

GM NOTE: CUSTOM SPELL

*Rot
7th-level necromancy
Range 30 ft.
Components V, S, C (1 piece of dried flesh, vial of fresh blood)
Duration 1 minute
Your spell inflicts a wave of necrotic destruction upon your target, cursing them and causing their flesh to rot. The creature must make a Constitution saving throw. On a failed save, the target is cursed and takes 3d8 necrotic damage, causing the target's flesh to rot and become vulnerable. On successful saving throw, the target takes half damage and is not cursed.

A cursed creature must make a Constitution saving throw at the end of each of its turns. If it successfully saves against the spell, the curse ends. Each time it fails, it takes 3d8 necrotic damage and becomes vulnerable to fire, cold, piercing, bludgeoning and slashing weapons. This spell has no effect on undead or constructs.

NECKLACE OF FEARLESSNESS

Wondrous item, rare (requires attunement)

This necklace grants the wearer protection from a dragon's Frightful Presence. While wearing the necklace, they are immune to the effect. The necklace also grants advantage to saves against a dragon's fearful presence to anyone within 5 feet of the creature attuned to this necklace.

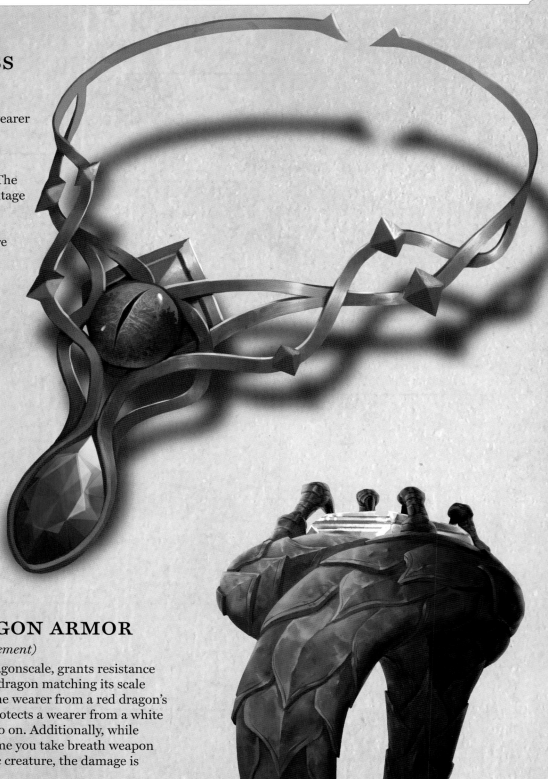

RING OF DRAGON ARMOR

Ring, rare (requires attunement)

This ring, crafted from dragonscale, grants resistance to the breath weapon of a dragon matching its scale type. A red ring protects the wearer from a red dragon's fire breath, a white ring protects a wearer from a white dragon's cold breath and so on. Additionally, while attuned to the ring, any time you take breath weapon damage from any draconic creature, the damage is reduced by 10.

TAPESTRIES OF PRESERVATION

Wondrous item, rare

These tapestries are usually found as a set of four, combining to create a single tableau. Each tapestry is 4 feet wide, 6 feet tall and weighs 4 pounds. The artwork on the tapestry is usually dragon-related, depicting epic battles and sometimes ancient airships. When the tapestries are hung and activated, they fill the room with preservation magic.

While the magic of the tapestries is activated, the room stays at a consistent temperature that is comfortable to most living creatures. They produce a radiance that can bathe a 40 x 40 foot room in daylight. Food, drink and dead creatures will not spoil provided they remain in the light emitted by these tapestries.

ONE-SHOT ADVENTURES

A SERIES OF SINGLE-SESSION
SHOWDOWNS WITH SOME OF THE
MOST ENGAGING DRAGONS IN THE
REALM. DOES YOUR PARTY HAVE
WHAT IT TAKES TO SURVIVE?

HOLD MY BEER

AFTER THE PARTY ENCOUNTERS AN ENTERPRISING ALCHEMIST AT AN AREA ALE FESTIVAL, THEY ARE TASKED WITH AIDING IN THE TRANSPORTATION OF A WAGON'S WORTH OF ALE ON BEHALF OF A BREW-OBSESSED BRONZE DRAGON.

AN ADVENTURE SUITABLE FOR LEVELS 3-6
BY JAMES FLOYD KELLY

BACKGROUND

Following the events of the area's beer festival, the party is hired to escort a few wagons loaded with ale barrels to the next town on behalf of a bronze dragon. On the journey, they'll encounter a bit of trouble on the road as well as discover just how valuable the cargo they are guarding could be—especially to the dangerous lich that's been tracking their every move.

ADVENTURE LOCATION

Silver Waters is a small village that does business up and down Harp River. About 50 families support the merchant boats that stop for food and water supplies at the midway point between the port cities of Blue Shard and Ocean's Gate. But once a year, Ale Fest turns this sleepy little village into a gathering of more than 5,000 visitors (and growing) who come for the games, the songs and to witness the naming of the realm's best ale, earning its creator the Brewer's Prize.

For the last 10 years, Ale Fest has become a significant celebration, with taverns sending representatives to find ales that will bolster their business. During its early years, the village started hiring qualified guards to keep thieves away and quell the inevitable drunken brawls, and the festival grounds have a "no weapons" policy. Families come for the food, the tavern games and a chance to break the monotony of small town life, while adventurers from all over visit to compete in the games, enjoy a day's respite from the dangers of heroism-for-hire and (let's face it) raise a pint or three of well-deserved ale.

The event lasts for one week, with the winner of the Brewer's Prize selected on the final day. The entire event takes place in a roped-off grassy area to the immediate east of the village. Weapons must be checked at the entrance, and any violation of this rule is swiftly dealt with by the 70+ guards patrolling the commons area.

SETTING UP

Hold My Beer is a stand-alone adventure for three to six level 4 characters, although the adventure can easily be dropped into an existing campaign with CRs and NPCs updated to reflect higher- or lower-level characters.

Hold My Beer focuses on a long-standing rivalry between a dragon and a **lich** (details on pg. 185), and the party could easily find themselves in the middle of the feud. The party will be recruited as escorts for the winner of an ale contest who needs to deliver his special recipe to Glitz, a legendary dragon. This ale, however, has some unusual properties, and a vain wizard-turned-lich believes the special brew could be the answer to her search for a "cure" for her desiccated and horrific physical form.

How the party find themselves in the little port village of Silver Waters can be easily answered by the GM using some of the Adventure Hooks (on pg. 186) or by changing the name of the village to match an existing one in an ongoing campaign. Ale Fest is well known in the area of Silver Waters and happens once a year; it's talked about in all the taverns, so the party will likely have heard about it or could simply stumble upon it during a trek.

How your party made it to Ale Fest is entirely at GM discretion. If running this adventure as a stand-alone, have each potential party member determine how they arrived at Ale Fest in Silver Waters to begin with. Perhaps they're already a company of adventurers looking to relax, or maybe they've all brought a brew of their own design to enter into the competition with hopes of claiming the Brewer's Prize as their own. The general mood around the festival is one of fun and freewheeling, as the beer flows as steady as the Harp River.

If the party has been journeying together as part of an ongoing campaign, you can easily drop Ale Fest into a town or city they're already adventuring around or utilize one of hooks outlined on pg. 186 to pull them closer to the action that's about to unfold.

GM NOTES: THE DRAGON AND THE LICH

Understanding the relationship between Glitz and Lady Divine is key to giving the players a true sense of the feud and the stakes of the job.

Keep in mind that Glitz is "hiding" in the form of Trefley Stonetrod; any special information the GM wishes to provide to the players can always be done through Trefley, who obviously knows the dragon's desires and motives. Likewise, remember that although Drake is a mercenary, he doesn't kill for sport. He observes rules and laws and attempts to make a living without breaking laws that would send him to jail. (His men, on the other hand...only the GM knows their true intentions.) And because Ale Fest is weapon-free, this is a good opportunity to run a brawl without fear of death. (The rules say nothing about spells, however!)

There are a number of clues and story points that can be used for future adventures or as jumping off points in an existing campaign. Ally's necklace, for example, is a MacGuffin that can easily be converted into an artifact that might lead to further adventure. And liches rarely die... their physical form just gets destroyed and they return to their phylactery. Nothing keeps players on their toes like the knowledge that they have found a lich for a nemesis. And finally, Glitz the dragon can become an ally who can provide not only new adventures and jobs, but also a source of information when researching or verifying rumors. Dragons know much, and they don't often like to be in debt to anyone.

A Rich History

The small elven village of Yylsa ("Charmed River") has remained hidden in the Tangled Oak Forest for centuries, long sought but never found. The elves there live quiet lives, hunting and foraging for their needs, relying on the flora and fauna for their magical components.

The special magic wielded by the Yylsa elves has been witnessed by outsiders over the years, typically when an elf leaves the village to explore and adventure. At those times, an awareness of the special components they use in their magic spreads among wizards who then search the Tangled Oak Forest, hoping to luck upon the special plants that convey such power. But the Tangled Oak Forest holds its secrets well, and few wizards have found what they go looking for...

For the last century, Glitz has made trades with the Yylsa elves, providing special brews that the elves enjoy in exchange for a mix of ingredients taken from the forest. His desire to use these ingredients in new brews has kept him returning year after year, although his attempts at creating magical brews from these ingredients have thus far been fruitless.

It was just over 60 years ago that the Tangled Oak Forest received another powerful visitor looking to discover the secrets of the forest's offerings. Lady Divine, a powerful lich, had hired a family of loggers to tear into the forest and take everything it could offer up.

The Yylsa elves, seeing a portion of their forest razed and the work continuing unabated, anxiously awaited Glitz's yearly arrival. They hoped the dragon might be able to scare off the loggers and end the damage being done to their home. When Glitz finally arrived, he agreed to do what he could and approached the loggers in peace, hoping to simply push them to another forest.

The loggers, fearful of the lich who hired them, explained they were hired to log this specific forest and could not stop their work. Glitz, understanding their fear, told them to inform their employer that any further damage to the forest would be ill-advised and that the forest was now under his protection. Glitz flew off, but not before vowing to return in a week to verify the work had stopped.

Three weeks without progress got the attention of Lady Divine, who traveled to the forest and killed the loggers for their lack of deliveries. With her research stalled, she began her search for the Yylsa elves, believing them to hold the key to repairing the damage that lichdom had done to her body. Unable to locate them, she began to burn and destroy portions of the forest in an attempt to draw them out.

The elves remained hidden. The dragon did not.

For weeks, the lich and the dragon did battle. The lich used the forest to hide and heal, and the dragon used the elves' knowledge of the forest to find each of Lady Divine's hiding places. After many more weeks of being thwarted at every turn, Lady Divine fled the forest and Glitz returned to his home.

Over the last 60 years, Lady Divine has continued her research, and once or twice a decade she returns to the Tangled Oak Forest to try and find new magical components. But the dragon always finds her and turns her away. Over the years, Lady Divine has grown in power, and now she is able to fight with Glitz more effectively.

Both dragon and lich know that the forest's continued survival is at stake. Lady Divine will hire the occasional wizard to go into the forest and collect for their individual aims, but it's a slow process.

Just over a year ago, word began to spread about a new ale being brewed using ingredients obtained from the Tangled Oak Forest. News of this ale and its entry into Silver Waters' Ale Fest reached both dragon and lich, and both made plans to attend.

Adventure Hooks and NPCs

The below story elements could be utilized to get your party closer to Ale Fest and the characters who create the inciting incidents of this adventure.

- During a trek through any type of terrain, the party encounters a handful of merchant wagons carrying large numbers of ale casks and barrels. One of the wagons has a broken wheel that the merchants are attempting to repair. A DC 12 Wisdom (Insight) check would allow the players to offer assistance by suggesting that two wagons be roped together to keep the three-wheel wagon balanced and allow it to roll. A spellcaster may also have a spell that could save the day. Information from the merchants during the encounter will mention Ale Fest and the rumor that a living, breathing dragon will be there!
- A childhood friend of a party member has gotten word to the group that he or she will be attending Ale Fest at Silver Waters. Silver Waters is only a day's journey from their current location, and the PC in question is owed a small debt of payment. The letter also mentions that the event always features a large collection of adventurers with news of the world, wizards with knowledge to share and wealthy patrons with maps and details of long lost ruins who are looking to hire adventurers.
- On the road to another adventure, the party encounters a large group of families walking and riding in the direction of Ale Fest. They casually offer up a solid night's meal and a small payment to the adventurers in exchange for escort duty. One of the travelers asks if the party is on its way to Silver Waters because of the rumors that a lich is allegedly skulking around the region.

This adventure features a few notable NPCs, including Aloysius Skylantern, Drake Devonair and the Gasp Gang, his band of mercenaries, and the lich Lady Divine. Profiles and stat blocks for these characters begin on pg. 196. Glitz the Rapscallion is also a major player in this adventure, and his profile starts on pg. 37. Glitz will spend some of this adventure in the guise of a halfling named Trefley Stonetrod (pg. 196).

The action of this adventure officially begins at the end of Ale Fest, when the Brewer's Prize is awarded, but a bit of preamble has been included in Part 1 to help set the scene. Use as much or as little as you feel is necessary.

Part 1: Ale Fest

> The sounds of reverie and the smells of a dozen different feasts greet you well before the glistening waters next to the port village of Silver Waters catch your eye. A gigantic banner—GREETINGS and WELCOME to ALE FEST!—flutters in the breeze between two large poles on the main road leading into town. Ships and small boats are moored at the dock, and the busy labors of the village mix with the obvious celebrations happening in the east commons area between the village and the nearby forest. But your attention turns from the clamor and casual work of the area laborers at the sight of a large dragon curled up and resting just outside the temporary fence line that has been erected around the festival.

This is Glitz the Rapscallion, legendary dragon and protector of ale. Glitz has a special interest in this year's event and has kindly offered his services both as protector of the festival and as a draw for travelers who wish to see a live dragon.

The festival requires all attendees entering the east commons area to relinquish weapons. They can be checked in at a special tent and will be returned when an individual leaves the area. Anyone causing trouble about the weapons rule will find themselves being glared at by a single open eye of the resting but still intimidating bronze dragon.

The village has also hired the services of 72 armed soldiers wearing green sashes (over armor). The soldiers will do everything in their power to escort troublemakers (and those deemed too inebriated) out of the commons area. Anyone producing a hidden weapon will be automatically detained and placed in the village jail until the event ends. Fighting or other attempts at causing trouble will be met with overwhelming force, with those deemed unseemly removed from the event without warning.

Glitz will only get involved if things look very bad. Otherwise, Glitz will nap until the contest begins. If the party wants to explore Ale Fest, they would find it's a celebration of all things beer.

A general Wisdom (Perception) check would reveal the following:

- Stalls selling ale, meats steamed in beer or both.
- Festival-goers wearing colors denoting their favorite area taverns, and some (so-called "Barrel Heads") wearing large beer barrels and little else as clothing.
- Guards enforcing the "no weapons" policy.
- An area cordoned off for Ale Fest's Tavern Games—tests of skill meant to challenge the heartiest of adventurers and a large draw for the festival.

A successful DC 15 Wisdom (Perception) check would also lead to recognition of a group of somewhat shifty-looking individuals wearing light armor that bears a flaming hourglass insignia and a suave-looking man who keeps eyeing them. Anyone with a military or mercenary background (or those succeeding on a DC 15 Intelligence [History] check) would know this insignia denotes members of the Gasp Gang—mercenaries for hire.

If the party wishes to explore what they've observed, allow scenes to unfold at GM discretion. As they walk about the grounds, the party may learn any of the following at GM discretion:

- There's a storm brewing on the horizon. Looks like it could rain very hard this evening, which is sort of strange for this time of year. Luckily the weather held for most of the festival! Cheers!
- Beer barrels aren't particularly flattering and don't do a very good job of covering up things clothes ought to. Most Barrel Heads don't care.
- All the ale here is good, but folks have been raving about one beer in particular, from a brewer named Aloysius Skylantern—a former alchemist.
- The suave but stern-looking man surrounded by the men in armor with hourglasses aflame is Drake Devonair, a local hotshot with ties to the criminal underground. He is watching the party any time they are watching him. He doesn't want trouble. But he could easily cause some.

When you're ready to move on to the next phase of this adventure, read the flavor text below:

> A great cheer can be heard from one specific section of the festival. Stacks of ale barrels make it easy for you to see that there is an ale contest, and it appears the contest is now over because the crowd is carrying one smiling individual, a nondescript man wearing the apron of a bartender. The crowd chants his name: "Al-ly! Al-ly! Al-ly!"

Aloysius Skylantern has been declared the winner of Ale Fest! Aloysius (Ally to his friends) will be provided with the trophy for this year's win. Normally an auction is held for any barrels left over from the contest, but it should be announced that Glitz has made a significant offer to Aloysius for all the remaining barrels and ownership of the recipe. After Aloysius accepts the offer, Glitz nods to the brewer, thanks the judges and takes flight. He disappears over the nearby hill amid the cheers of the festival attendees. But not everyone is pleased with the results...

You can allow the players to wander and mingle, and maybe even try some of the other vendors' ales. During their wanderings, however, it should become apparent that some troublemakers are making their way toward Aloysius now that the dragon has left. Once the players

OPTIONAL: TAVERN GAMES

If your party would like to participate in any of the tavern games at Ale Fest, these are on offer.

BARREL TOSS *Entry Fee 5 silver pieces*
Players can join in to see who can toss an empty barrel the farthest. A simple Strength (Athletics) check can allow a player to set the distance to beat, with the GM rolling for a few NPCs who will attempt to beat the record. **Winner receives 10 gp.**

BARREL BALANCE *Entry Fee 5 silver pieces*
Players will stand on barrels (with heads removed) that are threaded over a long log that floats in a pit filled with muddy water and, from the smell of it, stale beer. Players will hold on to a rope for balance until the game begins. The rope is dropped and the log is spun and shaken by a crew of sturdy-looking dwarves. Last person remaining on their barrel is the winner. A Dexterity check is made by the player(s) along with four or five rolls made by the GM to represent the other 4–5 competitors—lowest roll falls off and then everyone rolls again. **Winner receives 10 gp.**

BARREL RACE *Entry Fee 5 silver pieces*
A pair of competitors must compete in this race, with one competitor (the roller) rolling a barrel from one end of a field to another with their partner (the rollee) inside.

The field is 100 feet from one end to another, meaning the rollers must travel a total of 200 feet. A roller can move their barrel with them at full speed and movement with a successful DC 15 Strength (Athletics) check. Otherwise, they move at half speed. If the roller fails two checks in a row, they lose control of their barrel and it tumbles down a nearby hill. Their race is over, and their partner ill.

Once this first leg of the race is complete, the partner in the barrel must get out of the barrel and consume a beer while standing on one leg. This requires a DC 15 Dexterity (Acrobatics) check to get out of the barrel, a DC 15 Wisdom (Survival) check to find the beer on a nearby table and a combined Constitution and Dexterity check to consume the beer on one leg without falling over (DC 25). While any number of teams of two can compete, a set of local twins—Porter and Pud Podwick—will set the pace to beat for the area's NPCs. It takes Porter a total of eight rounds per initiative to roll the barrel from one end of the field to the other and four rounds per initiative for Pud to pop out and drink the ale on one leg. **Winners split 20 gp.**

ALE FEST MAIN STAGE

Site of the Brewer's Prize contest. This year's contest is won by Aloysius Skylantern. He is thrilled. A few local thugs are not. The judges aren't sure what to do—they're just here for the free beer.

JUDGES' TABLE

The main stage (*1*) features a judges' table as well as several steins of half-drunk ale. The stage's surface is 8 feet off the ground, and requires a DC 10 Strength or Dexterity check to leap onto without using the hay bales as a boost.

A GATHERED CROWD

As the most anticipated aspect of Ale Fest, the announcement of the Brewer's Prize always piques the interest of attendees in the area. At GM discretion, this entire area could be considered difficult terrain, as throngs of common folk mill about, unsure of what to do once a fight breaks out.

NO BLADES, NO BOWS

As this area is part of Ale Fest, no weapons are allowed. Drake Devonair and his Gasp Gang mercenaries aren't trying to get thrown in the clink, and would abide by the rules against carrying arms in this part of town. But that doesn't mean they're against using some of the available items in the area as improvised weapons.

Hay Bales (*2*). There are stacks of hay in the area, and each weighs roughly 20 pounds. A bale of hay can be used as an improvised ranged weapon (1d6 bludgeoning). The attacker uses Strength to make the attack. If the attack hits, roll 1d4. On a 1, the bale breaks apart, kicking up dust in a 10-foot area, centered on the target. Vision is obscured in this area until the top of the next round.

Tables and Benches (*3*). There are several wooden benches as well as a few long tables that could be utilized as bludgeoning devices by able-bodied adventurers. Benches and tables have a reach of 15 feet and a range equal to twice creature's Strength score. A creature attempting to utilize a bench (1d10) or table (1d12) as a weapon must first succeed on a DC 15 Strength (Athletics) check to wield it. Given their awkward size, attacks with a bench or table are made at disadvantage.

Beer Barrels (*4*). There are several barrels in the area that could be utilized as improvised weapons. Lifting a barrel requires a successful DC 17 Strength (Athletics) check. A barrel has a range equal to twice the wielder's Strength score. A barrel deals 2d6 bludgeoning damage on a hit. Any time a barrel is thrown, roll 1d4. On a 1-2, the barrel bursts and any creature within 10 feet of the busted barrel must succeed on a DC 15 Dexterity saving throw, or slip and fall in the puddle of booze.

have had an opportunity to look around, it's time for Drake and his Gasp Gang mercenaries to start trouble.

> Over the noises of the happy crowd, you can make out the distinct sound of an angry voice. A slim, sharply dressed individual is pointing his finger at Aloysius and gesturing towards the barrels that Ally is having loaded into two wagons. "I don't care!" shouts the fancy-looking gentleman. "You don't bring a winning ale to the contest and then sell it all to a dragon! Give me two barrels. Now!"

Ally will find one of the player's eyes and appeal for help with a hopeful look. If the players intervene, Drake and four of his mercenaries will start a fight (unarmed) with the players. If the players do not intervene, Drake will catch one of the players watching and toss an insult (specific to either the race or class of the player). He's looking for a fight and hoping the distraction will allow two of his mercenaries to sneak away with a few barrels.

If the party doesn't start a fight, Drake would.

Guards would intervene at GM discretion or after four rounds of initiative. Drake is smart. He'll find another way to get what he wants.

Once Drake and his men are chased away, a halfling (Trefley Stonetrod) will approach Ally and a discussion will begin.

> As the fracas breaks up, you notice a stout-looking halfling approaching Ally, who bends down to hear what the halfling has to say. The halfling then motions you all over to him and says, "You individuals look like you might be able to assist me. My master, Glitz, has purchased these 10 barrels and needs them escorted to a rendezvous spot just outside of town. Given the trouble Ally just had with those men, I was wondering if I might be able to hire you for two days to escort Ally and his barrels? My master pays well, and, let's be honest...gaining the favor of a dragon is never a bad thing, I can tell you."

If the players take the job, Trefley will negotiate a fee (25–50 gp for each barrel delivered, at GM discretion) and provide them with directions to the rendezvous spot—they will travel as far as possible tonight, camp and then finish the trip in the morning.

Trefley wants Ally and the barrels to hit the road and would give the party a few minutes to prepare. Trefley suggests at least one party member ride along in each of the wagons carrying barrels, though they have room for two passengers apiece. A third wagon is available to carry Ally, any remaining party members and their equipment. Camping gear has been provided by Trefley along with some food and drink for the night.

> After gathering in the wagons and leaving the commons area, you can see townsfolk waving to Ally and yourselves as you round a bend and head into the nearby forest. It will be dark soon, but you can get a few hours of travel in before you'll need to make camp.

Part 2: On the Road

> For the last few hours, you and your companions have enjoyed the calm of your ride through the forest. Aloysius, although shy, has shared a few things with your group regarding his ale and his surprise when Glitz extended an offer to buy his remaining barrels.

At GM discretion, Ally would reveal (or can now share) the following:

- Ally isn't sure why Glitz was so eager to purchase his ale or why Drake and his mercenaries were so keen to acquire it.
- He brewed the ale using a few special ingredients he found in a glen not far from the fabled location of the Tangled Oak Forest, but (if he's being honest) he's not sure he could make more even if he had all the ingredients...he sort of made the concoction up as he went along, a variation on the recipe his mother created.
- He has, of course, sampled the ale. It's very good.
- A DC 15 Wisdom (Perception or Insight) check would reveal that Ally keeps touching a medallion around his neck. If asked about it, he would reveal that it was given to him by his mother, the renowned brewer Emilia Skylantern. Her proprietary recipe is embossed on the back, a fact he may keep to himself.

As the party continues to journey along the road, they would run into a bit of trouble. Choose two of the encounters detailed below (and note the other for use in Part 4 of this adventure) and present them as happening en route to a spot to make camp for the night:

- A large oak tree has fallen into the center of the road. The party can try to maneuver the wagons around it with a successful DC 15 Wisdom (Animal Handling) check, but failure will require that the tree be removed with 30 minutes of labor. During this work, a group of 1d4 + 2 bandits (who felled the tree) will demand 10 gp for "safe passage." The party can pay up, parlay or put up a fight. The GM can adjust the number of bandits to augment the encounter.
- Coming around a curve in the road, a large bear and a pack of wolves are growling and posturing around the carcass of a deer. The party caught both the bear and the wolves by surprise, and the animals now see more food they can fight over. Combat can occur here, but there may be some roleplaying and magical solutions that can help the party avoid it.
- The party members become aware at some point that they are being watched from the woods. A half-elf ranger (Jesse Fee) has been following them (not for nefarious reasons), hoping to gain some insight into whether or not they can be trusted. If she deems the party to be safe, she will exit the forest and ask for assistance, hoping a cleric is in the party. The ranger's ally, a half-orc fighter, has been injured in a fight with a "horrible, foul-looking creature traveling in a horse-drawn hearse." If the party are willing to follow her and heal her ally, the ranger and fighter may be convinced to join the party for the rest of the trip; both will easily spot the hearse later in the adventure and be able to provide the party with more details on the lich. If the party lacks a cleric or other healer, the ranger will ask if they can carry her ally in the wagon to the next town that has an apothecary; the half-orc will not be of help in any combat, but the ranger is at full health and will assist as she can.

Following the second encounter, read the following flavor text:

> As you gather yourselves and continue the journey forward, the sun drops behind a pitch-black gathering of clouds, and you can see the rain coming from miles away. Aloysius nods in agreement that it's time to make camp. It looks to be a cold and drizzly night.

GM NOTE: FROM A DISTANCE
Unknown to Ally or the PCs, the party has been followed by some of Drake's mercenaries. It is their intention to attack the party in the morning and take as many barrels as they can grab. They've also been instructed to take Aloysius captive and bring him to Drake's campsite nearby. These mercenaries are using Drake's familiar, an invisible imp, to scout the party's journey from an unobservable distance.

PART 3: BEDDING DOWN

> After securing the horses and wagons and building a cozy fire, Aloysius breaks out the food provided by Trefley, before smiling wide. "Trefley told me we could break into one of the barrels on our journey as long as we didn't drink it all!"

A slight breeze will kick up, and Aloysius will pour mugs of ale for each member of the party, offering a toast to his escorts and his dearly departed mum. Any party members who choose to drink will discover that the ale's win was well deserved. It is an incredible brew that begs for another drink, and Aloysius is willing to offer up a single refill.

After a party member has a drink, make a roll on the Ally's Ale Special Effects table and inform the player that something unusual is happening. If a player has a second mug, roll again. Effects will stack.

GM NOTE: ALLY'S ALE SPECIAL EFFECTS

Any time a creature consumes a mug of Ally's ale, roll on this table to determine how they are impacted. These effects last for 24 hours.

1d6	This mug of brew offers…
1	**…enhanced hearing.** Wolf-like hearing allows the imbiber to hear the chant of a spellcaster more than a mile away. The sound of a large pair of wings in the sky is also heard.
2	**…enhanced vision.** The imbiber is able to pick out movement and details of a hearse that is parked on a hilltop over a mile away. A dark shadow is visible behind the clouds in the sky.
3	**…enhanced speed.** The imbiber gains 15 feet of movement.
4	**…enhanced strength.** The imbiber adds +4 to their Strength stat (to a max of 24).
5	**…mind reading.** The imbiber gains the ability to cast *detect thoughts* at will. Using this ability on Ally would reveal that he is excited and also somewhat shocked by the effects of the ale and wishes he could accurately remember how to replicate the recipe.
6	**…magic detection.** The imbiber can cast *detect magic* at will and senses a strong source of necromantic energy emanating from the hills beyond.

As the party discovers the unusual properties of the ale, the light drizzle from earlier becomes a full-blown thunderstorm. When the meal is done, Aloysius will suggest they get some rest. If one or more party members volunteer for watch duty, make note of how many drinks they had: zero, one or two.

As the party drops off to sleep, the ale's aftereffect (severe drowsiness) begins to take hold. All who had a drink will be unable to wake when Drake's mercenaries move in to kidnap Ally and take the wagons. Any who had one ale must make a DC 17 Constitution saving throw to stay awake while on watch. Any party member who had two ales will make this save at disadvantage.

If any party members are awake, a DC 17 Wisdom (Perception) check—made at disadvantage due to the rainfall—would reveal a group of 10 mercenaries quietly slipping into camp at GM discretion. The mercenaries would try to subdue any party member still awake and would be careful not to wake any other party members. If the mercenaries are successful in this endeavor, they would flee with Ally, the wagons and the barrels. If the mercenaries fail, any left alive would reveal they were sent specifically to kidnap Ally and the ale on behalf of Drake and his mistress, the powerful lich Lady Divine. They would suggest any attempt to flee without Lady Divine knowing would be impossible: her spies are everywhere. Adjust the flavor text at the top of part 4 as necessary based on the outcome of this part.

PART 4: THE MORNING AFTER

> As the sun begins to rise, you awaken to a disturbing sight. The horses are gone. Two wagons are gone. The ale? Gone. Aloysius is too. You feel well-rested, but something in that ale made you sleep so soundly you never heard the noise of the horses and wagons riding away. As you examine the campsite, you notice dozens of boot impressions in the mud that the night's rain made. And there, in the mud as well, are two perfect sets of wagon tracks that lead back the way you came.

If a party member was knocked out, that PC can validate that the wagons were stolen and Ally kidnapped. If no PCs were able to stay awake, the only clue that Ally was kidnapped is the medallion he wore around his neck that is found in the fresh wagon wheel impressions in the mud with a successful DC 15 Intelligence (Investigation) check. An examination of the medallion will reveal two bits of information:

- On the back is inscribed the special recipe that Ally uses for his ale (though without the ingredient found in the Tangled Oak Forest).
- The chain is thick and unbroken. Ally would have had to remove it himself, and he told the party he never takes it off.

If the party wishes to find Ally and retrieve the barrels, they will have no problem following the muddy tracks of the wagons. They'll have to go on foot, as the third wagon lacks horses. It's possible that the PCs may have received the right effects from the ale to discern the presence of a powerful spellcaster about a mile away and possibly a dragon in the sky. They may also make guesses that the hearse and Ally's disappearance are related.

If the party chooses to follow the tracks, they will find Ally, Drake and his men after two hours of travel. During these two hours, the third (of the three earlier encounters from part 2) will occur. The forest will protect the party from observation and the soft mud will cover the sound of their movements.

If the party abandons Ally and the barrels, word will get back to Glitz and the party will find they are unwelcome at many nearby towns as the dragon shares their cowardice with the population.

PART 5: DRAGON VS. LICH

> The muddy trail has led you back through the forest and then onto a branching roadway that you passed yesterday evening. The forest has grown thicker here, blocking much of the sunlight.

The party may or may not choose to scout ahead, but if they do, they would find Drake and his mercenaries at the top of a steep hill, waiting for the arrival of the lich known as Lady Divine, the individual who hired Drake to capture Ally and take the barrels of ale. Lady Divine will be coming from the opposite direction in her hearse. The party will most likely arrive ahead of Lady Divine and spot the mercenaries; their behavior and actions will hint that they are waiting on someone to arrive from the road running down the other side of the hill.

It is up to the party to determine a course of action, but attacking Drake and his men before the lich arrives is the best move. If the party wait until the lich arrives, Glitz will reveal himself as detailed later to ensure the party isn't immediately wiped out.

If the players choose to attack Drake and the Gasp Gang, they will have a difficult time approaching stealthily. The Gasp Gang (numbers at GM discretion) will spot them and (assuming the kidnapping was successful) gather in front of Ally, tied up alongside Drake who will speak:

> "You couldn't just leave it alone, could you? I told my men to spare your lives as you slept, but now you've forced my hand. Kill them. Now."

BARTON'S HILL

A slightly craggy outcropping named after Horace Barton, a nobleman who left the region after being snatched up by harpies that once roosted here, Barton's Hill is a known meeting place for the transfer of stolen goods among the area's less reputable citizens. It's a great spot for a fight as well, if that's what you're into.

HILLTOP

A bare expanse elevated above the rest of this region, the hilltop (*1*) offers advantage to those attacking from the high ground. Scrambling to its top, roughly 20 feet higher than the surrounding area, costs twice as much movement.

CRAGS AND COVER

Barton's Hill has plenty of places to hide (things or people). At GM discretion, the rocky outcroppings (*2, of many*) offer half to full cover depending on the height of the combatant and angle of the attack. The trees and shrubs (*3, of many*) in the area are also useful as a means of protecting oneself. They constitute difficult terrain and offer half cover.

Hidey Hole (*4*). A portion of this rock features a large gap between its underside and the ground upon which it sits, making it a quality hiding spot. A creature standing within 5 feet of this rock would notice a bit of cloth sticking out of it. Further investigation would reveal a hidden magic item, determined by rolling on the table below. The owner of this item may come looking for it in the future, at GM discretion.

1d6	This hole is hiding...
1	**...a necklace of weak fireballs.** The necklace has 1d4 beads. It functions as a *necklace of fireballs* but each bead deals half the damage of a level 3 casting of the spell.
2	**...a ring of spell storing.** This ring currently holds a level 4 *fly* spell. It has been tinkered with to offer immediate attunement to the first person who slips it on.
3	**...a potion of greater healing.** Potions come and potions go.
4	**...a cape of the mountebank.** This item was pinched from Straightline March, the Left Wand of the Marble Spire. She will come looking for it once she's finished nursing her hangover.
5	**...a tan bag of tricks.** The original owner of this bag was devoured by feral goats. But the man who was meant to claim it from this hidey hole will certainly wonder where it went.
6	**...a potion of *revivify*.** Not the worst thing to have on hand when you're an assassin who shoots first and checks the description on the bounty note later.

Drake will not attack with his men. The party may feel outnumbered or overpowered, but after a few blows between the two groups, two things will occur to interrupt the battle:

- A loud roar will be heard from the sky.
- A horse-drawn hearse will appear around the bend.

The mercenaries will retreat to Drake and await orders. If the players continue to fight the Gasp Gang, a lightning bolt will strike in the center of the fight and knock prone anyone within 25 feet of the strike.

The lid to the hearse will open.

> Wearing the dress of a noblewoman, a female form emerges from the hearse. Her skin is gray and stretched thin, revealing a grim rictus with teeth exposed, a look typically reserved for the very, very dead. In her right hand is a staff that glows green at its tip, and on her left hand is a single ruby ring that catches the eye. "Drake, I was clear in my instructions that there would be no witnesses to this meeting..." A single lightning bolt will strike Drake in the chest, and you watch him crackle then burst into a pile of ash. "If you don't want to join your leader, I suggest you dispatch these interlopers immediately." As the Gasp Gang turns to rush you, you hear a voice booming from the rocks behind you. "Not today, Divine." Trefley Stonetrod, the halfling who hired you, emerges from the woods with a smile on his face. "I had a suspicion you'd be interested in the ale."

The party may choose to rush the mercs or stand and wait to see what happens, but the mercs are confused and will stand their ground and wait for instructions from Lady Divine.

Lady Divine will begin walking towards Trefley (who shows no fear).

The lich will give the party a few looks that should make them nervous, but ultimately she is interested in Trefley.

> The lich glares at Trefley. "I told you that the next time we met, one of us wasn't going to walk away." Trefley bellows "Well, then...let's see who that will be," as he spreads his arms and his form shifts—scales cover his skin and his head and neck extend as the halfling changes form into a massive bronze dragon. You smell hops and malted barley in the breeze as he flaps his wings, surging toward the lich, grabbing her in his claws and soaring into the sky.

The mercs will now attack the players. As GM, you can control the danger to the players by allowing Glitz or the lich (or both) to take opportunity attacks against the players. The 10 mercenaries are skilled, and if they appear to be winning, Glitz can always dive down and grab one in his mouth. Likewise, if the players are winning, the Lady Divine may send a lightning strike down that will knock prone anyone within 25 feet of the strike.

The dragon and the lich will do battle in the sky. Lady Divine has teleport abilities and can control the weather. Her strikes against Glitz, however, will never be enough.

After two rounds per initiative, Glitz will release Lady Divine; she will fall but cast a spell to teleport herself down to the ground. In her injured state, she is not going to be able to assist the mercenaries as Glitz will continue his attacks against her.

If the players attempt to attack the lich, she will perform one of the following two diversions before turning her attention back to Glitz:

- A lightning bolt will strike one of the wagons, catching it on fire. The party will need to find a way to extinguish the flames while also dealing with any remaining mercenaries. While Divine wants the barrels, she will satisfy herself with Ally and his recipe if she can deny both to the dragon.
- The lich will focus on the least injured PC who is not within 30 feet of Ally and cast *fireball*. If this spell is successfully cast, all mercenaries within range of the spell will be killed. Glitz will re-engage with the lich.

After four rounds per initiative, read the following flavor text:

> The sky crackles with energy that suddenly surges against the massive dragon, and you watch as Glitz tumbles hard into the ground ahead of you. "Get Ally out of here," he growls, as the lich hovers overhead.

Lady Divine would cast *fireball* on the area near the wagons, setting them ablaze to spite Glitz, before turning her attention to him.

- Glitz will continue to ask the party to protect Ally and check him for any injuries.
- Glitz will request the party try to move the wagons and Ally out of range of the battle above them.

The mercenaries will fight to prevent the party from rescuing Ally and putting out the flames around the wagons, which will consume one barrel of ale per round starting at the top of round 6.

If the party is victorious against the mercenaries, Glitz

will finish off the physical body of the lich with a burst of his powerful breath weapon, before diving to crush her hearse. This isn't the end of the lich, but it does end the immediate threat.

If Aloysius is alert, he can be released from his bonds and will complete his bargain with Glitz (who would help bring him back from death using *revivify* if necessary). After things settle down, Glitz would thank the party.

> "Greetings, my friends. And thank you! You have brought me the prized ale I have so looked forward to having in my collection. I just wanted to say thank you for your aid in securing these ales. And if you ever find yourselves in need of a favor, I'm only a pub crawl away."

PART 6: LAST CALL

Glitz would pay the party the agreed upon amount per barrel saved.

If Ally's medallion is returned (and he will insist on it), the party will have access to an ally with access to unusual magical components in the future. Ally may also be able to occasionally provide unusual potions for testing.

Lady Divine will not forget this event; the party will have gained a powerful nemesis who can appear at various times in future adventures.

Ally will reach out to the party in one year to request escort services to Ale Fest (if the party is available). It is also possible that Glitz may hire the party again in six months' time to meet with Ally for a delivery of 20 barrels. This will be known to Lady Divine, who may use the opportunity for revenge.

NPCs

The following NPCs make appearances as part of this adventure.

GLITZ, THE RAPSCALLION, PURVEYOR OF ALE

This legendary dragon is well known from the many songs and tales told across the world about the dragon that brews ale. It is widely known that Glitz owns shares in many taverns near and far, and his own brewery keeps several beer halls filled with visitors looking to taste the dragon's special brews. It's not uncommon for Glitz's customers to forget that they are dealing with a dragon, and the tales told of Glitz's hospitality are matched in number by those of thieves who chose to rob the wrong tavern or the wrong merchant caravan carrying Glitz's special ales. More details as well as stats for Glitz are available on pg. 37.

TREFLEY STONETROD

This smiling halfling purports to work as Glitz's hireling, but the truth is they are one and the same. When Glitz desires to interact with the world, he often chooses to change form and become Trefley Stonetrod. Trefley is known near and far as a fair person to deal with, and he pays well, too. His infectious laugh is enjoyed by all he meets (though many think it has a bit of a charm spell applied), and his appetite in the taverns for food and ale is legendary.

ALOYSIUS SKYLANTERN

Aloysius (or Ally to his friends) is an alchemist from a long line of brewers. Although his ales have always been noteworthy, it is his latest brew that he brings to Ale Fest that has everyone talking. A secret recipe he has developed has won the Brewer's Prize, but there's something else in this ale that seems to have a minor effect on adventurers who have seen combat and experienced magic up close. Aloysius is unaware that an ingredient he added to the brew has been used by both Glitz and Lady Divine in their own experiments (with no luck); for this reason, his knowledge and barrels of his ale have become valuable to both parties.

DRAKE DEVONAIR

Hired by Lady Divine to kidnap Aloysius and to take his remaining barrels, this warlock mercenary was picked for his skill with the sword as well as his discretion. Drake, however, isn't so wise when it comes to picking henchmen to assist. Drake desires nothing more than his reward from Lady Divine (a magical blade she has promised to trade for Ally and the barrels), but he does not want to grab the attention of any militias or sheriffs in his travels as he's spent enough time in a handful of jails to know he wishes to avoid them. For this reason, Drake is hesitant to kill even with Lady Divine's instructions to leave no witnesses.

ALOYSIUS SKYLANTERN

Medium humanoid (Human), lawful good

Armor Class 10
Hit Points 4 (1d8)
Speed 30 ft.

STR	DEX	CON	INT	WIS	CHA
10 (+0)	10 (+0)	10 (+0)	16 (+3)	10 (+0)	10 (+0)

Senses passive Perception 10
Languages Common
Challenge 0 (10 XP)

ACTIONS

Unarmed Strike. Melee Weapon Attack: +0 to hit, reach 5 ft., one target. *Hit*: (1) bludgeoning damage. (Aloysius is unarmed)

DRAKE DEVONAIR

Medium humanoid (Human), neutral good

Armor Class 15 (studded leather)
Hit Points 97 (15d8 + 30)
Speed 30 ft.

STR	DEX	CON	INT	WIS	CHA
13 (+1)	16 (+3)	14 (+2)	10 (+0)	12 (+1)	18 (+4)

Saving Throws Dex +6, Cha +7
Skills Acrobatics +6, Deception +7
Senses passive Perception 11
Languages Common, Abyssal
Challenge 5 (1,800 XP)

Charismatic Attacker. Drake uses his Charisma modifier for his melee attacks.
Devilish Smile. Drake makes Charisma (Deception and Persuasion) checks at advantage.
Pact Familiar. Drake can summon a familiar, an imp named Quizbit, to do his bidding as in the *find familiar* spell.

ACTIONS

Multiattack. Drake makes two melee attacks, one of which can be Eldritch Pass.
Rapier. Melee Weapon Attack: +7 to hit, reach 5 ft., one target. *Hit*: 8 (1d8 + 4) piercing damage.
Eldritch Pass. Melee Weapon Attack: +7 to hit, reach 5 ft., one creature. *Hit*: 9 (2d4 + 4) slashing damage. On a hit, Drake gains 15 feet of movement and can move away from the target without provoking attacks of opportunity.

REACTIONS

Parry. Drake adds 3 to his AC against one melee attack that would hit him. To do so, Drake must see the attacker and be wielding a melee weapon.

The Gasp Gang

A group of mercenaries for hire, these ne'er-do-wells are dumb, but effective. And dumb. They wear armor featuring an hourglass aflame, meant to suggest that their enemies' time is running out (and also in homage to their founder, Klaus, who accidentally burned down their first fortress when he was roasting a boar and didn't check the timer).

Gasp Gang Mercenary

Medium humanoid (any race), any alignment

Armor Class 17 (Splint)
Hit Points 58 (9d8+18)
Speed 30 ft.

STR	DEX	CON	INT	WIS	CHA
16 (+3)	13 (+1)	14 (+2)	8 (-1)	11 (+0)	10 (+0)

Skills Athletics +5, Perception +2
Senses passive Perception 12
Languages Common
Challenge 3 (700 XP)

Actions

Multiattack. The mercenary makes two longsword attacks. If the mercenary has a shortsword drawn, they can also make a shortsword attack.

Longsword (Two-handed). Melee Weapon Attack: +5 to hit, reach 5 ft., one target. *Hit:* (1d10 + 3) slashing damage.

Longsword. Melee Weapon Attack: +5 to hit, reach 5 ft., one target. *Hit:* (1d8 + 3) slashing damage. one handed

Shortsword. Melee Weapon Attack: +5 to hit, reach 5 ft., one target. *Hit:* (1d6 + 3) piercing damage.

Shersha "Lady Divine" Darkfist

No one knows how long Shersha Darkfist lived as a wizard, but most agree it must have been to a ripe old age as few wizards have the knowledge or skill to become a lich upon death. Lady Divine, so named by those who knew of her exceeding beauty in life, succeeded in her attempt at lichdom. But the horrific changes to her lich body were unacceptable, and she now spends a significant portion of her undead life researching methods for reversing the physical effects she chose so long ago. Lady Divine possesses the abilities of a lich, but for the purposes of this adventure, she should exist more as an existential threat than an immediate one (as she could easily dispatch a low-level party with a flick of her wrist). The party should understand dealing with Lady Divine is at their discretion, and if their discretion suggests they should attack, then they ought to get their heads examined.

DRAGON HUNT

THE PARTY MUST ORGANIZE A HEIST, THEN TAKE TO THE SKIES TO HELP A RETIRED DRAGON HUNTER TAKE DOWN A RISEN ELEMENTAL EVIL.

AN ADVENTURE SUITABLE FOR LEVELS 8–12
BY CELESTE CONOWITCH

BACKGROUND

A mighty dragon is reborn, and two dragon hunters have set their sights on defeating their past nemesis once again.

A red dragon named Cenere has been resurrected by its loyal kobold minions. Forging itself a new body surging with elemental flame, Cenere has taken on a new moniker, Thrice-Born, and set its sights on reshaping the world in fire and blood. When Cenere last stalked the Earth, two legendary dragon hunters, Bellanus Yanorin and Rynden Aethedorn, slew the vicious creature. Now that Cenere has been brought back to life, these hunters are committed to taking up arms once again to stop the dragon before its reign of terror descends.

Successful partners when they faced Cenere more than 100 years ago, the dragon hunters have since splintered into rival factions. Now separated, each needs to find assistance from adventurers brave enough to defy both a creature of legend as well as the laws that forbid dragon hunting.

OVERVIEW

The adventure's story is spread over four parts and takes approximately five hours to play. This adventure is designed for three to seven 8th-to-12th-level characters and is optimized for five characters with an average party level of 10.

> • **Part 1: Dangerous Game (15 mins)**
> The party receives a mysterious message that leads to a rendezvous with dragon hunter Bellanus Yanorin. Bellanus recruits the party for a dangerous mission.
> • **Part 2: The Dragon Vault (90 mins)**
> The party must break into the vaults of Rynden Aethedorn and his followers, The Dragons Swords, to retrieve a prototype, an elemental engine, from Rynden's workshop.
> • **Part 3-5: Getting Warmer, Double Trouble, Get a Clue (120 mins)**
> With the elemental engine in tow, the crew sets off on the trail of their quarry. Threats try to impede them

from below and above as they draw nearer to the dragon.
> • **Part 6: Last Stand (90 mins)**
> The party reaches their final destination, only to run into the angered Dragon Swords. Between dragons and rivals, the situation is an all-out brawl.

ADVENTURE HOOKS

Dragon hunting is highly illegal in most civilized societies, unless of course that's not true in the world you've created. If your party has been adventuring together for some time, any of the below scenarios can be incorporated into the storylines you have in place:

> • Rumors of violent dragon attacks have started to circulate. Hundreds of people will continue to lose their lives and homes if the dragon responsible isn't stopped, and word that the party is interested in putting a stop to it has reached the ears of a talented (if somewhat retired) dragon hunter.
> • Local clerics and soothsayers have begun to speak of dark magic brewing nearby: Something has been brought back from death, and it is no paltry thing. Whatever it is, the gods want it stopped, which is why they communed with the retired dragon hunter who will make contact with the party.
> • A mage college reports a red dragon's burning heart has been stolen from their collection. They hire an adventuring party to retrieve it (or at least apprehend the thief), but want insurance on their investment, so they've hired a dragon hunter to go along for the ride.
> • A local official hires the party to use whatever means necessary to take down the dragon ravaging their lands (even if that means resorting to illegal means, i.e., involving some dragon hunters off the books). The official knows two dragon hunters reportedly have been seen in the backwoods town of Pontybridge and recommends the group starts there.

If running this adventure for a new party or as a one-shot, any of the previously mentioned would do, or you can have the party agree to meet the dragon hunter Bellanus in a town called Pontybridge at the Jaded Rose. If the party members don't know one another, they will have been contacted individually by the dragon hunter, who knows the appearance of Cenere is a horrible turn of events that cannot be left unchallenged.

PART 1: DANGEROUS GAME

> The shriek of a falcon rings through the air as the bird swoops to land just before you. The creature opens its beak, but instead of a squawk or screech you hear a smooth feminine voice say:
>
> "My name is Bellanus Yanorin, and I need skilled adventurers. If you are interested in gold and glory, meet me at the Jaded Rose in Pontybridge."
>
> As the message finishes, the falcon shakes its head and takes off into the air.

The message is from Bellanus Yanorin, leader of The Green Swords faction of dragon hunters. She has used the *animal messenger* spell to reach out to the party after hearing rumors of an adventuring band in the area. Any characters who succeed on a DC 15 Intelligence (History) check to recognize the name would know the information given in the Roleplaying Bellanus sidebar (pg. 200).

When the party receives this message, they should be no more than a day's journey away from the town of Pontybridge, where The Green Swords are currently waiting.

GM NOTE: THE TOWN OF PONTYBRIDGE

Pontybridge is a quiet little town, easily dropped into any campaign setting. Unremarkable in nearly every way, it's the perfect place to hide a dragon-hunting base.

Population: Around 1,000.
Government: A democratically elected town council handles decisions concerning Pontybridge. The council reports to the lord of the region for more important matters.
Defenses: Pontybridge does not have any traditional defenses. If trouble arises, Pontybridge can rally a small militia of 50 capable fighters.
Inns and Taverns: The Jaded Rose Tavern, The Pleasant Pheasant Inn, Shining Span Meadery.
Other Notable Locations: Ponty's Bridge, Foundations (a general store), plenty of pear orchards.

At GM discretion, help your party make their way to the town of Pontybridge, a small town so exceedingly uneventful that the militia was once dispatched when a bushel of pears went missing from the general store (turns out they were there the whole time—someone just moved them to the other side of the shop. Whoopsie!). The Jaded Rose is the nicest of the pubs in town, but that's only because they have one extra stool. When the players enter the Jaded Rose, read the following:

> Red-stained tables and chairs crowd this rustic tavern. A few patrons buzz about the space, but an elven woman in a royal blue frock coat is the most striking among them. She looks up from her mug directly at you, a smile on her face. She winks, then raises her glass your way before introducing herself.

The elf dressed in blue is Bellanus Yanorin. She recognizes the party by description and cheerily introduces herself. She'd buy a round of drinks then direct them to a private room to chat about the job. Once out of earshot of the other patrons, Bellanus lays out her proposition.

> "Glad you had the mettle to hear my offer! Here's the job: I have a dragon to hunt. Cenere...nasty red dragon. Put him down once before but now it seems he's been...reborn. I don't know how to express just how devastating the very notion of that is. The fact that it's a reality, well. I need capable people to help me take him down. It's going to be dangerous, it's going to be illegal and it's going to involve stealing from my old partner. If you can't agree to that, well... there's the door."

If the party wants to hear more, Bellanus would lay out the following information at GM discretion:

- The leader of a group called The Dragon Swords is a dwarf named Rynden Aethedorn. They have a hidden base in town.
- Bellanus wants to hire the party to sneak into this base, find the vaults contained within and steal a magical prototype called an elemental engine.
- Once the party has the engine, they have to get it out of the base without attracting the locals' attention.
- Bellanus knows that Rynden is currently away on business, so she needs the party to steal the engine as soon as possible or they risk interference from the dwarf.

If the characters have additional questions for Bellanus, here is what she knows:

• The base is inside an old boarding house that Rynden rents. As far as the town is concerned, the boarding house is permanently closed for business.

• Rynden lives in the boarding house alone but occasionally meets there with other members of The Dragon Swords. There likely won't be people, but Bellanus is sure the wily dwarf will have some magical protections in place.

• The elemental engine is some kind of prototype the dwarf has been building. It's rumored to be more potent than the airship engines of old.

• The town has no regular guard, so as long as the party doesn't make too much noise, they should be able to get in and out of the building without rousing suspicion.

Bellanus answers whatever questions she can before suggesting the characters get ready to break into the boarding house as soon as possible. She instructs them to take the engine to a rendezvous point in the forest just outside of Pontybridge, where her crew will be waiting to leave town.

GM NOTE: ROLEPLAYING BELLANUS

Bellanus Yanorin is a thrill seeker who found her calling battling the most dangerous dragons the world has ever seen. She is a charismatic and capable leader who inspires others by laughing in the face of adversity. Bellanus created the dragon hunting faction known as The Green Swords when she got fed up with the stuffy policies Rynden Aethedorn employed while leading The Dragon Swords. Through daring ventures and morally ambiguous decisions, Bellanus made The Green Swords the richest dragon hunting faction in the business. She has no qualms mentioning this fact to anyone at any time, whether she's told them already or not.

When dragon-hunting was officially outlawed, Bellanus experienced a long melancholic period as The Green Swords were forced to step into the shadows. She sees this new hunt as the first real opportunity to show the world that dragon hunters need to be put back on the map. As such, she is focused on taking down Cenere, almost to the point of obsession.

CASING THE JOINT

At GM discretion, after taking the job from Bellanus, the party may wish to investigate the boarding house before sneaking in. When the players scope out the boarding house for the first time, read or paraphrase the following:

> The boarding house is a rectangular wooden structure close to the edge of town. Its two-story frame of mortared stone is set with boarded-up windows. There are two sets of wooden entry doors and an open-air bell tower that appears to be an easy entry point.

There are several ways to get inside the boarding house. Both sets of doors on the ground level are locked but can be picked with a successful DC 15 Dexterity (Thieves' Tools) check. The bell tower is 20 feet tall and can be climbed with a successful DC 15 Strength (Athletics) check to reach an unlocked trap door. Alternatively, a Small or Tiny creature could crawl through the ground floor windows after prying off the boards.

As long as the party doesn't draw attention to themselves with loud noises or flashy spells, at GM discretion, no townsfolk come to investigate. If the party does cause a stir, 2d6 militia members (use **veteran** stat block) arrive at the scene and wait to apprehend the characters when they leave the boarding house.

Once the party is inside the boarding house, proceed to Part 2.

PART 2: THE DRAGON VAULT

The Dragon Swords' secret hideout is harder to infiltrate than its boarding house facade. The party must contend with the vault's magical defenses to reach Rynden's workshop. Once arrived, they must assemble the engine parts and deliver them to Bellanus.

VAULT LAYOUT

Rynden keeps the top floor of the building empty and hasn't changed much about the layout. The dwarf has maintained the dusty and empty floor to discourage any would-be thieves from hunting for valuables. The bottom floor contains several magic defenses to protect The Dragon Swords' stored secrets.

VAULT LOCATIONS

The following locations are shown on the Vault map (pg. 201–202). Flavor text is presented as if a creature is entering the space for the first time through its main entryway. Adjust at GM discretion.

1. COMMON AREA

> This musty common room hasn't seen use in quite some time. Long wooden dining tables and chairs neatly line the floor, ready to seat dozens. Many closed doors line the walls.

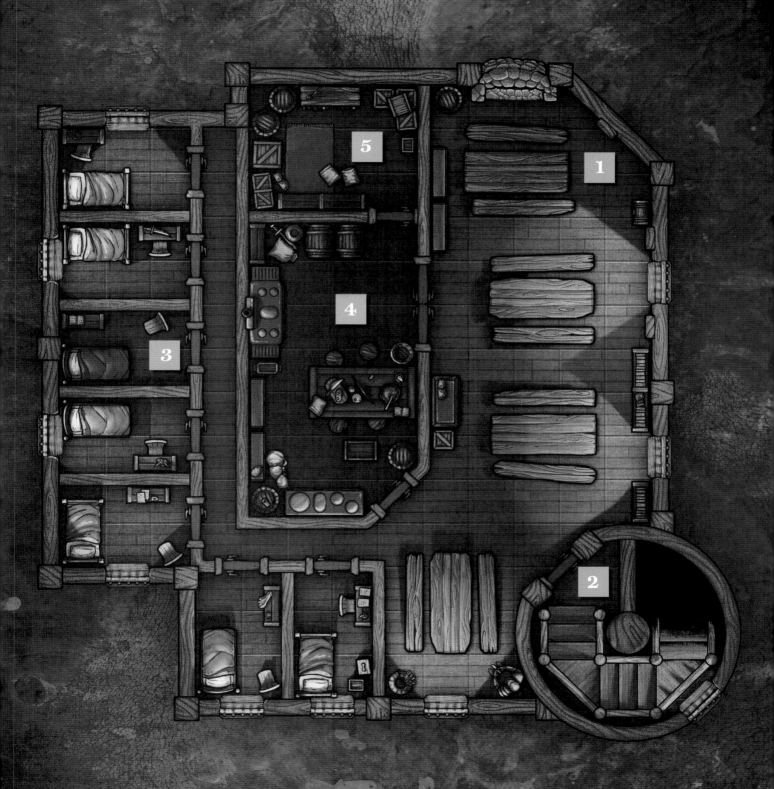

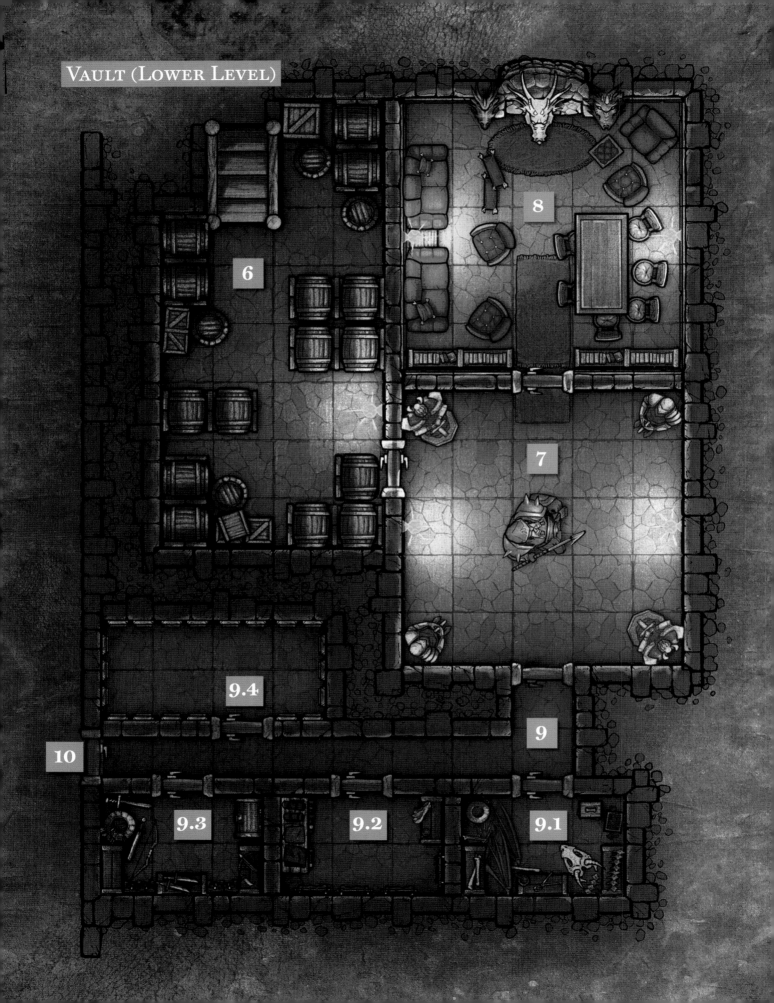

VAULT (LOWER LEVEL)

6

8

7

9.4

9

10

9.3

9.2

9.1

This room is a common area designed for the boarders to relax and take their meals. There is nothing of value in this room, and Rynden takes great care not to leave any footprints in the dust when he comes and goes.

2. BELL TOWER

A wooden spiral staircase fills this simple tower made of stone. The tower's top is flat and set with a trap door housed by a rustic belfry, though the bell has long since been removed. Before Pontybridge expanded, this tower alerted the workers when dinner was ready. Rynden doesn't bother to keep the trap door at the top of the tower locked. He figures anyone eager enough to break into the boarding house should do so, then be disappointed by the empty first floor.

3. BEDROOMS

> This simple room is equipped with a carved bed frame, a wooden chest and a stone washbasin. A fine layer of dust covers the furniture. There appear to be six more boarding rooms similar to this one.

These seven bedrooms are identical. They once were rented to boarders but have not seen use in years. There is nothing of real value in these rooms, at GM discretion.

4. KITCHEN

> This industrial kitchen is equipped to make large amounts of food. The cabinets, jars and shelves lining the walls all appear to be empty.

This kitchen has not seen use since before Rynden bought the place. Any visiting members of The Dragon Swords eat in the Trophy Room on the lower floor.

There is a stone door in the northern wall that leads to the pantry.

5. PANTRY

> This small pantry reeks of garlic, though the shelves are empty. A moldy rug covers the floor.

This pantry has not been used to store food in quite some time, but Rynden keeps the rug in place to hide any footprints.

A DC 15 Intelligence (Investigation) check in this room would reveal a small trap door-shaped square imprinted on the rug. If the party looks underneath the rug, they find an unlocked trap door leading to the cellar.

6. CELLAR

> A set of stone steps leads down into a large cellar filled with wooden racks supporting several enormous barrels. The whole room reeks of sour wine.

This cellar once housed wine and other goods that needed cold storage. It now serves as the decoy entryway to the vaults. All of the barrels in this room are empty, but one hides a secret door into the vaults. Anyone searching the room for secret doors and succeeding on a DC 15 Wisdom (Perception) check discovers the doorway hidden behind one of the barrels.

A *glyph of warding* spell is cast on this secret entrance. The glyph triggers a *cloudkill* spell (save DC 15) when any creature other than Rynden opens the door to Area 7.

7. ENTRYWAY

This square room is built of intricate stonework with vaulted ceilings. Magnificent suits of dwarven armor decorate the corners, but they are overshadowed by an impressive statue of a dwarf holding a harpoon. Two doors lead out of this room. One has a red woven doormat, and the other doesn't appear to have any handles. This room is the beginning of the vault proper, which Rynden dug out and built for The Dragon Swords. It is filled with myriad dangers designed to protect the vault's treasure.

- Northern Door. The door in the Northern wall is locked by conventional means and can be picked with a successful DC 15 Dexterity (Thieves' Tools) check. A spare key to this door is hidden under the red mat (Rynden left it there for his last guests and forgot to remove it). These doors lead into the Trophy Room.
- Southern Door. The western door is magically sealed and can only be opened using the key obtained in the Trophy Room.
- Guardians. Both the statue and the suits of armor are guardians created by Rynden to dispatch trespassers. If a creature spends more than one minute in the room without saying a specific passphrase, the **stone golem** statue and two suits of **animated armor** attack. These constructs only fight within the confines of this room. Notes for how to adjust this encounter are on pg. 204.

GM NOTE: ADJUSTING THE ENCOUNTER

• If your party is weaker than the recommended five-person party at 10th level, consider removing one or both animated armor constructs from this encounter.

• If the party is stronger than the recommended five-person party at 10th level, consider adding one or more animated armor constructs to the fight.

8. TROPHY ROOM

> As you enter the room, you see a stylish lounge, its walls and furniture made of rich red wood, with one corner hosting a long table carved from a single piece of spruce. Overstuffed chairs, dart boards and plush rugs make the space feel cozy, if a little butch. Hanging on the walls are various marvels, including intricately woven tapestries and three mounted dragon heads hung conspicuously above the fireplace.

THE DRAGON HEAD SONG

Once one of the dragon head names is spoken aloud, all three heads come to life and present their challenge.

> The mounted heads suddenly begin to twitch, moving their jaws and blinking their eyes as if awakening. The white dragon in the center speaks in a slurred tone: "Eh, what's this? More visitors, aye. Well, you know the game. Finish the song, and we'll show ye the way."
>
> The three heads all begin to sing together:
>   "Oh, once I was a drunken lout
> So me mum she threw me out
>   And so I set to wander that day
> And what did I find on the way?"
>
> The dragons then pause and look expectantly at all of you.

Some Dwarven friends of Rynden's enchanted these dragon heads to be entertainment for visiting guests. Rynden has since decided they make excellent stewards of the key to the sealed southern door in area 7.

To solve this puzzle, the party must make up a verse that follows the first verse's rhyme scheme. The dragons are not picky about the content of the lines (as many of Rynden's guests are deeply inebriated when they play this game). The verse simply must be four lines, composed of two rhyming couplets. The last words of the line must rhyme with each other in this pattern:

A
A
B
B

Once someone puts forward a qualified verse, the dragons all let out a merry cheer, and the green dragon head spits out a key that can open the door in area 7.

If your party is struggling to figure out the solution to the dragon head puzzle, here are some ways to help move things along:

• If the party has no idea how to solve the riddle. The black dragon head helpfully whispers: "You've got to make up a verse, laddie. And it's got to rhyme."

• If the party refuses to be creative, or panics, you can allow them to make a check to see if their characters would be able to finish the verse. A successful DC 15 Charisma (Performance) check allows them to make up the example verse below. A successful DC 15 Intelligence (History) check allows them to recall the next verse in this popular Dwarven drinking song.

> Near and far I wandered around
>   Until I heard a lovely sound
> So I stumbled over the hill
>   And thar she was with looks to kill

• If the situation is truly dire, consider allowing the party to find the key by destroying the heads. In the ruined stuffed remains of the green head, they can find the key.

This room is the regular meeting place for The Dragon Swords. The trophy room is kept comfortable, stocked with food, drink and board games and hides the key to access the vaults.

- **Tapestries.** The tapestries on the walls are tapestries of preservation woven to depict epic battles with dragons. They keep the atmosphere of the trophy room eternally pleasant.
- **Talking Heads.** The three stuffed dragon heads are enchanted to speak when spoken to, and they hold the clue to the location of the vault key. Each dragon head is mounted on a carved board that has its name carved into a brass plaque. On the right is the head of a black dragon named Vegha, in the center is the head of a white dragon named Wyrith and on the left is the head of a green dragon named Cryn. If any of the names are spoken aloud, the heads animate and present their song (pg. 204).

9. VAULTS

> A narrow, unlit hallway stretches before you, eventually disappearing around a bend. Many identical doors line the walls.

This is the vault proper, with almost every door leading into a small storage room. The door on the northern wall leads to the workshop.

Each of the storage room doors is locked with a mundane key (Rynden himself has the only key ring) and requires a successful DC 15 Dexterity (Thieves' Tools) check. If the characters investigate each vault, they find numerous treasures and oddities, at GM discretion.

VAULT 9.1. This vault is kept just above freezing by inlaid enchantments. It contains shelves and racks of preserved dragon parts. A cursory search of the room reveals scales and blood of an adult blue dragon, the tongue and wings of a young red dragon and the skull and blood of an ancient black dragon. The moment any of these components leave the vault, the spoilage countdown begins (see "Dragon Hunting Economies" in Legendary Dragons).

VAULT 9.2. This vault is kept magically dry and has no light or moving air. It contains racks of textiles and four magnificent tapestries on the walls. The fabrics are bolts of leather, silk and other valuable padding used to make armor. A successful DC 18 Intelligence (Investigation) check allows a character to identify one of the cloaks hanging in this room as magical. Spells like *detect magic* would also allow a character to find the ***cloak of the dragon*** (pg. 176) hanging on a wall peg amongst other mundane items.

VAULT 9.3. This vault serves as a small armory. Well-made weapons of every variety are stored here in wooden racks. None of the weapons are magical, but if a character searches for a specific simple, martial or more exotic weapon, they can find it here.

VAULT 9.4. This vault has 20 safe deposit boxes set into the wall. Eight of the boxes have a circular indentation, each with a different symbol carved into its recesses.

The boxes are each sealed with a different *arcane lock* spell. They can be dispelled or opened with the signet ring corresponding to each box (members of The Dragon Swords wear such rings). A successful DC 20 Dexterity (Sleight of Hand) check made with a forgery kit allows a character to make a seal close enough to a signet ring to open one of the boxes.

For every box the party manages to open, roll on the table to determine what they find. Reroll any duplicate roll results.

SAFETY DEPOSIT BOXES

D8	Contents
1	A half-finished manuscript of a romance title called Copper Embrace
2	A memory box containing interesting but worthless trinkets
3	A bag of 100 platinum pieces
4	Three large amethysts (worth 100 gp each)
5	A black opal (worth 1,000 gp)
6	Two **arrows of dragon slaying**
7	A necklace of fearlessness
8	A sack of 30 platinum pieces. A DC 15 Intelligence (Investigation) check would reveal they are counterfeit.

10. WORKSHOP (PG. 206)

> An impressive workshop stretches out before you. Long stone counters wind around the room along with worktables, bookcases and racks crammed with all manner of treasures, both biological and mechanical. Suspended from the ceiling are the bleached bones of a dragon posed in flight. A low humming fills the room, coming from a monolithic metal contraption, a 30 feet tall metal shaft, resting in the middle of an arcane circle.

This is Rynden's workshop, where he tinkers away perfecting weapons, armor and other curiosities he has utilized in his long career as a dragon hunter. The workshop is very unorganized, but anyone who takes the time to search it finds various spell components, alchemical ingredients and two full sets of dragon tools (see "Magic Items" pg. 177). More detail for Rynden's workshop, as well as what the party ought to do now that they're inside, is provided on pg. 207.

WORKSHOP

10

RYNDEN'S WORKSHOP

Though the party has made it through most of Rynden's exterior defenses at this stage, his workshop is not without dangers of its own.

SPECIAL FEATURES

Elemental Engine. The device in the center of this room, a metal shaft about 8 feet long with a 4 feet square base, is the elemental engine Bellanus hired the party to steal from the workshop. An **air elemental** and two **fire elementals** swirl and dance around it, almost as if they are being drawn into it. A DC 14 Wisdom (Perception) check would reveal these creatures to be non-hostile (at present) and would also suggest that they are seemingly bound to the object in some way.

Magic Circle. A creature who succeeds on a DC 14 Intelligence (Arcana) check understands the arcane circle around the engine is meant to keep elemental creatures inside. A creature who succeeds on a DC 14 Wisdom (Perception) check can see that the elemental engine does not look finished in the way Bellanus described it would be.

A DC 15 Intelligence (Investigation) check to search the workshop for clues about the circle or the engine reveals schematics and logbooks explaining how Rynden is currently activating the machine (and how to speed up the process: "The elementals could be subdued, forcing their matter to flow more readily into the device, but the circle and engine will work their magic in time, no need to singe my knuckles swinging at living flame").

Dragon Skeleton. The dragon skeleton hanging from the ceiling can be harvested and sold for components, but the process of taking it down and carrying it out will require several hours of work.

Arcane Wards. Rynden is no fool and at GM discretion would have worked to protect his interests within his workshop from intruders. These wards are detailed below and can be dismissed with a successful casting of *dispel magic* (level 4) or by flicking a switch hidden in the fireplace found with a DC 15 Intelligence (Investigation) check.

WORKSHOP WARDS

If the party attempts to disrupt the elemental engine, they would set off the wards protecting it. On initiative count 20, choose one of the wards below. These wards continue to impact the space until dismissed.

Skeletal claw. The dragon skeleton sweeps a claw at a creature within the magic circle, dealing 10 (2d6 + 3) slashing damage on a failed DC 15 Dexterity saving throw.
Bludgeoning books. A book flies off the shelf and makes a +5 ranged attack against a creature in the workshop. On a hit, the target suffers 5 (2d4) bludgeoning damage.

ACTIVATING THE ENGINE

When the party arrives in the workshop, the elemental engine is not in a usable state. Before the engine can be used, the elemental creatures that fuel it must be bound to the device. Rynden has ringed the engine in a more advanced version of *magic circle* and left the conjured elementals to bind to the device slowly over time.

To get the engine in working order and back to Bellanus quickly, the party must speed up the process by weakening the elementals designed to power the engine.

The magic circle surrounding the engine is a 30-foot-radius, 30-foot-tall cylinder. The elemental engine sits in the exact middle of the cylinder. Characters can physically pass through the circle, but magical effects (such as a spell cast from outside the circle to a target inside) do not pass through the barrier.

When a character enters the circle, two **fire elementals** and one **air elemental** emerge from the engine. The elementals are agitated by being trapped in the circle and attack relentlessly.

The elementals cannot leave the confines of the circle and cannot attack targets beyond the circle. If an elemental's hit points drop to 20 or fewer, it is instantly teleported inside the engine and then bound, where it is no longer a threat. The engine becomes active (and ready to deliver to Bellanus) once all three elementals have been bound to the device.

LEAVING THE VAULTS

Once the elementals have been bound to the engine, the party can successfully remove the elemental engine. The machine itself is bulky like a large chest, but surprisingly light (as the air elementals add a bit of buoyancy).

As long as the party didn't cause a stir entering the building (see "Casing the Joint"), they have no trouble exiting the boarding house and meeting Bellanus at the rendezvous point. Once the party has made it to the outskirts of Pontybridge, proceed to Part 3.

> **GM NOTE: ADJUSTING THE ENCOUNTER**
> • If your party is weaker than the recommended five-person party at 10th level, consider removing the second fire elemental from this encounter.
> • If the party is stronger than the recommended five-person party at 10th level, consider adding one air elemental to the fight.

PART 3: GETTING WARMER

Once the party reaches the rendezvous point with the activated elemental engine, they are met by a thrilled Bellanus who introduces them to her first mate, a grizzled half-orc veteran named Cambria Felix (Bellanus just calls him Felix).

The two are waiting with a covered wagon ready to transport the engine to the waiting ship. Bellanus has hidden the airship in a forest clearing about an hour's ride away from Pontybridge. When the characters first see the airship, read the following:

> Resting in the clearing ahead is a sleek vessel encased in burnished green metal. Decorative sails resembling delicate moth's wings are currently battened down, and the whole affair is crowned by a figurehead of an elven maiden spun from green glass. The impressive ship could easily host 15 crew members.

Since dragon hunting is both incredibly dangerous and highly illegal, Bellanus has managed to secure just three crew members (which is why she needed the assistance of capable adventurers). She would introduce the crew at GM discretion:

**GM NOTE:
ROLEPLAYING THE CREW**

Since the crew aboard the *Maiden* is so small, the party is likely to have a great deal of interaction with them. Here are some general suggestions for roleplaying each crew member.

• Arnarra Yanorin is much younger than her sister Bellanus and has only recently completed her arcane studies. She is apathetic about most things in life since she graduated. While she and Bellanus have never been close, Arnarra has agreed to assist her sister in hopes of finally doing something exciting.

• Cambria Felix was trained as a gladiator from a young age. When he aged past his prime, he suddenly found himself out of work and struggling to get by. After a chance encounter with Bellanus, Felix has stuck by her side through many of the odd jobs the captain has pulled since her dragon hunting career was cut short. He is desperately loyal to Bellanus and highly suspicious of anyone else.

• Randal Smith is the newest addition to Bellanus's crew and keeps his personal history close to his chest. Despite his shady past, he is exceptionally skilled in the subtle arts and remains loyal as long as the captain pays him well. Randal is charming to newcomers but intentionally torments Felix, who dislikes him immensely.

- Arnarra Yanorin, an apathetic elven mage who is Bellanus's younger half-sister.
- Cambria Felix, a grizzled half-orc gladiator who has loyally served Bellanus on several missions through the years.
- Randal Smith, a charismatic human assassin newly hired by Bellanus.

Once introductions are made, Bellanus gets to work installing the engine. She allows the characters to look around her airship, the *Emerald Maiden* (pg. 210).

With the crew assembled and the engine installed, the airship can begin its journey. When the party is ready to fly, the captain gathers the crew to explain her plan:

> "All right, me hearties, we're clear to fly this old girl, so here's our plan. First things first, we have to find where Cenere is hiding. To do that, we're going to head to the site of his last attack and hope we find a clue. We'll take off now and put as much distance as possible between us and this town before the sun comes up, then we'll land and fly again at night. Pray it stays dark. Once we're sighted, we're likely in for a fight.
> It's two days' flight to Amiens, so mind your stations and let's get flying."

Bellanus's destination is the Duchy of Amiens (or another location at GM discretion), the region reporting recent attacks by a red dragon. As the captain predicted, it takes the remainder of the first night and two additional nights of travel to reach the destination (with the ship parked from dawn to dusk). Because this aspect of the adventure is randomized, it's difficult to judge exactly how long each encounter could last. If short on time, the party could experience safe passage for their entire journey to Cenere's last known whereabouts, in which case you should jump to Part 5.

FIRST LEG (OPTIONAL)
During the partial first night of travel, roll once on the "Aerial Encounter" table to determine if an encounter occurs. While the ship docks during the day, roll twice on the "Land Encounter" table to determine if an encounter occurs. Reroll any duplicates that occur.

SECOND LEG (OPTIONAL)
During the second night of travel, roll three times on the "Aerial Encounter" table to determine if an encounter occurs.

While the ship docks during the day, roll four times to determine if an encounter occurs. Reroll any duplicates that occur. See text following the tables for roll result descriptions.

GM NOTE: AIRSHIP MECHANICS
The party will likely find themselves in a combat encounter as part of their journey aboard the *Emerald Maiden*. While you're welcome to wing it all as problems arise, for more in-depth coverage of the ups and downs of airship combat, including boarding mechanics, specifics related to the ship's overall hit points and more, turn to pg. 171.

THIRD LEG (OPTIONAL)
During the third night of travel, roll once on the "Aerial Encounter" table to determine if an encounter occurs. Reroll any duplicates.

Whether or not a random encounter is rolled, Part 4: Double Trouble (pg. 215) would take place toward the end of the third night.

AERIAL ENCOUNTERS

1d20	Contents
1–15	No encounter occurs
16	Freedom Fighter
17	Air Patrol
18	Engine Trouble
19	Rough Weather
20	Misty Night

LAND ENCOUNTERS

1d20	Contents
1–14	No encounter occurs
15	Local Officials
16	Ship for Sale
17	Now You See Me
18	Bite-Sized
19	Sympathetic Parties
20	Perfect Cover

AIR PATROL

> Three winged, lion-like creatures with knights in armor mounted on their backs burst from the cloud line, soaring toward the ship. One of the knights raises a white flag, waving it toward you.

A band of three **knights** riding **griffon** mounts flies to meet the airship. One of the knights flies a white banner hoping to speak with the captain. The griffon riders work for a local lord and are tasked with demanding the airship leave the area before it attracts the attention of the dragon (lest it cause trouble in the area).

The *Emerald Maiden* could outrace the knights to avoid a confrontation. If the party chooses to do so, the griffon riders would attempt to inflict whatever damage they could before being outpaced.

If the party allows the griffon riders to board and speak with the crew, the knights deliver their message but don't cause any further trouble (as they would personally like to see Cenere brought down).

BITE-SIZED

> The *Emerald Maiden* suddenly rocks as the sound of grating metal comes from below decks. Something is crunching through the hull.

The rare metals the airship comprises have attracted the attention of a hungry **xorn**. The creature has burrowed inside the ship and bitten a large hole out of the stern. The munching xorn can be driven off with attacks or bribed to stop eating the ship if given better treasure to consume.

The hole made by the xorn can be repaired with a few hours of work by any character proficient with mason's tools, smith's tools, or tinker's tools. Until repaired, the hull has 50 points of damage.

ENGINE TROUBLE

> You hear a grinding, sputtering sound from the engine compartment. Sparks fly and a gout of fire shoots from the hatch, tossing flames at the ship's wooden elements. A flickering fire elemental rises from the elemental engine.

While Rynden's elemental engine prototype is generally superior, it possesses several small flaws. One of the **fire elementals** has broken out of its confinement to destroy the ship in its rage. If the elemental is reduced to 20 hit points or fewer, it is pulled back into the engine. For each round that the fire elemental is active, the *Emerald Maiden* takes 10 points of damage. Roll to randomly determine which part of the ship is damaged, at GM discretion.

SHIP DAMAGE

1d4	Area
1	Hull
2	Helm
3	Elemental Engine
4	Airship Cannon

THE *EMERALD MAIDEN*

A small but mighty vessel utilized for the hunting of dragons will also be where the party catches a few winks over the course of this adventure. The map provided here can be utilized for any of the encounters that involve the airship (Part 3 onward) when it's airborne. More detailed airship mechanics can be found on pg. 171, including details on controlling the elemental engine and captain's features, but the below will serve you well if you're looking to simplify those aspects in the name of brevity or ease of use within your game.

ABOVE DECK

The area above deck features access to the steering mechanism as well as the airship's two long range cannons. A hatch leading below deck is located toward the stern.

Long Range Cannon. These cannons require a bonus action to load and an action to fire. Moving the cannon toward a new target requires 10 feet of movement or a successful DC 15 Strength (Athletics) check. They have a range of 150/300 feet, are +10 to hit and deal 22 (5d8) bludgeoning damage.

BELOW DECK

The living quarters for the *Emerald Maiden*, such that they are, can be found below deck. The crew sleeps in the common area, which also features a few small tables for chow and conversation. The captain's quarters is little more than an elevated bedroll and a few walls, but is also home to a small chest that protects any meaningful loot uncovered during various adventures.

ELEMENTAL ENGINE

The elementals that power the airship are mostly contained and subdued within the elemental engine, encased in a housing at the ship's stern, and accessible via a small topside hatch. The captain steers their combined power utilizing a small headset that requires an unclouded mind to use effectively.

If the engine is damaged, or if the ship takes more than 50 damage in one round, the captain must make a Wisdom saving throw to maintain control of the elementals.

DC	The elementals...
16	...remain under the captain's control.
12	...begin to break free of the engine. The next check to maintain control over the elemental engine is made at disadvantage.
8	...break free of the engine. The ship will begin a free fall from its current height if the elementals are not forced back into the engine. The elementals will recede back into the engine if they suffer 15 damage in one turn.

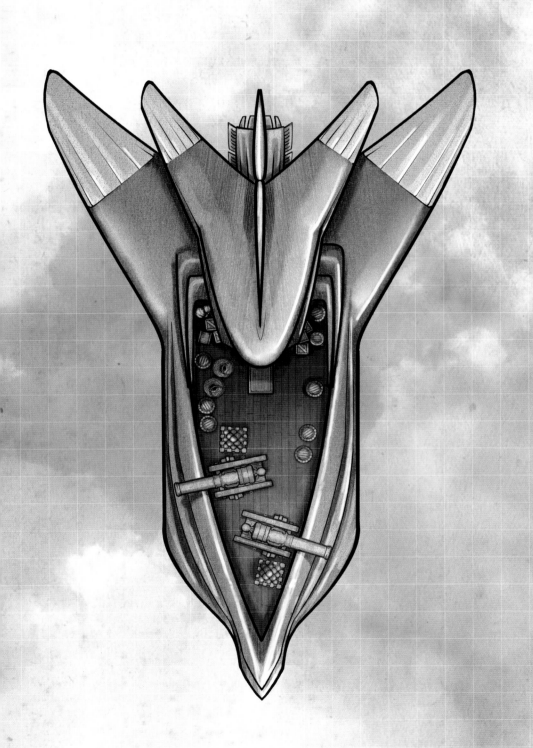

FREEDOM FIGHTER

> The *Emerald Maiden* is knocked off course by a blast of wind. The airship struggles against a series of gales as a blue-skinned figure flies into view and calls out in a voice that booms like thunder:
>   "You enslave my kind to power this hideous vessel? It is time you pay for your hubris."

The blue-skinned figure is a **djinni** who has sensed the trapped elementals' presence in the engine and come to investigate. The djinni does not particularly care for the well-being of the elementals but resents any who would imprison them.

The djinni fights until it has 40 or fewer hit points remaining, then it uses *plane shift* to escape.

KOBOLD SURPRISE
(OPTIONAL ENCOUNTER)

After securing the lead that points them towards the volcanic islands, the party is welcome to spend the day helping the villagers. Whenever they return that night to the ship, they walk into an ambush:

> The top deck is alight with action as you see a wounded Felix clashing weapons with two small lizard-like creatures. Looking down from the helm is a third red-scaled figure standing over Arnarra's crumpled form.

A kobold organization known as the Hand of the Dragon (pg. 138) has caught word of the dragon hunting ship and sent an elite team to dispose of the crew. The Hand of the Dragon is the group responsible for resurrecting Cenere and is determined to slaughter any threats to their master before he is able to recover his full power. Two **kobold brutes** (pg. 140) are currently engaged in fighting Felix, while a spell-slinging **schemer** (pg. 141) stands over an unconscious Arnarra. Two **scoundrels** (pg. 142) are hidden on deck, waiting to surprise attack new arrivals.

GM NOTE: RUNNING THE FIGHT

This fight is challenging and can easily lead to death if not run judiciously. First ensure both Bellanus Yanorin, Randal Smith (use **assassin** statistics) and Cambria Felix (use **gladiator** statistics) help the party during the fight. Consider allowing one of your players to control these NPCs so that you can focus your efforts on managing the threats on the board.

The two kobold scoundrels are hiding when the fight begins. They wait to take their turn in initiative until it is most advantageous for them to make a surprise attack.

Once combat begins, the kobold schemers use their actions to reach an advantageous position out of melee range. Ideally, they escape to a spot where they can fire spells but still be in at least partial cover.

If the fight starts to go poorly for the party, The Hand only drops characters until they are unconscious. They then destroy the elemental engine and run away.

If this happens, it takes the crew an entire day to repair the ship, which cannot fly without the engine. While repairs are taking place, roll on the Land Encounters table four times to represent the extra attention the airship draws.

GM NOTE: ADJUSTING THE ENCOUNTER

• If your party is weaker than the recommended five-person party at 10th level, consider removing the schemer from the fight (they watch the attack but don't engage).

• If the party is much weaker than the recommended five-person party at 10th level, consider removing one brute and one scoundrel from the fight.

LOCAL OFFICIALS

> Thundering hoof beats come from the area around the ship as six armor-clad riders gallop into view. All are astride horses, and one waves a white flag towards your vessel.

A band of six **knights** riding horses approaches the parked airship. One of the knights flies a white banner hoping to speak with the captain. The knights work for a nearby lord and are tasked with demanding the airship leave the area before it attracts the ire of Cenere.

The *Emerald Maiden* could outrace the knights to avoid a conversation, but the knights attempt to do as much damage as they can before being outpaced.

If the party allows the knights to board and speak with the crew, they deliver their message but don't cause any further trouble (they would personally like to see Cenere brought down). If the crew agrees to land the ship somewhere else, you must roll twice on the Aerial Encounters table to represent the extra attention caused by flying in daylight.

MISTY NIGHT

> Thick fog forms an obscuring layer beneath the *Maiden*. Bellanus calls out from the helm: "All right, you can put your boots up. Should be a safe night if this keeps up."

The night grows thick with clouds, granting the airship full cover. No further encounter rolls must be made for the rest of the night.

NOW YOU SEE ME

> A blue blurred shape flashes along the ground while another quickly follows suit on the other side of the ship. Whatever is moving out there, they're fast.

Four **drakes of displacement** (pg. 133) loyal to Cenere were sent to locate the airship and have finally caught up. The creatures burst from the tree line and use their breath abilities to try and separate the crew in order to attack them one by one.

PERFECT COVER

> The ship tilts as it suddenly descends. Bellanus calls out from the helm: "Finally! A decent spot to land. Not even a dragon could spot us down there."

Bellanus finds a perfectly sized ravine in which to hide the airship. No further encounter rolls must be made for the rest of the day.

ROUGH WEATHER

> Crashing thunder roars through the air and lightning streaks the gray clouds quickly rolling in. Crew members race to their stations as Bellanus calls out over the rising wind, "ALL HANDS ON DECK! STORM COMING!"

The *Emerald Maiden* has encountered a storm. Review the rules for flying an airship in a storm (see "PC Actions on An Airship," pg. 173).

Three successful Captain maneuvers must be completed or Bellanus will be forced to land the ship. Upon landing, roll on the Land Encounters table.

SHIP FOR SALE

> A shrill battle cry carries through the air as 20 goblins spring from behind the brush and rocks. A goblin wearing a coonskin cap calls out to you:
> "Pirates, the Black Stripe clan offers to buy your vessel. We have three crystals of power to trade."
> As the first goblin finishes speaking, a second voice comes from the opposite side of the clearing. Twenty more goblins emerge from hiding, and one wearing feathered headdress calls, "Do not trade with the traitorous Black Stripes! The Tail Feather clan offers you FOUR crystals of power for your ship."

Both sides begin jeering at one another, and it looks like a fight is brewing.

Bellanus has landed the ship in the middle of disputed goblin territory. The Black Stripe and the Tail Feather clans are bitter rivals who squabble over all the region's resources. Each clan is composed of **20 goblins.**

If the players do absolutely nothing, the two goblins clans ignore the crew and fight each other. If this fight breaks out, the airship takes 16 (3d10) points of collateral damage as the brawl commences around, on and beside the ship.

Roll to randomly determine which part of the ship is damaged:

SHIP DAMAGE

1d4	Area
1	Hull
2	Helm
3	Elemental Engine
4	Airship Cannon

This damage can be avoided if the ship takes off, but you must roll twice on the Aerial Encounters table to represent the extra attention caused by flying in daylight.

If the party manages to calm things down with the goblins through magic or diplomacy, at GM discretion, the clans continue their attempts at purchasing the ship. Bellanus refuses any such offers, and if the goblins feel insulted, both sides team up to attack the crew.

SYMPATHETIC PARTIES

> A puff of purple smoke suddenly appears on the deck, swirling around a figure swathed in black robes. The figure holds out a hand and rasps, "Do not fear. I have come to help."

SCARRED LANDING

The area outside Amiens where the *Emerald Maiden* is currently docked is pocked with scars created by the powerful claws of a dragon matching Cenere's description. It's also the perfect spot for an ambush.

FINDING COVER

The natural landscape here offers plenty of locations to hide or take cover.

Forest Trees. These trees offer half cover to any creatures attempting to avoid melee damage and three-quarter cover from ranged attacks. Creatures attempting to hide in these trees gain +2 to Stealth for the duration.

Flaming Trees. These trees are suitable for half cover from melee and ranged attacks, but a creature that starts its turn within 5 feet of these trees suffers 3 (1d6) fire damage. A creature that suffers this damage twice in a row will start to notice any flammable items on their person are on fire. If they do not spend an action to drop prone and roll around to put out the flames they will suffer 6 (2d6) fire damage at the start of each of their turns as long as their items continue to burn.

Carved Ruts. The claw marks created by a mighty dragon are difficult terrain. A creature that is prone in these ruts gains three-quarter cover from ranged attacks.

TAKING OFF (OPTIONAL)

At GM discretion, getting the airship off the ground from this location could also prove a difficult task. Once the encounter ends, roll on the Mild Complications table below to determine the challenge facing the party.

MILD COMPLICATIONS

1d4	The party discovers...
1	...the airship has sunk into the ground and will need to be dug out.
2	...a pair of **owlbear** cubs has managed to crawl inside the elemental engine to get warm. Firing it up with them still inside would be bad for the cubs and the engine.
3	...two **treants** hidden among the grove refuse to budge, meaning the ship will need to take off in reverse if the treants can't be reasoned with.
4	...during the fight it seems one of the **fire elementals** got loose and is now floating around below deck, burning all the good bedrolls. The ship will fly at half speed until the elemental is returned to the engine.

The **mage** does not reveal his name and keeps his face hidden by his robes. He claims he was sent by a party interested in seeing the dragon brought down, no questions asked. If the party is not hostile, the figure hands over two *potions of resistance (fire)* and a *dragon slayer longsword*. After he hands off these gifts, the figure disappears once again in a puff of smoke. If the party is hostile to the figure, he disappears without bestowing any gifts.

PART 4: DOUBLE TROUBLE

As the third night of travel is about to end and the final destination is only an hour away, a dragon attacks the *Emerald Maiden*:

> The crew has gathered on the top deck, preparing to land as the first rays of dawn appear. Randal shouts as he points towards the forests on the horizon. A flash of green scales shines in the light as a pair of dragons soar toward the ship.

A pair of **young green dragons** who previously warred over the area's thick forest have formed an unlikely alliance in the wake of Cenere's attacks. These dragons, Eitur and Nimhe, were already patrolling the region when they spotted the *Emerald Maiden*. Outraged by the sight of a dragon hunting airship, the pair immediately attack.

Before this fight begins, make sure the players have access to the rules for controlling an airship (see "Aerial Combat and Airship Options," pg. 170).

If one of the dragons is felled, the other attempts to flee.

GM NOTE: ADJUSTING THE ENCOUNTER

• If your party is weaker than the recommended five-person party at 10th level, consider having the dragons flee after losing 70 hit points.
• If the party is stronger than the recommended five-person party at 10th level, consider having both dragons fight to the death.

PART 5: GET A CLUE

With the trials of the journey now past, the party can land in the ruined area of Amiens:

> As the *Emerald Maiden* soars overhead, the massive tracts of devastation look like a lattice of black scars. Lines of scorched earth cross the rolling green hills with the remains of structures and farmland still smoldering.

The devastation of Amiens was the work of Cenere, who has been flexing his abilities since he awakened. This is just the latest in a series of attacks made by the vicious red dragon.

To determine where to head next in the search for Cenere, the party must gather clues from the area. There are many groups of survivors in these parts. It is not difficult to find these people in their makeshift camps or combing through ruins of their homes.

While most civilized folk scorn talking to dragon hunters, the people of Amiens have very little left to lose by doing so. Kind words and offers of food, medical aid or coin can convince the locals to divulge the following information at GM discretion:

• The dragon flew in from the southwest, and it headed back in the same direction after the attack.
• There are several volcanic islands off the western coast of Amiens. Even though no one lives out there, they are big enough to hide a dragon. This is the primary clue.
• The dragon didn't look like a typical red dragon. Parts of its body seemed to be made of fire.
• The dragon didn't take any people or livestock. Maybe it wasn't hungry.

After learning this info, the party should return to the ship.

PART 6: LAST STAND

Once The Hand is dealt with, or at GM discretion, the party can fly the ship toward the volcanic islands where Cenere is hiding. Felix has several sea charts of the area and can determine which of the islands is big enough to house a dragon.

As the *Emerald Maiden* approaches Cenere's island, read or paraphrase the following:

> Only a few hundred feet away, an island of black rock rises from the crystal water. Thin trails of magma slowly drip down its surface, which is dotted with crevices and caves.
> As your ship draws near, the air off your starboard side begins to shimmer, revealing a gargantuan golden airship on course to collide with your own!

The second airship is the *Golden Talon*, which belongs to none other than captain Rynden Aethedorn. After returning from his fact-finding mission to discover his prototype missing—and his vaults ransacked—he assembled a crew and raced to confront Bellanus.

The *Golden Talon* is a larger vessel than the *Emerald Maiden*. It has the benefits of several advanced pieces of magic technology (including the ability to cloak the ship with invisibility).

Rynden intends to take over the *Emerald Maiden*, lock Bellanus in the *Talon's* brig, then deal with Cenere himself. The damage done to both Rynden's vaults and pride have pushed him past the point of finding a diplomatic solution.

GM NOTE: RYNDEN'S TACTICS
When Rynden attacks the *Emerald Maiden*, his goal is to take over the ship rather than destroy it. His first goal is to get in a position where his crew can board the *Maiden* (see "Boarding" [pg. 172] for rules on how this works) then take out Bellanus, the party and the other NPC crew members.

Once boarding conditions are met, three of Rynden's hired toughs (use **gladiator** statistics) attempt to get on the *Emerald Maiden* while the dwarf provides covering fire.

BIGGER PROBLEMS

Once this inter-ship combat reaches the beginning of the third round per initiative, Cenere makes his entrance:

> A rumble comes from below as the rocky island begins to shake violently. A large shape emerges from the exploding volcano, and from the mushroom of ash comes a red dragon whose wings are formed from flame.

Cenere's kobold guardians have alerted the dragon to the fight, and he has decided to take this opportunity to attack while the captains tear each other apart. Cenere joins the initiative for the third round of combat.

If both captains are alive, both airships can battle Cenere during this fight. To make things easier on yourself, consider handing off control of the second airship to your players while you run Cenere.

If either of the captains still lives, they both order their respective crews to stand down. Bellanus and Rynden are not foolish enough to continue their squabbling when there is a dragon to fight. For this fight, at least, they begrudgingly work together.

AFTERMATH

If Cenere is defeated, read or paraphrase the following:

> As Cenere's body explodes into a wave of fire, a single smoking ember plummets into the sea below. The sulfurous volcanic smoke dissipates, and the island falls quiet once again.

Unless the characters take action, Cenere's heart ember sinks to the ocean depths where it continues to burn until discovered. Until then, the elemental dragon is no longer a threat.

If either captain is still alive, they agree to extend their truce until the airships are safely back on the mainland and their crews have recovered. With their mission accomplished, the party can collect their payment and ride off into the sunset, knowing at least (for now) there is one less murderous dragon in the world.

FURTHER ADVENTURES

If your party would like to continue their Dragon-Hunting adventures, here are a few suggestions:

• The Hand of the Dragon failed to make Cenere ruler of all things, so they will have to try again. The party could hear rumors of more dangerous kobold activity or even try to take down the organization at its source.
• If Bellanus or Rynden survive the adventure, either one might call on the party again when another evil dragon causes trouble. Check out the rest of *The Game Master's Book of Legendary Dragons* to get ideas about potential draconic villains.
• The party has engaged in officially illegal dragon hunting activities, despite their objectively good intentions. A local lord or other faction might hunt them down to bring them to justice.
• If one of the green dragons managed to escape, they swear vengeance upon the party. The green dragon collects a band of vicious monsters and plans to take down the party when they least expect it.
• This bold victory inspires either The Dragon Swords or The Green Swords to start building their operations once again (although in secret). These factions might need help acquiring the materials to build another ship, and that ship will need a new crew...

NPCs

These stat blocks will prove useful when running this adventure.

BELLANUS YANORIN
Medium high elf, chaotic neutral

Armor Class 19 (studded leather)
Hit Points 123 (19d8 + 38)
Speed 30 ft., fly 30 ft. (when her boots are active)

STR	DEX	CON	INT	WIS	CHA
12 (+1)	20 (+5)	14 (+2)	18 (+4)	16 (+3)	18 (+4)

Saving Throws Dex +9, Int +8
Skills Acrobatics +9, Deception +8, Perception +7, Sleight of Hand +9
Senses passive Perception 17
Languages Common, Elvish, Dwarvish, Draconic
Challenge 12 (8,400 XP)

Brave. Bellanus has advantage on saving throws against being frightened.

Breath Weapon Avoidance. Bellanus has advantage on saving throws against breath weapon attacks.

Evasion. If Bellanus is subjected to an effect that allows her to make a Dexterity saving throw to take only half damage, Bellanus instead takes no damage if she succeeds on the saving throw and only half damage if she fails. She can't use this trait if she's incapacitated.

Fey Ancestry. Bellanus has advantage on saving throws against being charmed, and magic can't put her to sleep.

Indomitable (3/day). Bellanus can reroll a saving throw she fails. She must use the new roll.

True Strike. Once per day, as a bonus action, Bellanus may use *true strike*.

Winged Boots. While Bellanus wears these boots, she gains a flying speed equal to her walking speed.

ACTIONS

Multiattack. Bellanus makes two weapon attacks.

Rapier. Melee Weapon Attack: +9 to hit, reach 5 ft., one target. *Hit:* 9 (1d8 + 5) piercing damage.

Longbow, +3. Ranged Weapon Attack: +12 to hit, range 150/600 ft., one target. *Hit:* 12 (1d8 + 8) piercing damage.

Rally (Recharges after a Short or Long Rest). For one minute, Bellanus can radiate a commanding presence that gives all allies that can see her advantage on saving throws against being frightened or charmed. If a creature is frightened or charmed already, the condition ends when Bellanus activates this ability. This effect ends if Bellanus is incapacitated.

Rynden Aethedorn
Medium dwarf, chaotic good

Armor Class 20 (magical red dragon leather coat)
Hit Points 144 (17d10 + 51)
Speed 30 ft.

STR	DEX	CON	INT	WIS	CHA
14 (+2)	11 (+0)	17 (+3)	18 (+4)	16 (+3)	18 (+4)

Saving Throws Strength, Constitution
Skills Animal Handling +8, Athletics +7, Intimidation +10, Perception +8
Resistances fire
Senses passive Perception 18
Languages Common, Draconic (limited to insults only), Dwarvish, Elvish
Challenge 16 (15,000 XP)

Brave. Rynden has advantage on saving throws against being frightened.

Breath Weapon Avoidance. Rynden has advantage on saving throws against breath weapon attacks.

Magic Resistance. Rynden has advantage on saving throws against spells and other magical effects.

Parry. As a reaction, Rynden adds 2 to his AC against one melee attack that would hit it. To do so, the captain must see the attacker and be wielding a melee weapon.

True Strike. As a bonus action, Rynden may cast *true strike* once per day.

Red Dragon Coat. Magical leather coat. Provides base AC of 17.

Ring of Dragon Armor (Red). This ring provides Rynden with damage reduction of 10 on any fire breath weapon attack.

Rynden's Ring of Feather Falling. Rynden's rate of descent slows to 60 feet per round for up to one hour. If Rynden lands before an hour, he takes no falling damage and can land on his feet.

Actions

Multiattack. Rynden makes two melee attacks or uses his Leadership action.

Longsword. Melee Weapon Attack: +7 to hit, reach 5 ft., one target. *Hit:* 6 (1d8 + 2) slashing damage or 7 (1d10 + 2) slashing damage if used with two hands.

Heavy Crossbow. Ranged Weapon Attack: +2 to hit, range 100/400 ft., one target. *Hit:* 5 (1d10) piercing damage.

Leadership (Recharge 6). For one minute, Rynden can utter a special command or warning whenever a friendly creature makes an attack roll or saving throw. The creature must be within 30 feet and able to see and hear Rynden. The creature can add 1d4 to its roll provided it can hear and understand him. A creature can benefit from only one Leadership die at a time. This effect ends if Rynden is incapacitated.

CENERE, THRICE-BORN

Huge elemental dragon, chaotic evil

Armor Class 19 (natural armor)
Hit Points 218 (17d12 + 108)
Speed 40 ft., climb 40 ft., fly 80 ft.

STR	DEX	CON	INT	WIS	CHA
25 (+7)	10 (+0)	23 (+6)	16 (+3)	13 (+1)	19 (+4)

Saving Throws Dex +5, Con +11, Wis +7, Cha +9
Skills Perception +12, Stealth +5
Damage Resistances bludgeoning, piercing and slashing from nonmagical attacks
Damage Immunities fire, poison
Senses blindsight 60 ft., darkvision 120 ft., passive Perception 23
Languages Common, Draconic, Ignan
Challenge 16 (13,000 XP)

Partial Elemental. Cenere doesn't require air, food, drink or sleep.

Eternal Ember. When Cenere dies, he explodes. Each creature within 60 feet of him must make a DC 21 Dexterity saving throw, taking 22 (4d10) fire damage on a failed save or half as much on a successful one. The fire ignites flammable objects in the area that aren't worn or carried.

The explosion destroys Cenere's body but leaves behind his heart, which is a smoldering ember weighing 5 pounds. The ember is immune to all damage, and with the proper rituals, it can be used to resurrect Cenere once again.

Flame Aura. At the start of each of Cenere's turns, each creature within 10 feet of him takes 10 (2d10) fire damage, and flammable objects in the aura that aren't being worn or carried ignite. A creature also takes 10 (2d10) fire damage if it touches Cenere or hits him with a melee attack while within 10 feet of him.

Illumination. Cenere sheds bright light in a 60-foot radius and dim light for an additional 60 feet.

Legendary Resistance (3/Day). If Cenere fails a saving throw, he can choose to succeed instead.

ACTIONS

Multiattack. Cenere can use his Frightful Presence. He then makes three attacks: one with his bite and two with his claws.

Bite. Melee Weapon Attack: +12 to hit, reach 10 ft., one target. *Hit:* 18 (2d10 + 7) piercing damage plus 7 (2d6) fire damage.

Claw. Melee Weapon Attack: +12 to hit, reach 5 ft., one target. *Hit:* 14 (2d6 + 7) slashing damage.

Tail. Melee Weapon Attack: +12 to hit, reach 15 ft., one target. *Hit:* 16 (2d8 + 7) bludgeoning damage.

Frightful Presence. Each creature of Cenere's choice that is within 120 feet and aware of him must succeed on a DC 19 Wisdom saving throw or become frightened for one minute. A creature can repeat the saving throw at the end of each of its turns, ending the effect on itself on a success. If a creature's saving throw is successful or the effect ends for it, the creature is immune to Cenere's Frightful Presence for the next 24 hours.

Fire Breath (Recharge 5–6). The dragon exhales fire in a 60-foot cone. Each creature in that area must make a DC 19 Dexterity saving throw, taking 66 (12d10) fire damage on a failed save or half as much on a successful one.

LEGENDARY ACTIONS

Cenere can take three legendary actions, choosing from the options below. Only one legendary action can be used at a time and only at the end of another creature's turn. Cenere regains spent legendary actions at the start of his turn.

Detect. Cenere makes a Wisdom (Perception) check.

Tail Attack. Cenere makes a tail attack.

Wing Attack (Costs 2 Actions). Cenere beats his wings. Each creature within 10 feet of him must succeed on a DC 22 Dexterity saving throw or take 15 (2d6 + 8) fire damage and be knocked prone. Cenere can then fly up to half his flying speed.

Living Furnace (Costs 3 Actions). Cenere radiates a wave of heat within 150 feet of himself. Each creature in the area in physical contact with metal objects (like carrying metal weapons or wearing metal armor) takes 6 (2d6) fire damage. Each creature in the area that isn't resistant or immune to fire damage must make a DC 19 Constitution saving throw or gain one level of exhaustion.

Hell Hath Fury

When the party descends into the lower planes on a rescue mission, they come face to face with one of the hells' most dangerous predators.

An Adventure Suitable for Levels 17-20
by Lysa Penrose

A wealthy benefactor secures the party's services to bring her son, Canti Loyola, home safe. There's just one caveat—he's trapped in the nine hells. Following a dangerous teleportation ritual that takes them straight to the gates of Canti's captor's home, the party quickly discovers he's being held prisoner by none other than Fury, the Dragon Queen of Hell. They also learn that Canti knows more than his mother let on (for starters, she's not his mother), and the information he possesses could upset the balance of power in the lower planes. That is, if Fury lets him live.

Adventure Location

This adventure begins in a metropolitan city where riches are plentiful and the nobility know how to grease a few palms in order to maintain or expand their wealth. Hiring thrill-seekers or proven adventurers to do their dirty work is not uncommon, and the rates are always fair (if often uncollected, given the danger associated with the gigs). If running this adventure as part of an ongoing campaign, it's entirely likely such a city already exists in your world. If not, or if you're running this adventure as a one-shot for a new party, the city is called Vaulteer. The city's wealth is immeasurable, its defenses impregnable and its citizenry as happy as any in the realm. But peace comes with a price, and in this case, a member of the nobility, Loveday Loyola, seeks to hire a group of able-bodied adventurers to rescue her son from the nine hells as part of keeping that peace (it's a long story). Following initial introductions in the city, the party is transported to the lower planes to fulfill their mission. Therefore, it's more accurate to say that while the adventure begins in a city like Vaulteer, the majority of the action takes place in an entirely different place

(and plane): hell. Determining how your party heard of the job being offered by Loveday Loyola is the first step in setting up this adventure. But since the starting location has little to do with the bulk of the adventure, if there's no convenient way to get your party to Vaulteer or a similar city, Loyola would happily find a way to connect with the party wherever they are, presuming they are for hire, through mutual acquaintances at GM discretion, offering transport to her estate overlooking the city.

Setting Up

The party has been approached by Loveday Loyola through a mutual friend. Perhaps they are told that one of the wealthiest families in the city seeks to hire exceptionally daring and skilled adventuring types, but everyone interviewed thus far has been rejected for the mission (which promises riches beyond belief). Or, if a party member comes from a noble background, a newly discovered distant relative reaches out with an urgent plea for help. However they get the message, it should be clear that the rewards are significant, but the job is dangerous.

The job features a few primary NPCs: Loveday Loyola/Joy Hultmark and Canti Loyola (pg. 231) and Fury, the Dragon Queen of Hell (pg. 28). Once the party journeys into the underplanes, they will encounter a collection of devils and other fiendish foes, with stat blocks at GM discretion.

The adventure begins in a quiet room in an estate owned by Loveday Loyola or another location at GM discretion.

GM NOTE: VIRTUE'S FIST

Unbeknownst to the adventurers, a secret order called Virtue's Fist plots to defeat the King of Hell himself: Asmodeus. Some fair-minded scholars might worry about how an event like this could upset the power balance of the universe, understanding that a "devil we don't know" could fill the ensuing void. But Virtue's Fist is single-minded in its hunt for justice. An agent of the Fist, a paladin named Canti Loyola, sacrificed portions of his soul making deals with devils until he learned the whispered secret of Asmodeus's weakness, but before he could return with this information, the totality of his soul by Fury, the Dragon Queen of Hell.

To extract Canti's soul and save him from captivity, Virtue's Fist has acquired the means of a ritual to travel directly into range of Fury's lair. Under the guise of a heartbroken, well-to-do benefactor—Loveday Loyola—an agent of the Fist named Joy Hultmark has reached out to the adventurers in order to hire them to "save the soul of a loved one." Hultmark wants to ensure Canti is spared, of course, but the information he's secured is far more valuable to her cause.

At GM discretion, if a member of the party seems to be aligned with the thinking of Virtue's Fist (which is to say "anti-Asmodeus"), Hultmark could reveal herself as a member of this oathsworn order if she thinks it will further her cause.

PART 1: NO PRICE TOO HIGH FOR LOVE

Answering a mysterious call for help, the adventurers begin in a noble family's townhouse, where they meet Loveday Loyola, the elderly matron of the household.

> An elderly woman, visibly distraught, looks out the window as she collects herself. Turning to face you, her powdered face and heavily rouged cheeks do little to hide her puffy eyes and only accentuate the trails of tears emanating from them. "I...I'm so glad you've come. I've heard you're the best adventurers money can buy, and, well, I have money. I need the job done. But I need to know that you're up for it. Tell me. What are your credentials?"

Loveday Loyola would interview the party to determine their skill sets. She might ask a wizard their most complex spell or a fighter their most daring deed. Ultimately, she decides this is the party up to the task. She would then alternate between strained stoicism and exaggerated

stifled sobs as she shares the following information at GM discretion:

- Her son, Canti, is a foolish young man with a gambling habit, tempted by anything that might give him an advantage. Unfortunately, one such temptation was a deal with a devil, and now Canti's soul is in hell.
- Canti is a good boy who doesn't deserve this fate for one silly mistake. Doesn't everyone deserve a second chance? Or fifth?
- The Loyola family is extremely wealthy (old money) but they also traffic in favors. Loveday was able to acquire a single scale from "some hellish dragon queen" and hired a wizard to create a ritual to transport adventurers to its infernal source: hell.
- Do the adventurers require gold? She can supply it. Magic items? She can pull some strings. But all of it pales in comparison to the riches hell holds. The adventurers can keep whatever they find in the home of the devil keeping her son captive. Loveday just wants Canti.

GM NOTE: THE REAL LOVEDAY

Loveday Loyola is Canti's mother's name, but this Loveday is an agent of Virtue's Fist named Joy Hultmark, disguised as Canti's dear mum. Joy's true personality is distinguished by a blasé attitude and monotone voice. She cares only about completing her mission, which is to convince adventurers to take the dangerous trip to hell to return Canti. She's willing to say anything to accomplish this, including telling the truth if all else fails.

For clarity, throughout this adventure, Joy Hultmark will be referred to as Loveday Loyola. If her identity is uncovered by the party, change her characterizations throughout the remainder of the adventure at GM discretion.

If the party suspects Loveday isn't being forthcoming with the truth, a successful DC 20 Wisdom (Insight) check would reveal she is hiding something, while a successful DC 25 Wisdom (Insight) check would reveal she is also concealing her true identity. If the party presses her for "the truth" or "the truth about her identity" respectfully, Loveday would reveal the following at GM discretion:

- Loveday is actually Joy Hultmark, a sworn paladin of Virtue's Fist. She wants to see the fiend Asmodeus removed from power.
- Canti is very much captured in hell, but the reason for the urgency regarding the rescue is that he was sent to hell to uncover Asmodeus's secret weakness and apparently struck paydirt. Unfortunately, he was ensnared by another fiend

before he could return. Attempts to communicate with him directly via arcane means have proved fruitless.

• Virtue's Fist has reason to believe Canti is being held prisoner by Fury, Dragon Queen of Hell and Asmodeus's former bride. Things could be worse, but not by much.

• Given this news, the benefactors associated with this mission are willing to double their rate.

If the party agrees to take the job, Loveday would inform them that the next step is a simple (though somewhat complicated) ritual that will allow them to travel directly to the place where Canti is allegedly being held captive. She would then hurry them toward the cellar of the estate, where a space has been prepared for the ritual.

PART 2: SAY IT WITH SOUL

> You journey down a set of spotless stone steps in this immaculate estate into a cellar that smells of musty earth and a bit of damp. Furniture has been pushed against the walls to leave a wide, open space with smooth stone floors. Wearing octagonal spectacles with thick lenses, Loveday reveals a neatly penned scroll with instructions to complete the ritual.

To complete this ritual, Loveday requires the adventurers' help. Their success with each step of the ritual will help or hinder them later in their mission.

GM NOTE: RITUALS HAVE CONSEQUENCES

For each of the ability checks associated with the ritual, if the result exceeds 20, mark a note in the party's favor. If the result is less than 20, mark a note in Fury's favor. If the result is less than 15, the party member performing this aspect of the ritual suffers 28 (8d6) psychic damage. This aspect of the ritual must be performed again. If the party fails in this way more than twice, Loveday would consider shutting down the operation entirely as these adventurers clearly aren't up for the task. A successful DC 20 Charisma (Persuasion) check would be required to get her to reconsider.

The ritual has three phases, as outlined below.

First, one character with a steady hand must sprinkle the powdered dragon scale in a perfect circle, in which the party will stand.

> "First, we need to form a perfect circle out of this powdered dragon scale. My hands are shaking just thinking about it! Someone else better take the lead..."

The chosen party member must succeed on a DC 15 Dexterity (Sleight of Hand) check to create the circle.

Next, one character of arcane might must improvise an incantation. Loveday, unfortunately, has smudged that part of the scroll!

> "Oh no—the scroll...the incantation...it's smudged. Do any of you know magic? I know we're supposed to state the goal of our ritual and include at least one rhyming pair. Like 'to hell, that's swell,'...but you know, with more arm movement."

To perform this aspect of the ritual, the chosen party member must succeed on a DC 15 Intelligence-, Wisdom- or Charisma-based (Arcana) check, depending on their spellcasting ability. They do so with advantage if they fulfilled the incantation's requirements.

The final part of the ritual is a little more complicated:

> "So, there is just one more part of the ritual...and I suppose I should have mentioned this up front. But, well...someone needs to give up their soul.... Not the whole thing, obviously, haha—*just* 1/128th of their soul!"

A chosen party member must willingly sacrifice the memory of their happiest moment. To perform this aspect of the ritual, the chosen party member describes the memory to the group. The character must roll a Charisma (Performance) check; they do so with advantage at your discretion based on their storytelling. If the check is below DC 15, this aspect of the ritual fails and, upon finishing their story, they have no recollection of sharing the memory or of experiencing it. Only a *wish* spell can help them recover the memory of this moment. At GM discretion, any time someone attempts to share this memory with the party member who sacrificed it, all the original memory holder will hear for the duration is depressing opera music.

Moments after the memory fades, the ritual is complete. At GM discretion, read the flavor text that follows:

The powdered dragon scale bursts into a searing blue flame that licks toward the ceiling, forming a fiery tornado around all of you. Through the inferno, you hear Loveday shouting, "You only have one hour before the ritual returns you to the material plane! Make the most of it! And do try to hang on to your souls!" As the flames tower higher, the rich blue shifts into a blood red, followed by pitch black—a magical darkness. Then, immediately, there is a shift in the air. It's hot. Very hot. And you're no longer in a gray stone cellar but within a massive obsidian fortress. Every few feet, molten gold cascades down the walls in slow-moving flows, filling the halls and rooms with a ubiquitous warm glow before dripping between cracks in the floor.

PART 3: FURY'S FORTRESS

The adventurers are in one of Fury's underground fortresses with walls of obsidian stone barely translucent enough to reveal dark shapes and shadows just below the glassy surface. At GM discretion, the party should feel as if they are trespassing and that any creature they encounter could blow their cover. The next portion of this adventure can be as long or as short as you like, offering opportunities for the party to explore in their search for Canti.

As characters navigate the twists and turns of Fury's fortress, choose two options from the random environmental encounters below and/or combat encounters presented on the next page or roll on each table at your discretion. On a repeat, roll again.

RANDOM ENVIRONMENTAL ENCOUNTERS

1d6 The party enters...

1 **...Fury's Archival Nest.** A room draped in velvet, with scrolls organized in several shelves throughout. A single desk sits in the center. Touching a scroll without first dispelling the glyph that protects it requires a DC 18 Dexterity saving throw. On a failed save, the target suffers 22 (5d8) necrotic damage. The scrolls are not spell scrolls but rather historical documents detailing the nature of the hells as well as the power held over the realm by Asmodeus. A successful DC 25 Intelligence (Investigation or History) check of these scrolls would reveal aspects of them have been altered, placing Fury, the Dragon Queen of Hell, on the throne as if part of a promised prophecy.

2 **...the Vault of Riches.** This entire chamber is full of treasure, piled high throughout the room. It represents more monetary value than any member of the party has ever seen. The treasure is cursed. Any creature who removes treasure from this horde, at GM discretion, will have their soul forfeited to Fury in 2d10 days, a fact that will wash over them the moment they walk through the chamber doors with the treasure in their hands. This curse can only be broken by a *wish* spell.

3 **...a Museum of Souls.** Fury's vast collection of souls is highly coveted among other fiends in the hells, and it is here where she displays some of her favorites to foster further jealousy. At GM discretion, if being included as part of an ongoing campaign, this chamber could also contain the souls of some of the party's favorite foes (or friends). The souls are presented as if displayed at a museum. They can speak, but only a few words at a time, but could reveal Fury is holding Canti, a soul she recently acquired, in her inner sanctum and is trying to determine what to do with it.

4 **...a Torturous Chamber.** This room features several fountains, the water within them glowing gold as it reflects the flowing light off the walls. Any creature who gazes at their reflection in these pools must succeed on a DC 20 Wisdom saving throw. On a failed save, they are confronted by their greatest fear, suffering 55 (10d10) psychic damage. They are paralyzed unless they are immune to the frightened condition. This paralysis can only be removed by *greater restoration* or a similar spell, at GM discretion.

A creature that succeeds on this saving throw would not see their own fears reflected in this fountain but rather one of Fury's. It is her wedding day, with Asmodeus by her side. She seems happy. A successful DC 20 Wisdom (Insight) check made after viewing this scene would help a creature comprehend that Fury must use this room to torture herself from time to time with visions of her past life—and love.

5 **...a Blazing Inferno.** This entire chamber, a corridor 10 feet wide and 100 feet long, is a roiling, swirling flame, as in the *firestorm* spell. Crossing it will require careful planning, the ability to *dispel magic* (7th level) or immunity to fire.

6 **...a Luxurious Lounge.** A four-person group of bards plays to an empty hall. This is Styx and Stones, which made a deal with Fury in another age in order to find musical success in the mortal realm and is now obligated to entertain Fury's guests. All day. And all night. For eternity. If the party agrees to cover for them for just one song (so they can take a quick smoke break) the bards would be willing to aid them in any way they can (they know the truth about Canti's whereabouts as well as the fact that he's been cursed). A successful DC 20 group performance check is required to not kill the vibe.

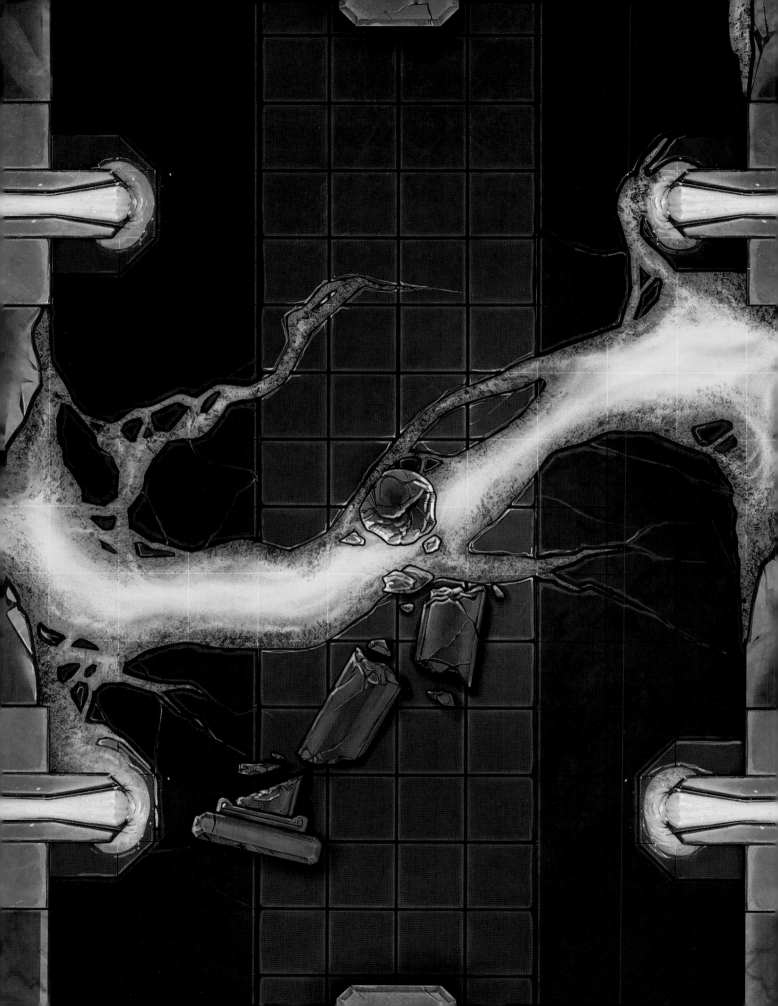

VARIANT COMBAT CHAMBER

This map is meant to aid you as you present a location for one of the random combat encounters below.

The lava flows from a height of 50 feet before spilling out into a flowing stream roughly 50 feet wide in most places. When a creature makes contact with lava or starts its turn in it, they suffer 55 (10d10) fire damage.

1d4	Random Combat Encounter
1	**Mean Erinyes** The party encounters a group of **erinyes** equal in number to the adventurers. Each erinyes happens to be similar to one of the adventurers; this might be a physical similarity (i.e., a signature piece of clothing) or a personality similarity (i.e., a nervous mannerism). Each erinyes attacks their matching adventurer.
2	**Opposites Attract Tension** The adventurers stumble across two arguing **pit fiends**. One of the pit fiends always tells the truth. The other always tells lies. Their conflicting communication styles are a major pain point. They attack the adventurers—at least they can both agree work comes first—but argue all the while.
3	**Ice Devil, Ice Devil, Baby** Two bored **ice devils** have discovered a devilishly adorable baby rat. They are unconcerned about the adventurers but very concerned about who gets to keep the rat as a pet, pleading their cases to the party (and putting the law in lawful evil). If the party decides neither ice devil gets the rat, they both attack immediately. Otherwise, the losing ice devil secretly follows the party, attacking when least expected. Unfortunately for both devils, the rat is a transformed **imp** who started the day pulling a prank and ended up getting in way over its head.
4	**Lemure, I Choose You** Four **horned devils** encircle four **lemures**. The lemures reluctantly shove and punch each other as the horned devils bet on the results. If uninterrupted, they pay no mind to the adventurers. If the adventurers attack the horned devils but spare the lemures, the lemures lead them to Canti Loyola, who is being held in Fury's throne room. Even imprisoned, this betting man has managed to get in on the lemure fighting action. If the party spares the lemures, this encounter leads directly to the start of Part 4.

PART 4: CANTI CAN'T, CAN HE?

> The next chamber you enter is open, vast, as if it were an aviary for a massive bird of prey. Your footsteps seem to echo even though you're stepping lightly. There is a throne of flame framed by what appear to be massive dragon's wings. Not far from this throne, within a 25-foot cube formed from shards that seem molded from the floor, is a man in ragged clothes. He is a bit run-down, but in relatively good spirits despite his situation.

Canti Loyola is currently trapped within a somewhat sentient cell, its features presented under Fury's Throne Room on pg. 229. Should the party try to free him (as they've been asked to do, after all) they will need to overcome this cell's defenses. Canti would hope for the best, but has resigned himself to the worst. He is in hell, after all. Canti did not get the memo that his devil deals to reveal Asmodeus's weakness were a secret mission. Once free, Canti would smile wide and share all he knows with the party. There's just one problem, which will soon become apparent:

> Canti smiles broadly, as if he knows exposing his teeth will bring you great pleasure and doing so is the most meaningful gift. "Thanks for saving me, chums! Quickly, back to the mortal plane, for I have learned Asmodeus's sole weakness. If you lean in close I shall share it as a whisper, for there are prying eyes and ears here. Asmodeus. King of hell. His secret is that he. That. Heeeee. Heeeeeeeeeeeeeeeeeeeee Haawwww."

At GM discretion, reveal the following:

- Canti is very proud of the information he's learned about Asmodeus and foolishly wishes to share his secret mission to bask in the adventurers' praise. However, his many devil deals have left him...very cursed. Whenever Canti tries to speak about his secret mission, he starts to bray like a donkey. If a character casts a spell such as *remove curse* to help Canti, the current curse would be replaced by something new (a watermelon head, a tongue the size of his body, a sudden loss of language) that prevents him from sharing his secrets. This includes the written word, sign language or features that allow for telepathic communication.
- Loveday's story was a cover, but there is some truth! Canti does have a gambling habit—part of why he dared to take on devil deals. He would be surprised and embarrassed if the adventurers mention his weakness.

FURY'S THRONE ROOM

Illuminated by deep lava flows that ring a central surface, the open, aviary-like throne room of Fury, Dragon Queen of Hell is carved from onyx and dense with heat. This space is presented for your convenience should you choose to create a more formal combat encounter within it once Fury and her accompanying army arrives. Otherwise, use the chase rules presented on pg. 230.

Living Cage (*1*)

This cage is the current home of Canti Loyola, and its bars present as a mouth full of razor-sharp teeth. The cage has been charged with keeping Canti alive, but trapped, and will lash out against any creatures who attempt to help him escape. Any creature that moves within 10 feet of the shards must succeed on a DC 20 Dexterity saving throw or take 28 (8d6) piercing damage and be grappled, pinned to the floor by the shards. On a success, a character takes half damage and is not grappled. To escape the grapple, a character must succeed a DC 15 Strength (Athletics) check.

Freeing Canti requires three consecutive DC 18 Strength (Athletics) checks, which bunches these shards together, allowing Canti room to escape. Any time a creature attempts this check they immediately suffer 14 (4d6) slashing damage.

Lava Flow (*2*)

The lava that flows throughout Fury's lair creates a hazard for any creature that isn't immune to fire damage. Any time a creature makes contact with the lava or starts its turn there, they suffer 55 (10d10) fire damage.

Fury's Throne (*3*)

When in her erinyes form, Fury will occasionally sit on this throne to consider ways through which she can subvert Asmodeus's aims. The throne has a pull to it, and any creature that desires power (at GM discretion) would feel an almost physical tug toward the throne. Any creature that feels this pull must succeed on a DC 16 Wisdom saving throw or must use their reaction to move as close to the throne as they can. Any creature (other than Fury) who attempts to sit on this throne must succeed on a DC 18 Dexterity saving throw or suffer 36 (8d8) psychic damage, as the lure of power corrodes their sense of self. They are blinded for one minute, the searing pain in their mind preventing them from opening their eyes.

- Canti thinks of himself as a hero, and although he is outmatched by most of the threats in Fury's fortress, that doesn't stop him from rushing into danger. Because of the nature of Canti's arrival in hell—"I think I might be dead, which makes my continued existence even more unimaginably heroic, don't you think?"—when Canti dies, he returns to "life" inside the obsidian cage after one minute.

As the party engages with Canti, his braying echoes off the walls in this chamber. The hees and haws are soon overwhelmed by a rush of wind and flame that surges around the party, heralding the arrival of Fury, the Dragon Queen of Hell.

PART 5: A FURIOUS ESCAPE

After Canti's rescue, his absence from the obsidian cage is noticed by Fury herself. Fury has kept Canti around until she can figure out how to extract the information that he has about defeating Asmodeus. Unfortunately, removing the curses are beyond her power. Fury appears before the adventurers with a guard of six erinyes.

> A rush of flame and wind surges around you then shifts into a central spot near the throne, as an alluring woman appears, her skin slightly scaled, her hair red as a burning ember. She is flanked on either side by a total of six winged beauties, each carrying a length of rope. "What, pray tell, are you all doing in my home? Don't you know it's rude to speak to someone else's food without permission?"

Fury is curious how the adventurers got into her fortress and for whom they're working, but once she has this information—or loses patience trying to acquire it—she would drop her somewhat charming persona and attack.

GM NOTE: POINTS IN FAVOR

Remember those points from the ritual in Part 2? For each point marked in the party's favor, the party gains a point of inspiration that can be used by any of the adventurers during this battle. For each note marked in Fury's favor, the game master gains a point of inspiration.

If the adventurers decide to flee (and they likely should) Fury pursues with an army of devils. The party must survive five total rounds before Loveday's ritual ends and helps them escape. Use the table on the following page for a more cinematic experience.

Each round, the adventurers battle their way through a mob (see chart below) of Fury's army while pursued by Fury herself. Each adventurer can attack Fury or the mob. Keep track of the damage dealt to the mob each round; by hitting thresholds of damage as a group, the adventurers can reduce or avoid damage or gain a boon.

Round	Mob
1	An unearthly clattering of chains fills the air as 50 **chain devils** (AC 16) surround the party. At the end of the round, characters must succeed on a DC 15 Strength saving throw or get tangled in the chains. Tangled adventurers make their next roll at disadvantage. If the party deals 100 damage, the DC is reduced by 2. If the party deals 200 damage, the DC is reduced by 4. If the party deals 300 damage, every adventurer's next roll is made with advantage.
2	A flock of 100 **erinyes** (AC 18) descend upon the party, a cloud of wings and steel. At the end of the round, each PC must succeed on a DC 15 Constitution saving throw or take 50 slashing damage and 50 poison damage. If the party deals 150 damage, this damage is reduced by half. If the party deals 300 damage, this damage is reduced to 0. If the party deals 500 damage, every adventurer's next roll is made with advantage.
3	Ten **pit fiends** (AC 19) form a foreboding barrier as the party flees. At the end of the round, characters must succeed on a DC 20 Dexterity saving throw or take 100 fire damage. If the party deals 200 damage, this damage is reduced by half. If the party deals 400 damage, this damage is reduced to 0. If the party deals 600 damage, every adventurer has an epic tale to tell. They make Charisma (Persuasion) checks with advantage while in taverns for the next 10 days.

After three rounds per initiative, there is a rush of blue flame that surrounds the party member who sacrificed their memory for the ritual, at GM discretion. If this creature is unconscious, the flames would still surround their body. If the creature is dead, these flames would surround another member of the party, at GM discretion.

> You see blue flame erupt around [insert party member name]. There is a flicker of recognition among each of you. You have about 12 seconds to enter these flames in order to be transported back to Loveday Loyola's estate.

After two rounds per initiative, or at GM discretion, the ritual spell that transported the party here would send them back. The party member that sacrificed their memory would recognize they have the power to offer teleportation to at least one other creature, possibly more, meaning they could extend a trip out of this plane to Canti as well. The creature must be willing to take this journey. Most fiends or devils would not be willing, though this fact is at GM discretion.

PART 6: MISSION ACCOMPLISHED

At the end of five rounds per initiative, all surviving members of the party who were able to make it to the swirling blue flames would be transported back to the Loyolas' townhouse. Loveday greets a confused Canti who floats ethereally, his soul detached from a physical form, as a doting mother would—or if Joy's true identity was revealed, she gives the party a brief back-handed compliment and payment.

Canti, for his part, would thank the party:

> "Such a shame we won't be able to go adventuring again, my friends, but I suppose I have now seen it all, and must therefore hang up my sword and my shield and my scabbard and my breastplate and my helm and my other sword and bid you all a fond farewell, for no adventure within the realm of my imagination could top the victory I snatched from the dragon's teeth this day." Canti smiles widely at you once more, as if awaiting applause. He leans forward, as if trying to share another secret, but once again finds his tongue is stilled. "I...hmm. Well. I know something. Special. And I'll need to. Spend time. Trying to figure out how to share it. And perhaps find a body I can borrow. Farewell."

NPCs

The following NPCs may prove useful during the course of this adventure.

LOVEDAY LOYOLA/JOY HULTMARK

An elderly woman with deep pockets and a flair for the dramatic, Loveday Loyola is also wearing a disguise: she is, in reality, Joy Hultmark, an agent of Virtue's Fist.

Armor Class 17 (studded leather)
Hit Points 104 (16d8 + 32)
Speed 35 ft.

STR	DEX	CON	INT	WIS	CHA
13 (+1)	20 (+5)	15 (+2)	15 (+2)	16 (+3)	16 (+3)

Saving Throws Dex +9, Int +6, Wis +7
Skills Acrobatics +10, Deception +11, Insight +7, Perception +11, Sleight of Hand +9, Stealth +13
Senses blindsight 10 ft., passive Perception 21
Languages Common, Elvish, Celestial, Thieves' Cant
Challenge 14 (11,500 XP)

Assassinate. During her first turn, Loveday has advantage on attack rolls against any creature that hasn't yet acted in combat. Any hit Loveday scores against a surprised creature counts as a critical hit.

Cunning Action. On each of her turns, Loveday can use a bonus action to take the Dash, Disengage or Hide action.

Evasion. If Loveday is subjected to an effect that allows her to make a Dexterity saving throw to take only half damage, she instead takes no damage if she succeeds on the saving throw and only half damage if it fails.

Virtue's Smite. Loveday's rapier attacks are infused with holy flame and deal an extra 4d8 radiant damage (included in the attack).

Unrivaled Impersonator. Loveday has advantage on any Intelligence ability check to disguise herself and advantage on any Deception checks made while in a disguise.

Sneak Attack (1/turn). Once per turn, Loveday deals an extra 31 (9d6) damage when she hits a target with a weapon attack and has advantage on the attack roll, or when the target is within 5 feet of an ally of her and she doesn't have disadvantage on the attack roll.

ACTIONS

Multiattack. Loyola makes two rapier attacks or two dagger attacks.

Dagger. Melee or Ranged Weapon Attack: +9 to hit, reach 5 ft. or range 20/60 ft., one target. *Hit:* 7 (1d4 + 5) piercing damage.

Rapier. Melee Weapon Attack: +9 to hit, reach 5 ft., one target. *Hit:* 9 (1d8 + 5) piercing damage and 18 (4d8) radiant damage.

Light Crossbow. Ranged Weapon Attack: +9 to hit, range 80/320 ft., one target. *Hit:* 9 (1d6 + 5) piercing damage.

CANTI LOYOLA

A confident champion of Virtue's Fist who has sold his soul up the fiend-chain in order to learn the secret weakness of Asmodeus, Canti Loyola is as self-assured as he is easily distracted.

Armor Class 20 (heavy plate, shield)
Hit Points 112 (15d8 + 45)
Speed 30 ft.

STR	DEX	CON	INT	WIS	CHA
18 (+4)	15 (+2)	16 (+3)	8 (-1)	12 (+1)	15 (+2)

Saving Throws Str +7, Dex +5, Con +6
Skills Athletics +10, Intimidation +5
Senses Passive Perception 11
Languages Common
Challenge 5 (1,800 XP)

Brave. Canti has advantage on saving throws against being frightened.

Brute. Canti deals one extra die of damage when he hits with it (included in the attack).

Virtue's Smite. Canti's attacks are infused with holy flame and deal an extra 4d8 radiant damage (included in the attack).

ACTIONS

Multiattack. Canti makes three attacks, two with his longsword and one with his shield.

Longsword. Melee or Ranged Weapon Attack: +7 to hit, reach 5 ft. and range 20/60 ft., one target. *Hit:* 11 (2d6 + 4) piercing damage and 18 (4d8) radiant damage.

Shield Bash. Melee Weapon Attack: +7 to hit, reach 5 ft., one creature. *Hit:* 9 (2d4 + 4) bludgeoning damage. If the target is a Medium or smaller creature, it must succeed on a DC 15 Strength saving throw or be knocked prone.

REACTIONS

Parry. Canti adds 3 to his AC against one melee attack that would hit him. To do so, Canti must see the attacker and be wielding a melee weapon.

FURY, DRAGON QUEEN OF HELL

A powerful, fiendish dragon and hoarder of souls, Fury seeks to topple and replace Asmodeus as ruler of the hells and has come into the possession of a valuable piece of information about his weakness. She just has to figure out how to get it out of a cursed Canti. Fury's backstory and stat block are presented on pg. 28.

AFTERWORD

AN UNDEAD DRAGON DRAPED IN RITUAL WRAPPINGS, serving as a dangerous cult's ultimate weapon; a vulture-like swarm of shadow and teeth that swoops into battlefields as a flock of terror and whose very name means surrender; a dragon covered in adamantine plate, its entire body serving as a siege weapon laying waste to walls and warriors in its path. Those are just the first three creatures presented in *The Game Master's Book of Legendary Dragons*, and already a campaign in a war-torn countryside overrun with zealotry and fear begins to take shape.

Not only did the team at Jetpack7 conceive of a host of horrific and awe-inspiring dragons, but they've been fully realized with breathtaking artwork meant to help you paint the picture at your table. As you undoubtedly know by now, each entry in this book could launch a dozen campaign hooks, and the lore, tactics and encounter conditions presented alongside each dragon are all the tools you'll need to build months of material for your party to dive into. Dragons are such an iconic part of fantasy lore (Dungeons & Dryads just doesn't have the same ring to it), and though there are numerous resources you can utilize to educate yourself on what dragons can be, most of them only offer a zoological breakdown. *Legendary Dragons* was created to establish psychological, historical, geographical and even economic considerations for each of these memorable monstrosities, granting you access to backstory fodder and tactical strategies for you to use in your game.

As a GM, you control the narrative of an ongoing story, and the most important character you bring to life each session is the setting of your world. That's why it's so refreshing to see a book in which the authors didn't just imagine how cool it would be to populate a region of the world with a dragon that spawns horrific creature hybrids each time it lays eggs, or a pus-dripping monstrosity that's gone into isolation because it knows it's the carrier of a deadly disease, or a dragon that methodically hunts dragonborn as part of a quest to rid the realm of all draconic races—they considered how each of these individual creatures would impact the world around them. Because the authors have done that work on your behalf, you can more readily include details for your players to sink their teeth into even as you prepare for your dragon to swoop in and deliver a few bites of its own. There is detail on how dragon parts can be used to improve or overwrite the entries in a wizard's spellbook, a race created when the powerful magical aura infused in dragonscale influences the unborn children in nearby towns and a playable class built around the ancient tradition of riding these great beasts. It's a horde of riches worth plundering.

But regardless of the work the authors did to help you at your table, the rest is up to you. You must decide which creature (or, if you're feeling feisty, creatures) you'll use to challenge your players. You must determine when to provide word of their existence. How to keep your players engaged. When to strike, or when to strike back. That's what makes you the Game Master. And with these dragons in your tool kit, your legend will continue to grow.

JEFF ASHWORTH
Author of The Game Master's Book of Random Encounters

CREDITS

Lead Designer, Creative Director, Art Director
Aaron Hübrich

Writing and Design
David Adams (Balaur, Kiennavalyriss, Naghi, Umunairu, Vyraetra), Rhys Boatwright, Daniel Colby (Glitz, Xavour), Dan Dillon (Volthaarius), James J. Haeck (Fury, Salathiir, Vanadon-Necroth), Sara Hübrich (Zuth), Aaron Hübrich (Jörmungand), Cody C. Lewis (Ilizinnii) and Jim Pinto (Anoth-Zuul, Aufgeben, Balleg, Gallomarg, Immryg-Umryss, Karnaggonn, Kundal, Kur, Kut-Echinae, Pellix, Tyrnin, Xylaarion)

One-Shot Adventures
James Floyd Kelly, "Hold My Beer"
Celeste Conowitch, "Dragon Hunt"
Lysa Penrose, "Hell Hath Fury"

Editing and Proofreading
Sara Hübrich, Aaron Hübrich, James Floyd Kelly

Map Illustrations Darryl T. Jones

Special Thanks Luke Gygax

Dragon Illustrations

Asep Ariyanto
Vanadon-Necroth

Agri Karuniawan
Salathiir

Leo Avero
Kiennavalyriss

Romain Kurdi
Karnaggonn

Tom Babbey
Tyrnin

Raph Lomotan
Zuth, Vyraetra

Brolken
Naghi, Xavour

Pius Pranoto
Ilizinnii, Umunairu

Milica Čeliković
Glitz

Kevin Sidharta
Kundal

Matheus Graef
Gallomarg, Pellix

Rudy Siswanto
Kur

Antti Hakosari
Anoth-Zuul

John Tedrick
Balleg

Maerel Hibadita
Immryg-Umryss, Jörmungand

Allison Theus
Volthaarius

Nathaniel Himawan
Balaur, Fury

Arif Wijaya
Xylaarion

Nino Is
Aufgeben, Kut-Echinae

Supplemental Illustrations
Javier Charro: *Dragonants, Drakes, Draken, Dragon Rider, Hand of the Dragon and Rynden Aethedorn*; Arif Restu: *Dragon Hunting Crew*; Jefrey Yonathan: *Bellanus—Female Elf Captain*

All others Shutterstock

Conceptopolis, LLC, Artwork
Major art contributions to Hasbro, Mattel, Marvel, DC, Wizards of the Coast, Lego, Sony, Square Enix, among others.

How to contact us
jetpack7.com
conceptopolis.com
Twitter: @Jetpack_7

Parts of this book were originally published in *Legendary Dragons* by Jetpack7.

Jetpack7 is a division of
Conceptopolis, LLC
8459F US Hwy 42
Suite 121
Florence, KY 41042

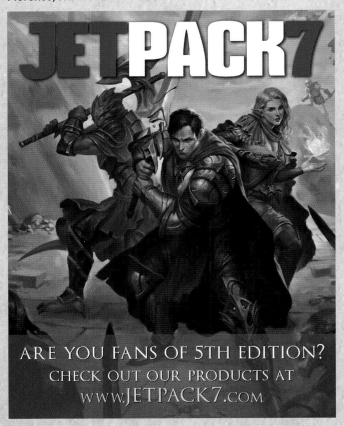

ARE YOU FANS OF 5TH EDITION?
CHECK OUT OUR PRODUCTS AT
WWW.JETPACK7.COM

Media Lab Books
For inquiries, call 646-449-8614

Copyright 2022 Jetpack7

Published by Topix Media Lab
14 Wall Street, Suite 3C
New York, NY 10005

Printed in Korea

ISBN-13: 978-1-956403-05-3
ISBN-10: 1-956403-05-1

CEO Tony Romando

Vice President & Publisher Phil Sexton
Senior Vice President of Sales & New Markets Tom Mifsud
Vice President of Retail Sales & Logistics Linda Greenblatt
Chief Financial Officer Vandana Patel
Manufacturing Director Nancy Puskuldjian
Financial Analyst Matthew Quinn
Digital Marketing & Strategy Manager Elyse Gregov

Chief Content Officer Jeff Ashworth
Director of Editorial Operations Courtney Kerrigan
Creative Director Susan Dazzo
Photo Director Dave Weiss
Executive Editor Tim Baker

Content Designer Glen Karpowich
Senior Editor Trevor Courneen
Associate Editor Juliana Sharaf
Assistant Managing Editor Tara Sherman
Designer Mikio Sakai
Copy Editor & Fact Checker Madeline Raynor
Junior Designer Alyssa Bredin Quirós
Assistant Photo Editor Jenna Addesso

Cover: Ilizinnii by Pius Pranoto

Additional artwork: Shutterstock: Cover, 10, 120, 129, 130, 157, 162, 169, 182, 232

YOUR GMs

AARON HÜBRICH: Writer/Artist/Designer. Publisher at Jetpack7. Creative director at Conceptopolis, a company that contributed hundreds of art pieces for the Dungeons & Dragons 5th Edition core books. Aaron has been playing Dungeons & Dragons since there were yellow character sheets that didn't take to erasers very well...and has fond memories of THAC0.

JAMES J. HAECK: Lead Writer at D&D Beyond. Co-author *Waterdeep: Dragon Heist* and *Critical Role Tal'Dorei Campaign Setting*/Darrington Press. DM of @WorldsApartShow.

DAN DILLON: Writer, *Tome of Beasts* and *Creature Codex* from Kobold Press, Dungeons & Dragons Adventurers League, Rogue Genius Games, Legendary Games, Rite Publishing. Dungeons & Dragons Designer at Wizards of the Coast.

CODY LEWIS: YouTube creator. D&D Twitch streamer. Dungeon Master. *youtube.com/taking20*. Mad mind behind *Save or Dice*.

JIM PINTO: Writer: *Legend of the Five Rings*, *Warlord, Protocol, Praxis, The Carcass, George's Children, World's Largest Dungeon, Gods and Goddesses* and *Masters and Minions* from Jetpack7.

JAMES FLOYD KELLY: Staff Writer, creator of The Tabletop Engineer Youtube channel, member of The Tabletop Crafters Guild, former author at *Geek Dad*, writer at Goodman Games, publisher of *Bexim's Bazaar RPG & Wargaming Magazine*.

DAVID GENE ADAMS: Writer. Has been pestering Dungeons & Dragons publishers for the past 12 years and managed to collect a myriad of credits in that time. He has had the good fortune of seeing his content published by the likes of Kobold Press and Wizards of the Coast in addition to other recognizable companies. David started playing D&D when he was 16, and the game has been an amazing outlet for creativity as well as a fascinating space to explore complex social issues while simultaneously slaying dragons in epic combat. Catch his stuff on the DMsGuild and Jetpack7's blog.

DANIEL COLBY: Writer. Daniel Colby has been an adventurer for over 20 years. As a Game Master, he hopes to bring some of his crazy machinations to the world of heroes and villains so they too can share his reality. Dungeon Master by day, mad illusionist by night! Blogger and design contributor to Jetpack7, Kobold Press and DMs Guild.

CELESTE CONOWITCH: A game designer based out of Seattle, she is the producer, DM and editor of the actual play podcast *Venture Maidens*. When not plotting behind the screen, you can see her championing femme lead shows as co-founder of the Penwitch Studio podcast network.

RHYS BOATWRIGHT: Designer and YouTube content creator at Jetpack7.

LUKE GYGAX: Writer, filmmaker and son of Dungeons & Dragons creator Gary Gygax, Luke is the founder of Gary Con, as well as the Head of Wizards of the Coast's Founders and Legends.

ACKNOWLEDGMENTS

First off, thank you to the quite demanding kid in sixth grade who slapped his character sheet onto my school desk and told me to draw his elf fighter. "What's this for? A game?" I asked. The kid seemed a little perplexed and told me, "Yeah, it's for a game called D&D." I immediately recalled the cartoon and even the toy line, never knowing there was an actual game, and instantly became intrigued. A half hour later, I completed his sketch and he walked away satisfied. No "thank you," but I knew he was happy, which was fine with me. That was my "official" intro to the game of D&D, and it wasn't long after that initial intro that I started getting books for Christmas and playing the game with my friends.

Of course, my parents were extremely supportive and they were excited to see the game expand my already vivid imagination. They helped cultivate that and I can't thank them enough.

Many years later I met my wife playing this amazing game. She is the backbone of Conceptopolis and Jetpack7, wearing any hat necessary to ensure our success. Without Sara, these creations do not come into existence and those ideas would still be swimming around in my head.

Of course, all the friends I met and gamed with over the years were also highly influential. I can recall many ideas from high school and beyond that have made it into several books we've published. From NPCs to epic battles, I always look back on those moments and recall how it was so fun—and use those times as a foundation in which to express within the products we make. When I ask myself as a designer, "Is this fun?" I think back to the days when we'd play every weekend—and if the answer is "yes," it usually stays.

During those early years, I became fascinated with the art for D&D, and this kid from Kentucky quickly learned several artists working for TSR were also from Kentucky. Jeff Easley, Larry Elmore and Fred Fields all worked for TSR when I was in high school and were a massive influence on me. I made it a mission to become the "next great D&D artist." That dream would become a reality decades later (albeit along a slightly different path) when we visited Wizards of the Coast around 2012, where Jon Schindehette gave us the opportunity of a lifetime. We had carved out some success working with Hasbro and their GI Joe line of toys a few years before and had expanded into game art. My studio (Conceptopolis) was hired to create the "art bible" for what would eventually become the next edition of D&D (5th Edition), and everything changed after that. I can't thank Jon enough for that opportunity, as it set in motion everything that makes us what we are today.

Of course, there are numerous people who are not accounted for here, but know that I thank everyone who helped us along the way. You know who you are.

Finally, I want to especially thank the Kickstarter backers who took a chance on Jetpack7, a tiny, unknown publishing company near Cincinnati that wanted to make books for 5e. Without you, I would not be writing this now. Thank you so much. We can't wait to show you what's coming out in the future. This community is amazing and it is an honor to be a part of it.

AARON HÜBRICH
Creative Director at Conceptopolis and Publisher at Jetpack7

Clockwise from top, concept art for Vyraetra (pg. 103), Salathiir (pg. 82), Anoth-Zuul (pg. 12) and Zuth (pg. 116)